INTERVENTIONS FOR CHILDREN EXPOSED TO VIOLENCE

Edited by:
Alicia F. Lieberman, PhD
Robert DeMartino, MD

Johnson & Johnson PEDIATRIC INSTITUTE L.L.C.

Every child deserves a healthy start in life. For almost a decade, the Johnson & Johnson Pediatric Institute, L.L.C. (JJPI) has been devoted to improving the lives of children and their families. From their first breaths through their early years, children are challenged to survive and thrive in the world. Every country, every family and every child face unique obstacles to the promise of a healthy life. At the forefront is JJPI—continually addressing the challenges and priorities in children's health.

A commitment to mothers and their babies has been at the heart of Johnson & Johnson for over 100 years. Reinforced by the Johnson & Johnson Credo that states, "We believe our first responsibility is to the doctors, nurses and patients, to mothers and fathers and all others who use our products and services," JJPI was established in 1998. Its mission is to save babies' lives and contribute to a healthy environment for children.

Collaborating with worldwide leaders from government, medicine, nongovernmental organizations and industry, JJPI addresses the local needs of children and their families. With our partners, we develop high-impact educational programs to:

- Ensure mothers have safe and healthy pregnancies
- Improve care for babies – from birth through the early years

Resources for professionals and parents are a vital part of the Johnson & Johnson Pediatric Institute's programming We hope you find the following educational material a valuable resource.

The Johnson & Johnson Pediatric Institute, L.L.C. (JJPI), gratefully acknowledges Karin Gillespie, MBA, for her dedicated efforts as technical editor of this publication. Her valued input and her persistence and devotion are greatly appreciated by both JJPI and the authors who worked with her on this project.

Publications in the Johnson & Johnson Pediatric Round Table Series

This series includes monographs for professionals and parent education materials.

1. *New Perspectives in Early Emotional Development*
   Edited by Steven P. Shelov, MD

2. *The Role of Early Experience in Infant Development*
   Edited by Nathan A. Fox, PhD and Lewis A. Leavitt, MD

3. *New Evidence on Unexplained Early Infant Crying: Its Origins, Nature and Management*
   Edited by Ronald G. Barr, MDCM; Ian St. James-Roberts, PhD; and Maureen R. Keefe, RN, PhD

4. *Emotional Regulation and Developmental Health: Infancy and Early Childhood*
   Edited by Barry S. Zuckerman, MD; Alicia F. Lieberman, PhD; and Nathan A. Fox, PhD

5. *Social and Moral Development: Emerging Evidence on the Toddler Years*
   Edited by Lewis A. Leavitt, MD and Professor Sir David M. B. Hall

6. *Interventions for Children Exposed to Violence*
   Edited by Alicia F. Lieberman, PhD and Robert DeMartino, MD

For more information, visit www.jjpi.com.

Table of Contents

Table of Contents (continued)

Participants

Victor G. Carrión, MD
Assistant Professor
Director, Early Life Stress Research Program
Division of Child Psychiatry and Child Development
Stanford University
401 Quarry Road
Stanford, California 95305 USA

Claude M. Chemtob, PhD
Clinical Professor of Psychiatry and Pediatrics
Mount Sinai School of Medicine
1132 Bishop Street, Suite 307
Honolulu, Hawaii 96815 USA

Michele R. Cooley, PhD
Assistant Professor
Department of Mental Hygiene
Bloomberg School of Public Health
Johns Hopkins University
624 North Broadway, Hampton House 8th Floor
Baltimore, Maryland 21205 USA

Robert DeMartino, MD
Senior Advisor
Office of the Associate Director for Medical Affairs
Center for Mental Health Services
Substance Abuse and Mental Health Services Administration
5600 Fishers Lane, Room 17C-26
Rockville, Maryland 20857 USA

Greg J. Duncan, PhD
Edwina S. Tarry Professor, School of Education and Social Policy
Director, Joint Center for Poverty Research
Institute for Policy Research
Northwestern University
2040 Sheridan Road
Evanston, Illinois 60208 USA

Nathan A. Fox, PhD
Professor
Department of Human Development
Institute for Child Study
University of Maryland
Room 4304, Benjamin Building
College Park, Maryland 20742 USA

Richard J. Gelles, PhD
Joanne T. and Raymond B. Welsh Chair of Child Welfare and Family Violence
School of Social Work, Caster Building
3701 Locust Walk
University of Pennsylvania
Philadelphia, Pennsylvania 19104 USA

Professor Sir David M. B. Hall
Professor of Community Paediatrics
University of Sheffield and the University of the NHS
Honorary Consultant Paediatrician
Sheffield Children's Trust
Storrs House Farm, Storrs Lane
Stannington, Sheffield, S6 6GY, UK

William W. Harris, PhD
Senior Fellow
Tufts University College of Citizenship & Public Service
Children's Research & Education Institute
2 Brighton Street, 2nd Floor
Belmont, Massachusetts 02478 USA

Nathaniel Laor, MD, PhD
Director, The Donald J. Cohen & Irving B. Harris Center for Trauma and Disaster Intervention, and Tel Aviv Community Mental Health Center
Professor of Psychiatry, Behavioral Science and Education in Medicine and of Philosophy
Sackler Faculty of Medicine and the Faculty of the Humanities
Tel Aviv University
Tel Aviv 67197 Israel

Participants (continued)

Lewis A. Leavitt, MD
Professor of Pediatrics
University of Wisconsin
Director of Developmental Pediatrics
Waisman Center on Human Development
1500 Highland Avenue
Madison, Wisconsin 53705 USA

Judge Cindy S. Lederman
Presiding Judge
11th Judicial Circuit, State of Florida
Miami-Dade Juvenile Court
3300 NW 27th Avenue
Miami, Florida 33142 USA

Sochua Mu Leiper, MSW
Minister
Ministry of Women's Affairs
Royal Government of Cambodia
3 Norodom Boulevard
Phnom Penh, Cambodia

Alicia F. Lieberman, PhD
University of California, San Francisco
Professor of Medical Psychology
Director of Child Trauma Research Project
San Francisco General Hospital
Building 20, Suite 2100, Room 2124
1001 Potrero Avenue
San Francisco, California 94110 USA

Steven Marans, PhD
Harris Associate Professor of Child Psychoanalysis
Child Development-Community Policing Program
Yale University School of Medicine
Yale Child Study Center
230 South Frontage Road
New Haven, Connecticut 06520 USA

Joy D. Osofsky, PhD
Clinical Psychologist and Psychoanalyst
Professor of Pediatrics, Psychiatry and Public Health
Louisiana State University Health Sciences Center
1542 Tulane Avenue - Room 315F
New Orleans, Louisiana 70112 USA

Robert S. Pynoos, MD, MPH
Professor
Department of Psychiatry & Biobehavioral Sciences
University of California, Los Angeles
Co-Director
National Center for Child Traumatic Stress
11150 West Olympic Boulevard, Suite 770
Los Angeles, California 90064 USA

Cynthia Cupit Swenson, PhD
Associate Professor
Family Services Research Center
Department of Psychiatry and Behavioral Sciences
Medical University of South Carolina
67 President Street, Suite CPP
PO Box 250861
Charleston, South Carolina 29425 USA

Philip B. Uninsky, JD
Executive Director
Cayuga County Safe Schools/Healthy Students Partnerships, Inc.
144 Genesee Street, Suite 410
Auburn, New York 13021 USA

Preface

The Johnson & Johnson Pediatric Institute, L.L.C., is pleased to present the most recent edition of its Pediatric Round Table series. These books are based on scientific conferences that explore important and timely topics pertaining to the earliest years of life. These meetings provide a forum for an international panel of professionals to openly exchange information about current research in the area of young child health development.

This Pediatric Round Table explored a topic of great importance *and* concern to child development professionals, childhood educators, healthcare professionals, law enforcement officials, parents and society at large — exposure to and experience with violence among children, the effects of that violence on future development and promising interventions for children exposed to violence. *Interventions for Children Exposed to Violence* brought together some of the world's most distinguished professionals in the arenas of health care, mental health, public policy, law and economics to share their perspectives, expertise and experiences.

Several themes emerged from the discussion:

- Violence experienced during childhood is a major, worldwide public health problem.
- Contrary to some common perceptions, infants and very young children are affected by exposures to and experiences with abuse and trauma. Disruptions of their basic developmental processes can occur. However, because preverbal or newly verbal children cannot articulate what they are experiencing, "the system" may overlook the extent of their suffering.
- The field of infant and child health lacks reliable and current information regarding the extent, nature and sequelae of childhood violence. Major epidemiological studies are needed to provide these data.
- There is a great need to develop partnerships among a variety of disciplines — including mental health, pediatrics, the legal system, economics and public policy — that involve research, practice and social policy in order to take constructive action on behalf of children who experience and/or are exposed to violence.
- Researchers and clinicians must begin to devote additional resources to empirically based treatments that deliver valid, reliable assessments that can be disseminated and replicated.

- Because financial and human resources are limited, the field of infant and child health would benefit from reliable screening tools that identify the most at-risk children. Once these children are identified, they must be directed to the most appropriate and cost-effective interventions in the continuum of social services.

These themes underscore the importance that both ***collaboration*** and ***science*** hold for assuring that all children have optimal conditions for daily living.

The Johnson & Johnson Pediatric Institute, L.L.C., is dedicated to saving babies through their focus on the continuum of care from pregnancy through early childhood. By working in partnership with leading professionals, the Pediatric Institute is able to provide programs that help shape the future of children's health around the world.

Johnson & Johnson Pediatric Institute, L.L.C.

Interventions for Children Exposed to Violence

Introduction

Introduction

Preventing and Treating Childhood Violence Worldwide: A Collaborative Effort

Karin Gillespie, MBA and Alicia F. Lieberman, PhD

Violence experienced during childhood — whether suffered directly or witnessed — has become a significant public health issue *worldwide*.[1] The statistics and accounts of childhood violence found throughout the chapters of this text, which takes the reader from Cambodia and Israel to California and New York, and to many other communities around the globe, confirm this finding. The sad accounts found daily in newspapers, of children who are maltreated and abused; victims of wars, famine and natural disasters; and growing up in communities rife with drugs, gunfire and gang warfare also support this conclusion.

Tragically, the most common and earliest trauma that children experience often occurs within their own homes and is perpetrated by a parent or caregiver.[2] In the United States alone, the statistics are staggering: Each year, between 3 million and 10 million children experience some form of domestic violence,[3] and among children 12 months of age and younger, child abuse is the number one cause of death.[4]

To further emphasize the scope of this problem, the injuries and deaths that *are* reported are just the tip of the iceberg. Many cases of abuse and neglect never see the light of day[5] (see Fig 1).

Fig 1. Magnitude of unreported and reported violence.[5]

The impact of early-life trauma on child development — from earliest infancy through adolescence — can prove to be significant.[6] Psychological and biological processes are disrupted, normal socialization is short-circuited and changes occur in normal brain development.[6]

Unfortunately, although early, ongoing intervention is key to recovery from abuse, many of the affected children never receive the mental health or healthcare services and treatment they need.[7] In fact, the ramifications of childhood violence are inescapable. Generations of traumatized children with behavioral, emotional, social, cognitive and academic problems are growing into traumatized adults[8] who suffer from high rates of depression, alcoholism, drug addiction and intimate partner violence.[1,4,8]

In addition, many adult *physical* illnesses are linked to childhood maltreatment.[8] The Adverse Childhood Event (ACE) study[8] looked at the prevalence of child abuse and household dysfunction and their effects as children grew into adults. The presence of one or more ACEs predicted a variety of health-risk behaviors and diseases, from chronic depression and alcoholism to smoking and chronic obstructive pulmonary disease.[8] According to Robert

DeMartino, MD, Senior Advisor at the Center for Mental Health Services of the Substance Abuse and Mental Health Services Administration (SAMHSA) and cochair of the Johnson & Johnson Pediatric Round Table (PRT) *Interventions for Children Exposed to Violence,* "These findings leap the boundary between mental health and physical health."[6] Adverse childhood experiences are directly linked to a variety of health-risk behaviors that have implications for the most important causes of death in the United States[6] (see Fig 2).

Fig 2. Adverse childhood experiences predict health-risk behaviors and disease conditions.[8]

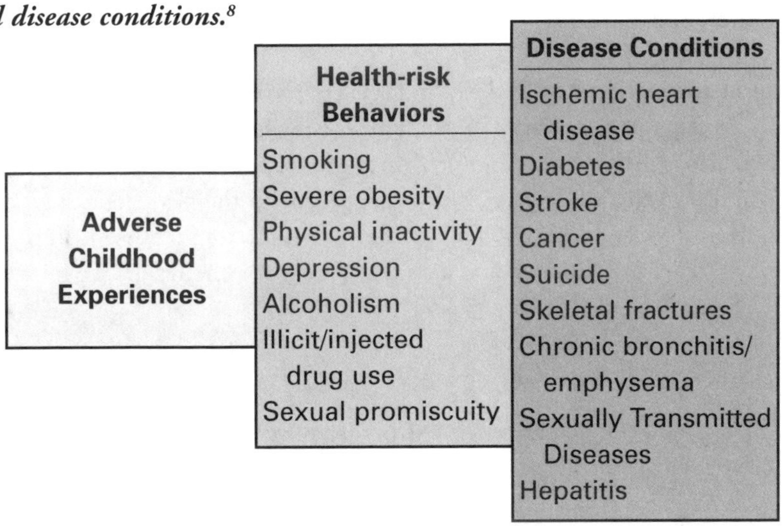

Source: Felitti VJ, et al. *American Journal of Preventive Medicine.* 1998;14:245-258.

As bleak as this picture may appear, a strong positive response has emerged. A committed group of physicians, researchers, academicians, economists, clinicians and leaders in public health and law have devoted their careers to making a difference for at-risk children so that future generations can grow into healthy, well-functioning adults. Such professionals were well-represented at the 2004 PRT. Over a 4-day period, internationally recognized experts engaged in a free flow of ideas, opinions, dialogue and didactics that produced and strengthened the outstanding chapters contained in this text. Quoting one participant, "The conference provided a unique opportunity to step back from the intensity of day-to-day work and join with knowledgeable and gifted colleagues... to think."

The PRT had the following objectives:

- explore the implications of children's exposure to family and community violence
- discuss models of collaboration between the mental health and legal fields with respect to children who are exposed to violence
- address the challenges to prevention and intervention for children exposed to violence and/or at risk for exposure to violence
- examine interventions that have taken place during natural and man-made disasters, including assessing and exploring planned, ad hoc and long-term clinical interventions

The ultimate goal of this PRT was to translate the current research presented by the participants into recommendations for those who care for at-risk children across disciplines. Through work groups and discussions held on the final day of this PRT, participants grappled with the next steps, the policy implications, the collaborative opportunities and the research needs in order to develop recommendations and a course of action. The results are presented in the "Summary" of this volume.

The chapters cover the following areas:

- Changes in brain chemistry and structure in children who have experienced childhood trauma

"Functional imaging will clarify how cognitive and emotional brain networks interact and help us identify altered brain circuitry. Once we identify these networks, we can then use functional MRIs [magnetic resonance images] before and after treatment to evaluate effectiveness and outcome."

— Victor G. Carrión, MD

- Violence prevention and intervention for children ranging in age from infancy through adolescence

"The long-term consequences of child physical abuse are too long-lasting and too grave not to venture beyond standard therapies to apply intensive treatments in an attempt to prevent adolescent and adulthood PTSD [posttraumatic stress disorder], violent crime, substance abuse, depression and an ongoing cycle of family violence."

— Cynthia Cupit Swenson, PhD
Lisa Saldana, PhD
Cathy Dodds Joyner, MEd
Scott W. Henggeler, PhD

"Battered women may prove unable to appraise danger signals realistically because of their own history of trauma, leaving them and their children vulnerable to repeated traumatic experiences. Joint mother-child therapeutic sessions provide an opportunity to focus on safety as the prerequisite for effective intervention; that is, working with the mother to mobilize her capacity for protecting herself and her child as the cornerstone of treatment."

— Alicia F. Lieberman, PhD
Allison Briscoe-Smith, PhD
Chandra Ghosh Ippen, PhD
Patricia Van Horn, PhD

"...not assessing levels of exposure to community violence among youth is a substantial oversight when mental health and primary care providers work with children and adolescents who are at high risk for exposure."

— Michele R. Cooley, MEd, PhD
Sharon F. Lambert, PhD

"There is a distinct need for more nuanced approaches to the issue of children's exposure to violence. Interventions should be problem-specific and should abandon the notion that exposure to family violence produces a robust outcome across behavioral domains."

— Richard J. Gelles, PhD

- Promising interventions undertaken in Cambodia and Israel for children who have experienced the trauma of war

"...mental health professionals working in the aftermath of a disaster must be willing and able to understand the problems at hand and work within both the mental health and healthcare systems, while they collaborate simultaneously with colleagues from a wide range of fields."

— *Nathaniel Laor, MD, PhD*
Leo Wolmer, MA
Smadar Spirman, MA
Ze'ev Wiener, MD

"The approaches taken by international and domestic organizations to respond to the immense needs of Cambodian children must include the fortification of family and community life, for it is in these settings that children receive the kind of security that they cannot get from therapy. New legislation to protect the rights of children and a commitment to judicial reform are also needed. Perpetrators of violence against Cambodian youth must be brought to a just court and the victims must be given justice. These are essential if the children of Cambodia are to regain control of their lives."

— *Sochua Mu Leiper, MSW*

- Comprehensive system change in entire communities to address the social and economic implications of children's experiences with violence

"... at-risk children and their families are compelled to navigate a fragmented system, accessing services by cycling through various entry points — from family court to social service agencies to the special education system. As a result, children's diagnoses are framed narrowly, interventions tend to be discontinuous and services offered are often incomplete."

— *Philip B. Uninsky, JD*

"...the advantages of safer, more affluent neighborhoods failed to translate into the kinds of family advantages that might have promoted the children's well-being: Adults who moved in conjunction with the Moving To Opportunity program remained similar to their control-group counterparts in terms of their employment status, welfare dependence, family income and parenting practices, as well as their connections to their children's schools and the parents of their children's friends...it appears that an intervention that is focused exclusively on

neighborhood — rather than also on child, family and school factors — is unable to solve the myriad health and behavioral problems of children growing up in violent urban neighborhoods."

— *Greg J. Duncan, PhD*
Elizabeth Clark-Kauffman, PhD
Emily K. Snell, PhD

- Innovative interventions established through collaborations between the mental health field and the legal field for children who have experienced violence

"Juvenile court judges often make monumental decisions that affect the future course of a child's life and well-being. A nexus between the law and science — which brings the knowledge of child development into the courtroom — could result in better decision-making.... Juvenile court can be the catalyst for a community to work together in a multidisciplinary fashion to help young children to heal."

— *Joy D. Osofsky, PhD*
Judge Cindy S. Lederman

"During their patrols, police officers confront routinely the psychological sequelae of violence and psychiatric illness.... because of their immediate and frequent contacts with children and families affected by violence, police officers could have a profound impact on the manner in which children experience violence and other adversities."

— *Steven Marans, PhD*
Robert A. Murphy, PhD
Robert L. Casey, PhD
Steven J. Berkowitz, MD
Miriam Berkman, JD, MSW

- A map of the multiple and overlapping levels of interventions needed to provide a cohesive approach to help traumatized children and their families

"As clinicians, researchers and advocates for traumatized children, our role is to serve as mediators for providing these children with the help they need to reach their full potential as healthy and productive citizens."

— *William W. Harris, PhD*
Frank W. Putnam, MD
John A. Fairbank, PhD

"...although parental overprotection is often linked with adverse developmental consequences, in some settings it facilitates and supports healthy child and adolescent development... Too often, our attachment considerations have not addressed the important developmental impact of the protective behaviors of parents in the face of dangers, in terms of real protection and in children's perceptions of their caretakers. There is a measurable added benefit to perceiving a parent as acting proactively; for example, by monitoring what an adolescent is doing or where an adolescent is going when living in a dangerous environment."

— *Robert S. Pynoos, MD, MPH*
Alan M. Steinberg, PhD

The authors offer their experiences, interventions, current research, evidence, opinions and recommendations in the hope of building a consensus on the prevention and treatment of childhood trauma as a global, front-and-center public health issue, as well as on the need for collaborative action.

Beyond the bounds of the Johnson & Johnson PRT and the pages of this text, much is already being done to ameliorate the effects of childhood violence and prevent additional violence:

- The World Health Organization has called for an international plan to prevent interpersonal violence and to improve the support and care of victims of violence.[1]
- Backed by federal and private funding, The National Child Traumatic Stress Network, a coalition of 54 treatment centers across the United States, is working to "... improve the quality, effectiveness, provision, and availability of therapeutic services delivered to all children and adolescents experiencing traumatic events."[9]
- The US Department of Health and Human Services guides and funds a variety of programs to combat domestic and youth violence, including: "No Child Left Behind"; "Safe and Drug-Free Schools"; "Safe Schools/ Healthy Students"; "Street Outreach"; and "Children of Substance-Abusing Parents."[5]
- The US Department of Justice, through its "Safe Futures" program, provides funding to local communities to prevent and control youth crime and victimization.[5]

As we continue to examine the significance of childhood violence on our worldwide community and to seek solutions, we are spurred by a recognition that, in the words of Alice Miller,

> "The truth about childhood is stored up in our bodies and lives in the depths of our souls. Our intellect can be deceived, our feelings can be numbed and manipulated, our perceptions shamed and confused, our bodies tricked with medication, but our soul never forgets. And because we are one, one whole soul in one body, someday our body will present the bill."[10]

References

1. Krug EG, Dahlberg LL, Mercy JA, Zwi AB, Lozano R, eds. World report on violence and health [World Health Organization Web site]. 2002. Available at: http://www.who.int/violence_injury_prevention/violence/world_report/en/full_en.pdf. Accessed March 16, 2005.
2. US Dept of Health & Human Services. *Child Maltreatment 2002.* Washington, DC: US Dept of Health & Human Services, Administration on Children, Youth and Families; 2004.
3. Carter LS, Weithorn LA, Behrman RE. Domestic violence and children: analysis and recommendations. *The Future of Children/Center for the Future of Children, the David and Lucile Packard Foundation.* 1999;9:4-20.
4. Gentry CE. *Crisis Intervention in Child Abuse and Neglect.* Washington, DC: US Dept of Health & Human Services, Administration for Children & Families, Administration on Children, Youth and Families, National Center on Child Abuse and Neglect; 1994.
5. Berkowitz SJ. Children exposed to community violence: the rationale for early intervention. *Clinical Child and Family Psychology Review.* 2003;6:293-302.
6. DeMartino R. The spectrum of prevention in response to violence. Presented at: Johnson & Johnson Pediatric Round Table: *Interventions for Children Exposed to Violence;* February 12-16, 2004; San Juan, Puerto Rico.
7. Guterman NB, Hahm HC, Cameron M. Adolescent victimization and subsequent use of mental health counseling services. *The Journal of Adolescent Health: Official Publication of the Society for Adolescent Medicine.* 2002;30:336-345.
8. Felitti VJ, Anda RF, Nordenberg D, et al. Relationship of childhood abuse and household dysfunction to many of the leading causes of death in adults. *American Journal of Preventive Medicine.* 1998; 14:245-258.
9. The National Child Traumatic Stress Network. Who we are: background, structure, and mission of the National Child Traumatic Stress Network. Available at: http://www.nctsnet.org/nccts/nav.do?pid=abt_main. Accessed March 16, 2004.
10. Miller A. Thou shalt not be aware: society's betrayal of the child. Translated from the German by H and H Hannum; with a preface by L deMause and a new introduction by the author. New York: Farrar, Straus and Giroux; 1998:315.

Section 1:
Foundation: What Factors Influence Resilience in Children?

Abstracts from Section 1: Foundation: What Factors Influence Resilience in Children?

Recovery of Children and Adolescents After Exposure to Violence: A Developmental Ecological Framework

Robert S. Pynoos, MD, MPH
Alan M. Steinberg, PhD

Exposure to violence in the United States is a major public mental health concern. Over the past decade, research efforts have moved beyond a simple examination of symptoms related to exposure to violence in children and adolescents to describe the influences of exposure on their development and functioning. A developmental psychopathology model of child and adolescent traumatic stress provides a useful framework with which to clarify the processes that fall under the rubric of *buffering* and *risk* for children and adolescents exposed to violence. This chapter elaborates on key concepts of such a model, including resistance, vulnerability, resilience and adjustment. As such, it can inform a discussion of the conceptual, empirical and methodological issues involved in the range of interventions that address the developmental ramifications of exposure to violence.

Understanding the Effects of Early Life Stress on Brain Development

Victor G. Carrión, MD

In the aftermath of violence or other trauma, posttraumatic stress disorder (PTSD) can impair children's academic and social abilities and disrupt normal development. This chapter, which descibes a multimethod evaluation of children with PTSD versus a control group, found that children with PTSD had higher diurnal salivary cortisol levels, lower cerebral volumes and an attenuation of frontal lobe asymmetry. Longitudinal analyses of behavioral, neuroendocrinological and anatomical markers will help shed light on the pathogenesis and progression of acute and chronic PTSD and facilitate the development of a more developmentally appropriate description of PTSD in pediatric populations.

Violence in Infancy and Early Childhood: Relationship-Based Treatment and Evaluation

Alicia F. Lieberman, PhD
Allison Briscoe-Smith, PhD
Chandra Ghosh Ippen, PhD
Patricia Van Horn, PhD

Interpersonal violence affects adults and children of all ages. Young children are particularly vulnerable because they are almost completely dependent on adults for their protection and well-being. Experiencing violence can profoundly disrupt normal developmental processes in infants, toddlers and preschoolers. Preliminary findings from an ongoing study of toddlers and preschoolers exposed to violence indicate that a relationship-based approach to the treatment of traumatic stress responses that includes both the mother and the child has beneficial effects on maternal functioning, child behavior problems, child readiness to learn and the quality of the mother-child relationship. The goal of child-parent psychotherapy is to return the child to a normal developmental course by restoring a sense of safety, trust and reciprocity in the parent-child relationship.

Recovery of Children and Adolescents After Exposure to Violence: A Developmental Ecological Framework

Robert S. Pynoos, MD, MPH
Alan M. Steinberg, PhD

Introduction

Every year, millions of children and adolescents in the United States experience firsthand or witness violence in their homes, schools and communities. The high rates of exposure to violence across the developmental life cycle experienced by the nation's youth are a major public mental health concern. Developmental, ecological studies have clarified the risk of exposure to different types of violence, trauma and loss during childhood and adolescence. These studies indicate that rates vary by culture, geographical location and historical context. These rates are also influenced by economic, political and social forces, as well as by individual, family, school and community environments.[1]

Social Factors Play a Role in Exposure Risk and Consequences

A variety of environmental factors can alter the effects of exposure to violence for both children and adolescents. Some factors may place the child at greater risk for psychopathologies related to exposure, while others may buffer the effects of exposure. Social forces, for example, can rapidly affect the analytical dimensions of both *buffering* and *risk.*

In 1986 and 1987, the introduction of crack cocaine into major metropolitan cities changed the nature of the illegal drug trade: It became a high-cash, street-corner economy that resulted in a greater need by neighborhood residents for guns for protection. Along with a general increase in the number of guns owned and carried by adult residents, these communities also experienced a greater access to guns by adolescents, rising rates of violent injuries and deaths among adolescents and young adults and, by necessity, changes in the dominant modes of protection practiced by families and schools. With regard to the latter point, neighbors began to scrutinize new families moving into the area to determine their risk for drug-related activities. Families sometimes radically changed their routines, even going to the extreme of eating family meals on the floor as a protective measure against gunfire. Due to fear of retaliation, community members also refused to cooperate with police investigations or to befriend a police officer. The ripples spread, leaving youth with significant rates of untreated chronic posttraumatic and traumatic grief reactions, ultimately compromising their academic achievement and motivation as well as their engagement with civil society through legitimate productive work.[2]

An ecological perspective of exposure to violence places the analyses of child and adolescent risks within a cross-generational and societal context. Typically, there is a lag period between adult psychopathology trends and resulting trends among children and adolescents: For example, in the 1960s and 1970s, documented increases in rates of suicidal behavior among parents, along with increasing rates of divorce and custody disputes, were followed shortly thereafter by increasing rates of suicidal behavior among children and adolescents.[3] A dramatic example involves school shootings. A careful review of the last 2 decades reveals that the first series of school shootings were committed by adults firing semiautomatic weapons on elementary school children. With little societal response, such as restrictions on the sale or possession of assault weapons, it was only a few years before such catastrophic violence was being perpetrated by high-school-age — and even younger — students.

We now have extensive knowledge about the impact of exposure to violence over the course of child and adolescent development. A model of developmental psychopathology[4,5] (see Fig 1) suggests that the impact of exposure to violence derives from the nature, intensity and consequence of exposure(s), the severity of postviolence adversities and the frequency of postviolence reminders of the trauma itself and the losses stemming from the trauma. In addition, there is an interplay between changes in the normal course of development and resulting psychopathology. Repeated and sequential exposures over one or more developmental periods impacts development significantly and contributes to a complex array of emotional, behavioral and health outcomes. Intrinsic factors in the child and the ecology of the child's life have a pervasive influence from the points of exposure through recovery and long-term adjustment.

Important components of the developmental model are maturation in the ability to appraise danger, the emotional response to it and efforts at regulation, as well as an evolving consideration of protective intervention. Child, family, peer and school appraisals of danger cannot be separated from their ecological contexts. Therefore, efforts directed at prevention, protection and intervention must engage not only the child, family, peer and school dimensions, but they must also incorporate social agencies and institutions, public policy and cultural values. The terrorist attacks of September 11, 2001, along with threats of weapons of mass destruction, have introduced additional unique aspects to a developmental psychopathology approach to exposure to violence.[6]

An Overview of Key Concepts Related to Child and Adolescent Exposure to Violence

Several theoretical works contribute to an understanding of key concepts that underlie this chapter, including *resilience, resistance* and *vulnerability.*[7-10] It is our hope that clarification of the developmental psychopathology model and these concepts will facilitate discussions about the etiology and consequences of violence, factors that influence adjustment and recovery, and intervention strategies.

***Fig 1. A developmental-ecological model for psychopathology.*[4]**

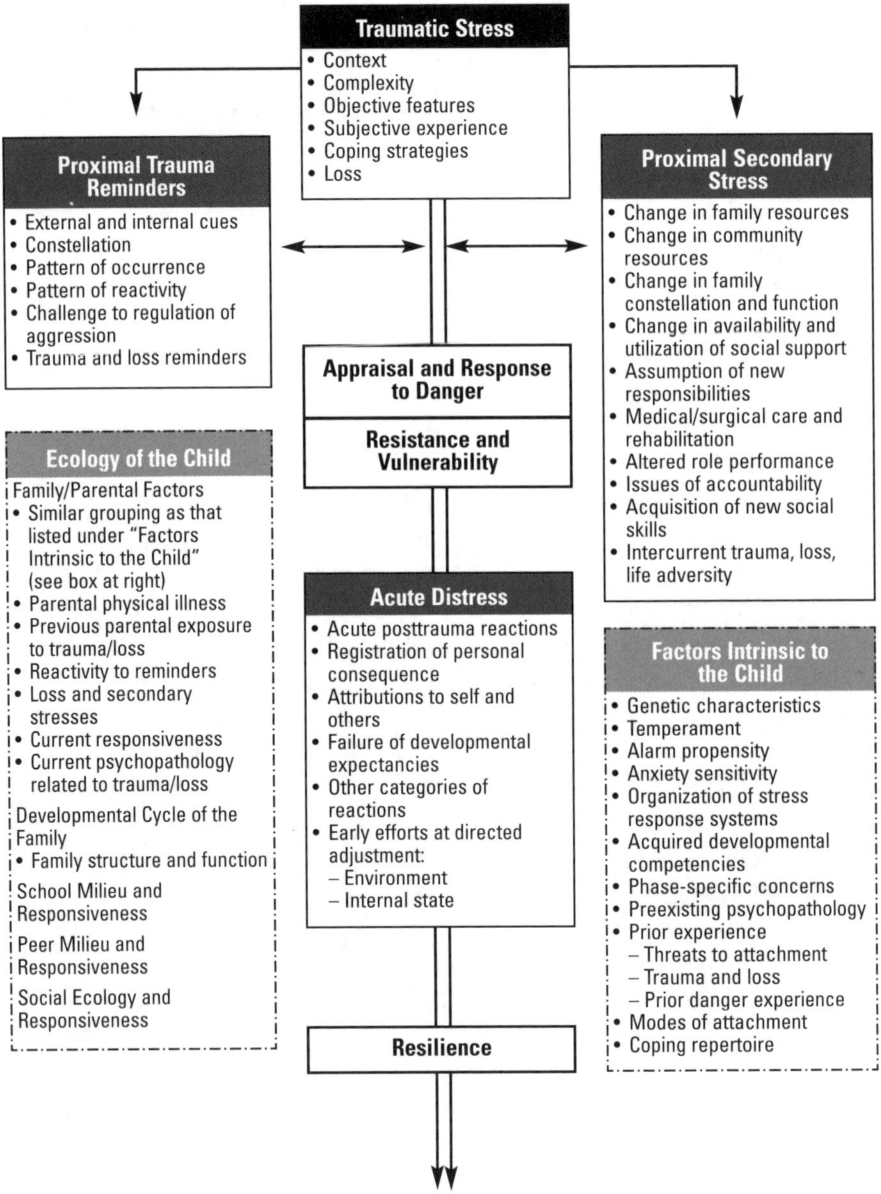

This material is used by permission of John Wiley & Sons, Inc. A developmental model of childhood traumatic stress; Pynoos RS, Steinberg AM, Wraith R; 1995; John Wiley & Sons, Inc.

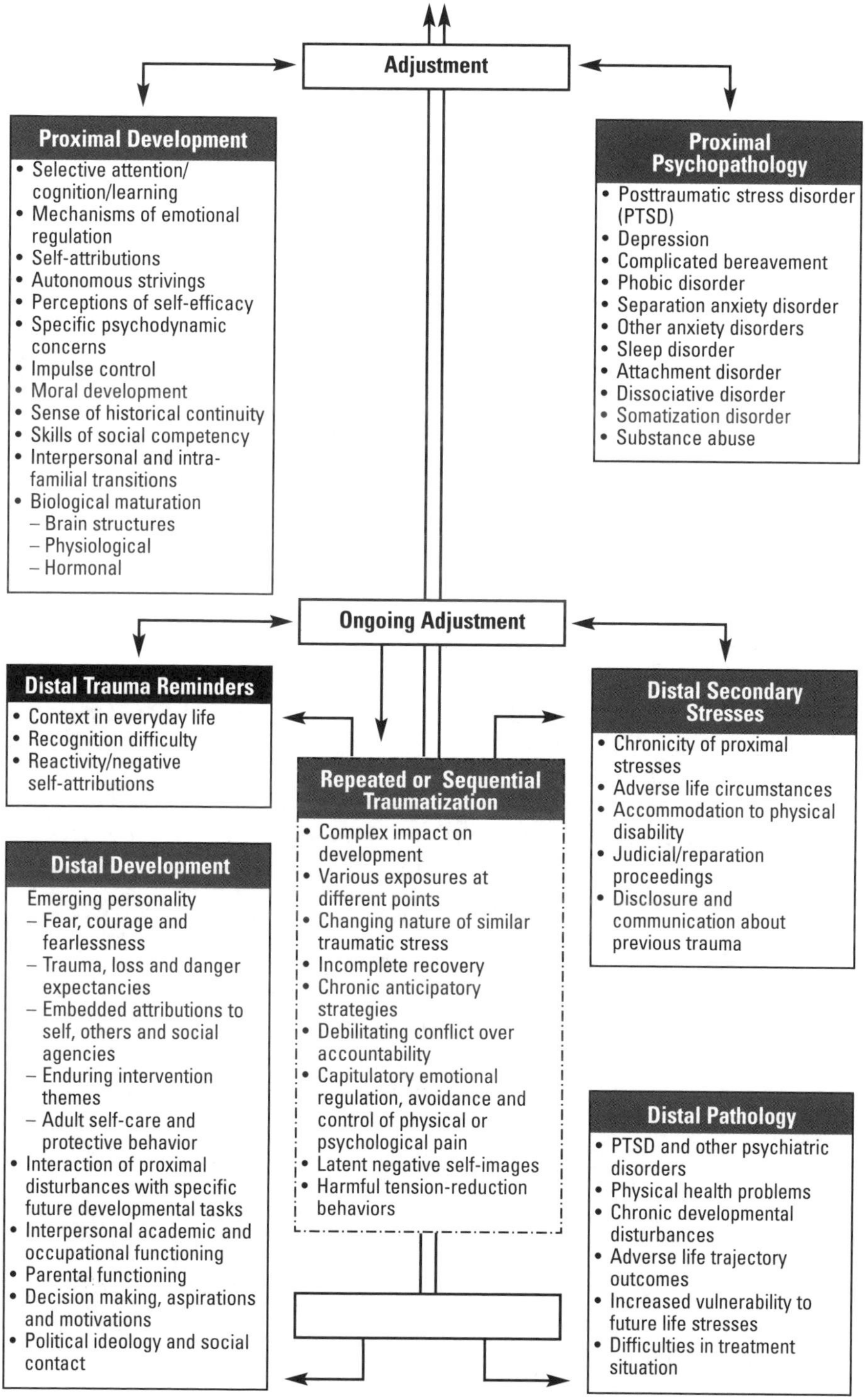
Adjustment
Proximal Development
• Selective attention/cognition/learning
• Mechanisms of emotional regulation
• Self-attributions
• Autonomous strivings
• Perceptions of self-efficacy
• Specific psychodynamic concerns
• Impulse control
• Moral development
• Sense of historical continuity
• Skills of social competency
• Interpersonal and intra-familial transitions
• Biological maturation
– Brain structures
– Physiological
– Hormonal
Proximal Psychopathology
• Posttraumatic stress disorder (PTSD)
• Depression
• Complicated bereavement
• Phobic disorder
• Separation anxiety disorder
• Other anxiety disorders
• Sleep disorder
• Attachment disorder
• Dissociative disorder
• Somatization disorder
• Substance abuse
Ongoing Adjustment
Distal Trauma Reminders
• Context in everyday life
• Recognition difficulty
• Reactivity/negative self-attributions
Distal Secondary Stresses
• Chronicity of proximal stresses
• Adverse life circumstances
• Accommodation to physical disability
• Judicial/reparation proceedings
• Disclosure and communication about previous trauma
Repeated or Sequential Traumatization
• Complex impact on development
• Various exposures at different points
• Changing nature of similar traumatic stress
• Incomplete recovery
• Chronic anticipatory strategies
• Debilitating conflict over accountability
• Capitulatory emotional regulation, avoidance and control of physical or psychological pain
• Latent negative self-images
• Harmful tension-reduction behaviors
Distal Development
Emerging personality
– Fear, courage and fearlessness
– Trauma, loss and danger expectancies
– Embedded attributions to self, others and social agencies
– Enduring intervention themes
– Adult self-care and protective behavior
• Interaction of proximal disturbances with specific future developmental tasks
• Interpersonal academic and occupational functioning
• Parental functioning
• Decision making, aspirations and motivations
• Political ideology and social contact
Distal Pathology
• PTSD and other psychiatric disorders
• Physical health problems
• Chronic developmental disturbances
• Adverse life trajectory outcomes
• Increased vulnerability to future life stresses
• Difficulties in treatment situation

Within the broader context of buffering the impact of a child's/adolescent's exposure to violence, the following processes deserve independent consideration:

- **Resistance:** This is the capacity to buffer the distress experienced following exposure to violence, thereby maintaining normal developmental processes.
- **Vulnerability:** This refers to the susceptibility to distress and disturbances during development.
- **Resilience:** This is the capacity to adapt to and recover from a given level of traumatic distress and acute developmental disruption quickly and effectively. The goal(s) of resilience building is to reduce the number of violence-related secondary adversities and/or to improve the child's and family's management of these adversities.
- **Restoration** and **progression:** These ideas underlie the concept of resilience; that is, returning to and moving forward with a normal course of development. In the absence of resilience, there may be multiple efforts at ongoing adjustment.
- **Attention** and **exertion:** From a developmental perspective, efforts at ongoing adjustment require these extensively by the child or adolescent, family and/or child-oriented institutions. These efforts can interfere with other areas of development.
- **Maladjustment:** Within a model of developmental psychopathology, such inadequate adjustment over time can initiate a cascade of changes that may result in a complex constellation of developmental outcomes, which may actually be better conceptualized as a trauma-related developmental disorder.
- **Risk:** It is important to distinguish clearly between children who are vulnerable to or *at risk for* adverse psychological, behavioral or biological outcomes and children whose adjustment responses are *compromised. Risk* also refers to the child's and adolescent's potential for exposure to violence.
- **Developmental compromise:** Traumatic experiences and their aftermath have developmental ramifications. Developmental progression can be compromised through different, yet often interdependent, pathways. There can be a direct loss of recently acquired developmental achievements, interference with the acquisition of developmental competencies, decreased developmental opportunities associated with failure to acquire age-related skills and a decreased initiative to accept developmental challenges.

The issues that accompany *risk exposure, vulnerability* and *developmental compromise* are more complex than commonly recognized: For example, although parental overprotection is often linked with adverse developmental consequences, in some settings it facilitates and supports healthy child and adolescent development. The UCLA Center for Community Health has conducted a multisite study of children of HIV-positive parents.[11] Lester, Rotheram-Borus and Ward have evaluated parenting and attachment extensively using the Parker Parental Bonding Scale (PPBS). On the PPBS, overprotection is associated with adverse developmental consequences. However, in this multisite study, children whose parents scored "high" on this dimension actually fared better. In an environment of community violence, an overprotective parenting approach could be understood to be ecologically sound.[11] Too often, our attachment considerations have not addressed the important developmental impact of the protective behaviors of parents in the face of dangers, in terms of real protection and in children's perceptions of their caretakers. There is a measurable added benefit to perceiving a parent as acting protectively; for example, by monitoring what an adolescent is doing or where an adolescent is going when living in a dangerous environment.

- **Dose of exposure:** This is a concept that is central to any discussion of *resistance, vulnerability, resilience* and *maladjustment.* Researchers and clinicians have typically drawn generalized conclusions from data across exposure groups that show that a majority of children or adolescents are *resilient* or only temporarily distressed, and experience an unproblematic course of recovery. In a study conducted in 1984 of children exposed to a sniper attack at an elementary school, along with our colleagues we found strong *dose-of-exposure* effects over time.[12,13] Those children who were in the direct line of fire on the playground were significantly more likely to have persistent posttraumatic reactions over the next year — a substantial period of time in the developmental life cycle of a child. Children who were trapped in classrooms, one step removed from the direct assault, showed nearly the same levels of distress initially, but they recovered at a much faster rate: By Year 1 after the attack, they had distress levels that were nearly indistinguishable from a group of children who were on vacation during the shooting incident. There was some variability in recovery among the most-exposed group, but not to the extent suggested by less-detailed, *dose-of-exposure* studies.[12,13]

Researchers must be careful not to overuse the concept of *resilience* without adequately analyzing *dose-of-exposure:* For example, in disasters it is generally held that 25% of children will remain distressed over time.[14] However, the rate can be greater than 75% for those trapped in an earthquake, and nearly 90% to 95% among children buried by a mudslide following a hurricane.[15] A structural equation model using data from a large cohort of adolescents exposed to war in Bosnia and Herzegovina shows that among the majority of adolescents who were exposed to the general conditions of war, deprivation, displacement and the unsatisfactory conditions of resettlement, postwar influences were the biggest determinants of current levels of distress and impairment. However, preliminary data analyses suggest that among those who experienced direct threats to their lives, injuries and/or traumatic war-related deaths of immediate family members, there was an unmoderated pathway to current distress and impairment.[16,17]

These findings have major implications for public mental health approaches to children exposed to violence. As researchers and clinicians, we must devote more resources to empirically based treatments that deliver proper assessments and algorithms of intervention strategies. The work of Lieberman and colleagues at the University of California at San Francisco (UCSF) is a good example of the clinical and social benefits of such an investment. (See the chapter authored by Lieberman and colleagues in this text.)

As the result of a series of studies and intervention programs undertaken with our colleagues, we have documented significant levels of untreated exposure to violence and traumatic loss in school-age children and adolescents. At a high school in the Los Angeles Unified School District, we identified more than 30 students who had suffered gunshot wounds. Despite having a sophisticated on-site health service, the school provided mental health services or other institutional support to very few of these students.[18] In a high-crime area of Pasadena, California, school-wide screenings at junior and senior high schools identified a pool of students who had a history of multiple exposures to extreme violence. These students were clearly overrepresented among students who had failing grades, but school administrators were not aware of this fact.[19]

There are numerous efforts being undertaken across the United States to enhance academic performance and motivation for learning in "underperforming" and "low-opportunity" schools. However, many of these initiatives, including the building of university partnerships with community agencies, businesses and schools, do not include complementary programs that address the real-life impact of the exposure to violence. In general, nationwide, there is a lack of public attention to the reservoir of exposure to violence that exists among students in these schools.

Before beginning an extensive discussion of possible mediators for exposure to violence, we must ensure that the principle of *dose-of-exposure* is reinforced in our public mental health approaches. Over the past 2 decades, the UCLA Trauma Psychiatry Program has placed dedicated staff members on-site in school violence recovery programs to assist school-based mental health teams with carrying out sustained programs for the most severely affected students and school personnel: For example, following the catastrophic school shooting in 2001 at Santana High School in Santee, California, a member of the UCLA program was principally responsible for acute and long-term mental health interventions on behalf of the students who were shot.[20]

Unfortunately, despite years of well-meaning public attention to youth and school violence, it has been our repeated experience that the mental health and school district commitment to providing the necessary direct care or rehabilitation services to students who have had the most direct exposures to violence remains spotty, at best.

Revisiting Resistance and Vulnerability: Opposite Sides of the Same Coin

Both resistance and vulnerability are neutral terms, connoting neither positive nor negative mental health attributes. Consider the following example: In 1987, the UCLA Trauma Psychiatry Program provided assistance to an elementary school where a psychotic woman took hostage a classroom of fifth-grade children. She forced the students to write her suicide note, and then she shot herself in the head. Some of the most empathic young students recognized her psychotic distress and understood the unpredictability of her behavior: Therefore, they did not believe her when she said that she would not harm them or their teacher. Meanwhile, other students were more naive in their appraisal of the situation and accepted her statement that she would not harm any of them. Interestingly, the first group demonstrated more acute distress, while the second group appeared more resistant, even though the empathy and psychological awareness exhibited by the first group was helpful in promoting their resilience.

Perceived self-efficacy can also buffer distress. We worked with a child who engaged what he learned during his earthquake preparedness drill — to "drop and cover" — during an actual shooting on a playground. He felt proud and effective in his protective action and demonstrated less acute distress compared with other children in this severe-exposure group.

The very same factor that contributes to resistance may also contribute to vulnerability, especially during circumstances of danger or violence: For example, a strong affiliation with or attachment to others who are present can help with the emotional regulation of fear, but at the same time it can create intense distress over harm to or loss of family, peer or group members.

Resistance and vulnerability may operate differently across different levels of exposure. The literature on children and disasters consistently reports that children who have prior anxiety conditions or anxiety sensitivity may demonstrate greater distress and worry beyond that predicted by their level of exposure.[14] This type of vulnerability may prove even more apparent during episodes of moderate or mild levels of exposure.[21]

Resistance and Vulnerability Vary Across Levels of Maturation

Resistance and vulnerability may also operate differently across various stages of neurobiological maturation, especially during periods of plasticity and consolidation.[22] It is critical to delineate specific neurodevelopmental processes that may be jeopardized by exposure to violence rather than simply refering to one developmental period as being a more vulnerable period than another. We are just beginning to understand the developmental neurobiology of danger and the special vulnerabilities exhibited as these systems slowly mature. Lieberman of UCSF and Carrión of Stanford are contributing heavily to this growing body of literature. (See the following 2 chapters in this text for discussions of their work.)

In general terms, the neurobiology of danger includes a period during early childhood when situation appraisal is dependent on social referencing and the response to cries of distress among caretakers, when emotional response is geared toward eliciting caretaking functions, and when protective responses depend upon interventions by parents or others. During this period, the startle reflex is not yet sufficiently modulated that it allows children to turn away from danger and seek out a protective other. During the school-age years, the development of greater inhibitive interneuron capacity leads to a maturation of the startle response that allows children to more accurately appraise danger, to monitor their emotions related to the danger and to evaluate whether to turn away from the danger or turn toward it to protect themselves and/or others. During adolescence, a developmental period of dynamic brain changes, the capacity to anticipate, assess and respond to dangers increases, as does the ability to train and regulate danger emotions — for example, through thrill seeking or watching horror movies — and to plan and take direct action by oneself or through others.

As we learn more about the intricacies of these maturational processes related to danger, we will be able to more accurately describe specific vulnerabilities that result in neurobiological alteration and alteration of the developmental trajectory. These vulnerabilities may include genetic–environmental interactions.[23]

Epidemiological surveys show that there is extensive exposure to violence and trauma during childhood and adolescence, and that repeated or serial exposures are not uncommon.[24] Along with our colleagues, we are just beginning, however, to investigate the mechanisms by which prior exposures to violence and danger influence later resistance or vulnerabilities to the same or even dissimilar experiences. Concurrently, we are investigating the impact of singular violent exposures within an ecology of ongoing danger. The National Child Traumatic Stress Network (NCTSN) is designing a comprehensive trauma history instrument that will provide a detailed characterization of the developmental profile of different types of violent exposures — including exposures that overlap and/or span a developmental period (eg, child abuse and witnessing of domestic violence) and singular extreme violent experiences — and the ecological factors related to dangerous environments, traumatic loss and extended separations (see Fig 2; NCTSN, in draft form, unpublished). The final version of this instrument will include Web-based data entry with drop-down screens that will capture more completely the salient features of trauma exposure. We believe that this trauma history profile will provide the information needed to understand the complex interplay among violence exposure, resistance and vulnerability.

*Fig 2. Proposed trauma/loss exposure profile**

Type of Trauma	Features of Trauma	Nature of Involvement	Primary Focus of Treatment? (check box if Yes)
Chronic/Repeated			
Neglect/maltreatment	☐ Physical ☐ Emotional	☐ Victim ☐ Witness	☐
Sexual abuse	☐ Penetration ☐ Nonfamily ☐ Intrafamily ☐ CPS report	☐ Victim ☐ Witness	☐
Physical abuse	☐ Serious injury ☐ Weapon used ☐ CPS report	☐ Victim ☐ Witness	☐
Emotional abuse	☐ Caregiver substance abuse ☐ Other: ________________	☐ Victim ☐ Witness	☐
Domestic violence	☐ Weapon used ☐ Reported ☐ Serious injury ☐ Report filed	☐ Victim ☐ Witness	☐
Community violence	☐ Gang related ☐ High crime ☐ Drug traffic	☐ Victim ☐ Witness	☐
War/political violence	☐ ______________________	☐ Victim ☐ Witness	☐
Life-threatening medical illness	☐ ______________________	☐ Victim ☐ Witness	☐
Circumscribed			
Serious accident	☐ Motor vehicle ☐ Hospitalized ☐ Dog bite ☐ Other: _________	☐ Victim ☐ Witness	☐
School violence	☐ Shooting ☐ Bullying ☐ Suicide ☐ Assault	☐ Victim ☐ Witness	☐
Disaster	☐ Earthquake ☐ Fire ☐ Flood ☐ Hurricane ☐ Tornado ☐ Other: _________	☐ Lost home ☐ Injured	☐
Terrorism	☐ Conventional weapon ☐ Biological ☐ Chemical ☐ Radiological		☐
Kidnapping		☐ Victim ☐ Witness	☐
Sexual assault/rape	☐ Weapon used ☐ Stranger ☐ Date rape ☐ Prosecution	☐ Victim ☐ Witness	☐
Interpersonal violence	☐ Robbery ☐ Assault ☐ Homicide ☐ Suicide ☐ Suicide attempt ☐ Bullying/discrimination	☐ Victim ☐ Witness	☐
Loss/Separation			
Traumatic bereavement	☐ Parent ☐ Sibling ☐ Friend ☐ Primary caregiver ☐ Other relative	☐ Violence ☐ Accident ☐ Illness ☐ Disaster ☐ Terrorism	☐
Divorce	☐ Amicable ☐ Adversarial		☐
Enforced separation	☐ Foster care ☐ Refugee ☐ Parent imprisoned ☐ Parent hospitalized		☐

CPS = Child Protective Services. *(continued)*

*At time of publication, unpublished by The National Child Traumatic Stress Network.

Fig 2. Proposed trauma/loss exposure profile * *(continued)*

Age(s) at Time of Trauma																			
1	2	3	4	5	6	7	8	9	10	11	12	13	14	15	16	17	18	19	20
☐	☐	☐	☐	☐	☐	☐	☐	☐	☐	☐	☐	☐	☐	☐	☐	☐	☐	☐	☐
☐	☐	☐	☐	☐	☐	☐	☐	☐	☐	☐	☐	☐	☐	☐	☐	☐	☐	☐	☐
☐	☐	☐	☐	☐	☐	☐	☐	☐	☐	☐	☐	☐	☐	☐	☐	☐	☐	☐	☐
☐	☐	☐	☐	☐	☐	☐	☐	☐	☐	☐	☐	☐	☐	☐	☐	☐	☐	☐	☐
☐	☐	☐	☐	☐	☐	☐	☐	☐	☐	☐	☐	☐	☐	☐	☐	☐	☐	☐	☐
☐	☐	☐	☐	☐	☐	☐	☐	☐	☐	☐	☐	☐	☐	☐	☐	☐	☐	☐	☐
☐	☐	☐	☐	☐	☐	☐	☐	☐	☐	☐	☐	☐	☐	☐	☐	☐	☐	☐	☐
☐	☐	☐	☐	☐	☐	☐	☐	☐	☐	☐	☐	☐	☐	☐	☐	☐	☐	☐	☐
☐	☐	☐	☐	☐	☐	☐	☐	☐	☐	☐	☐	☐	☐	☐	☐	☐	☐	☐	☐
☐	☐	☐	☐	☐	☐	☐	☐	☐	☐	☐	☐	☐	☐	☐	☐	☐	☐	☐	☐
☐	☐	☐	☐	☐	☐	☐	☐	☐	☐	☐	☐	☐	☐	☐	☐	☐	☐	☐	☐
☐	☐	☐	☐	☐	☐	☐	☐	☐	☐	☐	☐	☐	☐	☐	☐	☐	☐	☐	☐
☐	☐	☐	☐	☐	☐	☐	☐	☐	☐	☐	☐	☐	☐	☐	☐	☐	☐	☐	☐
☐	☐	☐	☐	☐	☐	☐	☐	☐	☐	☐	☐	☐	☐	☐	☐	☐	☐	☐	☐
☐	☐	☐	☐	☐	☐	☐	☐	☐	☐	☐	☐	☐	☐	☐	☐	☐	☐	☐	☐
☐	☐	☐	☐	☐	☐	☐	☐	☐	☐	☐	☐	☐	☐	☐	☐	☐	☐	☐	☐
☐	☐	☐	☐	☐	☐	☐	☐	☐	☐	☐	☐	☐	☐	☐	☐	☐	☐	☐	☐
☐	☐	☐	☐	☐	☐	☐	☐	☐	☐	☐	☐	☐	☐	☐	☐	☐	☐	☐	☐

Interventions That Address Exposure to Violence

Interventions that address resistance and vulnerability typically focus on preparation skills or improved competencies: Some are directed at children's intrinsic factors. Wendy K. Silverman, PhD, a member of the Terrorism and Disaster Branch of the NCTSN, is currently developing a protocol to enhance resistance among children who have anxiety sensitivity and are living in hurricane-prone areas. Because youth development programs employ a positive psychology that enhances personal attributes that relate to danger — eg, building courage[25] or interpersonal skills that can be used in dangerous circumstances — they may add to resistance.

Family, school and community programs that minimize violence or its consequences, even *after* its onset, enhance resistance. Whatever decreases distress during danger fortifies resistance, while, on the other hand, whatever increases distress adds to vulnerability. Therefore, an effective intervention employed during the violence can reduce distress, whereas a failed intervention increases distress. Failures in the "protective shield" are especially distressing to young children and their parents. In response to violence, the actions of a family member or friend that are perceived as further endangering self or others increase distress.

The interaction of event-specific features and newly acquired competencies represents another dimension of vulnerability: For example, we have evaluated young children who were proud of their newly acquired bladder control but subsequently felt intense shame at wetting themselves during a violent incident.

When Does the Violence End?

Clearly, the ramifications of a violent event do not end when the violence itself ends. Preventing unnecessary secondary exposures to distressing sights will reduce vulnerability. In the immediate aftermath of a violent incident, the management of reunions between children and their parents/other caretakers may contain or exacerbate the appraisal of danger that underlies the emotions of danger.

The NCTSN site at the Yale Child Study Center is studying how developmentally informed responses made by first responders to children, youth, their families and schools during or after a violent incident may significantly help control the physiological responses to danger, regulate intense negative emotions and prevent insensitive or inappropriate actions that can worsen distress. The Wendt Center for Loss and Healing in Washington, DC, another NCTSN site, provides assistance to children and families at the DC coroner's office, helping to minimize a potentially horrific experience following violence. As another method to enhance resistance, the NCTSN site at the Boston University Medical Center is studying the effects of immediate and sustained pain management for severe injuries or burns.

Effective steps taken to create or restore a safe and secure environment are prerequisites to providing relief from threat and minimizing the high level of responses to danger. These steps often require the involvement and actions of a broad range of social agencies; for example, an arrest by police, emergency safety provided by a domestic violence shelter or the removal of a child from the parent by Child Protective Services (CPS).

A New Perspective on Resilience

As discussed previously, resilience refers to the following 2 interdependent processes:

- the ability to better tolerate a given level of distress without major disturbances in function
- a lessening of distress accompanied by early, effective restoration of psychological, emotional, behavioral and biological functions

There is currently increasing interest in resilience and resilience building at the level of the individual child, the family, the school and the community. The primary goal of resilience building is to preserve developmental competencies in the face of violence-induced distress. In contrast, the primary goal of adjustment is to promote recovery in affected areas of functioning in parallel with a more prolonged recovery from postviolence reactions.

Some resilience-building interventions fall under the rubric of "psychological first aid."[26] In a developmentally appropriate manner, psychological first aid for a child validates the seriousness of an event or events so that it corresponds with the child's level of distress. These interventions also often provide the following:

- skills for regulating violence-related negative emotions and physiological reactions
- skills for increasing verbal capacity in order to talk about the event more easily
- assistance with contextual discrimination of reminders of the traumatic event
- clarifications of misunderstandings, confusions and distortions about the event that exacerbate distress
- corrections of myths, misconceptions and rumors regarding the event that add to fears of recurrence
- assistance with challenging issues of human accountability, including special attention given to attributions of excessive responsibility by self and others
- help with bridging estrangements among family members and/or friends that may arise from shifting concerns for self and others

Examples of the last intervention mentioned include addressing a 4-year-old girl's rejection of her father after witnessing him tied up and made to watch the rape of the mother, and a 3-year-old boy's fear of his mother after watching her use a knife to ward off a domestic violence assault.[27,28] Early intervention for these types of estrangements can significantly enhance the child's and family's recovery.

As part of resilience building, throughout the early course of recovery the courage displayed by the child or adolescent should be fortified and praised, as the violence itself may have induced a sense of terror, cowardliness, ineffectualness, failure to protect and/or helplessness.

Other emotions that may require special attention and intervention are the anger and rage that often occur during a violent incident and the intense preoccupation with thoughts of protection and revenge immediately following the exposure. In such cases, psychoeducation is an appropriate resilience-building strategy because it provides developmentally on-target information about common reactions. It also helps children, families, schools and communities gain an understanding of and tolerance for the variations in the course of recovery and the tools that are appropriate to monitor recovery: For example, within a family or classroom, increasing mutual understanding and tolerance for different courses of recovery encourages more flexible responses, which, in turn, increase the positive milieu and thereby foster resilience.

Resilience-building strategies must include steps to restore the child's disrupted sense of a "protective shield." This often requires a temporary "regression" or an enhancement in protective behaviors through such avenues as greater police presence at a school or in the community or increased monitoring behaviors by family members. The immediate implementation of strategies to assist with specific posttraumatic and loss reactions, as well as with problematic behaviors such as reckless actions, are also part of a resilience-building strategy.

Violent events are typically embedded within an ecology of adversity and/or initiate a cascade of changes in a child's life. Resilience building can increase the ability of the child, family, school and/or community to problem solve in the face of adversity. Assistance with decision making and advocacy, as provided by social agencies, can prevent a series of secondary adversities that can further compromise recovery. Enhancing specific social and communication skills, such as what to say to others about the violent event and how to protect oneself against ill-timed retellings of the trauma, are often overlooked ingredients of resilience building.

Resilience building may also include assisting families with resource-allocation issues, such as balancing parenting responsibilities and attending to secondary adversities. Resilience building for schools, from preschool through high school, must include crisis-management strategies *and* adjustment strategies for students affected by violence. For students affected by violence, schools must provide unqualified support that includes absolutely no undue stigmatization or misleading deviant labeling as students recover from changes in their academic performance and/or behavior.

Adjustment: Life After Violence

As we have discussed, violence results in many changes that affect the child, family, school and community, and it often requires interventions that move beyond resilience building to promote ongoing *adjustment.* Evidence-based, adjustment-focused interventions include the following[29]:

- efforts directed at obtaining social justice
- realignments of schemas of danger and protection
- physical rehabilitation
- recovery of developmental progression
- constructive actions aimed at improving the ecology of danger, trauma reminders and adversities for the child, family, school or community

The goals of adjustment are twofold:

- to address the cascade of developmental consequences as an outgrowth of violence-related adversities
- to minimize, address and manage intercurrent trauma, loss and adversities that can disrupt ongoing adjustment

Modern neurobiology suggests that a long-term strategy is needed to promote ongoing contextual discrimination between prior trauma or frightening experiences and aspects of the child's or adolescent's current or future environment.[30,31] This contextual discrimination involves specific neuroinhibitory processes that are separate from those underlying fear conditioning. Essentially, with each subsequent reminder of the violence, opportunities for new learning can increase flexibility and the appropriateness of appraisal, emotional regulation and considerations of protective intervention. The trauma narrative portion of structured treatments for posttraumatic stress disorder has the potential for learning, especially for introducing new responses to often ubiquitous reminders of trauma. As Bowlby pointed out over 25 years ago, a conspiracy of silence, a disavowal of the violent experience and a lack of attention to the long-term consequences for children can inhibit opportunities for this critical aspect of ongoing adjustment.[32]

Adjustment strategies should also include specific individual, family and school plans whose aims are to improve developmental recovery in the biological functions affected by exposure to violence, such as sleep, attention capacity, regulation of aggression and hypervigilance. In the school arena, the use of a graduated curriculum geared toward the recovery course of affected students can help promote adjustment. A graduated curriculum matches attention demands to improvements in attention capacity while adjusting for anticipated and unanticipated reminders of trauma, such as criminal proceedings and/or CPS hearings.

More research is needed regarding the use of appropriate psychopharmacological interventions as part of an adjustment strategy. Pharmacological agents could target neurobiological changes that directly affect adjustment, such as violence-induced sleep disturbances that contribute to learning impairment.

Using resilience building, as we have discussed, to manage potential subsequent adversities can be a critical component of successful adjustment to an exposure to violence. The following case study is an example of a cascade of developmental consequences that were managed through appropriate intervention:

CLINICAL CASE 1: High school athlete recovers from cascade of events following violence

A 17-year-old high school athlete unexpectedly became a hero when he "took a bullet" while protecting the lives of schoolmates during a school shooting. As he was not a strong academic student, a sports-related scholarship had been his avenue to college. However, since he was now unable to compete in sports due to physical injuries he sustained during the shooting, he lost the scholarship he had earned, as well as the opportunity to be the first in his family to go to college. He subsequently became despondent and, in conjunction with severe ongoing posttraumatic stress, he began to engage in atypical public behavior that prompted action by law enforcement. Fortunately, a keen district attorney, noting that this student did not match the profile for this behavior, followed the advice of school officials and consulted with our trauma team at UCLA. As a result, school-based and outpatient treatment interventions were substituted for prosecution and imprisonment.

continued

CLINICAL CASE 1: High school athlete recovers from cascade of events following violence ***(continued)***

Subsequently, this adolescent received specialized, trauma-focused intervention, with additional family sessions, and experienced remediation of posttraumatic stress and depressive reactions and showed increased academic motivation. After graduation from high school, he went on to attend a local community college.

Consequences of Failure of the Social Contract

Adjustment after violence must also address issues of *social justice* and an investment in the *social contract.* We have done work in an elementary school where the mothers of 5 children were murdered — without any subsequent arrests. The schoolmates of these children struggled with the developmental task of following rules because, for them, the most important rule of society had been broken — with no apparent accountability. Social justice is an important aspect of constructive adjustment to preoccupations with revenge. In one of our clinical programs, we learned the importance of intervening in the developmental cascade that can follow the failure of social justice (see box below):

CLINICAL CASE 2: Father-son intervention following failure of the social contract

During a combined psychotherapy-mentorship intervention program for elementary school children exposed to chronic violence, we followed an 11-year-old boy whose paternal uncle was shot and killed while walking home from a grocery store. During the initial weeks following the murder, this child demonstrated expected traumatic grief reactions and illustrated in drawings his preoccupation with fantasies of protective actions that could have averted the fatal consequence. However, he showed no accompanying hypervigilance or concern over possible future danger to himself. Over the subsequent weeks, the police failed to collect sufficient evidence to arrest any suspects and, because of warranted fears of perpetrator retaliation, no witnesses came forward. There was much community talk about who committed the crime. As time passed, the father's own traumatic grief reactions led him to openly express his desire to seek revenge for his brother's death. The father

continued

CLINICAL CASE 2: Father-son intervention following failure of the social contract ***(continued)***

neither had real plans to do so, nor did he have any history of criminal behavior. In response to his father's desire for revenge, the son showed a dramatic change in demeanor and preoccupations. He spoke of envisioning that when he was older he would become the target of a similar retaliatory attack by a presumed son of his uncle's murderer. The boy had a sudden shift in his relationship with his father, whom he now viewed as less protective and more willing to endanger his future safety. The son began to fantasize about the violent force he would need to combat the imagined future threat. As a consequence, he became frightened and hypervigilant, particularly when walking on his own to and from school. Observing this change, we intervened to help the father and son achieve a more constructive course for their traumatic grief.

Physical and/or sexual abuse of a child is another example of failure of the social contract between parent/caregiver/authority figure and child. There are similar adjustment issues (to the previous Clinical Case; see box) involved in the recovery process from this form of interpersonal violence. Failure to intervene, or returning a child to an abusive setting, constitutes a critical breach in the social contract. As detailed in *When a Child Kills: Abused Children Who Kill Their Parents*[33] and *All God's Children: The Bosket Family and the American Tradition of Violence*,[34] these breaches can trigger catastrophic youth violence both inside and outside the home.

Conducted with our colleagues, a study of adolescents who were exposed to catastrophic loss of life and destruction during and following the 1988 Spitak earthquake in Armenia introduces a moral dimension into adjusting to exposure to violence.[35] We found that with increased dose of exposure, chronic posttraumatic stress reactions and secondary adversities, affected adolescents showed accelerated moral development but impaired moral functioning. Simply, exposure to disaster or to violence affects the adolescents' will to use moral reasoning and judgment.

As emphasized in the emerging literature on normative developmental adjustment and positive youth development,[25] a central feature of adjustment to violence is the promotion of constructive actions that are prosocial and aimed at improving the social ecology of the child or youth. Such actions can steer the progression of intervention thoughts that often follow violence from a preoccupation with revenge towards socially adaptive, reparative efforts that invest in social institutions and agencies, and rely on the social contract.

We have worked with youth who witnessed the shootings of their closest friends, and, after participating in school-based, trauma-loss, adolescent group treatment, subsequently wanted to volunteer at a hospital and pursue a career in the health professions. Unfortunately, we have also seen how the ecology of poverty, inadequate community and educational resources, cultural divides and prejudice can limit opportunities severely for these kinds of constructive programs. With an increased sense of hopelessness, children and youth often become locked into less-adaptive modes of recovery, including making maladaptive peer choices or becoming a member of a gang in order to deal with ongoing concerns about danger and violence.

A major developmental accomplishment is the progressive capacity for self-care, a competency that exposure to child and adolescent violence can compromise.[36] The promotion of long-term adjustment after exposure to violent incidents includes forward-looking or developmentally *pulsed* interventions to rebuild this capacity, including strategies designed to handle violence or loss-related reminders that could prompt drug use, a relapse into reckless behavior or renewed restrictions on appropriate developmental activities.

Such pulsed interventions might extend through adolescence, dating and marriage and into adulthood, and eventually even target parenting issues that may arise because of expectancies stemming from early childhood experiences of violence. The following narrative highlights an intervention that addressed parenting expectations based on exposure to childhood violence:

CLINICAL CASE 3: Intervening to adjust a father's parenting expectations helps son recover

To protect his family during an armed robbery of their business, a father brandished a legally registered handgun. Subsequently, over the objections of the mother and his 10-year-old son, the father insisted on teaching his son to shoot a gun. However, the father was openly dismissive of his son's wish to have the police find, arrest and punish the perpetrators. Because of how he was raised, the father did not believe in

continued

CLINICAL CASE 3: Intervening to adjust a father's parenting expectations helps son recover ***(continued)***

the social contract of the family or society. He had been badly abused by his mother and subsequently went to live with his uncle, who was an enforcer for an organized crime ring. As a result, the father did not believe that society's laws deterred violence or that agents of the law protected or insured justice. The father wanted his son to see the world through his eyes. But the son was only becoming more symptomatic. With assistance, the father came to understand that because he had raised his son in a loving, nonabusive home, and in a law-abiding community, his son's expectations were inevitably different from his own. Indeed, these divergent expectations were a sign of his success as a father. He gained a more empathic understanding of his son's responses to the robbery and a respect for his son's investment in the social contract. The son improved quickly.

Adopting Effective Interventions

The "Learning From Research and Clinical Practice Core" of the NCTSN focuses on a legislative agenda that would increase the standard of care through the development, dissemination and adoption of evidence-based treatments for different types of trauma for children and adolescents of all ages. Treatment is often an essential component of successful adjustments to exposures to violence, especially for those who have high levels of exposure *and* for those who have complicated courses of recovery. Today, many interventions have incorporated the resilience-building and adjustment strategies discussed in this chapter.

As we transition from demonstrating the overall efficacy of interventions towards delineating the relative contributions of the components of an intervention, we must apply the appropriate metrics to capture the wide range of mental health outcomes. Furthermore, when evaluating the benefits of a treatment, we must look at the degree of symptom reduction as well as at other critical adjustment measures: For example, school-based treatments for adolescents exposed to violence and traumatic loss can be associated with significant improvements in academic performance and behavior.[37-39] Treatment can move adolescents from failing to passing grade-point averages, thereby reengaging them in sports, after-school programs and other normal school-related activities that affect youth development positively. Based on a dose-of-exposure model, special efforts should be directed at addressing barriers to care and improving the provision of evidence-based treatments for individuals who have high levels of exposure, ongoing distress and complicated courses of recovery. For adolescents, school-based and group interventions have shown promise for engagement, compliance and effectiveness, as well as for reduced stigma.

Complementary and pulsed interventions to facilitate developmental transitions and the acquisition of developmental competencies require the integration of evidence-based treatment using positive youth development programs, such as mentoring, academic enrichment, after-school activities and community service. Mentoring, in particular, assists adolescents with the transition to young adulthood, an age range replete with challenges to ongoing adjustment. Refugee and recent immigrant student populations face unique challenges to adjustment, including the following:

- the immigration and resettlement process itself
- integration into an expanded or new peer group and new school setting
- a lack of peer and school understanding of their cultural issues and perhaps even their families' experiences of war and political violence
- new cultural expectations that introduce conflict into the family

Both a rehabilitation model and a habilitation model are currently under investigation by the Complex Trauma and Adolescent Task Forces of the NCTSN. These approaches recognize that successful long-term adjustment requires specialized interventions that build or restore developmental competencies (eg, in emotional regulation) that were not achieved adequately or were consolidated because of exposures to violence over a significant developmental period.[40] This type of remedial strategy is gaining in importance as we increase our knowledge of the critical roles that child sexual and physical abuse can play in the onset and course of other psychiatric disorders, including bipolar disorder and its associated risk of suicidal behavior.[41]

Conclusion

As we improve our conceptual models for understanding buffering and risk for children and adolescents who have been exposed to violence and seek to translate these models into effective clinical interventions we will need to integrate our knowledge of the following: developmental epidemiology;

economics; social, cultural and historical perspectives; developmental psychology and neurobiology; gene-environment interactions; clinical investigations; systems of care; and public policy. This chapter, including the 3 clinical case examples, provides one framework with which to address the complex interactions among these forces and the multidimensional strategies for the prevention of violence, and interventions that protect or restore the future of children and families after incidences of violence. We hope that this integration will add to the current expanded discussion of the environmentally-mediated risks for developmental psychopathology.[42]

References

1. Crouch JL, Hanson RF, Saunders BE, Kilpatrick DG, Resnick HS. Income, race/ethnicity, and exposure to violence in youth: results from the national survey of adolescents. *Journal of Community Psychology.* 2000;28:625-641.
2. James B. Changing patterns in the ecological landscape of juvenile delinquency: availability of crack cocaine, handguns and increased pathological gang activity among high school adolescent boys in Los Angeles County, 1987-92. Paper presented at: Third International Conference on Delinquent Behavior; May 1994; Philadelphia, Pa.
3. Pynoos RS, Eth S: Children traumatized by witnessing acts of personal violence: homicide, rape and suicide behavior. In: Eth S, Pynoos RS, eds. *Post-Traumatic Stress Disorder in Children.* Washington, DC: American Psychiatric Press; 1985:17-44. Progress in Psychiatry Series.
4. Pynoos RS, Steinberg AM, Wraith R. A developmental model of childhood traumatic stress. In: Cicchetti D, Cohen DJ, eds. *Developmental Psychopathology: Risk, Disorder, and Adaptation.* Vol 2. New York, NY: John Wiley & Sons; 1995:72-93.
5. Pynoos RS, Steinberg AM, Piacentini JC. A developmental psychopathology model of childhood traumatic stress and intersection with anxiety disorders. *Biological Psychiatry.* 1999;46:1542-1554.
6. Pynoos RS, Steinberg AM, Schreiber MD, Brymer M. Children and families: a new framework for preparedness and response to danger, terrorism and trauma. In: Schein LA, Spitz HI, Burlingame GM, Mushkin PR, eds. *Group Approaches to the Psychological Effects of Terrorist Disasters.* New York, NY: Haworth Press. In press.
7. Heller SS, Larrieu JA, D'Imperio R, Boris NW. Research on resilience to child maltreatment: empirical considerations. *Child Abuse & Neglect.* 1999;23:321-338.
8. Luthar SS, Cicchetti D, Becker B. The construct of resilience: a critical evaluation and guidelines for future work. *Child Development.* 2000;71:543-562.
9. Robinson JL. Are there implications for prevention research from studies of resilience? *Child Development.* 2000;71:570-572.
10. von Eye A, Schuster C. The odds of resilience. *Child Development.* 2000;71:563-566.
11. Lester P, Rotheram-Borus MJ, Ward MJ. The intergenerational impact of parental HIV illness. Symposium presented at: American Academy of Child and Adolescent Psychiatry 50th Annual Conference; October 2003; Miami Beach, Fla.
12. Pynoos RS, Nader K, Frederick C, Gonda L, Stuber M. Grief reactions in school age children following a sniper attack at school. *The Israel Journal of Psychiatry and Related Sciences.* 1987;24:53-63.
13. Nader K, Pynoos R, Fairbanks L, Frederick C. Children's PTSD reactions one year after a sniper attack at their school. *The American Journal of Psychiatry.* 1990;147:1526-1530.
14. Vogel M, Vernberg EM. Psychological responses of children to natural and human-made disasters: I. Children's psychological reactions to disasters. *Journal of Clinical Child Psychology.* 1993;22:464-484.
15. Goenjian AK, Molina L, Steinberg AM, et al. Posttraumatic stress and depressive reactions among Nicaraguan adolescents after hurricane Mitch. *The American Journal of Psychiatry.* 2001;158:788-794.

16. Legerski JP, Layne CM, Isakson B, Saltzman WS, Djapo N, Kutlac M. Post-war psychosocial adjustment in war-exposed Bosnian youths: a SEM analysis. Poster presented at: 19th Annual Meeting of the International Society for Traumatic Stress Studies; November 2003; Chicago, Ill.

17. Layne CM, Pynoos RS, Saltzman WR, et al. Trauma/grief-focused group psychotherapy: school-based postwar intervention with traumatized Bosnian adolescents. *Group Dynamics: Theory, Research, and Practice.* 2001;5:277-290.

18. Layne CM, Pynoos RS, Cardenas J. Wounded adolescence: school-based group psychotherapy for adolescents who have sustained or witnessed violent interpersonal injury. In: Shafii M, Shafii SL, eds. *School Violence: Assessment, Management, Prevention.* Washington, DC: American Psychiatric Press; 2001:163-186.

19. Saltzman WR, Pynoos RS, Layne CM, Steinberg AM, Aisenberg E. Trauma- and grief-focused intervention for adolescents exposed to community violence: results of a school-based screening and group treatment protocol. *Group Dynamics: Theory, Research, and Practice.* 2001;5:291-303.

20. Brymer M, Steinberg A, McGlenn R, Pynoos R. Santana High School shooting: a public mental health response. Paper presented at: 18th Annual Meeting of the International Society for Traumatic Stress Studies; November 7-10, 2002; Baltimore, Md.

21. Asarnow J, Glynn S, Pynoos RS, et al. When the earth stops shaking: earthquake sequelae among children diagnosed for pre-earthquake psychopathology. *Journal of the American Academy of Child and Adolescent Psychiatry.* 1999;38:1016-1023.

22. Pynoos RS, Steinberg AM, Ornitz EM, Goenjian AK. Issues in the developmental neurobiology of traumatic stress. *Annals of the New York Academy of Sciences.* 1997;821:176-193.

23. Suomi SJ. How gene-environment interactions influence emotional development in rhesus monkeys. In: García Coll C, Bearer EL, Lerner RM, eds. *Nature and Nurture: The Complex Interplay of Genetic and Environmental Influences on Human Behavior and Development.* Mahwah, NJ: Lawrence Erlbaum; 2003:35-52.

24. Cook A, Blaustein M, Spinnozola J, van der Kolk B, eds. Complex trauma in children and adolescents [white paper]. Washington, DC: Complex Trauma Task Force, National Child Traumatic Stress Network. 2003.

25. Peterson C, Seligman ME. The positive psychology of youth development. In: Evans DL, Foa EB, Gur RE, et al, eds. *A Call for Treatments and Preventions that Work for Adolescents: A Research Agenda in Mental Health.* Oxford, England: Oxford University Press. In press.

26. Pynoos RS, Nader K. Psychological first aid and treatment approach for children exposed to community violence: research implications. *Journal of Traumatic Stress.* 1988;1:445-473.

27. Pynoos RS, Nader K. Children who witness the sexual assaults of their mothers. *Journal of the American Academy of Adolescent Psychiatry.* 1988;27:567-572.

28. Lieberman AF, Comptom NC, Van Horn P, Ghosh Ippen C. *Losing a Parent to Death in the Early Years: Guidelines for the Treatment of Traumatic Bereavement in Infancy and Early Childhood.* Washington, DC: Zero to Three Press; 2003.

29. Layne CM, Warren JS, Saltzman WS, Fulton J, Steinberg AM, Pynoos RS. Retraumatization and posttraumatic adjustment: the roles of distressing reminders, secondary adversities and resilience. In: Schein LA, Spitz HI, Burlingame GM, Mushkin PR, eds. *Group Approaches for the Psychological Effects of Terrorist Disasters.* New York, NY: Haworth Press. In press.

30. Bouton ME. Context, ambiguity, and unlearning: sources of relapse after behavioral extinction. *Biological Psychiatry.* 2002;52:976-986.

31. Cain CK, Blouin AM, Barad M. L-type voltage-gated calcium channels are required for extinction, but not for acquisition or expression, of conditional fear in mice. *The Journal of Neuroscience: The Official Journal of the Society for Neuroscience.* 2002;22:9113-9121.

32. Bowlby J. On knowing what you are not supposed to know and feeling what you are not supposed to feel. *Canadian Journal of Psychiatry. Revue Canadienne de Psychiatrie.* 1979;24:403-408.

33. Mones P. *When a Child Kills: Abused Children Who Kill Their Parents.* New York, NY: Pocket Books; 1991.

34. Butterfield F. *All God's Children: The Bosket Family and the American Tradition of Violence.* New York, NY: Avon; 1996.

35. Goenjian A, Stilwell BM, Steinberg AM, et al. Moral development and psychopathological interference in conscience functioning among adolescents after trauma. *Journal of the American Academy of Child and Adolescent Psychiatry.* 1999;38:376-384.

36. Wyatt GE, Guthrie D, Notgrass CM. Differential effects of women's child sexual abuse and subsequent sexual revictimization. *Journal of Consulting and Clinical Psychology.* 1992;60:167-173.

37. Saltzman WR, Steinberg AM, Layne CM, Aisenberg E, Pynoos RS. A developmental approach to school-based treatment of adolescents exposed to trauma and traumatic loss. *Journal of Child and Adolescent Group Therapy.* 2001;11:43-56.

38. Saltzman WR, Layne CM, Steinberg AM, Arslanagic B, Pynoos RS. Developing a culturally and ecologically sound intervention program for youth exposed to war and terrorism. *Child and Adolescent Psychiatric Clinics of North America.* 2003;12:319-342.

39. Stein BD, Jaycox LH, Kataoka SH, et al. A mental health intervention for schoolchildren exposed to violence: a randomized controlled trial. *JAMA: The Journal of the American Medical Association.* 2003;290:603-611.

40. Cloitre M, Koenen KC, Cohen LR, Han H. Skills training in affective and interpersonal regulation followed by exposure: a phase-based treatment for PTSD related to childhood abuse. *Journal of Consulting and Clinical Psychology.* 2002;70:1067-1074.

41. Leverich GS, McElroy SL, Suppes T, et al. Early physical and sexual abuse associated with an adverse course of bipolar illness. *Biological Psychiatry.* 2002;51:288-297.

42. Rutter M. Environmentally mediated risks for psychopathology: research strategies and findings. *Journal of the American Academy of Child and Adolescent Psychiatry.* 2005;44:3-18.

Understanding the Effects of Early Life Stress on Brain Development

Victor G. Carrión, MD

Introduction

Many children who experience physical and/or sexual abuse and/or witness domestic violence suffer subsequently from a group of common emotional conditions or sequelae that affect their social, academic and emotional development. Unfortunately, children in the United States are experiencing this triad of trauma — known as interpersonal violence — in epidemic proportions. According to statistics published in 1998 by the US Department of Health and Human Services, more than 3 million cases of child abuse were reported in 1996; 1 million of these cases were substantiated.[1] A 1995 Gallup poll of 1000 parents suggests that 44 of every 1000 American children experience physical abuse by their parents, and anywhere from 1.5 million to 3.3 million witness domestic violence.[2]

Posttraumatic Stress Disorder

It has been estimated that slightly more than 33% of children who experience interpersonal violence will develop symptoms of posttraumatic stress disorder (PTSD),[3] which, as outlined in 1994 by the American Psychiatric Association,[4] include the following:

- reexperiencing the trauma through intrusive thoughts, dreams or hallucinations
- avoiding people, places, things and other contexts related to the trauma
- emotional numbing and physiological hyperarousal

As PTSD progresses, the symptoms increase in severity and are complicated by comorbidities, such as depression, cognitive difficulties and suicidal tendencies. However, our knowledge of the neurobiological underpinnings of this progression is limited.

Early identification of children who are at the highest risk for developing PTSD in the aftermath of interpersonal violence holds the promise of meaningful intervention by mental health professionals. Using sophisticated diagnostic methods, such as magnetic resonance imaging (MRI), the field of developmental traumatology has begun critical evaluations of the biological markers of risk.[5,6] Identifying and understanding these markers could help guide the development of more targeted and more focused interventions. Nevertheless, and as noted in an article by Pfefferbaum in 1997, effective interventions for this group of children await empirical support.[7]

Animal research related to stress and its effects on the brain currently focuses on the stress hormone corticosterone; cortisol in mammals. High levels of this glucocorticoid demonstrate a cytotoxic effect on neurons in critical brain regions, including the hippocampus, a medial-temporal lobe structure involved in memory encoding and retrieval.[8]

Memory retrieval and experienced stress are core elements of PTSD. Current research of PTSD, including the study described in this chapter, is using neuroimaging to investigate cortisol levels, brain structure and brain function. A primary aim of this research is to chart the behavioral outcomes of individuals who have a history of trauma with the typical triad of symptoms of PTSD.

This chapter highlights the methodology and results of the "Brain Development in PTSD" study currently underway at the Stanford University (SU) Early Life Stress Research Program. This study is a multimethod assessment of children who have a history of interpersonal trauma and the symptoms of PTSD. The SU research team, of which I am a member, is using a combination of behavioral and cognitive assessments, neuroimaging and measures of salivary cortisol and psychopathology to examine changes related to PTSD and their possible effects on brain development. To date, the investigators have published their methodology and preliminary findings in the following peer-reviewed journal articles:

- Carrion VG, Weems CF, Ray R, Reiss AL. Toward an empirical definition of pediatric PTSD: the phenomenology of PTSD symptoms in youth. *Journal of the American Academy of Child and Adolescent Psychiatry.* 2002;41:166-173.
- Carrion VG, Weems CF, Ray RD, Glaser B, Hessl D, Reiss AL. Diurnal salivary cortisol in pediatric posttraumatic stress disorder. *Biological Psychiatry.* 2002;51:575-582.

- Carrion VG, Weems CF, Eliez S, et al. Attenuation of frontal asymmetry in pediatric posttraumatic stress disorder. *Biological Psychiatry.* 2001;50: 943-951.

Understanding Pediatric PTSD

The most recent edition of the *Diagnostic and Statistical Manual of Mental Disorders (DSM-IV™)* took several steps forward with the introduction of developmental modifications to criterion A2 ("experience of trauma with disorganized or agitated behavior") and symptom cluster B criteria ("reexperience of the trauma through repetitive play or frightening dreams") of PTSD (see Table 1).[9] Symptom clusters C (avoidance and numbing) and D (hyperarousal), however, did not receive developmental modifications.[9] Based on the *DSM-IV*, physicians must determine that each of the symptom cluster criteria B through D are met before assigning a diagnosis of PTSD to children or adolescents.

There is little empirical evidence that the diagnostic criteria of PTSD, noted in the *DSM-IV*, characterize pediatric PTSD appropriately. In fact, *partial* symptomatology is quite common[10,11]: Children and adolescents often have just 1 or 2 of the symptoms associated with PTSD, yet they are sufficiently disabled to require treatment.[7] Additional information about impairment in individuals who have only some symptoms of PTSD may prove to be a catalyst for future developmental modifications to the current diagnostic criteria.

Cortisol and Pediatric PTSD

Research has shown that children who experience trauma may have altered limbic-hypothalamic-pituitary-adrenal (LHPA) axis circadian rhythmicity: For example, maltreated children diagnosed with PTSD demonstrated increased urinary free cortisol levels after 24-hour urinary collection, as compared with matched controls.[12] In addition, Goenjian and colleagues evaluated adolescents 5 years after the 1988 earthquake in Armenia and found that the youngsters who were geographically close to the epicenter who still had symptoms of PTSD had lower basal salivary cortisol levels.[13] This finding[13] is similar to those observed in some studies of adults, but is different from that found by De Bellis and colleagues.[12]

Table 1. Diagnostic Criteria for Posttraumatic Stress Disorder[9]

A. The person has been exposed to a traumatic event in which both of the following were present:
   (1) The person experienced, witnessed or was confronted by an event or events that involved actual or threatened death or serious injury, or a threat to the physical integrity of self or others.
   (2) The person's response involved intense fear, helplessness or horror. (In children, this may be expressed instead by disorganized or agitated behavior.)

B. The traumatic event is persistently reexperienced in one (or more) of the following ways:
   (1) recurrent and intrusive distressing recollections of the event, including images, thoughts or perceptions (In young children, repetitive play may occur in which themes or aspects of the trauma are expressed.)
   (2) recurrent distressing dreams of the events (In young children, there may be frightening dreams without recognizable content.)
   (3) acting or feeling as if the traumatic event was recurring (includes a sense of reliving the experience, illusions, hallucinations and dissociative flashback episodes, including those that occur on awakening or when intoxicated) (In young children, trauma-specific reenactment may occur.)
   (4) intense psychological distress at exposure to internal or external cues that symbolize or resemble an aspect of the traumatic event
   (5) physiological reactivity on exposure to internal or external cues that symbolize or resemble an aspect of the traumatic event

C. Persistent avoidance of stimuli associated with the trauma and numbing of general responsiveness (not present before the trauma), as indicated by 3 (or more) of the following:
   (1) efforts to avoid thoughts, feelings or conversations associated with the trauma
   (2) efforts to avoid activities, places or people that arouse recollections of the trauma
   (3) inability to recall an important aspect of the trauma
   (4) markedly diminished interest or participation in significant activities
   (5) feeling of detachment or estrangement from others

(continued)

Table 1. Diagnostic Criteria for Posttraumatic Stress Disorder[9] (continued)

(6) restricted range of affect (eg, unable to have loving feelings)
(7) sense of foreshortened future (eg, does not expect to have a career, marriage, children or a normal life span)

D. Persistent symptoms of increased arousal (not present before the trauma), as indicated by 2 (or more) of the following:
(1) difficulty falling or staying asleep
(2) irritability or outbursts of anger
(3) difficulty concentrating
(4) hypervigilance
(5) exaggerated startle response

E. Duration of the disturbance (symptoms in criteria B, C and D) is more than 1 month

F. The disturbance causes clinically significant distress or impairment in social, occupational or other important areas of functioning.

Reprinted with permission. Carrion VG, Weems CF, Ray R, Reiss AL. Toward an empirical definition of pediatric PTSD: the phenomenology of PTSD symptoms in youth. *Journal of the American Academy of Child and Adolesent Psychiatry.* 2002;41:166-173.

Investigators have also examined levels of salivary cortisol in traumatized children who were not evaluated systematically for PTSD: For example, King and colleagues collected morning salivary cortisol samples in girls ages 5 years to 7 years who were scheduled for a physical examination.[14] They found that girls who had a history of sexual abuse within the previous 2 months had lower cortisol levels than did control subjects. Even when these results do not prove consistent, taken together they suggest a differing adrenal response in children exposed to traumatic experiences.

The investigation at SU of cortisol levels in children with PTSD and subthreshold symptoms of PTSD addressed our theory that the eventual alterations in the adrenal responses of adults with PTSD result from chronic hyperactivity of the LHPA axis during development. Thus, we hypothesized that children with a history of interpersonal trauma and symptoms of PTSD would demonstrate higher levels of basal cortisol than would age- and gender-matched controls.

Neuroimaging and Pediatric PTSD

A growing body of research suggests that stress and the glucocorticoids secreted during stress can damage the hippocampus.[8,15] In fact, when neuroimages of the hippocampus were compared between 22 adults who had no psychiatric history and 26 American combat veterans of Vietnam who had PTSD, the latter group had a right hippocampal volume that was 8% smaller; a statistically significant finding.[16] A similar group of authors investigated patients with PTSD who had a history of interpersonal trauma: They found that these patients had a left hippocampal volume that was 12% smaller than that of a control group.[17] Findings of reduced hippocampal volumes have now been replicated in several other laboratories.[18,19] Different findings, however, have been reported for other samples: For example, a study by De Bellis and colleagues found no differences in hippocampal volumes in children with PTSD secondary to maltreatment.[6] In adults, Golier and colleagues reported no hippocampal changes in adult Holocaust survivors who had been diagnosed with PTSD.[20]

Current Study of PTSD in Children

In the "Brain Development in PTSD" study, the laboratory at the SU Early Life Stress Research Program examined imaging data from 24 children who had a documented history of interpersonal trauma. All of these children experienced posttraumatic symptoms after the traumatic event, and 12 children (50%) met *DSM-IV* diagnostic criteria for a diagnosis of current PTSD. Based on the findings of De Bellis and colleagues,[6] my coinvestigators and I hypothesized that children with a history of trauma and symptoms of PTSD would not demonstrate the decreased hippocampal volumes found in most of the studies of adults with PTSD.[16-19]

Methodology

Recruitment and demographics

My colleagues and I recruited study participants from local social service departments and mental health clinics. All of the children referred to the project by therapists and caseworkers had a history of exposure to interpersonal trauma. We included in the study only those children who met each of the following criteria:

- had at least one episode of exposure to trauma, as defined by *DSM-IV* criterion A1 (see Table 1)
- experienced the trauma episode (or episodes) at least 6 months prior to referral
- had no known history of neurological disorders
- had no known history of alcohol or drug abuse/dependence

Therapists and caseworkers referred 60 children to this study. We obtained consent from the courts in the participating counties for children who were in foster placement (n = 27). Most of the children and adolescents referred to the study (n = 35) had prior involvement with Child Protective Services. Any suspected cases of ongoing maltreatment would be reported: However, no such cases were identified. Participants' caretakers, regardless of prior court consent, signed an institutional review board-approved informed consent form prior to study enrollment. All referred children underwent screening using both the Clinician-Administered PTSD Scale for Children and Adolescents (CAPS-CA)[21,22] and the Child Posttraumatic Stress Disorder Reaction Index.[23,24] Only one subject was unable to complete the CAPS-CA, due to scheduling problems, and therefore was not included in this analysis.

The final sample included 34 boys and 25 girls. The children's mean age was 10.6 years, with a range of 7 years to 14 years. More than 50% of the children had experienced multiple traumatic events, including separation and loss, witnessing violence, physical abuse, sexual abuse, physical neglect and emotional abuse.

Almost half of the study participants reported family incomes between 0 and \$31,000; 15% had incomes between \$31,000 and \$76,000; 14.9% reported incomes over \$76,000; and 21.7% reported no income data because the child was in foster care, residential treatment or another nontraditional rearing environment.

Education levels among the participants' caregivers ranged from some high school to completion of graduate school: 3.3% reported having a partial high school education; 21.7% had completed high school; 18.3% reported a partial college education; 11.7% had completed college; and 16.7% had completed graduate school. There was no educational background available for 28.3% of the sample.

The ethnic composition of the study participants included the following: European American (n = 25), African American (n = 26), Hispanic (n = 5), Asian (n = 2) and other (n = 1).

Behavioral assessment

We conducted a behavioral assessment of all 59 study participants using the following instruments:

- **CAPS-CA** — a structured clinical interview that is a developmentally sensitive counterpart to the CAPS for adults.[21,22] The CAPS-CA facilitates assessment of exposure to trauma, the individuals' experiences of the trauma and the frequency and intensity ratings for each of the 17 symptoms for PTSD clustered in thc *DSM-IV*.
- **Child Posttraumatic Stress Disorder Reaction Index** — a 20-item, self-report instrument used to assess symptoms of PTSD after exposure to violence.[23] This index, used widely, has proven to be a valid and reliable measure of the symptoms of PTSD in pediatric populations.[24]
- **Schedule for Affective Disorders and Schizophrenia for School-Age Children — Present and Lifetime Version** — a semistructured clinical interview designed to identify Axis I *DSM-IV* disorders, such as depression or schizophrenia.[25] A certified child psychiatrist conducted these evaluations.
- **Wechsler Abbreviated Scales of Intelligence** — an instrument that yields verbal, performance and IQ scores to determine the intelligence levels of children and adolescents.[26]

In addition, current caretakers completed the Child Behavior Checklist, a 113-item rating scale that assesses children's behavioral and social problems.[27]

Neuroendocrinological evaluation

Fifty-one study participants underwent neuroendocrinological evaluation. We obtained salivary cortisol samples from the study participants using home collection procedures. Participants collected samples 4 times per day (prebreakfast, prelunch, predinner and prebedtime) over a 3-day period. To collect each sample, participants placed a cotton swab in their mouths for 1 minute. The swab was then placed inside a sterile plastic tube and was sealed.

We also assessed pubertal development using self-reports. From a group of drawings that represent the 5 Tanner Stages of puberty, participants selected the one that best represented their current pubertal stage.[28]

Neuroanatomical evaluation

For 24 study participants, we obtained high-resolution magnetic resonance imaging scans using a General Electric (Milwaukee, Wis) Signa 1.5T scanner. The data collected included a coronal 3-dimensional volumetric spoiled gradient echo series (TR = 35; TE = 6; flip angle = 45°; number of excitations = 1; FOV = 24; matrix = 256 × 192; 124, 1.5-mm contiguous slices), which was used for all measurements and analyses discussed in this chapter.

The Psychiatry Neuroimaging Laboratory at SU completed a morphometric analysis of each participant using the software program BrainImage.[29] Volumetric assessment of segmented image data using this software consists of a sequential process of data importation, removal of nonbrain voxels, correction of image nonuniformity, positional normalization and fuzzy-tissue segmentation.

To assess the volumes of the amygdala and hippocampus using BrainImage, we delineated regions of interest manually. Brain tissue was isolated, and coronal images were then oriented perpendicular to the anterior commisure–posterior commisure plane. Two trained raters, blind to diagnoses, performed interrater reliability testing to assure measurement accuracy.

Main Findings

Behavioral outcomes

Fourteen of the 59 evaluable children (24%) met the *full* diagnostic criteria for PTSD based on CAPS-CA results. The following were the 5 most frequent comorbid *DSM-IV* conditions found among the participants:

- depressive disorder–not otherwise specified (12%)
- major depressive disorder (11%)
- attention deficit-hyperactivity disorder (11%)
- specific phobia (9%)
- separation anxiety disorder (7%) and social phobia (7%)

The frequency and intensity of each of the *DSM-IV* PTSD symptoms associated with the trauma are presented in Table 2.[30] The 5 most frequent symptoms included the following:

- avoidance of thoughts, feelings and conversations (83.1%)
- distressing recollections (69.5%)
- inability to recall important aspects of the event (69.5%)
- distressing dreams (64.4%)
- difficulty concentrating (64.4%)

The 3 most intense symptoms reported were irritability/anger, distressing dreams and detachment from others.

My colleagues and I conducted separate regression analyses on the frequency and intensity for each symptom in the CAPS-CA and the PTSD diagnosis (see Table 2).[30] As the table illustrates, for some symptoms, symptom "Intensity" alone predicted a diagnosis of PTSD or functional impairment regardless of the "Frequency" of the symptoms.

Table 2. Frequency and Intensity of* DSM-IV *PTSD Symptoms and Their Relation to PTSD[30]

Diagnosis and Overall Impairment

	Frequency n (%)	Intensity Mean (SD)	PTSD-Dx R^2-		Impairment R^2	R^2
DSM-IV Criteria			F	I	F	I
B) Reexperience						
(1) Distressing Recollections	41 (69.5)[B]	1.98 (1.3)[K]	.128*	.065	.230‡	.260‡
(2) Distressing Dreams	38 (64.4)[C]	2.37 (0.9)[B]	.079†	.111†	.203*	.281‡
(3) Feeling of Reoccurrence	24 (40.7)[J]	1.67 (1.1)[O]	.011	.138*	.144*	.160*
(4) Distress at Exposure to Cues	34 (57.6)[E]	2.26 (1.0)[E]	.008	.041	.044	.084†
(5) Physiological Reactivity to Cues	19 (32.2)[L]	1.95 (1.1)[L]	.017	.059	.014	.017
C) Avoidance and Numbing						
(1) Avoid Thoughts, Feelings and Conversations	49 (83.1)[A]	2.18 (1.2)[F]	.004	.065	.017	.303‡
(2) Avoid Places and People	35 (59.3)[D]	1.86 (1.1)[M]	.016	.081†	.014	.044
(3) Inability to Recall Important Aspects of Event	41 (69.5)[B]	2.00 (1.1)[J]	.100†	.111†	.194*	.230‡
(4) Diminished Interest	22 (37.3)[K]	1.68 (0.9)[N]	.064	.060	.117†	.185*
(5) Detachment from Others	30 (50.8)[F]	2.30 (1.0)[C]	.346‡	.215‡	.123*	.109†
(6) Restricted Range of Affect	30 (50.8)[F]	2.07 (0.9)[H]	.054	.010	.109†	.032
(7) Foreshortened Future	18 (30.5)[M]	2.28 (1.0)[D]	.028	.024	.078†	.044
D) Hyperarousal						
(1) Sleep Problems	35 (59.3)[D]	1.86 (1.0)[M]	.075†	.087†	.160*	.058
(2) Irritability/Anger	26 (44.1)[I]	2.73 (1.0)[A]	.004	.012	.026	.006
(3) Difficulty Concentrating	38 (64.4)[C]	2.11 (0.9)[G]	.034	.111†	.096†	.102†
(4) Hypervigilance	29 (49.2)[G]	2.03 (0.9)[I]	.380‡	.270‡	.102†	.078†
(5) Exaggerated Startle	28 (46.6)[H]	2.07 (0.9)[H]	.196*	.256‡	.008	.017

F = frequency of symptoms; I = intensity of symptoms.

*$P \leq .01$; †$P < .05$; ‡$P \leq .001$.

Superscript letters represent rank.

Reprinted with permission. Carrion VG, Weems CF, Ray R, Reiss AL. Toward an empirical definition of pediatric PTSD: the phenomenology of PTSD symptoms in youth. *Journal of the American Academy of Child and Adolesent Psychiatry.* 2002;41:166-173.

A full diagnosis of PTSD was associated most strongly with the following 3 symptoms based on either their frequency or their intensity: detachment from others, hypervigilance or exaggerated startle.

Table 2 also shows the results from separate regression analyses for "Symptom Frequency," "Symptom Intensity" and "Clinical Impairment," as assessed by the CAPS-CA composite clinical impairment index. Overall impairment was associated most strongly with the following 3 symptoms based on either their frequency or their intensity: distressing recollections, distressing dreams or the inability to recall important aspects of the traumatic event.

Lastly, the intensity of some symptoms predicted a diagnosis of PTSD or functional impairment when frequency did not and, vice versa, the frequency of some symptoms predicted the diagnosis of PTSD or functional impairment when intensity did not.

To examine the importance of meeting each of the symptom cluster criteria in a diagnosis of PTSD, we conducted analyses of variance (ANOVAs) with Fisher's post hoc tests to compare children meeting all 3 *DSM-IV* PTSD symptom cluster criteria (PTSD-3; n = 14), children meeting criteria for 2 of the symptom clusters (PTSD-2; n = 23) and children meeting criteria for one of the symptom clusters (PTSD-1; n = 14). Nine children did not meet criteria for any one symptom cluster, and therefore were not included in the current analyses. Likelihood chi-square tests were used to compare the groups on the bases of categorical variables.

These 3 groups of participants did not differ in terms of demographics, comorbidity, pubertal stage, number of traumatic experiences, amount of time since the first trauma, amount of time since the most recent trauma or the types of traumas experienced. As Table 3 demonstrates, the PTSD-2 and PTSD-3 groups did not differ significantly from each other on any of the noted variables, but each differed significantly from the PTSD-1 group in terms of distress of symptoms, social impairment, school impairment, overall impairment and the percentage (%) meeting Criterion F of the *DSM-IV* PTSD, which is "Clinically Significant Impairment." In other words, participants in the PTSD-2 and PTSD-3 groups experienced more distress from their symptoms and greater social, school, overall and clinical impairment than did participants in the PTSD-1 group. "Developmental Impairment" and the PTSD "Reaction Index Score" did not differ significantly across the 3 groups.

Table 3. Comparison of the 3 PTSD Symptom Groups in Symptom Distress and Impairment[30]

Met Criteria for	1 Symptom Cluster (PTSD-1) (n=13)	2 Symptom Clusters (PTSD-2) (n=23)	3 Symptom Clusters (PTSD-3) (n=14)		
Measures	**Mean (SD)**	**Mean (SD)**	**Mean (SD)**	***F* or χ^2**	***P***
Distress of Symptoms*	1.54 (0.9)	2.39 (1.0)	2.57 (1.1)	4.30	.019
Social Impairment*	0.54 (0.8)	1.52 (1.1)	1.79 (1.1)	5.67	.006
School Impairment*	0.69 (0.9)	1.76 (1.3)	2.14 (1.2)	5.38	.008
Developmental Impairment	0.38 (0.8)	0.91 (1.2)	1.29 (1.1)	2.36	.106
Overall Impairment*	3.15 (2.0)	6.64 (3.4)	7.79 (3.0)	9.06	<.001
Reaction Index Score	26.14 (9.2)	35.59 (12.7)	33.86 (18.1)	2.16	.126
% Meeting Criterion F*	64.3	91.3	100.0	8.96	.011

Note: Means with standard deviations in parentheses or percentage.

*Significant differences (P<.05) on Fisher's post hoc test or paired χ^2 with individuals meeting criteria for one symptom cluster significantly less than individuals meeting criteria for 2 or 3. There were no significant differences found between the group meeting criteria for 2 symptom clusters and the group meeting criteria for 3 symptom clusters.

Reprinted with permission. Carrion VG, Weems CF, Ray R, Reiss AL. Toward an empirical definition of pediatric PTSD: the phenomenology of PTSD symptoms in youth. *Journal of the American Academy of Child and Adolesent Psychiatry.* 2002;41:166-173.

Salivary cortisol findings

We examined cortisol levels using a mixed-design, repeated-measures analysis of covariance (ANCOVA) with "condition" (PTSD versus control) as the between-subjects independent variable and time of day or "time" (prebreakfast, prelunch, predinner and prebedtime) as the within-subjects independent variable, controlling for family income level. However, we found that family income was not a significant covariate [F (1,68) = .846, P>.10] in this model. Therefore, we used an ANOVA for the analysis, which revealed a significant effect of time [F (3,78) = 111.75, P<.0001] and condition [F (1,80) = 4.09, P<.05; Cohen's d = .46], independently, but no time-by-condition interaction [F (3,78) = 0.57, P>.10]. The effect of condition was significant when controlling for family income, as well.

For both the PTSD group and the control group, cortisol levels followed the normal circadian rhythm. For both groups, there was a decrease in cortisol levels over the course of the day (see Fig 1). However, the PTSD group had higher cortisol levels than did the control group at each sampling period.[31]

Follow-up Mann-Whitney U (rank sum statistic) tests revealed a significant difference in predinner and prebedtime levels of salivary cortisol ($P = .02$; $P = .03$, respectively) between the PTSD group and the control group. The control group experienced a greater drop in salivary cortisol levels from predinnertime to prebedtime when compared with the PTSD group.

Fig 1. Cortisol levels as a function of condition and time of collection.[31]

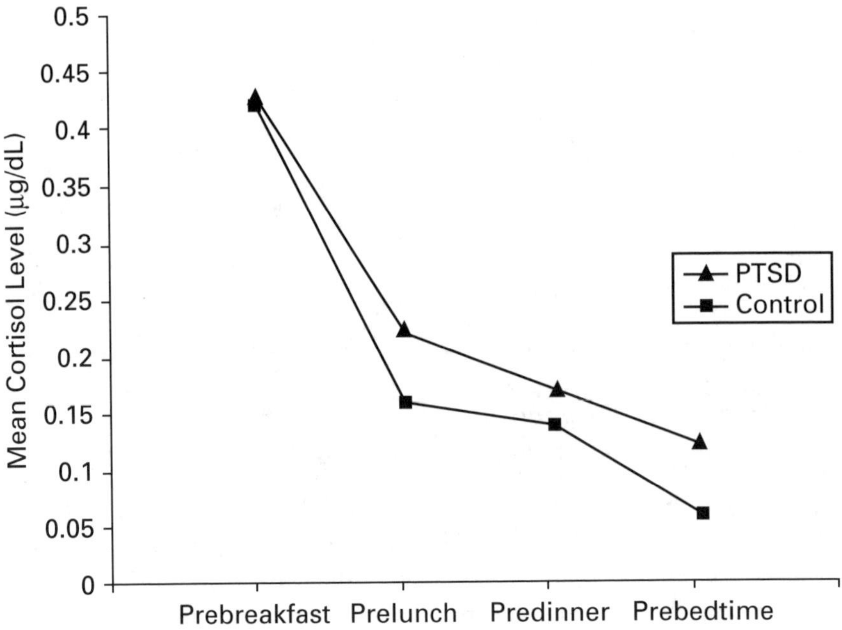

Reprinted from *Biological Psychiatry*, 51:575-582; Carrion VG, Weems CF, Ray RD, Glaser B. Hessl D, Reiss AL; Diurnal salivary cortisol in pediatric posttraumatic stress disorder; 2002 with permission from Society of Biological Psychiatry.

Because prior research[32] has demonstrated a relationship between cortisol levels and depressive symptoms, my colleagues and I looked at whether the children in the current study who had both depression and symptoms of PTSD had higher cortisol levels than did children with just symptoms of PTSD alone. We found no significant differences between these groups [F (1,46) = 0.01, *P*>.10].

Within the PTSD group, a mixed-design, repeated-measures ANOVA — with gender as the independent variable and time of day as the within-subjects variable, and with follow-up Mann-Whitney U tests — showed that the girls had significantly higher levels of prebedtime salivary cortisol [z = 2.20, *P*<.05] than did the boys. We found no significant gender differences within the control group.

Structural MRI findings

Table 4 shows the means and standard deviations for PTSD and control participants for all brain regions of interest.[5] Children with PTSD had significantly smaller total brain volumes than did age- and gender-matched controls [t(46) = 3.19, *P*<.005]. In addition, t-tests indicated that children with PTSD had significantly smaller volumes of total brain gray matter than did control-group children [t(46) = 2.81, *P*<.01]. Subsequently, we used total brain gray volume as a covariate in all between-group comparisons involving gray-matter subregions, such as lobar volumes.

To investigate differences in brain morphology, we conducted a multivariate analysis of variance with each of the cerebral lobes (frontal, parietal, temporal, occipital) and the cerebellum for each hemisphere's (right and left) respective gray-matter volumes as dependent variables; total brain gray volume was the covariate. These analyses revealed that diagnostic status (PTSD versus control) had a significant effect on the variables [multivariate F (10,36) = 2.44, *P* = .024] while controlling for total brain gray. (Total brain gray was a significant covariate.) Univariate results indicated that only the left frontal gray matter differed significantly between the 2 groups [F (1,47) = 12.00, *P*<.005]. Interestingly, although the unadjusted means (as shown in Table 4) showed that the control group had larger left frontal volumes, the covariate (ie, total brain gray) adjusted means showed that the control group had proportionately smaller left frontal gray volumes than did the PTSD group. We did not observe similar results for comparable analyses focused on white-matter volumes.

Table 4. Means and Standard Deviations for Brain Regions of Interest[5]

	Control		PTSD	
	Mean	**SD**	**Mean**	**SD**
Total Brain Tissue*	1297.7	109.2	1191.1	118.2
Right*	651.4	55.5	594.0	58.0
Left*	646.3	54.3	597.1	60.6
Cerebrum Tissue*	1125.1	96.1	1041.9	104.0
Right*	565.9	48.9	521.0	51.3
Left*	559.2	48.3	520.9	53.0
Amygdala Total	4.2	0.7	4.0	0.6
Hippocampus Total	7.8	1.0	7.2	1.3
Gray (G) Regions of Interest				
Total Brain — G*	780.2	64.9	724.2	73.2
Right*	392.9	32.4	361.7	35.3
Left*	387.3	33.6	362.5	38.3
Cerebrum — G*	677.4	52.0	633.3	65.0
Right*	342.1	27.2	315.5	31.4
Left*	335.3	25.8	317.8	34.0
Frontal Lobe — G†	242.4	20.1	231.8	23.3
Right	123.9	10.6	115.4	10.9
Left*	118.5	10.7	116.4	12.7
Parietal Lobe — G	160.7	14.5	152.2	15.3
Right	80.3	7.7	75.8	7.6
Left	80.4	7.1	76.4	7.9
Temporal Lobe — G	153.1	14.9	141.6	17.5
Right	77.2	8.0	70.0	8.9
Left	75.9	7.7	71.6	8.8
Occipital Lobe — G	75.4	9.0	65.2	14.4
Right	37.8	4.8	33.2	7.1
Left	37.6	4.5	31.9	7.5
Cerebellum — G	85.3	18.9	77.5	11.8
Right	42.1	9.0	39.5	6.1
Left	43.2	10.2	38.0	6.0

*Significant effect of group.
†Significant group-by-hemisphere interaction.
Analysis of lobar regions was conducted while controlling for total brain gray volume.

Reprinted from *Biological Psychiatry*, 50:943-951; Carrion VG, Weems CF, Eliez S; Attenuation of frontal asymmetry in pediatric PTSD.

Due to the results we found with the subjects' frontal lobes, we subsequently conducted a 2 (diagnostic status; PTSD versus control) by 2 (hemisphere; right versus left) mixed factorial ANCOVA with total brain gray matter as the covariate. The ANCOVA for the frontal lobe revealed a significant interaction between diagnostic status and brain hemisphere [F (1,45) = 16.04, *P*<.001]. Simple effect analyses for frontal-lobe gray matter showed that control children had significant volume differences between the hemispheres [(R>L): t(23) = 3.79, *P*<.001], with the right hemisphere volume being greater than the left. We found no significant difference in frontal hemisphere volumes for the PTSD subjects.

Average hippocampal volume in PTSD subjects was 8.3% smaller than in control subjects. Amygdala volume in PTSD subjects was 5% smaller than in the controls. Since total brain volume differed between controls and PTSD children, we conducted a series of ANCOVAs to test the statistical significance of mesial temporal region differences after controlling for total brain volume, total gray matter and temporal lobe volume. No significant group differences were observed in these analyses. In addition, we conducted several 2 (diagnostic status; PTSD versus control) by 2 (hemisphere; right versus left) mixed factorial ANCOVAs for the temporal lobe subregions and found no significant differences or asymmetry between the 2 groups. Because the severity of the symptoms of PTSD may be responsible for hippocampal differences, we compared the subsample of children meeting complete *DSM-IV* PTSD diagnostic criteria (n = 12) with their matched control group (n = 12). Again, we found no significant differences in the amygdala or hippocampus, regardless of whether we controlled for total brain gray.

Due to the potential role of IQ on our main findings, we reanalyzed our data after excluding 3 subjects who had the lowest IQ scores (between 65 and 70). Nevertheless, we obtained the same pattern of findings. Again, t-tests indicated that PTSD participants had significantly smaller total brain gray volumes than did control subjects [t(40) = 2.24, *P*<.05]. Covariate-adjusted (ie, total brain gray) means showed that the control group had proportionally smaller left frontal gray volumes than did the PTSD group [F(1,42) = 11.12, *P*<.005]. Results from the frontal lobe again revealed a significant diagnostic-status-by-hemisphere interaction [F(1,42) = 13.65, *P*<.001]. We found no significant differences in the amygdala or the hippocampus.

Discussion

The results of this study suggest that the process of making a definitive diagnosis of pediatric PTSD should include an evaluation of symptoms, their intensity and their relationship to functional impairment. An important clinical implication of these findings is that children who experience trauma and exhibit posttraumatic symptoms should be evaluated for functional impairment and given appropriate treatment regardless of the number of *DSM-IV* PTSD criteria they meet.

Additional research is needed to understand the consequences of elevated cortisol levels during critical developmental stages. This potential marker may serve as a guide when treating anxiety and depression in an at-risk population. If evidence continues to accumulate indicating that an elevated level of cortisol is a potential biological marker for PTSD, this may help clinicians treat and follow-up children who have been diagnosed with PTSD.

Increased vulnerability to PTSD in women has been linked to exposure to trauma in early development.[33] Our finding of higher cortisol levels in girls with symptoms of PTSD may be related to this diathesis. In girls, in particular, elevated cortisol levels during development may be a contributing factor to their higher risk of developing PTSD following trauma.

It is still not clear if the elevated levels of cortisol in children with PTSD cause the neuroanatomical findings of lower cerebral volume and attenuated frontal asymmetry. Perhaps these anatomical differences are risk factors for the development of PTSD, thus indicating a type of stress vulnerability. Elevated cortisol may augment the risk because of its neurotoxic potential.

The laboratory at SU has continued to follow this cohort through examinations and evaluations administered 12 months to 18 months after the initial evaluation. The longitudinal analyses of behavioral, neuroendocrinological and anatomical markers will help shed light on the pathogenesis and progression of acute and chronic PTSD, as well as facilitate the development of a more developmentally appropriate description of PTSD in pediatric populations. Both, in turn, will help investigators design better and more targeted interventions for clinical use by mental health professionals.

Conclusion

New methodology, such as functional neuroimaging, will help investigators better understand the significance of the structural findings reported by my coinvestigators and me. Currently, using functional MRIs, we are assessing adolescents who have PTSD as they complete 2 different tasks; one of response inhibition and one of emotional valence. Functional imaging will clarify how cognitive and emotional brain networks interact and help us identify altered brain circuitry. Once we identify these networks, we can then use functional MRIs before and after treatment to evaluate effectiveness and outcome.

References

1. US Department of Health and Human Services. *Child Maltreatment 1996: Reports from the States to the National Child Abuse and Neglect Data System.* Washington, DC: US Government Printing Office; 1998.
2. Gallup Poll: Child Abuse Study, 1995. Ithaca, NY: Cornell University, College of Human Ecology, Family Life Development Center, National Data Archive on Child Abuse and Neglect [NDACAN]; 2005. NDACAN Dataset Number 106.
3. Widom CS. Posttraumatic stress disorder in abused and neglected children grown up. *The American Journal of Psychiatry.* 1999;156:1223-1229.
4. American Psychiatric Association. *Diagnostic and Statistical Manual of Mental Disorders.* 4th ed. Washington, DC: American Psychiatric Press; 1994:428-429.
5. Carrion VG, Weems CF, Eliez S, et al. Attenuation of frontal asymmetry in pediatric posttraumatic stress disorder. *Biological Psychiatry.* 2001;50:943-951.
6. De Bellis MD, Keshavan MS, Clark DB, et al. Developmental traumatology. Part II: Brain development. *Biological Psychiatry.* 1999;45:1271-1284.
7. Pfefferbaum B. Posttraumatic stress disorder in children: a review of the past 10 years. *Journal of the American Academy of Child and Adolescent Psychiatry.* 1997;36:1503-1511.
8. Sapolsky RM. Potential behavioral modification of glucocorticoid damage to the hippocampus. *Behavioural Brain Research.* 1993;57:175-182.
9. American Psychiatric Association. *Diagnostic and Statistical Manual of Mental Disorders: Text Revision.* 4th ed. Washington, DC: American Psychiatric Press; 2000:467-468.
10. Aaron J, Zaglul H, Emery RE. Posttraumatic stress in children following acute physical injury. *Journal of Pediatric Psychology.* 1999;24:335-343.
11. Cuffe SP, Addy CL, Garrison CZ, et al. Prevalence of PTSD in a community sample of older adolescents. *Journal of the American Academy of Child and Adolescent Psychiatry.* 1998;37:147-154.
12. De Bellis MD, Baum AS, Birmaher B, et al. Developmental traumatology. Part I: Biological stress systems. *Biological Psychiatry.* 1999;45:1259-1270.
13. Goenjian AK, Yehuda R, Pynoos RS, et al. Basal cortisol, dexamethasone suppression of cortisol, and MHPG in adolescents after the 1988 earthquake in Armenia. *The American Journal of Psychiatry.* 1996;153:929-934.
14. King JA, Mandansky D, King S, Fletcher KE, Brewer J. Early sexual abuse and low cortisol. *Psychiatry and Clinical Neurosciences.* 2001;55:71-74.
15. Watanabe Y, Gould E, McEwen BS. Stress induces atrophy of apical dendrites of hippocampal CA3 pyramidal neurons. *Brain Research.* 1992;588:341-345.

16. Bremner JD, Randall P, Scott TM, et al. MRI-based measurement of hippocampal volume in patients with combat-related posttraumatic stress disorder. *The American Journal of Psychiatry.* 1995;152: 973-981.
17. Bremner JD, Randall P, Vermetten E, et al. Magnetic resonance imaging-based measurement of hippocampal volume in posttraumatic stress disorder related to childhood physical and sexual abuse — a preliminary report. *Biological Psychiatry.* 1997;41:23-32.
18. Gurvits TV, Shenton ME, Hokama H, et al. Magnetic resonance imaging study of hippocampal volume in chronic, combat-related posttraumatic stress disorder. *Biological Psychiatry.* 1996;40: 1091-1099.
19. Stein MB, Koverola C, Hanna C, Torchia MG, McClarty B. Hippocampal volume in women victimized by childhood sexual abuse. *Psychological Medicine.* 1997;27:951-959.
20. Golier J, Yehuda R, Grossman R, De Santi S, Convit A, de Leon M. Hippocampal volume and memory performance in holocaust survivors with and without PTSD. Paper presented at: 39th Annual Meeting of the American College of Neuropsychopharmacology; December 11, 2000; San Juan, Puerto Rico.
21. Nader KO, Kriegler JA, Blake DD, Pynoos RS, Newman E, Weathers FW. *Clinician Administered PTSD Scale, Child and Adolescent Version.* White River Junction, Vt: National Center for PTSD; 1996.
22. Blake DD, Weathers FW, Nagy LM, et al. The development of a Clinician-Administered PTSD Scale. *Journal of Traumatic Stress.* 1995;8:75-90.
23. Pynoos RS, Frederick C, Nader K, et al. Life threat and posttraumatic stress in school-age children. *Archives of General Psychiatry.* 1987;44:1057-1063.
24. Nader K, Pynoos R, Fairbanks L, Frederick C. Children's PTSD reactions one year after a sniper attack at their school. *The American Journal of Psychiatry.* 1990;147:1526-1530.
25. Kaufman J, Birmaher B, Brent D, et al. Schedule for Affective Disorders and Schizophrenia for School-Age Children–Present and Lifetime Version (K-SADS-PL): initial reliability and validity data. *Journal of the American Academy of Child and Adolescent Psychiatry.* 1997;36:980-988.
26. The Psychological Corporation. *Wechsler Abbreviated Scale of Intelligence.* San Antonio, Tex: Harcourt Brace; 1999.
27. Achenbach TM. *Manual for the Child: Behavior Checklist and Revised Child Behavior Profile.* Burlington, Vt: University of Vermont Department of Psychiatry; 1991.
28. Marshall WA, Tanner JM. Variations in the pattern of pubertal changes in boys. *Archives of Disease in Childhood.* 1970;45:13-23.
29. Subramanian B, Hennessey JG, Rubin MA, Beach LS, Reiss AL. Software and methods for quantitative imaging in neuroscience. In: Koslow SH, Huerta MF, eds. *The Kennedy Krieger Institute Human Brain Project in Neuroinformatics: An Overview of the Human Brain Project.* Mahwah, NJ: Lawrence Erlbaum; 1997:335-360.
30. Carrion VG, Weems CF, Ray R, Reiss AL. Toward an empirical definition of pediatric PTSD: the phenomenology of PTSD symptoms in youth. *Journal of the American Academy of Child and Adolescent Psychiatry.* 2002;41:166-173.
31. Carrion VG, Weems CF, Ray RD, Glaser B, Hessl D, Reiss AL. Diurnal salivary cortisol in pediatric posttraumatic stress disorder. *Biological Psychiatry.* 2002;51:575-582.
32. Heim C, Newport JD, Bonsall R, Miller AH, Nemeroff CB. Altered pituitary-adrenal axis responses to provocative challenge tests in adult survivors of childhood abuse. *The American Journal of Psychiatry.* 2001;158:575-581.
33. Breslau N, Davis GC, Andreski P, Peterson EL, Schultz LR. Sex differences in posttraumatic stress disorder. *Archives of General Psychiatry.* 1997;54:1044-1048.

Violence in Infancy and Early Childhood: Relationship-Based Treatment and Evaluation

Alicia F. Lieberman, PhD
Allison Briscoe-Smith, PhD
Chandra Ghosh Ippen, PhD
Patricia Van Horn, PhD

Introduction

Interpersonal violence affects adults and children of all ages. Young children are particularly vulnerable because they are almost completely dependent on adults for their protection and well-being. Preverbal or newly verbal children cannot articulate what they are experiencing: For this reason, adults may overlook the extent of their suffering and mistakenly believe that an infant, toddler or preschooler is too young to understand or remember what is happening.

In this chapter we provide highlights of the literature on the effects of exposure to violence in infancy and early childhood and describe a relationship-based approach to the treatment of traumatic stress responses that result from such exposure.

Interpersonal Violence: Scope of the Problem

Violence directed at children is a pervasive national problem in the United States. Child abuse is the leading cause of death in the first year of life.[1] The United States ranks third among 27 industrialized countries in the number of deaths among children due to maltreatment.[2] Young children are at particular risk: Half of all victims of child abuse are younger than 7 years of age,[3] and 85% of fatalities from maltreatment occur among children under the age of 6 years.[1]

Different types of violence tend to overlap, subjecting children to traumatic stressors from multiple sources: For example, the rate of child abuse among children who witness domestic violence is 15 times higher than the national average.[4] Children who witness domestic violence are also at serious risk for sexual abuse.[5] In fact, it has been estimated that 30% to 70% of children who witness domestic violence also experience child abuse.[6-8] This convergence of forms of violence is a particular concern because psychiatric disorders among children increase significantly as the number of adverse events accumulate.[9,10] In addition, traumatic events tend to generate secondary stresses, including family disruption, economic hardship and relocation — issues that can further compromise a child's ability to rely on protective environmental factors to weather the developmental impact of trauma.[11]

Developmental Impact of Violence in Infancy and Early Childhood

Experiencing violence can profoundly disrupt normal developmental processes in infants, toddlers and preschoolers. The empirical literature documents higher levels of internalizing and externalizing problems in groups of children who have experienced violence than in control groups of children without violence exposure. These difficulties include affect dysregulation, bouts of intense fear and uncontrolled crying, sleep disturbances, heightened aggression, regression in developmental achievements, affect constriction, social withdrawal and traumatic play.[8,12-17]

Young children's responses to violence bear the imprint of their developmental stage. During the first year of life, infants are unable to use language or mobility to express their inner state. Instead, they express their distress through sensorimotor disorganization and the disruption of biological rhythms,[18] including the following:

- frequent and prolonged bouts of crying, unresponsiveness to soothing, muscle flailing, rigidity, agitation and restlessness
- feeding disturbances, such as refusal to eat or excessive appetite
- sleeping disorders, such as difficulty falling asleep, frequent night awakenings and night terrors

- lack of interest in the environment, as evidenced by sadness, withdrawal, apathy and lack of social responsiveness
- somatic problems, such as weight loss, diarrhea, vomiting and skin rashes that have no detectable organic cause

Toddlers and preschoolers, in contrast, are mobile and may engage in "fight-or-flight" mechanisms when they perceive danger.[19] These mechanisms include recklessness and proneness to accidents, inhibition of exploration and precocious competence in self-care — behaviors that are a hallmark of disruption in the normative pattern of secure-base behavior that is characteristic of the second and third years of life.[20] Toddlers and preschoolers also increasingly use language and symbolic play to understand causality. However, their cognitive immaturity and self-oriented perception of cause-effect relations often lead them to misinterpret the causality of events and to blame themselves when they are frightened by an event: For example, after months of treatment, a 3-year-old girl who witnessed the battering of her mother by an intruder whispered, "If I closed the door, he couldn't come in." She attributed the attack on her mother to her failure to avert it by closing the door. This example illustrates young children's remarkable capacity to infer what is needed to influence a situation, as well as their tendency to assume that they should be able to take this action even when it is beyond their developmental capacities — and to feel intense guilt and self-reproach for their perceived failure to act.

These internal processes unfold without adult reinforcement, but parents often compound their children's unfounded sense of responsibility by blaming them for behaviors that are either developmentally appropriate or an inevitable by-product of immaturity. Many parents blame their child for triggering marital fights, and the child internalizes these negative parental attributions.[21,22] In our assessments of young children who have witnessed domestic violence we have observed that during their playtime preschoolers often reenact the conflicts between their parents and blame themselves for these conflicts[23]: For example, when we asked a 4-year-old girl what was happening when the mother and the father dolls she was manipulating were fighting over who lost the keys, she made the child doll respond, "I lost the keys, mommy. It wasn't daddy." If we consider that her play is a reflection of her perception of her family's relationships, we may surmise that she took the blame for the lost keys in a courageous effort to restore harmony between her parents.

Violence and Traumatic Stress

Children's responses to violence may be so intense and pervasive that they constitute "traumatic stress disorder," a diagnostic category for mental health disorders of infancy and early childhood[24] that is characterized by the following symptoms:

- reexperience of the traumatic event through posttraumatic play, recurrent recollections of the event outside of play, repeated nightmares, distress upon exposure to reminders of the trauma and/or episodes with objective features of a flashback or dissociation
- numbing of responsiveness or interference with developmental momentum, including social withdrawal, restricted range of affect, temporary loss of previously acquired developmental skills and/or a decrease or constriction in play
- increased arousal, as evidenced in night terrors, difficulty falling asleep, repeated night awakenings, difficulty paying attention and concentrating, hypervigilance and exaggerated startle responses
- development of troubling symptoms that were not present prior to the traumatic event, such as aggression toward peers, adults or animals, separation anxiety, fear of the dark or other new fears, motor reenactments and/or precociously sexualized behavior

These symptoms do not develop within a vacuum. Their intensity and persistence are associated frequently with the inability of parents to provide protective care and a developmentally appropriate child-rearing environment. As van der Kolk noted, "The earliest and possibly most damaging psychological trauma is the loss of a secure base."[25] Children who witness family violence or experience maltreatment themselves are very often unable to develop and maintain the developmentally appropriate expectations that their parents will protect them and ensure their well-being.[26,27] Violence-prone parents may become the child's attacker when angered, rather than the unwavering source of protection and reassurance. The child is then confronted with a seemingly unsolvable psychological dilemma: a simultaneous struggle between fear of the parents and a desire for their protection.[28] As a result, the child experiences contradictory impulses to run from the parents to avoid harm and to approach the parents for protection — as well as overlapping but competing emotions, including fear, anger, protectiveness and identification with both the aggressor and the victim.[29] These emotions, in turn, are manifested in the internalizing and externalizing behaviors observed frequently in the maltreated young children described previously in this chapter.

There is a striking similarity in the responses to traumatic stress experienced by young children, older children, adolescents and even adults. The symptom clusters of reexperiencing the trauma, avoidance/numbing and hyperarousal are common to both the diagnostic category of "traumatic stress disorder" described in the *Diagnostic Classification of Mental Health and Developmental Disorders of Infancy and Early Childhood (DC: 0-3)*[30] and the diagnostic category of "posttraumatic stress disorder" (PTSD) elucidated in the most-recent edition of the *Diagnostic and Statistical Manual of Mental Disorders-IV (DSM-IV™)* published by the American Psychiatric Association.[31] However, it is important to note that the specific behaviors resulting from traumatic stress that are shown in these 2 diagnostic manuals differ: The *DSM-IV* is more relevant to adolescents and adults, while the *DC: 0-3* is geared specifically to children in the first 5 years of life.

Current classification systems do not adequately describe the full range of developmental disruptions, the emotional, social and cognitive difficulties, and/or the behavioral problems that children experience when they are traumatized multiply by violence, maltreatment and abuse. As a result, there is a tendency to emphasize comorbidity in the form of co-occurring diagnoses. In addition to PTSD, children exposed to violence and maltreatment are often diagnosed with the following:

- mood disorders, such as depression or anxiety
- attention deficits
- hyperactivity
- a conduct disorder, such as oppositional conduct disorder
- an attachment disorder, such as separation anxiety or reactive attachment disorder

Using multiple overlapping diagnoses increases the risk of treatment fragmentation because clinical attention focuses on specific symptoms rather than on the core deficits common in children traumatized repeatedly by violence. To remedy this situation, the Complex Trauma Task Force of The National Child Traumatic Stress Network published a white paper entitled *Complex Trauma in Children and Adolescents.*[32] The following are the 7 domains that this task force identified:

- attachment
- biology
- affect regulation
- dissociation
- behavior regulation
- cognition
- self-concept

In each domain, impairment occurs within a developmental context — affecting different children differently depending on their particular developmental stage — and continues to affect development from that point forward. This conceptualization advances the theory outlined by Pynoos and Steinberg in this text that children exposed to multiple and complex trauma may suffer subsequently from a trauma-related developmental disorder.

This multifaceted, developmentally informed model is supported by accumulating evidence that repeated exposures to violence have a significant impact on a child's actual biological makeup.[33-38] Maltreated children and children diagnosed with PTSD showed higher levels of cortisol than did a control group of well-adjusted children. They also exhibited an adrenocorticotropic hormone-blunted response to corticotropic-releasing hormone as well as significantly reduced brain volumes, particularly in the area of the corpus callosum. The duration of maltreatment, the severity of the child's symptoms of PTSD and the presence of dissociative symptoms correlate positively with the loss of brain volume.[35] These findings indicate that experiences of abuse and trauma suffered during childhood affect the child's neurobiology in lasting and complex ways which ultimately affect functioning in a variety of areas and shape the child's core sense of self distinctly.

While understanding fully the profound impact that trauma has on early personality development will require significant and sustained investigation, it is important to note that trauma does not affect all children in the same way: For example, Kitzmann and colleagues reported that 63% of children exposed to domestic violence had worse outcomes in terms of both internalizing and externalizing behavior problems than did children who were not exposed to violence. However, the remaining 37% did not differ from the control group.[39] Clinicians have used the concept of "resilience" — defined in terms of a child's ability to achieve or maintain positive adaptation despite exposure to significant stresses or traumatic experiences — to explain differences in individual responses to adverse circumstances.[40] Although the concept of resilience is indispensable for understanding the resourcefulness, strength and adaptability of individuals who cope effectively with potentially damaging circumstances, it has several definitional inconsistencies and measurement problems,[41] including the following:

- disagreement about whether resilience is a personality trait or a transactional process
- uncertainty about the type and number of functioning domains that should be considered when examining resilience
- questions about the stability of positive adaptation over time

These issues notwithstanding, there is remarkable uniformity in the following empirically identified factors that predict resilience:

- the child-centered factors include above-average cognitive abilities, high self-esteem, an internal locus of control, ego flexibility and high ego control.[42]
- the key environmental factor is a consistent, caring relationship with an adult. This fosters resilience by decreasing the symptomatology of the child, thereby enhancing the child's school performance and bolstering the child's social skills with both peers and adults.[43-45] The significant role that a nurturing adult plays in promoting resilience in a child is consistent with basic theoretical premises from both psychoanalysis[46] and attachment theory[26] regarding the centrality of the caregiving relationship in healthy personality development.[47] This convergence of theoretical tenets and empirical evidence has important implications for the treatment of children exposed to violence.

Ecology of Violence: Implications for Treatment of Young Children

It is now accepted widely that the emotional health of children is shaped by complex transactional processes that exist among a variety of risk and protective factors, with cumulative risk factors increasing the potential for emotional and behavioral problems.[48-51] As noted previously, research has identified many of these risk and protective factors,[52] which include the following:

- **parental characteristics:** mental health, educational level, sense of efficacy, resourcefulness and competence in parenting
- **family factors:** quality of the parent-child relationship, quality of the emotional relationship among family members and quality of the marital relationship
- **community cohesiveness factors:** social support systems for parents, social resources and children's peer relationships
- **neighborhood factors:** availability of resources, adequacy of housing, and presence and level of violence

The predictive validity of these factors across multiple studies led to the development of transactional–ecological models that conceptualize the relative contributions of proximal and distal risk and protective factors to the developmental outcomes in children.[11,53]

With rapid advances in genetics and the mapping of the human genome, many clinicians and researchers were hopeful that the developmental outcomes and mental health profiles of children could be predicted from their genetic makeup. However, scientific data[54,55] do not support an emphasis on genetic factors as the primary engine for development and mental health. On the contrary, genes engage in complex transactions with the variety of internal environments that surround them within the body. The cellular environment influences which of the tens of thousands of genes are turned "on" or "off."[54,55] In other words, according to Shonkoff and Phillips, "It is impossible to think of gene expression apart from the multiple environments in which it occurs. It is impossible to think of the manifestation of hereditary potential independently of the hierarchy of environments that shape its appearance."[56]

The result of this intricate interplay between nature and nurture is illustrated graphically in a longitudinal study of children raised in a variety of environmental conditions.[57] In their first year of life, infants were classified as "low-competence" or "high-competence" based on 13 measures, including physical health, cognitive performance and temperamental characteristics. The investigators found no positive correlation between infants' Year 1 competence scores and their IQ or mental health scores at age 4 years. Most notably, highly competent infants who were raised in "detrimental" environments functioned more poorly as preschoolers than did less-competent infants raised in "favorable" environments. These findings suggest that environmental risk factors may, as a rule, be a more accurate predictor of developmental course than may factors intrinsic to the child.[52]

These considerations are key to understanding the impact of violence on the development of young children. Because violence is associated so frequently with conditions stemming from poverty, children growing up in poor families are significantly more likely than children growing up in higher-income families to live in chronically violent environments and to become victims of violence themselves.[58] In fact, violence is so prevalent in some neighborhoods that the term "inner-city war zone" has been coined to describe them.[58-60] There is strong evidence that the higher incidence of violence reported among ethnic minority groups may be attributed to poverty because, when socioeconomic status is controlled, few differences in rates of violence emerge among ethnic groups.[58]

In conditions of poverty, adults are traumatized, as well, because the stresses of living and raising a family are compounded by the chronic risk of physical danger to themselves *and* their children. Parents' efforts to adapt to these dangers may result in particular kinds of child-rearing strategies — such as harshly punitive discipline and constrictions on the child's autonomous explorations — that interfere with secure attachment and the child's readiness to learn.[61]

In this context, helping young children cope effectively in the aftermath of exposure to violence must necessarily involve supporting the parents, as well. When parents' internal resources are depleted by multiple sources of stress, including exposure to and victimization by violence, they may have difficulty providing emotional priority to their child and/or to their parenting roles. Furthermore, they may not be motivated to cooperate with a treatment format that excludes them, such as with individual child psychotherapy or play therapy. Waiting outside a psychotherapist's office while the child and the therapist meet alone can be a lonely and alienating experience for a needy or traumatized parent. It may rekindle feelings of being left out, and these feelings may be compounded by the confidentiality of the child-therapist therapeutic relationship, which prevents the parent from knowing what transpired during the therapeutic sessions. Parents from disempowered cultural groups may be especially threatened by child-centered forms of intervention that do not include them.

There is extensive evidence that a therapeutic format that includes both the child and the parent in the treatment leads to statistically significant more positive outcomes for high-risk families with young children, including those with maltreated toddlers and preschoolers.[62-66] We have adopted this approach in treating infants, toddlers and preschoolers who have witnessed their father or father figures battering their mothers.[29] Battered women may prove unable to appraise danger signals realistically because of their own history of trauma, leaving them and their children vulnerable to repeated traumatic experiences. Joint mother-child therapeutic sessions provide an opportunity to focus on safety as the prerequisite for effective intervention; that is, working with the mother to mobilize her capacity for protecting herself and her child as the cornerstone of treatment. The father or father figure is included in treatment *only* when he has acknowledged the violence he has instigated or caused, expressed contrition, made an explicit commitment to not repeating it and is receiving concurrent therapy in a program that specializes in the treatment of violent behavior.

Recognizing and addressing the damaging effects of violence are other prerequisites to recovery from exposure to trauma. Parents often underestimate the impact that "exposure" to violence has on their child.[67] Joint child-parent therapeutic sessions offer an opportunity for both the youngster and the adult to overcome their resistance to speaking about the violence. Toddlers and preschoolers often reenact the violence in their play, which serves as a form of nonverbal communication to the therapist *and* the parent about the child's experience.

Child-Parent Psychotherapy After Exposure to Violence

The goal of child-parent psychotherapy is to return the child to a normal developmental course by restoring a sense of safety, trust and reciprocity in the parent-child relationship. The targets of intervention and treatment are the shared or jointly constructed systems of meaning that may be trauma-related and may have devalued the child, the parent and/or their relationship.[68] Even different approaches to the treatment of trauma share commonalities in their goals and in the mechanisms to achieve them.[69] These commonalities, described below, address the main symptoms of a response to trauma[69]:

- encouraging a return to normal development through adaptive coping and engagement with developmentally appropriate activities and goals
- fostering an increased capacity to respond realistically to threats by evaluating accurately whether a situation is safe or poses a danger
- maintaining appropriate levels of affective arousal by containing and redirecting unmodulated emotional responses
- reestablishing trust in bodily sensations by encouraging expressions of affection between parent and child — using touch as a source of protection and care — and by promoting the achievement of developmentally appropriate milestones, such as mobility, toilet training and autonomous exploration
- restoring reciprocity in the parent-child relationship by helping each partner recognize and respond empathically to the other's signals
- normalizing the response to trauma by establishing a framework of meaning that is accepted as universal and legitimate
- encouraging a differentiation between "reliving" and "remembering" the trauma by helping the child and parent recognize when they are being flooded by traumatic memories and subsequently restoring a sense of connection with present circumstances
- placing the traumatic experience in perspective by encouraging a frame of mind where memories of the trauma are counterbalanced by engagement in and appreciation for rewarding life events and daily activities

In child-parent psychotherapy, these goals are applicable to both the child and the parent because, as discussed previously, effective parental functioning is considered essential for a successful outcome for the child. Although these goals are pursued through various therapeutic modalities, the parent-child interaction is the organizing focus of the therapy sessions. The uses of play, language and physical contact are encouraged to promote all of the following: reciprocity and exploration; to contain, process and redirect negative affect; to resolve conflict; and to clarify feelings. Unstructured developmental guidance is provided to the parents, as needed, to increase their knowledge about age-appropriate behaviors and interventions. Whenever the family ecology is threatened with disruption, crisis intervention, case management and concrete assistance with problems of living are provided, as are advocacy with social systems and agencies that can provide assistance with issues relevant to the family's well-being.

Toward Evidence-Based Treatment: Effectiveness Data

To evaluate the effectiveness of child-parent psychotherapy with toddlers and preschoolers who witnessed domestic violence, we assessed 59 children and their mothers. The assessments occurred at the time of referral and after 1 year of weekly psychotherapeutic treatment. The court, child protective services, child care centers, mothers' attorneys and community agencies serving families in need referred children to our practice. Treatment, however, was voluntary. The children ranged in age from 3 years to 6 years, with a mean age of 4.19 years, and they were split almost evenly by gender. In all cases, the child was living with the mother after marital separation resulting from domestic violence.

Maternal education varied widely: 29% of mothers had less than a high school diploma, 26% had completed high school, 41% had started or completed college and 4% had some postgraduate education. Annual incomes ranged from $4800 to $100,000, with a mean income of $22,062. The majority of mothers (67%) were employed, while 12% received public assistance and 35% received child support from the child's biological father.

There was also substantial ethnic diversity among these mothers and children. Among the mothers, 47% were Latin American, 25% were white, 15% were African American, 11% were Asian American and 2% were of another ethnic heritage. Among the children, 37% were of mixed ethnicity, 32% were Latin American, 14% were African American, 8.5% were Asian American and 8.5% were white.

We excluded mother-child dyads from the study if the mother and child still lived with the perpetrator of the violence. Other exclusionary criteria included maternal psychosis, maternal substance abuse, homelessness or child mental retardation or autism. (Each of these risk factors requires specialized intervention.) These exclusionary factors were selected to increase the uniformity of the child-parent psychotherapy intervention for all members of the sample.

Prior to providing treatment, we assessed both the child and the mother using clinical and play interviews, structured and semistructured measures and observations of mother-child interactions. This assessment took place over the course of 4 sessions. We used the same multimethod assessment 1 year later, after termination of treatment.

The clinicians who provided psychotherapeutic treatment came from diverse backgrounds: psychology and social work interns; psychiatry residents who had no previous experience with infant and early childhood mental health; and Master's-level and PhD-level psychologists who had significant experience in child-parent psychotherapy. Unlicensed clinicians received clinical supervision, an essential ingredient for treatment fidelity.

In this chapter, we focus on findings from one instrument administered at the time of referral and 4 measures assessed before and after treatment. During the initial assessment, we interviewed mothers, using the revised Life Stressor Checklist (LSC),[70] about their histories of exposure to stressful events. In addition, immediately after referral and then after treatment, we assessed the mothers to determine if, using the Clinician-Administered PTSD Scale, they had PTSD.[71] Using the revised Wechsler Preschool and Primary Scale of Intelligence (WPPSI), we also assessed the children's cognitive functioning and readiness to learn. Using the Parent-Infant Relationship Global Assessment Scale (PIRGAS), we assessed the quality of the mother-child relationship.[24] Clinicians observed mother-child interactions to assess the latter. Each mother completed the Child Behavior Checklist (CBC)[72,73] to provide information about the child's symptoms. We selected these measures for the study for 2 reasons: They were relevant to the domains that were the focus of the intervention and they have robust psychometric properties. Maternal responses to the revised LSC demonstrated a high incidence of lifetime exposure to traumatic stressors: The mean number of stressors reported by the mothers was 12.5, with a range from 4 to 25. Of particular note is the prevalence of childhood traumatic events: 51% of mothers reported that they had witnessed domestic violence between their parents while growing up, 36% reported childhood physical abuse and 36% reported sexual molestation or assault before the age of 16 years. Mothers also reported a high frequency of interpersonal violence and loss in their adult lives: 56% reported the traumatic death of someone close to them, 36% reported coerced intercourse and 37% reported having been robbed or mugged. These figures are consistent with research that reports that the cycle of domestic violence often carries over into the next generation and co-occurs with child maltreatment and community violence.[39]

Findings from the initial assessment indicated a substantial level of distress among these children and their mothers:

- Children's performance on the WPPSI was below the norm on the full scale (mean IQ = 92), the verbal scale (mean IQ = 90) and the performance scale (mean IQ = 97).
- PTSD was diagnosed in 54% of the mothers, with high frequency and intensity of symptoms found in the following 3 clusters: reexperiencing the trauma, avoidance and hyperarousal.
- The mean score for the group with regard to the quality of the mother-child relationship ranked as "disturbed," placing the dyad at "significant risk for dysfunction" according to interpretation of the PIRGAS findings.

1 Year Later

After 1 year of an average of one session per week, the assessments of the mothers and children showed substantial improvement. There was a statistically significant increase in the IQ scores of the children on all 3 scales: performance ($P<.001$), verbal ($P<.05$) and total ($P<.001$). There was also a statistically significant decrease ($P<.01$) in the children's behavioral problem scores, based on mothers' responses on the CBC. The percentage of mothers who met the criteria for PTSD after 1 year of treatment dropped by more than half, to 23%, with statistically significant decreases in the frequency and intensity of all 3 symptom clusters: reexperience ($P<.001$), avoidance ($P<.05$)

and arousal symptoms ($P<.01$). According to the PIRGAS criteria, the quality of the mother-child relationship improved significantly to the level of "...strained in some way but still largely adequate and satisfying to the partners."[24]

Our interpretation of these results is that, after treatment, the children improved significantly: They had fewer behavioral symptoms and better cognitive functioning. We are in the process of analyzing videotapes of the administration of the WPPSI to determine whether the improvements in IQ are related to improvements in any of the following: children's ability to concentrate on tasks; children's persistence in their efforts to find the correct answer; the children contain their negative feelings in response to not knowing an answer; and/or the children cooperate with the assessor. Clinical examination of the videotapes suggests that the improved cognitive performance exhibited by the children after treatment is associated with improvements on all of these parameters. If these clinical impressions are confirmed by quantitative analyses, the findings would indicate that the cognitive performance of young children is influenced strongly by their emotional well-being, and that timely therapeutic intervention can simultaneously improve their emotional well-being and their readiness to learn.

The findings of improvements in the mothers' symptoms were well-received, but unexpected because child-parent psychotherapy does not focus on the parents' psychopathology. These results are particularly rewarding, as they indicate that a focus on the mother-child relationship also has beneficial effects on the mother's mental health. We believe that these findings indicate that an increase in the mother's feeling of competence in her maternal role as well as a sense of reciprocity and pleasure in her relationship with her children are important parts of her individual mental health. If this proves so, child-parent psychotherapy emerges as an effective treatment approach for both the child and the mother through the vehicle of the mother-child relationship.

Conclusion

Exposure to violence that results in severe distress in young children has the potential to derail their normal course of development. There is an urgent need to develop, implement and assess the efficacy of culturally appropriate, developmentally informed interventions that can be offered in accessible community settings. There is increasing evidence that a therapeutic focus on the mother-child relationship facilitates functional improvements in the child in the emotional, social and cognitive domains. The current study presents preliminary evidence that shows that this approach may also improve the mother's psychological functioning, thereby supporting the child's trajectory towards normalized development.

References

1. Gentry CE. *Crisis Intervention in Child Abuse and Neglect.* Washington, DC: US Dept of Health & Human Services, Administration for Children and Families, Administration on Children, Youth and Families, National Center on Child Abuse and Neglect; 1994. Available at: http://nccanch.acf.hhs.gov/pubs/usermanuals/crisis/index.cfm. Accessed May 20, 2004.
2. UNICEF Innocenti Research Centre. *Child Abuse Leads to 3,500 Deaths Each Year in Developed Countries, New Research Finds: First Comparative Analysis of Child Maltreatment in Rich Nations.* Berlin, Germany: UNICEF Innocenti Research Centre; September 18, 2003. Available at: http://www.unicef-icdc.org/presscentre/presskit/repcard5/rc5_pr_en.pdf. Accessed May 20, 2004.
3. Administration for Children & Families. *Child Maltreatment 2001.* Washington, DC: US Dept of Health & Human Services, Administration for Children and Families, Administration on Children, Youth and Families, Children's Bureau; March 21, 2003. Available at: http://www.acf.hhs.gov/programs/cb/publications/cm01/outcover.htm. Accessed May 20, 2004.
4. *Women and Violence: Hearings Before the US Senate Judiciary Committee.* August 29, 1990 and December 11, 1990. Senate Hearing 101-939. pt. 2, p. 142.
5. McCloskey LA, Figueredo AJ, Koss MP. The effects of systemic family violence on children's mental health. *Child Development.* 1995;66:1239-1261.
6. Osofsky JD. Prevalence of children's exposure to domestic violence and child maltreatment: implications for prevention and intervention. *Clinical Child and Family Psychology Review.* 2003;6:161-170.
7. Edleson JL. Children's witnessing of adult domestic violence. *Journal of Interpersonal Violence.* 1999;14:839-870.
8. Margolin G, Gordis EB. The effects of family and community violence on children. *Annual Review of Psychology.* 2000;51:445-479.
9. Rutter ML. Psychosocial adversity and child psychopathology. *The British Journal of Psychiatry; the Journal of Mental Science.* 1999;174:480-493.
10. Sameroff A. Models of development and developmental risk. In: Zeanah CH Jr, ed. *Handbook of Infant Mental Health.* New York, NY: The Guilford Press; 1993.
11. Pynoos RS, Steinberg AM, Piacentini JC. A developmental psychopathology model of childhood traumatic stress and intersection with anxiety disorders. *Biological Psychiatry.* 1999;46:1542-1554.
12. Davidson T. *Conjugal Crime: Understanding and Changing the Wifebeating Pattern.* New York, NY: Penguin Press (USA); 1978.
13. Eth S, Pynoos RS. *Post-Traumatic Stress Disorder in Children.* Washington, DC: American Psychiatric Press; 1985.
14. Gaensbauer TJ. Therapeutic work with a traumatized toddler. *The Psychoanalytic Study of the Child.* 1994;49:412-433.
15. Parson ER. Post-traumatic stress and coping in an inner-city child. Traumatogenic witnessing of interparental violence and murder. *The Psychoanalytic Study of the Child.* 1995;50:272-307.
16. Pynoos RS, Nader K. Children who witness the sexual assaults of their mothers. *Journal of the American Academy of Child and Adolescent Psychiatry.* 1988;27:567-572.
17. Terr LC. "Forbidden games": post-traumatic child's play. *Journal of the American Academy of Child and Adolescent Psychiatry.* 1981;20:741-760.

18. Margolin G, Gordis EB. The effects of family and community violence on children. *Annual Review of Psychology.* 2000;51:445-479.
19. Cannon W. *Effects of Strong Emotions.* Oxford, England: University of Chicago Press; 1932.
20. Lieberman AF, Zeanah CH. Disorders of attachment in infancy. *Child and Adolescent Psychiatric Clinics of North America.* 1995;4:579-588.
21. Lieberman A. Negative maternal attributions: effects on toddlers' sense of self. *Psychoanalytic Inquiry.* 1999;19:737-756.
22. Silverman RC, Lieberman AF. Negative maternal attributions, projective identification, and the intergenerational transmission of violent relational patterns. *Psychoanalytic Dialogues.* 2000;9:161-186.
23. Lieberman AF, Van Horn P. *Don't Hit My Mommy! A Manual for Child-Parent Psychotherapy With Young Witnesses of Family Violence.* Washington, DC: Zero to Three Press, 2005.
24. National Center for Clinical Infant Programs. *Diagnostic Classification — 0-3: Diagnostic Classification of Mental Health & Developmental Disorders of Infancy & Early Childhood.* Arlington, Va: National Center for Clinical Infant Programs; 1994.
25. van der Kolk BA. *Psychological Trauma.* Arlington, Va: American Psychiatric Publishing; 1987.
26. Bowlby J. *Attachment.* 2nd ed. New York, NY: Basic Books; 1982.
27. Ainsworth MDS, Blehar MC, Waters E, Wall S. *Patterns of Attachment: A Psychological Study of the Strange Situation.* Hillsdale, NJ: Lawrence Erlbaum Associates; 1978.
28. Main M, Hesse E. Parents' unresolved traumatic experiences are related to infant disorganized attachment status: is frightened and/or frightening parental behavior the linking mechanism? In: Greenberg MT, Cicchetti D, Cummings EM, eds. *Attachment in the Preschool Years: Theory, Research, and Intervention.* Chicago, Ill: University of Chicago Press; 1990:121-160.
29. Lieberman AF, Van Horn P. Attachment, trauma, and domestic violence. Implications for child custody. *Child and Adolescent Psychiatric Clinics of North America.* 1998;7:423-443.
30. DC 0-3: Zero to Three/National Center for Clinical Infant Programs. *Diagnostic Classification of Mental Health and Developmental Disorder of Infancy and Early Childhood.* Arlington, Va: Zero to Three/National Center for Clinical Infant Programs; 1994.
31. American Psychiatric Association. *Diagnostic and Statistical Manual of Mental Disorders: Text Revision.* 4th ed. Washington, DC: American Psychiatric Association; 2000.
32. Cook A, Blaustein M, Spinazzola J, van der Kolk B, eds. *Complex Trauma in Children and Adolescents* [white paper]. Rockville, Md: US Dept of Health & Human Services, Substance Abuse and Mental Health Services Administration, Center for Mental Health Services, The National Child Traumatic Stress Network; 2003.
33. De Bellis MD, Chrousos GP, Dorn LD, et al. Hypothalamic-pituitary-adrenal axis dysregulation in sexually abused girls. *The Journal of Clinical Endocrinology and Metabolism.* 1994;78:249-255.
34. Putnam FW, Trickett PK. Psychobiological effects of sexual abuse. A longitudinal study. *Annals of the New York Academy of Sciences.* 1997;821:150-159.
35. De Bellis MD, Baum AS, Birmaher B, et al. Developmental traumatology. Part I: Biological stress systems. *Biological Psychiatry.* 1999;45:1259-1270.
36. Cicchetti D, Rogosch FA. The impact of child maltreatment and psychopathology on neuroendocrine functioning. *Development and Psychopathology.* 2001;13:783-804.
37. Carrion VG, Weems CF, Ray RD, Glaser B, Hessl D, Reiss AL. Diurnal salivary cortisol in pediatric posttraumatic stress disorder. *Biological Psychiatry.* 2002;51:575-582.
38. Teicher MH, Ito Y, Glod CA, Andersen SL, Dumont N, Ackerman E. Preliminary evidence for abnormal cortical development in physically and sexually abused children using EEG coherence and MRI. *Annals of the New York Academy of Sciences.* 1997;821:160-175.
39. Kitzmann KM, Gaylord NK, Holt AR, Kenny ED. Child witnesses to domestic violence: a meta-analytic review. *Journal of Consulting and Clinical Psychology.* 2003;71:339-352.

40. Masten AS. Resilience in individual development: successful adaptation despite risk and adversity. In: Wang MC, Gordon EW, eds. *Educational Resilience in Inner-City America: Challenges and Prospects.* Hillsdale, NJ: Lawrence Erlbaum Associates; 1994:3-25.
41. Luthar SS, Cicchetti D, Becker B. The construct of resilience: a critical evaluation and guidelines for future work. *Child Development.* 2000;71:543-562.
42. Heller SS, Larrieu JA, D'Imperio R, Boris NW. Research on resilience to child maltreatment: empirical considerations. *Child Abuse & Neglect.* 1999;23:321-338.
43. Egeland B, Jacobvitz D, Sroufe LA. Breaking the cycle of abuse. *Child Development.* 1988;59: 1080-1088.
44. Herrenkohl TI, Huang B, Tajima EA, Whitney SD. Examining the link between child abuse and youth violence: an analysis of mediating mechanisms. *Journal of Interpersonal Violence.* 2003;18: 1189-1208.
45. Spaccarelli S, Kim S. Resilience criteria and factors associated with resilience in sexually abused girls. *Child Abuse & Neglect.* 1995;19:1171-1182.
46. Freud S. *Inhibitions, Symptoms, and Anxiety.* Strachey J, trans-ed. London, England: Hogarth Press; 1959. Freud S. *Standard Edition of the Complete Psychological Works of Sigmund Freud;* vol 20.
47. Fairbairn WRD. *An Object Relations Theory of the Personality.* New York, NY: Basic Books; 1954.
48. Cicchetti D, Sroufe LA. The past as prologue to the future: the times, they've been a changin'. *Development and Psychopathology.* 2000;12:255-264.
49. Rutter M. Maternal deprivation, 1972-1978: new findings, new concepts, new approaches. *Child Development.* 1979;50:283-305.
50. Rutter M, Sroufe LA. Developmental psychopathology: concepts and challenges. *Development and Psychopathology.* 2000;12:265-296.
51. Sameroff AJ. Developmental systems and psychopathology. *Development and Psychopathology.* 2000; 12:297-312.
52. Sameroff AJ, Fiese B. Models of development and developmental risk. In: Zeanah CH Jr, ed. *Handbook of Infant Mental Health.* 2nd ed. New York, NY: The Guilford Press; 2000.
53. Cicchetti D, Lynch M. Toward an ecological/transactional model of community violence and child maltreatment: consequences for children's development. *Psychiatry.* 1993;56:96-118.
54. Greenough W. Experience as a component of normal development: evolutionary considerations. *Developmental Psychology.* 1991;27:14-17.
55. Greenough WT, Black JE. Induction of brain structure by experience: substrates for cognitive development. In: Gunnar MR, Nelson CA, eds. *Developmental Behavioral Neuroscience.* Hillsdale, NJ: Lawrence Erlbaum Associates; 1992:155-200.
56. Shonkoff JP, Phillips D. *From Neurons to Neighborhoods: The Science of Early Childhood Development.* Washington, DC: National Academy Press; 2000.
57. Sameroff AJ, Bartko WT, Baldwin A, Baldwin C, Seifer R. Family and social influences on the development of child competence. In: Lewis M, Feiring C, eds. *Families, Risk, and Competence.* Mahwah, NJ: Lawrence Erlbaum Associates; 1998:161-186.
58. American Psychological Association. *Violence & Youth: Psychology's Response. Summary Report of the American Psychological Association Commission on Youth and Violence.* Vol 1. Washington, DC: American Psychological Association, Commission on Violence and Youth; 1993.
59. Dubrow NF, Garbarino J. *Living in a War Zone: Mothers and Young Children in a Public Housing Development.* Washington, DC: Child Welfare League of America; 1989.
60. Garbarino J, Kostelny K, Dubrow N. What children can tell us about living in danger. *The American Psychologist.* 1991;46:376-383.
61. Fick AC, Osofsky JD, Lewis ML. Perceptions of violence: children, parents, and police officers. In: Osofsky JD, ed. *Children in a Violent Society.* New York, NY: The Guilford Press; 1997:261-275.
62. Cicchetti D, Toth SL, Rogosch FA. The efficacy of toddler-parent psychotherapy to increase attachment security in offspring of depressed mothers. *Attachment & Human Development.* 1999;1:34-66.

63. Heinicke CM, Fineman NR, Ruth G, Recchia SL, Guthrie D, Rodning C. Relationship-based intervention with at-risk mothers: outcome in the first year of life. *Infant Mental Health Journal.* 1999; 20:349-374.
64. Lieberman AF, Weston DR, Pawl JH. Preventive intervention and outcome with anxiously attached dyads. *Child Development.* 1991;62:199-209.
65. Toth SL, Maughan A, Manly JT, Spagnola M, Cicchetti D. The relative efficacy of two interventions in altering maltreated preschool children's representational models: implications for attachment theory. *Development and Psychopathology.* 2002;14:877-908.
66. Dunn JD, Levenstein P, Levenstein S, Temple P, Olds D. Long-term effects of home visits on children's behavior. *JAMA: The Journal of the American Medical Association.* 1999;281:1375-1377.
67. Peled E, Davis D. *Groupwork With Children of Battered Women: A Practitioner's Manual.* Thousand Oaks, Calif: Sage Publications; 1995.
68. Lieberman AF. Child-parent psychotherapy. In: Sameroff AJ, McDonough SC, Rosenblum KL, eds. *Treating Parent-Infant Relationship Problems: Strategies for Intervention.* New York, NY: The Guilford Press; 2004:97-122.
69. Marmar CK, Foy D, Kagan B. An integrated approach to treating posttraumatic stress. In: Pynoos RS, ed. *Posttraumatic Stress Disorder: A Clinical Review.* Lutherville, Md: Sidran Press; 1993:239-272.
70. Wolfe JW, Kimerling R, Brown PJ, et al. Psychometric review of the life stressor checklist — revised. In: Stamm BH, ed. *Measurement of Stress, Trauma, and Adaptation.* Lutherville, Md: Sidran Press; 1996.
71. Blake DD, Weathers F, Nagy L, et al. Clinician administered PTSD scale. *The Behavior Therapist.* 1990;18:12-14.
72. Achenbach TM. *Manual for the Child: Behavior Checklist and Revised Child Behavior Profile.* Burlington, Vt: University of Vermont Department of Psychiatry; 1983.
73. Achenbach TM. *Manual for Child Behavior Checklist 4-18, 1991 Profile.* Burlington, Vt: University of Vermont Department of Psychiatry; 1991.

Section 2: Models of Collaboration: The Mental Health and Legal Systems Working Together

Abstracts from Section 2: Models of Collaboration: The Mental Health and Legal Systems Working Together

Mental Health and Judicial Partnerships: Collaborating to Reduce the Effects of Abuse on Children and Families

Joy D. Osofsky, PhD
Judge Cindy S. Lederman

Juvenile court judges often make monumental decisions that affect the future course of a child's life and well-being. A nexus between the law and science — which brings the knowledge of child development into the courtroom — could result in better decision-making. The Miami-Dade (Florida) Juvenile Court is conducting groundbreaking work on the relationship between child maltreatment and domestic violence. This work includes the development and implementation of a parent-child treatment model that supports and enhances the crucial bond between a young child and the primary caregiver. It is one of the first programs in the United States that brings together prevention and intervention efforts, research and community collaboration to address the dual issues of child maltreatment and domestic violence through the auspices of the juvenile court. Three years of data from this pilot program show improvements in parental sensitivity, child and parent responsiveness during play and parental responsiveness to children's behaviors and affect.

Mental Health-Law Enforcement Collaborative Responses to Children's Exposure to Violence

Steven Marans, PhD
Robert A. Murphy, PhD
Robert L. Casey, PhD
Steven J. Berkowitz, MD
Miriam Berkman, JD, MSW

Each year, millions of children are exposed to violence in their homes and communities. Beginning in the 1970s and gathering momentum in the late 1980s, leaders in law enforcement recognized the need for a change in the existing reactive models of policing: They recommended community-based policing as an alternative. Community-based policing integrates police officers within the community, where they are known as individuals rather than just by their role, and, likewise, the officers come to know the people they serve as individuals. This chapter examines the Child Development-Community Policing (CD-CP) program — as adopted by the community of New Haven, Connecticut — which is a partnership among the area's mental health system, the police department, the juvenile justice system, the schools and Child Protective Services. Recent studies have yielded promising evidence that youth-oriented community policing and the CD-CP model are having a positive impact on children's lives by promoting feelings of safety and security, decreasing levels of exposure to domestic and community violence, enhancing perceptions of the police as a responsive and benevolent authority, improving access to acute clinical intervention and follow-up and decreasing repeat calls for police services in cases of domestic violence.

Mental Health and Judicial Partnerships: Collaborating to Reduce the Effects of Abuse on Children and Families

Joy D. Osofsky, PhD
Judge Cindy S. Lederman

Introduction

Every day in the United States, juvenile courts make crucial decisions that affect the health, safety and well-being of many children and adolescents. Frequently, juvenile courts are the places of last resort — where children and families end up when all else has failed.

Children's Voices in the Courtroom

Increasingly, within the child welfare system, younger and younger children are coming under the jurisdiction of the US court system. In fact, among the nearly 600,000 children in foster care in 2002, 1 in 5 entered the system initially during the first year of their life.[1] Of significant concern is the unprecedented increase of infants in foster care: 5% first enter the foster care system sometime between birth and 3 months of age.[2] Their families often struggle with poverty, emotional deprivation and other such cumulative disadvantages. Since children who enter foster care at a younger age often stay in foster placement longer,[3] it is crucial that everyone in the child welfare system who comes into contact with these very young children and infants — judges, lawyers, court-appointed special advocates (CASAs), court personnel and others — understand how to protect them and promote their healthy development.

In some states, children have a right to legal representation by a court-appointed guardian or attorney during dependency hearings: For example, Arkansas requires that the court appoint an attorney to represent children in dependency and neglect (D&N) cases.[4] Colorado has a similar requirement.[5] California requires that the court appoint an attorney and a CASA to each child involved in D&N proceedings.[6] However, there are still a few states where children have no right to any form of legal representation. Unfortunately, even in states where children have a legal entitlement, the court systems are sometimes so underfunded — or even totally unfunded — that children end up with no legal representation of any kind during dependency proceedings. Or, equally disturbing, when attorneys are appointed to represent dependent children in court, the attorneys are often overburdened, frequently have little knowledge about child development and the needs of these children and have limited opportunities to meet the children before representing their interests in court. In these cases, young children truly are the "silent victims" of the system. They, themselves, have no legal voice, their parents often cannot or do not recognize their needs and the already overburdened court system is unable to do what is in the best interests of these children.

With the passage of the Adoption and Safe Families Act of 1997 (ASFA),[7] the child became the center of the child welfare system: Finally, the health and safety of the child became the paramount concerns of the dependency judge. ASFA regulations require the court, through its rulings, to meet the physical and mental health needs of dependent children — and to monitor the effects of judges' rulings. However, this legal mandate often has no teeth for the protection of infants, toddlers and preschoolers, the largest and youngest cohort of children in the child welfare system. The Child Abuse Prevention and Treatment Act (CAPTA),[8] passed in 1988 (and amended in 1989), does have teeth. In order to receive federal funding, CAPTA requires states to provide representation for children in dependency and neglect cases. CAPTA, however, does not specify whether the child's representative must be an attorney.

These very young children, who frequently are not well-served by the courts, are often the most amenable to intervention. Infants and toddlers (because of their adaptability at such a young age) who receive targeted, careful and consistent interventions — more so than older children and adolescents — can often be helped to achieve their full potential. Unfortunately, the many decision-makers in the family law and mental health fields remain largely ignorant of decades of research regarding child development. Child custody decision-makers, especially judges, and child development researchers rarely intersect, and therefore the opportunity for one to learn from the other is almost nonexistent.[9] By necessity, not by choice, judges are forced to make monumental decisions in minutes; decisions that will have a significant impact on the future course of a child's life and well-being. Judges often must make these decisions having limited, inadequate and sometimes incorrect information. They also decide without the benefit of having a guardian or an attorney speaking on behalf of the child. Based on the information provided and on their legal training — not on the science of child development — the judge must discern what is in the best interest of the child. At times, their task is akin to riding a bicycle blindfolded.

A nexus between the law and science — which would bring the knowledge of child development into the courtroom — could result in better decision-making. This nexus could provide more informed answers to the following very challenging and potentially life-altering questions that judges in the juvenile court face almost every day:

- When is joint custody with 2 domiciles *not* in the best interest of a young child?
- When a relative comes forward after an infant has been placed in a loving foster home for nearly 1 year, should the judge change the placement of the baby?
- How often and under what circumstances should a domestic violence perpetrator who harmed the mother severely in the child's presence be permitted visitation with the child?
- Should different optimal requirements for visitation time, place and manner be based on the age of the child?
- When is a teenage mother ready to be reunified with (and care for) her baby?
- Is it better to keep siblings together in one mediocre foster home or place the children in separate, superior foster homes?

Children's Exposure to Maltreatment and Domestic Violence

It is difficult to estimate how often maltreatment of children and domestic violence co-occur in the homes of children who end up in the child welfare system. Differences in definitions and interpretations of the problem, as well as variations in research methodologies by multiple disciplines, account for much of this quandary.[10] There are significant differences across studies regarding estimates of the prevalence of the co-occurrence of child abuse and domestic violence, ranging from less than 10%[11] to more than 90%.[12] Edleson concluded that because of serious methodological shortcomings in the available studies, existing knowledge about the co-occurrence of child abuse and domestic violence is actually scant.[13] However, regardless of these definitional and methodological issues, there is considerable evidence that both moderate and severe domestic violence occur frequently,[14] and within these same homes parents also abuse their children.[14]

Miami Juvenile Court Initiative Works With Victims of Domestic Violence and Child Maltreatment

The Miami (Fla) Juvenile Court is conducting groundbreaking work on the relationship between child maltreatment and domestic violence through the Dependency Court Intervention Program for Family Violence (DCIPFV), a national demonstration project funded by the Violence Against Women Grants Office of the US Department of Justice (USDOJ). The DCIPFV addresses the safety-related, legal and emotional needs of adults and children who are victims of family violence. It is the first program in the United States that brings together family violence prevention and intervention efforts, research and community collaboration to address the dual issues of child maltreatment and domestic violence within a juvenile court setting. Using domestic violence victim *advocates*, the program identifies battered mothers within the child protection system and provides intensive outreach-based advocacy services, which include domestic violence screening, risk assessment and safety planning, counseling, case management and crisis intervention. Victim advocates work collaboratively with the Florida Department of Children and Families, the state judiciary, domestic violence victim shelters, mental health professionals, researchers and a host of community agencies to promote the safety of mothers and their dependent children.

As part of the research component of this project, for the first time in a judicial court setting, the DCIPFV developed an empirical estimate of the co-occurrence of child abuse and domestic violence: More than one of every 3 cases in Miami juvenile dependency court at any one time involves *both* child maltreatment and domestic violence.[15]

The mission of the DCIPFV — to promote the safety and well-being of maltreated children by supporting the safety and self-efficacy of their mothers who have experienced domestic violence — was built into the advocacy protocol from the program's inception. To fulfill its mission, the DCIPFV employs the aforementioned domestic violence victim specialists, called advocates, who, in dependency cases, approach mothers at the initial court hearings to discuss their safety and to offer *voluntary and confidential* services if they are, in fact, identified as victims of domestic violence.

In 1997, the DCIPFV became the first court-based research project in the United States to provide psychological assessments to dependent children who had been exposed to domestic violence. Subsequently, the DCIPFV expanded on the court-ordered psychological evaluations of maltreated children by including a broader assessment of the extent and the impact of the violence on their young lives. A team of experienced forensic psychologists designed a structured interview for children and they administered a questionnaire to parents regarding their children's experiences with community and family violence.[16] Data from the first year of these assessments indicated that 50% of children ages 5 years to 17 years in just one division of dependency court were exposed to high levels of interparental violence, and that most of the children had experienced more than one form of maltreatment.[16]

Through these assessments, it became readily apparent that the Florida child welfare system, including the courts, did not recognize or appreciate the impact of violence on infants and toddlers, and therefore was failing to address the critical needs of this growing population.[16] The commonly held perspective just a few years ago was that very young children were not really harmed by interparental violence. To rectify this situation, in 1999 the DCIPFV created the Prevention and Evaluation of Early Neglect and Trauma program (PREVENT) to assess child-parent bonding and attachment and the cognitive and developmental functioning of maltreated children less than 5 years of age.

Findings from the PREVENT program revealed that more than 50% of children under the age of 5 years in Miami's dependency court suffered significant cognitive and language development delays.[16] Based on these findings, the DCIPFV developed a parent-child treatment model that supports and enhances the crucial bond between a young child and the primary caregiver: The Miami-Dade County (Fla) Safe Start Initiative administers the PREVENT evaluation and dyadic therapy models, now known as Early Childhood Relationship Assessments, developed through the DCIPFV for children less than 4 years of age. Miami-Dade Safe Start is a targeted expansion grant to increase the capacity of Miami to provide early intervention services for infants and children through 6 years of age who have witnessed or been the victims of domestic violence.

The services that DCIPFV advocates provide to their clients are unique because they further the dependency system's overarching goal of promoting child safety and well-being by supporting battered mothers. Helping these mothers to help themselves — by educating them about domestic violence and the cycle of victimization — provides support during a critical time, thereby enabling them to take the necessary steps towards recovery and to regain control of their lives. This effort, in turn, promotes the safety and well-being of their children.[17]

Looking at DCIPFV Through the Lens of Risk and Protective Factors

A "risk and protective factors" model is a useful framework for understanding the impact of children's exposure to domestic violence and maltreatment. In the aftermath of exposure to violence or abuse, a child may develop behavioral, cognitive, social and/or emotional problems — even a full-blown psychopathology.[18]

Protecting children and facilitating their development are a family's most basic functions. Mothers who end up in dependency court have often tried to protect their children, but in ways that may be easily overlooked. Some mothers involved in the DCIPFV program have told their advocates that when they are being beaten, they will not scream because they do not want their children to hear their cries.[15]

Regardless of their composition, families are structured uniquely to provide the attention, nurturing and safe environment that children need to grow and develop in healthy ways. When parents are unable (or unwilling) to protect their children from violence, they are likely to feel frustrated and helpless. In addition, when parents are exposed to violence or are themselves the victims of violence, they often find it difficult to remain emotionally available, sensitive and responsive to their children. In these latter cases, it is important for the traditional societal protectors of children — schools, community centers, houses of worship and others — to help provide safe environments for the children.

Children who are victims of or who are exposed to violence need these additional sources of protection for immediate support and guidance, as well as for longer-term support because they face increased risks of becoming victims and/or perpetrators of violence as they grow older.[19] An unsafe environment may exacerbate this risk. In the Spousal Assault Replication Program (SARP), Fantuzzo and colleagues reported the findings of a major multicity research effort involving children exposed to family violence.[20] Law enforcement officers and university researchers provided the data for the study. This program highlighted the advantages of building partnerships between public agencies, such as law enforcement and universities, to collect and evaluate detailed information about violent incidents, including who was in the home at the time of the incident, who made the call to the police and who else in the household was assaulted.

Data from this multicity study showed that households where domestic violence occurred were more than twice as likely as comparable nonviolent households to have children in them.[20] In addition, children under the age of 5 years were more likely than older children to experience multiple exposures to incidents of domestic violence and to episodes of parental substance abuse over a 6-month period. Other risk factors that were present in homes where domestic violence occurred included poverty, households with single parents and lower educational levels. While these researchers did not gather data on child maltreatment, it is likely that the children included in this study were at considerable risk.

In 2001, more than 26% of the victims of child maltreatment in the United States were under the age of 3 years, and more than 25% were between the ages of 4 years and 7 years.[21] Data from the SARP and other studies indicate that very young children, who are the most dependent on their caretakers, are more likely than older children to experience domestic violence and other risk factors in their homes.[22]

Although clinicians, educators, policy makers and interested others are increasingly more cognizant of the impact of maltreatment and/or exposure to domestic violence on children,[19,23-27] further research is surely needed.

To understand fully the effects of domestic violence and child abuse on children — especially young children — it is crucial to consider the developmental issues and the particular vulnerabilities of infants and toddlers. Their developmental immaturity can be a double-edged sword. On the one hand, based on her clinical experience as Director of the Child Witness to Violence Project at Boston (Mass) City Hospital, Groves emphasizes that domestic violence may be particularly damaging to young children, as they are witnessing a violent confrontation between the people they love.[24,28] However, very young children have not yet developed the capacity to understand and cope with trauma in the same way as would older children.[19] On the other hand, they may be partially protected from the full effects of exposure to a traumatic incident because they do not fully appreciate the potential danger.[29] Researchers and clinicians are still trying to tease out the truth from these 2 different perspectives.

There is consistent evidence[21,30] that children's psychological reactions to trauma vary in intensity based on the following:

- their proximity to the violence
- their familiarity with the victim(s) and/or perpetrator(s)
- their temperament
- their developmental stage
- the severity and frequency of the violence
- the support available to them to moderate the effects of the violence

The Significant Impact of Interparental Violence

In research done with our colleagues, we have found that parents *and* police perceive that witnessing violence against a parent has a much greater impact on a child than does witnessing violence against a stranger.[31,32] What a child remembers about a violent experience ultimately affects whether, when and how posttraumatic symptoms develop.[33] Again, without intervention, younger children seem to be more vulnerable in terms of both the immediate effects of violence and the longer-term risks for developing psychological problems. Because of the developmental concerns for younger children, early intervention after an exposure to violence is imperative.

In a 2001 survey of police officers in New Orleans (La) regarding their perceptions of the effects of domestic violence on young children, more than 75% reported that they believe that even very young children are affected by violence in their homes and that exposure to domestic violence can be just as traumatizing to the young child as can abuse.[31] Several studies have documented that after witnessing domestic violence, infants and toddlers often exhibit emotional distress, immature behaviors, somatic complaints and regressions in toileting and language.[25,33-39] Furthermore, the potential protective influence of not being totally aware of the full scope of the violent incident appears to fail for young children when *severe* trauma occurs; as, for example, when they witness one of their parents as either a victim or perpetrator of violence.[36-38] The symptoms of posttraumatic stress, including sleeplessness, disorganized behavior and agitation, are often observed in such circumstances, even if the children's caretakers downplay them.[33] Among children, in general, aggressive behaviors, as well as reduced social competencies, depression, sleep disturbances, learning problems, fears and anxieties, are common after exposures to violence.[19,40-42] Posttraumatic fears and anxieties may include the fear of death of the child him-herself and fear of the loss of a parent.[43] Children may also experience intense rage, feelings of guilt and a sense of responsibility for the violent event, even if *they* are the victims.[24]

The complexity of providing protection and additional support to young children who are abused and/or exposed to domestic violence emerges because often the parents cannot (or are unable to) provide a safe environment. In a study by Huth-Bocks, Levendosky and Semel in a community sample of 3- to 5-year-old children (N = 100), the investigators found that exposure to domestic violence had a direct effect on children's verbal abilities and an indirect effect on the quality of their home environment because of maternal stress, depression and the mothers' emotional unavailability to their children.[43] More recently, McIntosh reported the relative lack of parental attention to children that often accompanies domestic violence.[44] Children must deal with the dual stresses of witnessing violence between people they trust and living in an unnurturing environment. The effect on children of continual exposures to violence, as well as to the psychopathology of their parents, cannot be ignored.

Our work through the DCIPFV with mothers who are victims of domestic violence and who have had their children removed from their homes because of child maltreatment has led to a disturbing realization: Mothers within the court system do not identify themselves as *victims* of domestic violence. Clearly, violence is simply a consistent part of their lives and the lives of their children[31,45]: Domestic violence is usually just one of the many problems in their difficult lives.

The ramifications of domestic violence and maltreatment extend far beyond the experience itself. Children learn from what they observe. Through exposure to abuse and domestic violence, children may learn that these behaviors are permissible and acceptable. Unfortunately, they also receive the confusing message that the people they trust to protect and nurture them also place them in harm's way. What is often underestimated in such children is the potential effect that growing up in an environment of violence and abuse has on later relationships and their own tendency towards violent and/or deviant behavior — and even psychopathology. The increased risk of developing problems in the short term, as well as later in life, highlights the need for effective early interventions for these children.

Based on available research, there is general agreement that much more data are needed regarding the extent and implications of exposure to both child maltreatment and domestic violence and its impact at different developmental stages.[14,19,23,25,27,41] Finally, careful studies are needed to identify and understand the risk and protective factors that may heighten children's vulnerability or, conversely, protect them, especially when they are exposed to both maltreatment and family violence in their home environment.

Parenting and the Intergenerational Transmission of Violence

Any consideration of risk and protective factors for children exposed to abuse and domestic violence must examine the potential for such experiences to become part of an intergenerational cycle of violence.[34] A study of more than 10,000 African American elementary school and high school children in inner-city Chicago (Ill) found that those youngsters who had witnessed and/or been victims of violence were more likely to subsequently become perpetrators of violence than were their peers who had not been exposed to violence and abuse.[46] Another study of more than 500 children in grades 2, 4, 6 and 8 linked children's physical aggression with witnessing family violence, primarily spousal abuse.[47] A 1995 report commissioned by the Massachusetts Coalition of Battered Women Service Groups provided the following important information about what children learn after witnessing domestic violence[48]:

- Violence is an appropriate way to resolve conflicts.
- Violence is part of family relationships.
- The perpetrator of violence in intimate relationships often goes unpunished.
- Violence can be used to control other people.

Based on "social learning theory," it has been a commonly held belief that behavior learned from a family history of violence is a leading cause of the transmission of child maltreatment from one generation to the next. However, there is more-recent evidence that shows that learned behavior alone is not sufficient to explain this phenomenon.[49] Rather, child maltreatment and harsh parenting often go hand in hand in transmitting domestic violence to the next generation. There is also emerging evidence that, within the family, violence by a partner or parent against the other partner or parent largely affects child antisocial behavior by way of parental harshness and poor parenting.[50] Therefore, witnessing domestic violence *and* poor parenting are contributors to the cycle of violence.

Using excessive physical punishment and inconsistent, authoritative punishment may increase a child's risk for behavior problems, aggressive behavior and interpersonal difficulties.[49] Coercive conflict resolution is learned by the child from the parent-child relationship and is later generalized to romantic partner relationships. Coercive conflict resolution may be learned even in families where partner violence does not exist.[51] Unskilled parenting, characterized by ineffective discipline and low monitoring, is a risk factor for coercive conflict resolution, as well: In a longitudinal study of boys and young men, Capaldi and colleagues found a significant relationship between youth aggression towards a partner in later adolescence and exposure to unskilled parenting during childhood and early adolescence.[52] Although maltreatment experienced as a child may be one clear pathway to entering conflictual and abusive romantic relationships, a history of generally hostile parenting may be sufficient by itself to create a risk for partner abuse.[51]

Corporal punishment tends to be part of a more general pattern of coercive social relationships. It can set into motion an escalating pattern of coercive interaction in which the child, who is the subject of the coercion, becomes resentful, hostile and ultimately physically violent towards the parent.[53] In particular, boys who experience abuse and who are exposed to erratic, coercive and punitive parenting are at risk of becoming violent offenders themselves.[54] Why some maltreated children ultimately engage in delinquent behavior, while most do not, is not completely understood. There is recent evidence that a functional polymorphism in the monoamine oxidase A gene moderates the impact of early childhood maltreatment on the development of antisocial behavior in males[55]: That is, some maltreated boys may actually have a genetic susceptibility to antisocial behavior.

It is clear that any effective effort aimed at stopping the intergenerational transmission of domestic violence can no longer focus on partner-partner violence alone. The process is much more complicated. The common thread linking child maltreatment, punitive parenting and exposure to violent parental conflict may reside in the serious disruption of relationships with caregivers, which, in turn, results in deficits in emotional regulation, faulty processing of social information and hostile expectations for intimate relationships.[56]

Although most of the evidence that verifies the intergenerational transmission of violence relies on retrospective studies and anecdotes, it has been well-established that the majority of youth in the juvenile justice system have experienced significant abuse early in their young lives.[54,56] This is especially true for girls[57]: A recent study of 493 girls incarcerated in the Miami-Dade County Juvenile Detention Center revealed that nearly 85% of them had experienced significant traumas in their lives.[57] On average, these girls reported experiencing 3 different kinds of trauma. Across all of the girls, the following were the 4 most frequently reported traumatic experiences:

- witnessing a violent attack — 50%
- thinking that they (or someone close to them) were going to be killed or badly injured — 40%
- being threatened with a weapon — 30%
- being sexually abused — 25%

In addition, 49% of the girls reported thinking about the experienced trauma within the past 12 months,[57] suggesting the presence of considerable distress and possible posttraumatic stress disorder.

Bell has elaborated on the contribution of exposure to violence to later negative outcomes: He has suggested that, as researchers, we have not yet fully conceptualized the impact of exposure to violence on children[34] as we have with our in-depth analyses of the impact of exposure to violence on other groups, such as veterans of the Korean and Vietnam Wars.[28] Children and adolescents who simply witness violence are themselves victims, and therefore experience significant stress. Based on work that he published with Jenkins, Bell believes that exposure to violence at a young age leads to high-risk behaviors in later youth.[34] As Margolin emphasized, it is not just that children *see* aggression; rather, it is that they learn how to *use* aggression in intimate relationships.[25] Thus, children perceive violence as an acceptable way — perhaps the only way — to resolve conflicts and may learn to rationalize its use.

Although witnessing domestic violence may not be perceived as life-threatening, it is disturbing enough to cause distress: For example, at least one study has shown that children who are exposed to domestic violence without experiencing concurrent maltreatment or abuse reported more symptoms of depression than did a nontraumatized control group.[58] In addition, the children exposed to domestic violence alone did not differ in the severity of their depressive symptoms when compared with children who had also been abused.[58]

In our clinical experiences with elementary school and even younger children who have been exposed repeatedly to family violence, we frequently observe disturbances in school behavior, commingled positive and negative feelings towards parents, difficulties forming intimate relationships in adolescence and adulthood and, ultimately, difficulties with parenting. In fact, Lederman, Malik and Aaron reported that one third of individuals who are abused and neglected as children can be expected to abuse their own children.[16]

When children experience severe violence, including witnessing the homicide of a loved one, questions must be raised about their immediate reactions — and how they will react over time. From a developmental perspective, very young children who witness horrific violence may subsequently perceive death quite differently than those youngsters who don't, and they may develop a sense of vulnerability as they grow older. Adolescents who are exposed to violence and/or who are maltreated as younger children may become perpetrators of violence themselves. In fact, for these youngsters violence may become a typical response to everyday situations, and they may not even consider the consequences of their violent behaviors. Often, children who are exposed to violence when they are young deal with aggression, sexuality and intimacy very differently when they reach adolescence than do children who have not been exposed to such violence.[59]

Without intervention, by the time these children reach school age they will likely be at risk for both social problems and learning deficits. Observations of very young children and infants exposed to violence, including abuse and neglect, reveal that even in infancy they may appear uninterested in adults and unable to play and explore the world around them.[60] Many of these children inevitably exhibit signs of traumatic stress, including withdrawn behavior, fearfulness, aggression and sadness.

Building Judicial-Mental Health Partnerships to Serve the Best Interests of Children

One of the most frustrating events for any juvenile court judge to witness is when an abused or neglected girl raised in foster care becomes a mother herself while still a young adolescent. All of the following questions run through the judge's mind:

- How will such a young mother, who never felt safe, nurtured or loved as a young child, create a healthy environment for and develop a loving attachment with her baby?

- How can the juvenile court fulfill its legal mandate under these circumstances, especially in what is essentially an adversarial system, within the limitations of huge caseloads and inadequate services?
- How can the juvenile court intervene to reduce the risk of transmission of child maltreatment from generation to generation in this young mother's new family?

Perhaps the most effective way to stop the intergenerational cycle of child maltreatment is to focus intensively on the youngest and largest cohort of children in the child welfare population immediately upon their entry into the jurisdiction of the court. That is exactly what the Miami-Dade County Juvenile Court has attempted to accomplish.

The law does not exist in a vacuum. Therefore, the court cannot operate independently from the world of social science. Laws alone will not solve the problems of chronic deprivation and impoverishment in families that face cumulative disadvantages. These are the very families that are disproportionately represented in the court population. The court and its representatives must work jointly with experts in the community who bring their interdisciplinary knowledge and skills into the courtroom setting in order to translate social science research into practice. Court decisions about assessment, care and planning must be made on the basis of adequate information about the unique strengths and challenges of each child.[61,62] Legal decisions should be informed by developmental theory and scientific research, including findings about vulnerability and resilience and how children are influenced by variations in the quality of care they receive.[63] This marriage of science and law is essential if the court is to fulfill its legal requirement of acting in the "best interest" of the child — a much more difficult determination for a judge to make than merely applying the law and determining the legal rights of each parent. To make thoughtful and appropriate decisions, the juvenile court judge must be able to call upon the expertise of an interdisciplinary team.

Beginning in 2000, based on the work done by PREVENT, the Florida Legislature designated the Miami-Dade Juvenile Court as an "Infant and Young Children's Mental Health Pilot Site." This pilot intervention program (designed by Dr. Osofsky and implemented by Judge Lederman and her team) provided the funding for parents and toddlers to participate in a relationship-based evaluation and a 25-session program of child-parent psychotherapy[63] with a trained infant mental health clinician. Child-parent psychotherapy is an evidence-based treatment designed to help young parents learn to play reciprocally with their children, to understand the emotional meaning of their children's verbal communications and nonverbal cues and to follow their children's lead to support their healthy development. Since many of the parents who participated in this program (and continue to) did not have positive or nurturing experiences in their own childhoods, this was (and is) unfamiliar territory for them.

Three years of interpreted data from this pilot program show the following improvements:

- increases in parental sensitivity towards their children
- increases in child and parent responsiveness during play
- increases in parental responsiveness to children's behaviors and affect

The children showed significant improvements in enthusiasm, persistence and positive affect, and a reduction in depression, anger, withdrawal and irritability. The parents involved in the pilot program have not committed any further acts of abuse or neglect, and the reunification rate is an extraordinary 86%.[14] The contention of Dr. Selma Fraiberg, an infant mental health pioneer who said that intervening with young children is "... a little like having God on your side,"[64] seems evident in these results.[64]

Funded by a grant from the USDOJ, Office of Juvenile Justice and Delinquency Prevention, the Miami-Dade Juvenile Court and the Linda Ray Early Intervention Center at the University of Miami (Fla) have implemented the Miami Safe Start Initiative (MSSI) jointly. The MSSI opened the first Early Head Start program for maltreated children in the United States. Maltreated toddlers who would not otherwise have access to early intervention programs are referred by the Miami-Dade Juvenile Court to this comprehensive Early Head Start program, which provides transportation, home visitation and dyadic therapy with the child's primary caregiver.

Infant and Young Children's Mental Health Pilot Project Helps Adolescent Mother and Her Child — A Case Study of Katrina and Charles

Katrina was born in 1984 into poverty and deprivation. She and her 6 siblings lived with their mother in a house that was filthy and infested with insects. All 7 children were often left unsupervised for long periods of time — including Katrina's mentally retarded sibling who was left alone in diapers for days. The children were dirty and hungry. The mother routinely gave her food stamps to her boyfriend, while the children begged for food. There was illegal drug activity in the house, and the mother's boyfriend was accused of physically abusing both the mother and the children.

In 1994, the Miami-Dade Juvenile Court removed all 7 children from the care of the mother because of clear evidence of abuse and neglect. After the mother attended a series of parenting classes, she was reunited with all of her children. However, the children were removed from the home again in 1997 when the case first came under the purview of Judge Cindy Lederman.

In February 1999, at the age of 15, after being sexually assaulted, Katrina gave birth to her son Charles. In May 1999, the court removed Charles from Katrina's custody because she ran away from her foster home and left the baby with her mother. In December 2000, the court began the process of filing a Termination of Parental Rights petition to remove Charles permanently from Katrina's custody. Before filing the petition, Judge Lederman referred Katrina to the "Infant and Young Children's Mental Health Pilot Project" intervention.

Charles, almost 2 years of age now, and Katrina participated in 25 sessions of dyadic therapy. Prior to therapy, Katrina did not know how to play or interact with her son. No one had played with her as a child. A baseline evaluation showed that there were minimal play interactions: Katrina's actions were intrusive and did not allow Charles to explore the environment or initiate play. There was no spontaneity or joy in their play.

(Continued)

Infant and Young Children's Mental Health Pilot Project Helps Adolescent Mother and Her Child — A Case Study of Katrina and Charles (continued)

After 16 sessions of dyadic therapy, the therapist began to see evidence of reciprocal interaction between Katrina and Charles. They were talking and laughing together, maintaining eye contact and having fun together. Katrina was "learning" to play with Charles.

A posttherapy evaluation showed that Katrina's actions were less intrusive, she was more responsive emotionally to Charles and she was using discipline in a more positive way. Charles' play was more enthusiastic. He appeared less angry, less irritable and less withdrawn, and he was more responsive to Katrina's actions. Both Katrina and Charles were more responsive emotionally to each other when they were reunited after being separated during therapy.

Overall, in this mental health pilot project, there was no recidivism for abuse and neglect among 92% of the parent-children dyads participating in the therapy. The reunification rate was 86% for the 14 children who were not in the custody of their parents at the beginning of therapy.

Conclusion

The experiences in Miami-Dade County have shown that the court can play a timely and crucial role in early intervention for the most at-risk children — ensuring that they are evaluated, treated and monitored, and have access to vital resources within the community. Juvenile court can be the catalyst for a community to work together in a multidisciplinary fashion to help young children to heal. For some children and some families, this will make all the difference in the world.

References

1. Wulczyn F, Hislop KB. Babies in foster care: the numbers call for attention. *Zero to Three.* 2002;22:14-15.
2. Wulczyn F, Hislop KB, Harden BJ. The placement of infants in foster care. *Infant Mental Health Journal.* 2002;23:454-475.
3. Dicker S, Gordon E. *Ensuring the Healthy Development of Infants in Foster Care: A Guide for Judges, Advocates, and Child Welfare Professionals.* Washington, DC: Zero to Three Policy Center; 2004.
4. Ark Code Ann §9-27-401.
5. Colo Rev Stat 19-1-111.
6. Cal Welfare Institutions Code §317(e).
7. The Adoption and Safe Families Act of 1997, Pub L No. 105-89.
8. The Child Abuse Prevention and Treatment Act, 42 USC §5101 et seq, 42 USC §5116 et seq.
9. Kelly J, Lamb M. Using child development research to make appropriate custody and access decisions for young children. *Family and Conciliation Courts Review.* 2000;38:297-311.
10. Appel AE, Holden GW. The co-occurrence of spouse and physical child abuse: a review and appraisal. *Journal of Family Psychology: JFP: Journal of the Division of Family Psychology of the American Psychological Association (Division 43).* 1998;12:578-599.
11. Hotaling GT, Sugarman DB. A risk marker analysis of assaulted wives. *Journal of Family Violence.* 1990;5:1-13.
12. Kolbo JR. Risk and resilience among children exposed to family violence. *Violence and Victims.* 1996;11:113-128.
13. Edleson JL. Children's witnessing of adult domestic violence. *Journal of Interpersonal Violence.* 1999;14:839-870.
14. Osofsky JD. Prevalence of children's exposure to domestic violence and child maltreatment: implications for prevention and intervention. *Clinical Child and Family Psychology Review.* 2003;6:161-170.
15. O'Riley CA, Lederman CS. Co-occurring child maltreatment and domestic violence. *The Florida Bar Journal.* 2001;75:40-43.
16. Lederman CS, Malik NM, Aaron SM. The nexus between child maltreatment and domestic violence: a view from the court. *Journal of the Center for Families, Children & the Courts.* 2000;2:129-135.
17. Maze CL, Klein SA, Lederman CS. The use of domestic violence advocates in juvenile court: lessons from the dependency court intervention program for family violence. *Juvenile and Family Court Journal.* 2003;54:16-19.
18. Osofsky JD, Thompson MD. Adaptive and maladaptive parenting: perspectives on risk and protective factors. In: Shonkoff JP, Meisels SJ, eds. *Handbook of Early Childhood Intervention.* 2nd ed. New York, NY: Cambridge University Press; 2000:54-75.
19. Osofsky JD. The impact of violence on children. *The Future of Children/Center for the Future of Children, the David and Lucile Packard Foundation.* 1999;9:33-49.
20. Fantuzzo J, Boruch R, Beriama A, Atkins M, Marcus S. Domestic violence and children: prevalence and risk in five major U.S. cities. *Journal of the American Academy of Child and Adolescent Psychiatry.* 1997;36:116-122.
21. Chalk R, Gibbons A, Scarupa H. *The Multiple Dimensions of Child Abuse and Neglect: New Insights Into an Old Problem.* Washington, DC: Child Trends; 2002.
22. Brown B, Bzostek S. *Violence in the Lives of Children.* Washington, DC: Child Trends; 2003.
23. Fantuzzo JW, Mohr WK. Prevalence and effects of child exposure to domestic violence. *The Future of Children/Center for the Future of Children, the David and Lucile Packard Foundation.* 1999;9:21-32.
24. Groves BM. Mental health services for children who witness domestic violence. *The Future of Children/Center for the Future of Children, the David and Lucile Packard Foundation.* 1999;9:122-132.
25. Margolin G. Effects of domestic violence on children. In: Trickett PK, Schellenbach CJ, eds. *Violence Against Children in the Family and the Community.* Washington, DC: American Psychological Association; 1998:57-101.

26. McCloskey LA, Figueredo AJ, Koss MP. The effects of systemic family violence on children's mental health. *Child Development.* 1995;66:1239-1261.

27. Zuckerman B, Augustyn M, Groves BM, Parker S. Silent victims revisited: the special case of domestic violence. *Pediatrics.* 1995;96:511-513.

28. Groves BM, Zuckerman B. Interventions with parents and caregivers of children who are exposed to violence. In: Osofsky JD, ed. *Children in a Violent Society.* New York, NY: The Guilford Press; 1998: 183-201.

29. Osofsky JD. Introduction: Different ways of understanding young children and trauma. In: Osofsky JD, ed. *Young Children and Trauma: Intervention and Treatment.* New York, NY: The Guilford Press; 2004:3-10.

30. Pynoos RS, Steinberg AM, Ornitz EM. Issues in the developmental neurobiology of traumatic stress. In: Yehuda R, McFarlane AC, eds. *Psychobiology of Posttraumatic Stress Disorder.* New York, NY: New York Academy of Sciences; 1997:176-193.

31. Osofsky JD, Hammer JH, Freeman N, Rovaris JM. How law enforcement and mental health professionals can partner to help traumatized children. In: Osofsky JD, ed. *Young Children and Trauma: Intervention and Treatment.* New York, NY: The Guilford Press; 2004:285-300.

32. Osofsky JD, Rovaris M, Hammer JH, et al. Working with police to help children exposed to violence. *Journal of Community Psychology.* 2004;32:593-606.

33. Drell MJ, Siegel CH, Greensbauer TJ. Post-traumatic stress disorder. In: Zeanah CH Jr, ed. *Handbook of Infant Mental Health.* New York, NY: The Guilford Press; 1993:291-304.

34. Bell CC, Jenkins EJ. Community violence and children on Chicago's southside. *Psychiatry.* 1993;56: 46-54.

35. Jaffe PG, Wolfe DA, Wilson SK. *Children of Battered Women.* Newbury Park, Calif: Sage Publications; 1990.

36. Osofsky JD, Fenichel E, eds. *Caring for Infants and Toddlers in Violent Environments: Hurt, Healing, Hope.* Washington, DC: Zero to Three: National Center for Infants, Toddlers and Families; 1994.

37. Osofsky JD, Fenichel E, eds. *Islands of Safety: Assessing and Treating Young Victims of Violence.* Washington, DC: Zero to Three: National Center for Infants, Toddlers and Families; 2002.

38. Osofsky JD, Fenichel E, eds. *Protecting Young Children in Violent Environments: Building Staff and Community Strengths.* Washington, DC: Zero to Three: National Center for Infants, Toddlers and Families; 2000.

39. Pynoos RS. Traumatic stress and developmental psychopathology in children and adolescents. In: Oldham JM, Riba MB, Tasman A, eds. *American Psychiatric Press Review of Psychiatry.* Washington, DC: American Psychiatric Association; 1993:205-238.

40. Margolin G. The multiple forms of aggressiveness between marital partners: how do we identify them? *Journal of Marital and Family Therapy.* 1987;13:77-84.

41. Holden GW, Geffner R, Jouriles EN. *Children Exposed to Marital Violence: Theory, Research, and Applied Issues.* Washington, DC: American Psychological Association; 1998.

42. Osofsky J. Children and youth violence: an overview of the issue. In: Osofsky JD, ed. *Children in a Violent Society.* New York, NY: The Guilford Press; 1997.

43. Huth-Bocks AC, Levendosky AA, Semel MA. The direct and indirect effects of domestic violence on young children's intellectual functioning. *Journal of Family Violence.* 2001;16:269-290.

44. McIntosh JE. Thought in the face of violence: a child's need. *Child Abuse & Neglect.* 2002;26: 229-241.

45. Lederman CS, Osofsky JD, Katz L. When the bough breaks the cradle will fall: promoting the health and well being of infants and toddlers in juvenile court. *Juvenile and Family Court Journal.* 2001;52:33-38.

46. Shakoor BH, Chalmers D. Co-victimization of African-American children who witness violence: effects on cognitive, emotional, and behavioral development. *Journal of the National Medical Association.* 1991;83:233-238.

47. Jenkins EJ, Bell CC. Exposure and response to community violence among children and adolescents. In: Osofsky JD, ed. *Children in a Violent Society.* New York, NY: The Guilford Press; 1998:9-31.
48. Massachusetts Coalition of Battered Women Service Groups. 1995. Report on domestic violence and women.
49. Cohen P, Brook JS. The reciprocal influence of punishment and child behavior disorder. In: McCord J, ed. *Coercion and Punishment in Long-Term Perspectives.* New York, NY: Cambridge University Press; 1995:154-164.
50. Tolan PH, Gorman-Smith D, Henry DB. Linking family violence to delinquency across generations. *Children's Services: Social Policy, Research, and Practice.* 2002;5:273-284.
51. Ehrensaft MK, Cohen P, Brown J, Smailes E, Chen H, Johnson JG. Intergenerational transmission of partner violence: a 20-year prospective study. *Journal of Consulting and Clinical Psychology.* 2003;71: 741-753.
52. Capaldi DM, Dishion TJ, Stoolmiller M, Yoerger K. Aggression toward female partners by at-risk young men: the contribution of male adolescent friendships. *Developmental Psychology.* 2001;37: 61-73.
53. Ulman A, Straus M. Violence by children against mothers in relation to violence between parents and corporal punishment by parents. *Journal of Comparative Family Studies.* 2003;34:41-61.
54. Rutter M, Giller H, Hagell A. *Antisocial Behavior by Young People.* New York, NY: Cambridge University Press; 1998.
55. Caspi A, McClay J, Moffitt TE. Role of genotype in the cycle of violence in maltreated children. *Science.* 2002;297:851-854.
56. Dodge KA, Bates JE, Pettit GS. Mechanisms in the cycle of violence. *Science.* 1990;250:1678-1683.
57. Lederman CS, Dakof GA, Larrea MA, Li H. Characteristics of adolescent females in juvenile detention. *International Journal of Law and Psychiatry.* 2004;27:321-327.
58. Sternberg KJ, Lamb ME, Greenbaum C, et al. Effects of domestic violence on children's behavior problems and depression. *Developmental Psychology.* 1993;29:44-52.
59. Osofsky JD. Community-based approaches to violence prevention. *Journal of Developmental and Behavioral Pediatrics: JDBP.* 1997;18:405-407.
60. Osofsky JD, ed. *Young Children and Trauma: Intervention and Treatment.* New York, NY: The Guilford Press; 2004.
61. American Academy of Pediatrics. Developmental issues for young children in foster care. *Pediatrics.* 2000;106:1145-1150.
62. Osofsky JD, Lederman CS, Maze C, Grace M, Dicker S. *Questions Lawyers and Judges Should Ask About Infants and Toddlers in the Child Welfare System.* Reno, Nev: National Council of Juvenile and Family Court Judges; 2002.
63. Lamb ME. Child development and the law. In: Lerner RM, Easterbrooks MA, Mistry J, vol eds. *Developmental Psychology.* New York, NY: John Wiley & Sons; 2003:559-577. Weiner IB, ed-in-chief. *Handbook of Psychology,* vol 6.
64. Fraiberg L, ed. *Selected Writings of Selma Fraiberg.* Columbus, Ohio: Ohio State University Press; 1987.

Mental Health-Law Enforcement Collaborative Responses to Children's Exposure to Violence

Steven Marans, PhD
Robert A. Murphy, PhD
Robert L. Casey, PhD
Steven J. Berkowitz, MD
Miriam Berkman, JD, MSW

Scope of Violence Against Children

Each year, millions of children are exposed to violence in their homes and communities[1-6]: As a result, their most basic developmental processes are disrupted. In the face of stabbings, beatings and shootings, the mental and neurophysiological systems that enable accommodation and assimilation by these children cannot contain and process such overwhelming stimulation. When these systems become immobilized, a cascade of psychological and neurophysiological alterations ensues that may subsequently lead to the development of posttraumatic symptoms, including hyperarousal, withdrawal and reexperiencing the traumatic events. Other children may develop more specific, circumscribed symptoms, such as disruptions in sleeping, eating and/or toileting.[7-16] Many children become distracted and are unable to concentrate or pay attention in school and/or at home.[7-16] Transient oppositional behavior may also emerge, and may represent both an attempt to reassert power in the face of feeling vulnerable and an effort to cope with the anxiety and hyperarousal caused by the dysregulation of their stress response systems.

Ultimately, this exposure to violence and related trauma can result in a broad range of childhood psychopathologies, including posttraumatic stress disorder, depressive disorders and antisocial and defiant behaviors: The prevalence rates of these psychopathologies are higher among urban youth who are confronted simultaneously with social and family adversities.[9,13,15,17-20]

Repeated exposures to violence may lead to enduring maladaptations and impairments across cognitive, emotional and physiological domains of development as affected children fail to develop adequate capacities for self-regulation and/or modulation of distress[21,22] As symptoms become chronic and maladaptive, they no longer serve the purposes of restitution and recovery. Ongoing exposures to violence, which are often punctuated by acute violent episodes, are associated with increased depression, anxiety and alcohol use and lower school achievement.[10,13,23-25] In densely populated, impoverished urban areas, where the prevalence of violence tends to be especially high, there may be a progression from witnessing violence to being the victim of and then engaging in violence.[26-28] This trend becomes more pronounced when children are exposed to multiple forms of family violence. Children who shoot and/or stab other children have all too often been exposed to abusive family relationships, and have been abused, maltreated and/or neglected themselves.[29]

Based on our current knowledge of the complex interplay between psychological and neurobiological responses to overwhelming events, there is ample reason for concern about the enduring effects of traumatic violence on children's maturation and development. When a child is exposed repeatedly to violence, a confluence occurs between the perception of the brain and the understanding of the mind.[26] When children can no longer anticipate and/or mediate the experience of overwhelming danger and threat, their capacity falters for neurophysiological mediation of stress via the central regulation of the noradrenergic system, resulting in dysregulated heart rate, respiration rate and startle reflexes.[30-32] During the acute, peritraumatic phase of violence, the child's insufficient efforts to process, anticipate and regulate stress and physiological excitation may result in varying patterns of intrusion, avoidance and/or motor agitation or motor retardation.[33] Cues and reminders of traumatic violent events engender further symptomatology, including hypervigilance, anxiety and dissociation.[34] While transient distress may lead to enhanced coping, in effect priming the child's psychological "immune" response, persistent distress from chronic exposure to violence limits the child's capacity to experience the preconditions of healthy development, such as psychological security, reciprocity of caring relationships and tolerance of routine frustrations.[35]

Children and families who are most vulnerable to the deleterious effects of violence may also have limited or no access to sufficient mental health care services. Families who contend simultaneously with violence, poverty, social disadvantage and individual and family psychopathology may not access traditional clinic- or office-based services — even when such services are readily available. As a result, those who have the greatest need may receive the least care. In response to this situation, there has been a proliferation of community-based services that provide mental health care in homes, schools and community settings — with emphases on acute stabilization of individual and family psychopathology and collaboration with other community providers.[36,37]

Community Policing and Effective Partnerships to Manage Violence Against Children

Beginning in the 1970s and gathering momentum in the late 1980s, leaders in law enforcement recognized the need for a change in the existing reactive models of policing. In the traditional, "911"-driven system, officers were dispatched to crime scenes from a central command point, and they departed from that area when their work was completed. They were not well known within the communities they served, and were often viewed as intruders in city neighborhoods. Lacking both a personal presence and a connection to residents, they could accomplish little in terms of establishing a sense of neighborhood security. Officers were often frustrated, and they felt alienated from citizens who viewed them as remote, ineffective and/or unconcerned.

To redress this situation, many police departments nationwide implemented community-based or problem-oriented policing.[38] In contrast with a reactive, crime-fighting response, community policing adopted a "proactive, solution-based and community-driven" perspective (R.A. Murphy, et al, unpublished data, 2005). The need to arrest offenders is integrated with a preventive approach to crime based on relationships with community residents and problem-solving efforts with a range of community constituencies. Research to date suggests that community policing may be particularly effective at improving residents' satisfaction with police services and subjective feelings of neighborhood safety and security.[39,40]

Despite variations across communities, police departments that have embraced community policing share several commonalities[38,41,42]:

- They emphasize the accessibility of officers to the citizens they serve through problem-solving and preventive approaches to policing.
- They utilize proactive order maintenance, which is designed to diffuse situations prior to receiving emergency complaints.
- They collaborate with community agencies.
- They involve the neighborhood in the policing effort.
- They sponsor community-based crime-prevention initiatives.

Community-based policing integrates police officers within the community. There they are known as individuals rather than only by their role, and, likewise, they come to know the people they serve as distinct individuals. Working directly in neighborhoods and police substations, officers observe firsthand the lives of children within their families and communities. Victims and witnesses of violence thus become known as individuals, and officers increasingly become engaged in proactive efforts to prevent or decrease violence and crime — and their subsequent effects. Because the community-policing model brings police officers into regular, ongoing contact with children and families within given neighborhoods, it requires a new type of police officer who has been given specialized training, and is being supervised and supported daily.

Law Enforcement and Public Mental Health Efforts: Working Hand in Hand

During their patrols, police officers confront routinely the psychological sequelae of violence and psychiatric illness. Despite decades of practical experience in responding to psychiatric crises, few police departments provide extensive training in the identification and/or management of acute mental health problems. Training officers to identify psychiatric symptoms and disorders, conduct mental-status evaluations, recognize the medical syndromes that may cause psychiatric symptoms, understand the legal and ethical aspects of involuntary commitment and utilize interpersonal and communicative strategies for interacting with seriously disturbed individuals has improved officers' abilities to respond to psychiatric disturbances.[43,44] Yet, traditionally, their role has been limited to evaluating individuals' danger to themselves or others, and subsequently arresting the offenders or committing them involuntarily for a psychiatric evaluation.[45,46]

Teplin noted that the likelihood of arrest by the police was 67% greater for criminal suspects who had signs of mental disturbance than for suspects who had no signs of mental disorder.[46] Police officers may not have sufficient training in responding effectively to psychiatrically disturbed citizens and, therefore, they may see arrest as their only option. Alternatively, they may resort to an arrest to secure mental health services for the offender if there is limited access to behavioral health care services in a community's public mental health sector. Officers may recognize the complex risks and needs within this population — a population that has not been served adequately by mental health organizations or law enforcement alone. From this perspective, an arrest may actually serve a therapeutic function: the application of police authority with the ultimate goal of securing necessary mental health care.

In a 1999 survey, the training needs of 174 urban police departments were highlighted as they pertain to responding to mental health crises.[47] More than half of the departments (55%) reported lacking specialized response procedures for mental health crises, even though such incidents comprised a significant proportion of all police service calls.[47] Among the police departments that reported having some type of procedures in place for responding to mental health crises, 3% (6 departments) relied on specific officers who had undergone crisis intervention training to act as liaisons with mental health providers. Another 11% (20 departments) retained civilians as mental health consultants or providers. The other 30% (52 departments) relied on referrals to non–police-affiliated mental health professionals. Although most of these police departments perceived their efforts on behalf of psychologically impaired citizens "as effective," none could point to specific positive outcomes or benefits for detained individuals who had mental health problems.

Among the 174 police departments surveyed, none had procedures in place to address the specific mental health concerns of children and adolescents, suggesting that the relative paucity of organized responses by police to psychiatric concerns is even more widespread with respect to youth.

In one of the few evaluations of law enforcement and mental health services, the joint identification of youth psychopathology by mental health clinicians *and* police detectives within an urban European police department resulted in enhanced treatment access and intervention.[48] After training detectives who specialized in youth crime to recognize risk factors for psychopathology among adolescents, the detectives began their daily rounds accompanied by mental health clinicians in order to discuss cases from the previous day involving juveniles so as to develop appropriate treatment recommendations. An analysis of this collaborative effort revealed a 74% concordance rate between youth identified by police as at-risk for serious psychopathology and those identified as at-risk using a standardized clinical screening instrument.[48] Although subsequent interventions were not well-operationalized, post hoc analyses suggested that at-risk youth who received the collaborative response by law enforcement and mental health professionals engaged more readily in treatment and experienced fewer psychiatric symptoms in the 6 months following referral.[48]

Despite progress in the development and implementation of community-based mental health interventions, as well as increased attention to the mental health needs of youth in the juvenile justice system, police officers still have limited ability to influence the mental health of acutely traumatized children and adolescents. Although they are often the first to respond to situations in which children may be in acute distress, police officers typically lack the resources and training to effect change at this critical time. Mental health providers, particularly those working in trauma-related fields, have extolled the importance of acute intervention and its catalytic effects. But the reality is that it is the police officers who respond at precisely the moment when previous defenses and coping methods have faltered, and children and families are perhaps more needy and more responsive to intervention.

The Child Development-Community Policing Program

The Child Development-Community Policing (CD-CP) program[21,49,50] uses the combined expertise of police officers and mental health professionals to intervene with children and families who have been exposed to violence and may be experiencing its posttraumatic effects. The Yale Child Study Center at Yale University in New Haven, Connecticut, and the New Haven (Conn) Department of Police Service initiated the CD-CP program in response to shared concerns about the paucity of policing and clinical responses to children and families at the greatest psychological risk because of violence within their homes, neighborhoods and schools.[50] Both groups recognized that, because of their immediate and frequent contacts with children and families affected by violence, police officers could have a profound impact on how children experienced and dealt with violence and other adversities. By collaborating with police and other first responders, mental health professionals could respond more appropriately to children's psychological distress following episodes of violence and move beyond the bounds of their traditional model of clinic-based care that resulted in consultation only when chronic symptoms or maladaptive behaviors brought these children to the attention of parents, teachers or juvenile court personnel. The CD-CP program brings together the strengths of both professions to maximize valuable opportunities to intervene at precisely the moment when joint, concerted contacts could provide both immediate stabilization and bridges to a variety of ongoing services. The program has since altered the ways in which policing, mental health and now other related services are delivered to children and families who are exposed regularly to community violence.[11,21,22,49,51,52]

The CD-CP program has 5 central components:

- **Seminars in child development and trauma** — The seminars in child development and trauma involve a minimum of 32 hours of didactic training and clinical observation for police officers, mental health clinicians, probation officers overseeing juvenile offenders, domestic violence advocates and child protective service (CPS) workers. Reflecting the collaborative nature of the CD-CP program, the seminars are led jointly by a senior/supervisory police officer and an experienced mental health clinician.
- **Clinical fellowships for police officers** — Officers who have completed the child development and trauma seminars participate in a clinical fellowship during which they attend weekly CD-CP case conferences, supervise rank-and-file officers who respond to acute episodes of violence involving children and families, coordinate follow-up police services and receive extended consultations from senior clinical faculty. These officers subsequently become local and national leaders in the CD-CP program and are centrally involved in program dissemination and replication through teaching, presenting and developing educational curricula.

- **Police fellowships for clinicians** — Just as police officers become familiar with aspects of child development, mental health clinicians learn about basic police practices through a police fellowship that includes attendance at CD-CP case conferences, the completion of 20 hours of seminars in police practices and protocols, participation in a minimum of 40 hours of accompanying police officers on patrol and involvement as an on-call clinician for the acute consultation service.
- **Acute consultation service** — Through the acute consultation service, clinicians are available to the police department, by pager, 24 hours per day, 7 days per week for consultations involving children, adolescents and families who have been involved in violence.
- **Weekly program case conferences** — Law enforcement officers, clinicians, probation officers overseeing juvenile offenders, domestic violence advocates and CPS providers meet weekly at a program case conference to discuss and plan coordinated interventions for cases that have been generated through the acute consultation service.

Seminars in Child Development and Trauma: An Overview

The seminars in child development and trauma provide a common language for police officers, clinicians and other related professionals to evaluate and understand the needs of children and families exposed to violence.[21,51,53] Through these seminars, police officers learn about the key concepts related to emotional, interpersonal, cognitive and motor development, and the effects that trauma can have on that development. With this knowledge, they can respond to domestic violence crises in a more informed manner. The seminars emphasize the ways in which children may experience and demonstrate traumatization according to their phase of development, psychological history, family circumstances and ecological circumstance. The senior police officer and mental health clinician who lead the seminars draw on scenarios encountered in police work, films and videotapes about children, as well as case histories from the acute consultation service, to help officers and others (eg, probation officers overseeing juvenile offenders, CPS workers and educators) discover new situationally and developmentally appropriate ways to respond to children.

The seminars address the various stages of child development:

- **Infancy:** An all-too-common police incident in which an officer responds to a dispute complaint and is greeted by an angry and hostile young mother provides an introduction to the topic of infancy in the child development and trauma seminars. In this scenario, police witness 3 young, unkempt and ill-cared-for children who are long overdue for diaper changes. When queried about their initial reactions, the officers express feelings of despair and anger. They proceed to identify concerns about infants who are unable to fend for themselves, about the infants' physical discomfort and about the notion that the mother doesn't care enough about her children. What emerges is an increased awareness of an infant's physical and emotional needs and the role of the mother in mediating distress and providing crucial care and affection. As the officers consider the results of a child's unmet basic needs, they realize that an infant in this situation — unable to feed, clothe, comfort itself or satisfy the demands of its feelings on its own — will be overwhelmed with pain, discomfort and despair. Through this example of a routine police encounter, class members are able to identify developmental capacities and vulnerabilities — the absence of verbal language, motor maturation and coordination, cognitive processes necessary for problem solving and, lastly, the absolute reliance of the infant on the mother for the experiences of physical and emotional well-being.

  Similar probing of the young mother's hostile greeting and the officers' resultant indignation allow seminar leaders to introduce the concept that complex clinical phenomena underlie presenting behaviors. The discussion turns to examples of those who experience depression, irritability and substance abuse, which offers the class an opportunity to discuss the complex biological and psychological relationships among stress, anxiety, depression and substance abuse. The process of "transference" is introduced as officers are asked to explore the mother's possible feelings about herself and her own competence, as well as how police, as societal representatives of authority, may engender responses that bear little relation to the situation at hand. The discussion culminates with a greater appreciation for the complexity of the scene, its interactions and potential points for response.

- **Toddlerhood and attachment:** Seminar members view the film *John, Seventeen Months: Nine Days in a Residential Nursery*[54] by Robertson and Robertson, about a 17-month-old child's efforts to soothe himself during a 9-day, enforced separation from his parents. Through the vehicle of the film, they observe a child's attempts to reach out for comfort from child care nurses, cuddly toys and research staff, as well as his utter despair when these efforts fail. In contrast, the children who have been raised in an institutional care setting exhibit predominately aggressive, driven and need-satisfying behaviors. In their attempt to understand why John may feel so vulnerable to the disruption in care, seminar participants begin to consider individual differences and the interactions among genetics, temperament and environment. As the discussion continues, the simple solution of removing a child from the home when parenting seems inadequate fades and is replaced by increasing recognition of the central importance of a child's attachment to his/her parents or other primary caregivers. The officers come to recognize the importance of maintaining consistent and continuous relationships between parents and their children, and the emotional damage that can occur when that relationship is disrupted.

The link between psychological processes, overt behavior and the observers' responses is pursued as the seminar focuses on toddlers' issues of power, body size and capacities. The officers discuss the ways in which the challenges and conflicts of early childhood are repeated later in life, particularly in situations where police authority is required to limit the impulses and actions of individuals who are unable to do this on their own. When officers intervene during fights, civil disorders, drug raids, traffic stops and other similar situations, they may often feel like parents attempting to set limits on the behavior and the intensity of toddlers' demands. In their positions of authority, it is at these times that police officers may easily become a lightning rod for individuals' explosive feelings toward having their power and capacities challenged and/or curtailed. Officers commonly report that understanding the dynamics of these encounters and the earliest origins of these emotions help them respond with greater emotional distance and calm. The ability of police officers to maintain professional distance can mean the difference between a short-lived initial confrontation and a protracted and dangerous battle.

- **Preschool:** Videotapes of 4- to 6-year-old children engaged in imaginative play provide participant officers with a vehicle to consider the preschool child's use of fantasy, identification and their burgeoning cognitive and physical resources to master new demands. During the viewing process, the officers begin to appreciate the fact that children's perceptions of and communications about real events often reflect an interplay between fact and fantasy: For example, the officers initially suspect a history of domestic violence when they witness a 5-year-old boy enact play scenarios characterized by fighting and violence. As they learn about the child's high level of psychosocial functioning and the mundane events of recent days, which included being involved in a very minor traffic accident, they see firsthand the interplay between the boy's experience of the accident and developmentally appropriate concerns about aggression, bodily damage and intimate feelings toward his parents. As a result, the officers acquire a greater appreciation for the multiple ways in which young children tell their stories about life events. With this knowledge, they can evaluate previous assumptions about children's testimony during police interviews and courtroom proceedings from an informed and critical developmental perspective, recognizing that children may invest their versions of events with more than just the simple facts needed for police investigations.[55,56]

- **School age and adolescence:** Subsequent seminars provide detail on the developmental tasks of school-age children and adolescents. Failures in negotiating oedipal conflicts surrounding issues of competition, envy, love and hate, and the often unstable, overstimulating home environments in which many children reside, are explored in discussions about latency-age children who come to the attention of the police because of their antisocial activities. Similarly, puberty is discussed in terms of the intensification of struggles over sexual and aggressive urges. Seminar discussions regarding each phase of development are used as additional opportunities to consider the impact of violence and trauma and the ways in which individual histories, normative tasks and challenges shape the child's experiences of events and the extent of their symptomatic responses to these events.

Seminar leaders introduce each developmental stage by asking the officers to describe the most salient issues, either observed or assumed, that play a part in that period of life. The officers will often invoke their own memories as vehicles for understanding the behaviors they observe and encounter on the street: For example, when discussing puberty and early adolescence, the officers may describe their concerns about provocative, tough, drug-involved or pregnant teens, as well as the frustration they experience when logic and warnings about consequences seem to have absolutely no impact on the teens' behaviors. However, as they begin to talk about their own experiences of this stage of development, their frustration and angry dismissal is tempered:

Stories of fighting, social isolation, school difficulties and losses alternate with the ones about best friends, romantic relationships, team sports and other positive experiences. They begin to perceive adolescence as a mix of both good and bad.

Boyz N the Hood,[57] a film by John Singleton, and the award-winning documentary film *Bangin'*, by Michael King,[58] prompt further discussions about the adolescent stage of development. The discussion of *Boyz N the Hood* moves from issues of race and inner-city socioeconomics to a focus on the internal and external contributions to the diverse fates of 2 brothers: One becomes a gun-toting drug dealer, while the other is a high school football star bound for college, until he is fatally shot by gang members. *Bangin'*, which focuses on the deaths of 2 adolescents who were victims of violence, features interviews with their peers and other teens who have been incarcerated because of their involvement in violent crimes.

As the seminars in child development and trauma conclude, officers discuss their reactions to the scenes of violence and suffering they confront on a daily basis: Some speak of minimizing their emotions, "getting used to it" and distancing themselves as much as possible from their troubling experiences, while others describe displacing their frustrations onto the citizens they interact with or their own family members. The wide range of responses made by these officers is discussed in terms of the defensive functions they may serve in warding off unwanted feelings of fear, inadequacy, sadness, despair and anger, as well as the potential interferences they may pose in achieving the desired goals of their interventions.

Practical Applications to Policing of the Seminars in Child Development and Trauma

The seminars in child development and trauma help police officers understand the unique experiences of individual children based on their ages, developmental stages and backgrounds.[59] With their newly gained knowledge, the officers have a framework for organizing information about children who previously may have been too overwhelming. The CD-CP program also provides officers with a group of colleagues with whom they may share the burden of responding to domestic crises at any hour. Officers in the program refer children for clinical evaluation and treatment regularly who have witnessed and/or experienced violence and, increasingly, children who have committed serious violent offenses. Similarly, officers in the program have become more attentive to the potential for dangerous confrontations when they deal with adolescents — especially juvenile offenders — in a harsh manner that may evoke feelings in the child of humiliation and undermine nascent feelings of independence and autonomy. As officers become better known within the neighborhoods they serve, their interactions with residents become informed by familiarity and individual relationships. CD-CP-trained officers recognize that because of their authority and uniformed presence, they will often bear the brunt of powerful emotions. Understanding the complex origins of such intense emotions has led to a more judicious and strategic use of police authority.

Since the inception of the CD-CP program, every police officer in New Haven, from frontline beat officers to senior supervisory officers, has received training in the principles of child development and acute traumatic responses. The officers, who have participated willingly in the program, report that it has enhanced their ability to function professionally as law enforcement officers. In addition, they report that collaborating with their mental health colleagues has helped them deal with feelings of alienation and burnout brought on by their continual confrontations with senseless pain and injury. Working alongside mental health professionals, police officers in New Haven and in other sites where the CD-CP program has been instituted are now able to respond more humanely and effectively to thousands of children who have witnessed and experienced violence, as well as to hundreds of children who have committed violent crimes.[60]

Collaborative Responses to Trauma: CD-CP Consultation Service

The CD-CP 24-hour acute clinical consultation service is staffed by a team of mental health clinicians who are available for immediate consultation — in many cases, immediate, on-site intervention. While some situations require emergency, community-based interventions, officers can handle others using a telephone referral.

The acute consultation service augments access to clinical services and may help prevent the onset of posttraumatic symptomatology in at-risk children by providing crisis-oriented and psychoeducationally focused on-site clinical assessment and intervention. Following a consultation, the police officers continue to play a central role in the intervention as representatives of control, authority and security in the face of traumatic or psychologically overwhelming circumstances. By brokering clinical services and addressing both physical and psychological security, officers — supported by clinicians — may enhance children's feelings of security and stability in the wake of trauma that often leaves children and their families feeling beleaguered and helpless.

The primary goals of the acute clinical intervention are to initiate a process of psychological stabilization following a violent event and to allow the child to gain a sense of control following a potentially traumatizing experience. In the face of ongoing realistic concerns about physical danger to the child, providing a psychotherapeutic intervention alone is both naive and counterproductive. The timing of a clinical response is often dependent on issues of safety, such as leaving the crime scene and relocating the child to another home or a police station. In some instances, the involvement of CPS is a prerequisite to any clinical intervention because the child will not benefit from it unless his/her safety can first be assured. Without due attention being given to physical and psychological safety following a traumatic encounter, the potential therapeutic benefits of the police-mental health response are compromised significantly. Informed consideration about these matters advances the initial clinical goal of restoring a sense of safety and predictability in the wake of violence or trauma.

Between 1997 and 2001, the CD-CP acute consultation service worked with 2361 children; 809 of these children (34.3%) received a direct, in-person response. Based on an analysis of data kept by the CD-CP program, Hispanic youth were more likely than Caucasian children to receive this form of response (OR = 1.36), as were children involved in gang-related incidents (OR = 8.12), accidents (OR = 5.21), felony assaults (OR = 2.97), property crimes (OR = 2.30), family violence (OR = 1.53) and psychiatric crises (OR = 1.29) (S.M., unpublished data, 1997-2001). Immediate, on-site clinical interventions were less likely when juvenile conduct problems (OR = 0.61), fires (OR = 0.59), child maltreatment (OR = 0.57) or domestic violence (OR = 0.44) was involved (S.M., unpublished data, 1997-2001). Analysis of the use of the CD-CP consultation service revealed that the greater the severity of the incident that police responded to, the greater was the use of CD-CP resources (S.M., unpublished data, 1997-2001). As this was the intent of the CD-CP program — to match services to needs — this analysis highlights the feasibility and success of this collaborative mode of law enforcement-mental health service delivery.

Police Officer's Role in the CD-CP Program

The consulting police officer serves as the liaison between the mental health clinician and the family in establishing the therapeutic relationship. This encourages the family to view the police and clinician as a team that promotes the child's psychological stability and physical security. In addition, it expands the role of the police beyond their traditional law enforcement response to include a recognition of and assistance with the mental health needs of children in the aftermath of violence. At any affected child's request, the officer may remain present during the clinical consultation to assure the youngster's physical safety and allow him/her the opportunity to experience and express dangerous or overwhelming emotions in a secure environment.

Clinician's Role in the CD-CP Program

Clinicians may meet with children individually or in small groups, depending upon the wishes of the family, the availability of additional clinicians and the developmental and psychological characteristics of the child (eg, age and/or age range; cognitive development; status as victim, witness or offender). The use of multiple clinicians who meet one-on-one with children allows for more in-depth assessments of individual children, although when groups of children of similar age share a common experience, a small group meeting led by a single clinician may foster more open communication and mutual support.

Concurrent preliminary discussions with adult caregivers focus on gathering relevant history about the child's and family's prior psychosocial functioning and trauma, as well as provide developmentally informed education and guidance about the child's responses to trauma and violence.

To help a child regain a sense of control in the face of potentially traumatic violence, the clinician typically follows the child's lead, as expressed in words, play or drawings. Through these media, the clinician helps the child elaborate his/her concerns. Associations with prior events or internal psychological responses are frequently more pressing or prominent than those related to the specific event that precipitated the intervention. The clinician's ability to listen quietly and empathetically, without telling or cuing the child about what he/she might wish to hear, permits the child to assume control in understanding the traumatic events and placing them into a framework that is consonant with his/her needs. Rather than becoming a passive recipient of generic strategies for coping with potentially traumatic events that the child endured, the child is encouraged to adopt an active role in communicating his/her unique concerns, which may or may not resemble the facts of the events that he/she has undergone or witnessed. Although the intervention is child-centered, the clinician is an *active* listener, asking for pertinent clarification. By the conclusion of the meeting(s), the clinician is able to provide the child and the family with information about a range of potential interventions, as well as details regarding responses to the violence and/or trauma that the child may exhibit.

Participating clinicians provide families with psychoeducational information, in both verbal and written forms, about children's possible responses to the violence and/or trauma, as well as possible coping mechanisms: The former facilitates the developing clinical relationship, while the latter provides a concrete reference that families can revisit at times of heightened concern or distress. The clinician also provides the family with contact information, asks for permission to follow up with a therapeutic visit or phone call (at the family's discretion) and offers information about longer-term consultation and treatment options, if needed. This concrete information, along with the immediate connection to a clinical expert, helps normalize the child's and the family's responses to their experiences, provides them with the knowledge that help is available and accessible and facilitates the development of a clinical relationship at a time when defenses are more malleable and receptiveness to intervention is heightened.

CD-CP: Implications for Policing and Mental Health Care

The CD-CP 24-hour acute consultation service is the most visible manifestation of the police-mental health partnership, as well as the clearest departure from the traditional activities of both police officers *and* mental health clinicians. The acute consultation actually changes the paradigm within which police and mental health professionals respond to the needs and concerns of affected children and families. It provides officers with the opportunity to expand their knowledge of child development and therapeutic interventions within a model of youth-oriented community policing. The collaboration with police has allowed child therapists to venture into a new setting and thereby increase their understanding of the impact of violence and trauma. It also provides for clinical care to youth proactively prior to the point at which symptoms crystallize into serious psychiatric disorders.

By following the unfolding stories of children exposed to violence, clinicians understand the specific features of a violent event, and its sequelae, that individual children experience as exceptional, overwhelming and, therefore, traumatizing. All too often, clinical assumptions and notions about the nature of a child's traumatization have been determined by observable features of the violence as it occurred. Yet, these assumptions may have little to do with the child's actual experience of the violence or their attributions generated in its aftermath.

Clinicians may not find it necessary to take the time to learn about the child and his/her previous psychological functioning as a basis for understanding unique responses to an experience of violence.

These responses can be understood only in the context of life history, temperament, family constellation, developmental stage and psychological defense configuration. Without this essential information, the clinician does not have sufficient data upon which to base recommendations for police and psychiatric interventions. For clinicians and police officers alike, paying closer attention to the details of the individual child's experience within the CD-CP program has prompted changes in their responses to affected children and allowed them to move beyond proscribed responses, which may not address the child's distress adequately. The following case study illustrates these important changes:

Case Study: CD-CP Program Responds to 7-Year-Old Witness to Violence

Sergeant G described an incident in which a 7-year-old girl witnessed a beloved female neighbor bleed to death after being stabbed fatally by another female neighbor. Believing he was protecting her from the gore of the crime scene, Sergeant G had the child wait on the porch outside while officers conducted their investigation. The intense gaze — a mixture of despair and rage — that the girl fixed on Sergeant G when he finally invited her back into the apartment haunted him. The next day the sergeant went back to the apartment and spoke with the girl and her grandmother. He began to understand that in his genuine attempt to be helpful, by shielding her from the crime scene, he had not considered what this girl was experiencing and what help she needed at the moment.

As Sergeant G later explained in the case conference: "Especially in the midst of so much blood and terror, what the girl needed was to be close to her grandmother — the most stable figure in her life — not to be stranded alone with images of the scene." Both the girl and her grandmother eagerly accepted Sergeant G's offer of a referral for clinical psychological services. During her treatment, what emerged was that being alone with frightening ideas and fantasies involving extremes of love and hate was common for this young girl. Her heroin-addicted mother moved in and out of her life capriciously. The girl was also burdened by her realistic uncertainty about her grandmother's health and longevity. Both internal and external conflicts were underscored boldly by her confusion of "loyalties" in the stabbing. Although she mourned the death of a beloved and idealized maternal substitute, she told her therapist anxiously about the love letters she was writing to the perpetrator, now in jail awaiting trial on murder charges, whom she viewed as safer and more available than her inconsistent and absent mother.

Expanding the CD-CP Approach: A Domestic Violence Intervention Project

Since the inception of the CD-CP program, approximately one third of the calls to the consultation service have involved children's exposures to domestic violence. These calls present unique challenges to responding officers: Incidents are often repetitive in nature and emotionally charged, and the scenes can be dangerous for all parties involved, including the responding police officers. Across the United States, more officers are injured while responding to domestic violence calls than when responding to any other type of police call.[61] Yet, because most domestic violence calls involve misdemeanor offenses, criminal justice remedies tend to be limited, and officers often find themselves stymied in their efforts to provide realistic assistance. Many officers also often find themselves frustrated when their efforts to assist battered women are met with suspicion, disbelief or resistance. Even when officers are aware that such women may have many good reasons for not calling the police or not actively pursuing prosecution of their abusers, it becomes very easy for action-oriented officers to feel angry and/or resentful. In this context, it is difficult for police officers to consistently notice and attend to the children they encounter.

To address the particular difficulties associated with responding to incidents of domestic violence, the CD-CP program implemented an enhanced police-mental health intervention based on principles of police-mental health collaboration. The cornerstone of this intervention involves a neighborhood-based, home-visit, follow-up project implemented at present in 4 of 10 police districts within the city of New Haven. Detectives who investigate reports of domestic violence identify households where an intimate-partner assault has been reported. Teams comprised of a patrol officer assigned to the target district and a clinically informed, domestic violence advocate are assigned to these households to provide follow-up home visits. During these visits, the teams monitor victim safety, improve the family's understanding and enforcement of court orders and increase access to information and supportive services for victims and their children. The intervention design is based on the hypothesis that regular personal contact between police officers and victims of domestic violence can increase the immediate physical safety of battered women and their children, and facilitate a better connection to supportive and therapeutic services — thereby improving the health and well-being of affected women and children over the course of their development.

In the CD-CP program, between September 2000 and December 2003, police-advocate teams made direct service contact with 780 adult (primarily female) victims in 612 households (S.M., unpublished data, 1997-2001). The majority of incidents involved physical injury as a result of the domestic assault. Relatively few victims sought additional medical attention beyond that available at the scene, perhaps highlighting their reluctance to access health care through traditional modes of service delivery.

A matched comparison of 102 victims receiving the police-advocate intervention (the intervention group) with a group of 102 victims from districts where the intervention had not been implemented (who received a standard police response; the control group) indicated that there was a significant decrease in the number of repeat calls for police service within the intervention group during the 12-month period following the police-advocate home visit: Police received only 20 "911" calls from the intervention group for repeat incidents of domestic violence, compared with 43 such calls for repeat incidents of domestic violence from the control group (S.M., unpublished data, 1997-2001).

The 23% decrease in calls to the police for repeat incidents of intimate-partner domestic violence in the intervention group is encouraging, although it does not definitively signify a reduction in domestic violence. Alternatively, the decrease in calls may reflect continued violence with decreased seriousness, such that the victim did not request assistance from the police, or it may reflect an increased reluctance of victims to report the violence. Preliminary data from a satisfaction survey administered to approximately 28% (218) of the 780 victims receiving the CD-CP intervention suggest that it is unlikely that the reduction in police calls resulted from increased inhibition of victims to report these crimes. Of the 218 victims who responded to this confidential telephone survey, 63% (137) reported feeling "safer" after the police-advocacy visit; 37% reported "no change in safety"; and none reported feeling "less safe." A total of 80% (174) reported that they would be more likely to call the police for help in the future as a result of the home-visit contact with the police-advocate team (S.M., unpublished data, 1997-2001).

Summary

The CD-CP program has resulted in a coordinated approach to the delivery of police and mental health services to children and families who are affected by violence in their homes and communities and who have historically lacked access to quality interventions. Mental health clinicians and police officers in New Haven now have a "common language" for assessing and responding to the needs of affected children and families. Learning from each other, these relatively unlikely partners have established close working relationships that have improved and expanded the range of available interventions for families — yet have preserved the areas of expertise and responsibilities of each profession. Immediate access to witnesses, victims and perpetrators of violent crimes through the acute consultation service enhances our knowledge of posttraumatic phenomena from the acute moment to longer-term adaptation, symptom formation and recovery. As a result, the CD-CP program has become an effective vehicle for the systematic study of basic psychological and neurobiological functions involved in traumatization, as well as for the investigation of the effectiveness of child- and systems-oriented interventions. Studies have yielded promising evidence that youth-oriented community policing and the CD-CP model are having a positive impact on children's lives in the following ways: promoting feelings of safety and security; decreasing levels of exposure to domestic and community violence; enhancing perceptions of police as a responsive and benevolent authority; improving access to acute clinical interventions and follow-up; and decreasing repeat calls for police services in cases of domestic violence.[5,6]

References

1. Costello EJ, Erkanli A, Fairbank JA, Angold A. The prevalence of potentially traumatic events in childhood and adolescence. *Journal of Traumatic Stress.* 2002;15:99-112.
2. Elklit A. Victimization and PTSD in a Danish national youth probability sample. *Journal of the American Academy of Child and Adolescent Psychiatry.* 2002;41:174-181.
3. Perez-Smith AM, Albus KE, Weist MD. Exposure to violence and neighborhood affiliation among inner-city youth. *Journal of Clinical Child Psychology.* 2001;30:464-472.
4. Richters JE, Martinez P. The NIMH community violence project: I. Children as victims of and witnesses to violence. *Psychiatry.* 1993;56:7-21.
5. Schwab-Stone ME, Ayers TS, Kasprow W, et al. No safe haven: a study of violence exposure in an urban community. *Journal of the American Academy of Child and Adolescent Psychiatry.* 1995;34: 1343-1352.
6. Schwab-Stone M, Chen C, Greenberger E, Silver D, Lichtman J, Voyce C. No safe haven. II: the effects of violence exposure on urban youth. *Journal of the American Academy of Child and Adolescent Psychiatry.* 1999;38:359-367.
7. Boney-McCoy S, Finkelhor D. Is youth victimization related to trauma symptoms and depression after controlling for prior symptoms and family relationships? A longitudinal, prospective study. *Journal of Consulting and Clinical Psychology.* 1996;64:1406-1416.
8. Foy DW, Goguen CA. Community violence-related PTSD in children and adolescents. *PTSD Research Quarterly.* 1998;9:1-6.
9. Gorman-Smith D, Tolan P. The role of exposure to community violence and developmental problems among inner-city youth. *Development and Psychopathology.* 1998;10:101-116.
10. Kilpatrick DG, Ruggiero KJ, Acierno R, Saunders BE, Resnick HS, Best CL. Violence and risk of PTSD, major depression, substance abuse/dependence, and comorbidity: results from the National Survey of Adolescents. *Journal of Consulting and Clinical Psychology.* 2003;71:692-700.
11. Marans S, Adelman A. Experiencing violence in a developmental context. In: Osofsky JD, ed. *Children in a Violent Society.* New York, NY: The Guilford Press; 1997:202-222.

12. McCloskey LA, Walker M. Posttraumatic stress in children exposed to family violence and single-event trauma. *Journal of the American Academy of Child and Adolescent Psychiatry.* 2000;39:108-115.
13. Pfefferbaum B. Posttraumatic stress disorder in children: a review of the past 10 years. *Journal of the American Academy of Child and Adolescent Psychiatry.* 1997;36:1503-1511.
14. Pynoos RS. Traumatic stress and developmental psychopathology in children and adolescents. In: Oldham JM, Riba MB, Tasman A, eds. *American Psychiatric Press Review of Psychiatry.* Vol 12. Washington, DC: American Psychiatric Press; 1993:205-238.
15. Pynoos RS, Steinberg AM, Piacentini JC. A developmental psychopathology model of childhood traumatic stress and intersection with anxiety disorders. *Biological Psychiatry.* 1999;46:1542-1554.
16. Terr LC. Childhood traumas: an outline and overview. *The American Journal of Psychiatry.* 1991;148:10-20.
17. Cooley-Quille M, Boyd RC, Frantz E, Walsh J. Emotional and behavioral impact of exposure to community violence in inner-city adolescents. *Journal of Clinical Child Psychology.* 2001;30:199-206.
18. Mazza JJ, Reynolds WM. Exposure to violence in young inner-city adolescents: relationships with suicidal ideation, depression, and PTSD symptomatology. *Journal of Abnormal Child Psychology.* 1999;27:203-213.
19. Miller LS, Wasserman GA, Neugebauer R, Gorman-Smith D, Kamboukos D. Witnessed community violence and antisocial behavior in high-risk, urban boys. *Journal of Clinical Child Psychology.* 1999;28:2-11.
20. Windle M. A latent growth curve model of delinquent activity among adolescents. *Applied Developmental Science.* 2000;4:193-207.
21. Marans S, Murphy RA, Berkowitz SJ. Police-mental health responses to children exposed to violence: The Child Development Community Policing Program. In: Lewis M, ed. *Child and Adolescent Psychiatry: A Comprehensive Textbook.* 3rd ed. Baltimore, Md: Lippincott Williams & Wilkins; 2002:1406-1416.
22. Murphy RA. Mental health, juvenile justice, and law enforcement responses to youth psychopathology. In: Marsh DT, Fristad MA, eds. *Handbook of Serious Emotional Disturbance in Children and Adolescents.* New York, NY: John Wiley & Sons; 2002:351-374.
23. Garbarino J, Dubrow N, Kostelny K, Pardo C. *Children in Danger: Coping With the Consequences of Community Violence.* San Francisco, Calif: Jossey-Bass Publishers; 1992.
24. Martinez P, Richters JE. The NIMH community violence project: II. Children's distress symptoms associated with violence exposure. *Psychiatry.* 1993;56:22-35.
25. Widom CS. Posttraumatic stress disorder in abused and neglected children grown up. *The American Journal of Psychiatry.* 1999;156:1223-1229.
26. Marans S, Berkman M, Cohen D. Child development and adaptation to catastrophic circumstances. In: Apfel RJ, Simon B, eds. *Minefields in Their Hearts: The Mental Health of Children in War and Communal Violence.* New Haven, Conn: Yale University Press; 1996:104-127.
27. Marans S. Psychoanalysis on the beat. Children, police, and urban trauma. *The Psychoanalytic Study of the Child.* 1996;51:522-541.
28. Thornberry T. *Violence, Families, and Youth Violence.* Washington, DC: US Dept of Justice, Office of Justice Programs, Office of Juvenile Justice and Delinquency Prevention; 1994.
29. Dodge KA, Pettit GS, Bates JE. How the experience of early physical abuse leads children to become chronically aggressive. In: Cicchetti, D, Toth SL, eds. *Developmental Perspectives on Trauma: Theory, Research, and Intervention.* Rochester, NY: University of Rochester Press; 1997:263-288. Rochester Symposium on Developmental Psychopathology: Proceedings. Vol 8.
30. Lipschitz DS, Rasmusson AM, Southwick SM. Childhood posttraumatic stress disorder: a review of neurobiologic sequelae. *Psychiatric Annals.* 1998;28:452-457.
31. Southwick SM, Krystal JH, Morgan CA, et al. Abnormal noradrenergic function in posttraumatic stress disorder. *Archives of General Psychiatry.* 1993;50:266-274.
32. Yehuda R. Post-traumatic stress disorder. *The New England Journal of Medicine.* 2002;346:108-114.

33. Bryant B, Mayou R, Wiggs L, Ehlers A, Stores G. Psychological consequences of road traffic accidents for children and their mothers. *Psychological Medicine.* 2004;34:335-346.

34. Pynoos RS, Frederick C, Nader K, et al. Life threat and posttraumatic stress in school-age children. *Archives of General Psychiatry.* 1987;44:1057-1063.

35. Marans S, Cohen DJ. Child psychoanalytic theories of development. In: Lewis M, ed. *Child and Adolescent Psychiatry: A Comprehensive Textbook.* 3rd ed. Baltimore, Md: Lippincott Williams & Wilkins; 2002:196-211.

36. Aber JL, Jones SM, Brown JL, Chaudry N, Samples F. Resolving conflict creatively: evaluating the developmental effects of a school-based violence prevention program in neighborhood and classroom context. *Development and Psychopathology.* 1998;10:187-213.

37. Woolston JL, Berkowitz SJ, Schaefer MC, Adnopoz JA. Intensive, integrated, in-home psychiatric services. The catalyst to enhancing outpatient intervention. *Child and Adolescent Psychiatric Clinics of North America.* 1998;7:615-633.

38. Thurman QC. Community policing: the police as a community resource. In: Adams P, Nelson K, eds. *Reinventing Human Services: Community- and Family-Centered Practice.* New York, NY: Aldine de Gruyter; 1995:175-187.

39. Catalano RF, Loeber R, McKinney KC. School and community interventions to prevent serious and violent offending. *OJJDP Juvenile Justice Bulletin.* Washington, DC: US Dept of Justice, Office of Justice Programs, Office of Juvenile Justice and Delinquency Prevention; October 1999.

40. Zhao J, Thurman QC. Community policing: where are we now? *Crime & Delinquency.* 1997;43: 345-358.

41. Goldstein H. Toward community-oriented policing: potential, basic requirements and threshold questions. *Crime & Delinquency.* 1987;33:6-30.

42. Novak KJ, Alarid LF, Lucas WL. Exploring officers' acceptance of community policing: implications for policy implementation. *Journal of Criminal Justice.* 2003;31:57-71.

43. Borum R. *Misdemeanor Offenders With Mental Illness in Florida: Examining Police Response, Court Jurisdiction, and Jail Mental Health Services.* Tampa, Fla: Dept of Mental Health Law & Policy, Louis de la Parte Florida Mental Health Institute, University of South Florida; 1999.

44. Hails J, Borum R. Police training and specialized approaches to respond to people with mental illnesses. *Crime & Delinquency.* 2003;49:52-61.

45. Redondo RM, Currier GW. Characteristics of patients referred by police to a psychiatric emergency service. *Psychiatric Services (Washington, DC).* 2003;54:804-806.

46. Teplin LA. Keeping the peace: police discretion and mentally ill persons. *National Institute of Justice Journal.* July 2000:8-15.

47. Deane MW, Steadman HJ, Borum R, Veysey BM, Morrissey JP. Emerging partnerships between mental health and law enforcement. *Psychiatric Services.* 1999;50:99-101.

48. Scholte EM. Identification of children at risk at the police station and the prevention of delinquency. *Psychiatry.* 1992;55:354-369.

49. Marans S, Adnopoz J, Berkman M, et al. *The Police-Mental Health Partnership: A Community-Based Response to Urban Violence.* New Haven, Conn: Yale University Press; 1995.

50. Marans S, Cohen DJ. Children and inner-city violence: strategies for intervention. In: Leavitt LA, Fox NA, eds. *The Psychological Effects of War and Violence on Children.* Hillsdale, NJ: Lawrence Erlbaum Associates; 1993:281-301.

51. Marans S, Berkowitz SJ, Cohen DJ. Police and mental health professionals. Collaborative responses to the impact of violence on children and families. *Child and Adolescent Psychiatric Clinics of North America.* 1998;7:635-651.

52. Marans S, Schaefer M. Community policing, schools, and mental health: the challenge of collaboration. In: Elliott DS, Hamburg BA, Williams KR, eds. *Violence in American Schools.* New York, NY: Cambridge University Press; 1998:312-347.

53. Berkowitz SJ, Murphy RA. Child development and education. In: *COPS in Schools: SRO Training Curriculum.* Westlake Village, Calif: National School Safety Center; 2000.

54. Robertson J, Robertson J. *John, Seventeen Months: Nine Days in a Residential Nursery* [film]. New York, NY: New York University Film Library; 1969.
55. Portwood SG, Grady MT, Dutton SE. Enhancing law enforcement identification and investigation of child maltreatment. *Child Abuse & Neglect.* 2000;24:195-207.
56. Wells GL, Malpass RS, Lindsay RCL, Fisher RP, Turtle JW, Fulero SM. From the lab to the police station. A successful application of eyewitness research. *The American Psychologist.* 2000;55:581-598.
57. Singleton J. *Boyz N the Hood* [film]. Los Angeles, Calif: Columbia Pictures; 1991.
58. King M. *Bangin'* [documentary film]. Boston, Mass: Boston Productions; 1999.
59. Child Development-Community Policing Program. *Case, Activity, and Patient Electronic Recording System (CAPERS).* New Haven, Conn: Yale Child Study Center, Yale School of Medicine; 1998.
60. Goldstein J, Solnit AJ, Goldstein S, Freud A. *The Best Interests of the Child: The Least Detrimental Alternative.* New York, NY: The Free Press; 1996.
61. FBI Press Room. Law enforcement officers killed and assaulted, 1999. Washington, DC: US Dept of Justice, Federal Bureau of Investigation, FBI National Press Office. March 15, 2001. Available at http://www.fbi.gov/pressrel/pressrel01/leoka031501.htm. Accessed May 20, 2004.

Section 3: Family or Community Violence: Exploring Prevention and Intervention for School-Age Children

Abstracts from Section 3: Family or Community Violence: Exploring Prevention and Intervention for School-Age Children

Exposure to and Experience With Family Violence: Issues for Intervention and Prevention

Richard J. Gelles, PhD

Children experience violence and are exposed to it in their schools and communities, among their peers and through the media. Often, children's first, most extensive and most persistent experience with and exposure to violence occurs in their families. The impact of exposure to and experience with violence in the home varies according to the gender and age of the child. However, the typical clinical intervention for children who are exposed to violence is a standardized, brief or low-dose, school-based intervention. Published evidence suggests that there is a need for more nuanced approaches to the issue of children's exposure to violence. Interventions should be problem-specific, gender-specific, age-graded and developmentally appropriate. This chapter analyzes the prevention strategies that aim to reduce children's experience with and exposure to violence, as well as the interventions that address the potentially harmful consequences of these experiences.

Ecological Treatment for Parent-to-Child Violence

Cynthia Cupit Swenson, PhD
Lisa Saldana, PhD
Cathy Dodds Joyner, MEd
Scott W. Henggeler, PhD

At present, there is no known single factor — or set of factors — that causes child abuse. Instead, an increased risk of child abuse is the result of a complex interaction among multiple factors within the child, parent, family, social and community network. This multifaceted etiology of child physical abuse demands a multifaceted, comprehensive treatment that focuses on numerous domains of functioning. To address all of the key problems that increase the risk of child abuse, this treatment must include the child, parent and family. A 5-year, randomized, controlled, effectiveness study of Multisystemic Therapy, an ecological model for the treatment of parent-to-child violence, developed originally to treat deeply entrenched antisocial behavior amongst youth, shows promise for its application to parent-to-child violence, and it is thus the focus of this chapter.

School-Based Interventions for Children and Adolescents Exposed to Chronic Community Violence

Michele R. Cooley, MEd, PhD
Sharon F. Lambert, PhD

Children and adolescents are exposed to community violence at alarming rates, often with adverse consequences for multiple domains of functioning — including depression, anxiety, posttraumatic stress symptoms, academic and achievement problems, substance abuse and health problems. However, exposure to violence in communities is not routinely assessed among children and adolescents, and, therefore, many youth do not receive the treatment they need. Moreover, there are few interventions designed specifically for this population. School-based interventions provide a means of increasing access to and utilization of services among youth exposed to community violence. This chapter reviews the suggested components of mental health interventions and summarizes 4 published school-based group interventions designed specifically for this population. Suggestions for future interventions are discussed, as well.

Exposure to and Experience With Family Violence: Issues for Intervention and Prevention

Richard J. Gelles, PhD

Introduction

Children experience violence and are exposed to it in a wide variety of settings, contexts and social groups — in their schools and communities, among their peers and through the media.[1] Often, a child's first, most extensive and most persistent experience with and exposure to violence occurs within the sphere of his/her family.[2] The first time a child is struck physically, irrespective of the reason, is usually in his/her home and at the hands of a caregiver.[2] Using his empirical research and historical evidence, Straus summarized the research on corporal punishment: He concluded that 90% of American parents hit their toddlers, and that most parents continue to strike their children into late childhood and even adolescence.[3]

This chapter examines the extent and behavioral consequences of children's experiences with and exposures to violence in the home. I define violence as "an act carried out with the intention or perceived intention of causing physical pain or injury to another person."[4] The pain caused by a violent act can range from slight — the result of a push or a slap — to excruciating, and can even include death.[4] I define "family" as "those individuals who share a blood or legal relationship, including parents or caregivers, children, intimate partners and siblings."[5] "Experience with violence" is defined as "being the individual against whom an act intended or perceived to cause harm and/or pain is directed."[4] "Exposure to violence" is defined as "witnessing or being aware of an act of violence that occurs between or among family members, but not being the direct object of the violent act."[4]

This chapter also analyzes the prevention strategies that aim to reduce children's experiences with and exposures to violence, as well as the interventions that address the potential harmful consequences of those experiences.

Extent of the Experience With and Exposure to Violence

Experience With Violence at Home

There are a variety of sources of data regarding the extent of children's experiences with violence: For one, the US Department of Health and Human Services (HHS) measures the incidence of physical abuse among children as part of the data it collects on child maltreatment. Based on these data, HHS reported that 895,569 children were the victims of some form of child maltreatment during 2002: Among this number, 166,920 youngsters were the victims of physical abuse — a rate of 2.3 children per 1000 children under the age of 18 years.[6]

Every 10 years, HHS also conducts a survey of the number of cases of child abuse and neglect reported to youth and family service agencies nationwide. The survey published most recently, conducted in 1993, found that nearly 3 million maltreated children were known by these agencies. Among these maltreated children, 381,700 youngsters were physically abused — a rate of 5.7 children per 1000 children under the age of 18 years.[7]

Social science surveys of the use of violence toward children by parents and caregivers also provide estimates of children's experiences with violence. The National Family Violence Surveys (NFVSs), conducted by myself and Straus, interviewed 2 nationally representative samples of families: 2146 family members in 1976[2] and 6002 family members in 1985.[8] The surveys measured violence and abuse by asking respondents to report their behaviors towards their children during the previous 12 months. "Mild" forms of violence — such as that thought of as "physical punishment" by most people — was the type reported most commonly. Yet, more than 80% of the parents/caregivers of children 3 years to 9 years of age reported hitting their children at least once during the previous year.[9] Among older children, the reported rates were lower: 67% of the parents/caregivers of preteens and young adolescents reported hitting their youngsters during the previous year, and slightly more than 33% of caregivers/parents of teenagers 15 years to 17 years of age reported hitting their adolescents during the prior year.[9]

Even with the most severe forms of violence, the reported rates were surprisingly high.[9] Slightly more than 20 parents in 1000 admitted to engaging in an act of "abusive violence" during the year prior to the 1985 survey. Abusive violence, which was defined as an act that had a high probability of injuring the child, included kicking, biting, punching, beating, hitting or trying to hit a child with an object, burning or scalding, and threatening to use or using a gun or a knife. Seven children in 1000 were hurt as the result of an act of violence directed at them by a parent or caregiver during the previous year. Based on these findings, it is projected that 1.5 million children in the United States under the age of 18 years who live with one or both parents are the victims of acts of abusive physical violence each year, and 450,000 children are injured annually as a result of parental violence.

In a more recent telephone survey of 900 parents regarding children's experiences with violence in the home, more than 28% of parents of 2- to 8-year-old children reported using an object to spank their child's bottom.[10] Incredibly, a 1995 Gallup survey found that 74% of children under the age of 5 years had been hit or slapped by their parent(s).[11]

Overall, children experience a broad range of violence — with mild to fatal outcomes — at varying rates across their childhood. "Corporal punishment," while not universal in the United States, is part of life for 70% to 80% of toddlers and for more than one third of older teens.[11] Between 2% and 6% of all children experience violence serious enough to cause them injury.[11]

Exposure to Violence at Home

Surprisingly, the data are scant regarding the number of children who are exposed to violence in their homes. However, extrapolating from the 2 NFVSs, Straus estimates that between 3.3 million and 10 million children are exposed annually to domestic violence in their homes.[12] In a more recent examination of data from the second NFVS, Silverman and I found that the reported rate of domestic violence among parents who had children 17 years of age or younger residing in the home was 155 exposures per 1000 children.[13] Based on data released by the US Census Bureau regarding the number of children residing with 2 parents or caretakers in 1984,[14] Silverman and I estimated that 7.2 million children were exposed to domestic violence, either directly or indirectly, during that year.[13]

Overall, we noted that children were exposed most frequently to minor forms of violence, such as pushing, shoving or slapping.[13] The overall rate of exposure to such minor violence was 91 children per 1000 children. Projecting this rate to the total population of children 17 years of age or younger living with 2 parents or caretakers, approximately 4.2 million children were exposed to minor forms of violence in the United States during 1985.[13]

In contrast, the rate of exposure to severe forms of violence was 62 children per 1000 children — for a total of approximately 2.9 million children exposed annually in the United States to severe violence.[13] A closer examination of exposure rates by the "direction" of the violence (ie, the individuals toward whom minor forms and severe forms of violence were directed), as reported in the 1985 NFVS, showed the following rates for minor forms of violence as described by the following categories[13]:

- husband to wife only = 27 per 1000
- wife to husband only = 25 per 1000
- bidirectional = 39 per 1000

For severe forms of violence, the rates were the following:

- husband to wife only = 16 per 1000
- wife to husband only = 27 per 1000
- bidirectional = 19 per 1000

Behavioral Consequences of Experience With and Exposure to Violence

In the field of family violence and child maltreatment there appears to be a strong tendency to "overdetermine" the consequences of children's experiences with and exposures to violence: That is, to assume that all or most children who experience or are exposed to violence or maltreatment will grow up to be abusive and violent to their children, partners and others. Early writings (1975) in the professional literature dealing with child abuse and neglect presumed that young victims of physical abuse would grow up to be delinquent, violent and/or homicidal.[15] The "cycle of violence" hypothesis contended that child maltreatment is transmitted across generations.[16] In fact, Widom noted that the "intergenerational transmission" hypothesis is the *premier* hypothesis in the field of child abuse.[17] However, Kaufman and Zigler noted that the intergenerational-transmission-of-violence hypothesis is often greatly overstated.[18,19] While the rates of violent and abusive behaviors among those who experienced physical abuse as children are considerably higher than are the rates of violent and abusive behavior among those who did not, best estimates, as noted by Kaufman and Zigler, are that approximately 30% of abused children grow up to be abusive adults themselves.[18,19]

Similarly, the behavioral consequences of children's exposures to intimate or domestic violence have been "overdetermined." A leading assumption is that the consequences of exposure to intimate violence are so harmful that exposure to domestic violence should, on its own, be considered a form of child maltreatment.[20] The combination of experiencing *and* being exposed to violence in the home is considered so harmful by some scholars that they have labeled it the "double whammy."[21] Their contention is that experience with *and* exposure to violence together are more than simply additive: In fact, they contend, it constitutes an exponentially greater risk for children with major harmful outcomes.

The overdetermination of the effects of violence on children has been accepted so widely that few scholars have taken an unbiased look at the *actual* consequences of experiences with and exposures to violence. In fact, Hughes, Parkinson and Vargo, who first coined the "double whammy" label, concluded that their data supported the "double whammy" hypothesis even though the data presented in their article actually failed to confirm it.[21] Furthermore, few investigators have examined the consequences of experience with and exposure to family violence by considering outcomes other than violent behavior, the differences in consequences across age groups and the different impacts that violence may have according to gender.

In a paper that I coauthored with Silverman regarding the "double whammy" hypothesis, we reexamined the data from the second NFVS.[13] (For a complete discussion of the methodology, see Silverman A, Gelles RJ.[13]) In brief, the survey consisted of a nationally representative sample of 6002 households, of which 3362 (56%) had children under the age of 18 years residing in the home.[2,8,9] *Experience* with violence was measured by having the respondent (a parent or caregiver of the child) complete the Conflict Tactics Scales (CTS)–Child Version, which contains questions pertaining to adult behavior towards the child.[8] *Exposure* to violence was measured by having each respondent complete the CTS–Adult Version, which contains questions about conflict tactics between intimate partners.[13] We assumed that if violence occurred between the partners, the children were *exposed* to intimate violence, whether or not they were direct or indirect witnesses to the incident. We assessed the behavioral consequences of experiences with and exposures to violence by asking each adult respondent to answer a series of questions about any troubles their child had experienced during the previous year. There were 4 types of behavioral troubles that children could have experienced during the previous 12 months: school troubles (eg, failing grades); delinquency (eg, stealing); problems with adults (eg, physical fights with adults who did not live in their house); and physical aggression (eg, temper tantrums, physical fights with other youth in the house and physical fights with youth not living in the house). The survey did not include questions that would have allowed us to examine the emotional consequences of experiences with and/or exposures to family violence.

Our Findings Regarding Experiences With and Exposures to Violence

The following summarizes the main findings[13]:

- Children who both experienced *and* were exposed to violence reportedly had more problems at school than did children who were only exposed to violence or who were neither exposed to nor experienced any family violence during the previous year. This finding provides some support for the "double whammy" hypothesis.
- Children who experienced violence were reportedly the most likely to engage in delinquent behaviors, as compared with children who experienced *and* were exposed to domestic violence, were only exposed to violence or who had neither experienced nor been exposed to family violence.
- The "double whammy" hypothesis was again supported by the findings regarding problems with adults: Children who had experienced *and* were exposed to domestic violence reportedly had more problems with adults

than did the children who only experienced violence, were only exposed to domestic violence or who had neither experienced nor been exposed to violence.

- Aggression was most common among children who only experienced family violence or who experienced *and* were exposed to violence, as compared with children who had only been exposed to violence or who had neither experienced nor were exposed to violence.

As these results suggest, there was some support for the "double whammy" hypothesis. Interestingly, exposure to family violence in the absence of experience with family violence did not significantly increase the likelihood of school problems, delinquency, problems with adults or physical aggression. Of course, there is the possibility that the "double whammy" effect could manifest itself as emotional or psychological problems; but these issues were not examined in the survey.

Gender as an Issue

In the absence of empirical research, the conventional and popular wisdom is that boys who have experience with and/or are exposed to family violence are at greater risk of acting out aggressively, while girls are more likely to internalize their reactions and exhibit signs and symptoms of depression, anxiety, withdrawal and social isolation. The only published research on gender and the consequences of abuse is a study of the consequences of sexual molestation on boys.[22]

Silverman and I disaggregated our data to examine the impact that experiences with and exposures to family violence had on males versus females.[13] Highlights of our findings include the following:

- Boys who only experienced family violence had more problems at school than did boys who had experience with *and* were exposed to violence, were only exposed to violence or who had neither experienced nor were exposed to violence. In contrast, girls who had experience with *and* were exposed to violence had more problems at school than did girls who only experienced violence, were only exposed to violence or who had neither experienced nor were exposed to violence.

- Boys were more likely than girls to be delinquent no matter what: Exposure to and experience with violence had no significant impact on this gender difference.
- As with delinquency, the only significant variable for aggression was gender: Overall, boys were more likely than girls to exhibit aggressive behavior. Neither exposure to nor experience with violence had an impact on this gender difference.
- Boys who only experienced violence, but were not exposed to violence, had more problems with adults than the following subjects:
  - boys who were only exposed to violence
  - boys who experienced *and* were exposed to violence
  - boys who had neither experienced nor were exposed to violence
- In contrast, girls who experienced *and* were exposed to violence had more problems with adults than did the other subgroup of girls.

Age as an Issue

Certain problems that children experienced were age specific. Our question was: Did experience with and/or exposure to family violence influence or exacerbate age-related problems? The following are our findings[13]:

- Latency-age children (ages 7 years to 11 years) who experienced *and* were exposed to violence had more school problems than did children who only experienced violence, were only exposed to violence or who had neither experienced nor were exposed to violence. Among adolescents, those who had experienced violence at the hands of their parents or caregivers had the most school problems.
- Not surprisingly, *only* adolescents who had experienced or were exposed to violence — and not younger children — were more likely to exhibit delinquent behavior. While exposure to violence alone was enough to increase delinquent behavior among teenagers, experiencing violence at the hands of parents or caregivers increased the risk of delinquent behavior significantly.
- There was no interaction effect for age and experience with and/or exposure to violence for aggression or problems with adults.

Combined Effects of Gender and Age on Child Problems

Examining the combined effects of gender and age on child problems caused by family violence produced some unexpected findings and modest support for the "double whammy" hypothesis.[13] The results are as follows:

- There were no interaction effects for gender and age for school problems or delinquency.
- Adolescent boys who experienced violence only had the highest rate of aggressive behavior.
- Adolescent girls who were exposed to *and* experienced violence had the highest rate of reported aggression.
- There was no gender-by-age interaction effect for adolescent boys with regard to problems with adults.
- Again, for adolescent girls, experience with *and* exposure to violence were associated with the highest rates of problems with adults.

As all of these results suggest, exposure to family violence clearly has no uniformly negative impact on all children. The impact of exposure to *and* experience with violence in the home varies with the gender and age of the child and the type of problem being examined (eg, delinquency, aggression, school problems and problems with adults). The hypothesized "double whammy" effect of exposure to *and* experience with family violence appears to exist only for girls — and then only for those girls who are older than 7 years of age and only for problems with adults and aggression. For girls who experienced *and* were exposed to family violence, especially latency-age and teenage girls, survey respondents reported a host of behavioral problems. Internalizing was not measured. For boys across the age span, experience with violence *only* increased the likelihood of behavioral problems.

The Intervention Dilemma

The field of family violence — research, practice and policy — is relatively new. The *newest* facet of this emerging field is the examination of the impact of exposure to violence on children. The development of a knowledge base, and best practices and policies has been limited by a persistent gravitation towards simplistic causal models and intervention strategies, as well as by the placement of research, practice and policy into victim-specific silos. In other words, there is very little cross communication between the researchers, clinicians, advocates and policy makers who focus on the problem of child maltreatment with the professionals and advocates whose primary concern is the abuse of women.[23]

One Size Fits All

For almost all violent relationships between individuals who are intimate, there are only elementary causal models that lead to one-size-fits-all interventions. During the first decade of public concern about child maltreatment (the 1970s), the causal model applied by most practitioners was *psychopathology,* and the intervention of choice was to remove the at-risk child from the dangerous environment.[24] Subsequently (in the 1990s), the psychopathology model was replaced by a *diathesis stress model,* which proposed that abuse and neglect grew out of 3 key factors: structural stress (eg, poverty, unemployment and inadequate housing and/or health care); the lack of psychological, social, economic and network resources; and social norms that approved of violence as an instrumental and expressive behavior.[24] The intervention of choice under the diathesis stress model was *family preservation,* which was achieved through intensive supportive services and parenting classes.[25]

Violence towards women was initially conceptualized using the diathesis stress model as a result of the 3 key factors noted. This conceptualization was replaced quickly by the *feminist model,* which conceptualized domestic violence as a form of coercive control that was the result of the patriarchal organization of societies.[26] Since eliminating patriarchy would require a macrosocial change, all of the interventions of choice would be forms of social control: for example, a policy of mandatory arrest of domestic violence offenders and referral to batterers intervention programs (BIPs). BIPs are comprised of profeminist psychosocial educational curricula aimed at requiring batterers to assume responsibility for their behavior and modify abusive, gender-based attitudes.[27]

None of these distinct silos recognized the possibility that there might be different types of offenders and that interventions might need to be tailored to fit these particular offenders and families — or even victims.[28] Not surprisingly, the legacy of simplistic causal models and one-size-fits-all interventions is evidence that no single prevention or treatment program is actually effective in all instances.[23] (The only apparent exception is the demonstrated effectiveness of home visitation programs, whose aim is to reduce the occurrence of child maltreatment in high-risk families.[23])

Silo Problem

Complicating the research, practice and policy issues of intervening effectively on behalf of children exposed to family violence is the "silo" problem discussed previously. A prime example of this problem is the response of those who work in the domestic violence/violence against women community to the whole issue of children who are exposed to domestic violence: Initially, they embraced as a critical issue the exposure of children to domestic violence and acknowledged these children as victims themselves. They felt that the presence of a second victim in cases of domestic violence — the child — would add credibility to the victimization of the woman. In addition, they reasoned that the presence of the affected child would tip the balance of services and legal responses in favor of women who had, for decades, been ignored by *both* the legal and the social service systems. However, the sadly unintended consequence of defining exposure to violence as a "social problem" and not just a "women's problem" was the resulting increase in nonoffending victims of battering (ie, those women who were abused by their partners who were not engaged in abusive or neglectful behavior toward their children) being labeled and treated as "*offenders*" for allowing their children to be exposed to domestic violence. This further resulted in the start of Child Protective Service agencies, who adopted policies that defined exposure to domestic violence as "prima facie evidence of maltreatment," and removed children from mothers whose only innocent "offense" was either living with or being married to an abusive man.

Low-Dose Interventions

Another limitation of current interventions is that they are typically "low dose" in nature. As noted previously, for cases of domestic violence, the typical intervention is arrest of the batterer, followed by their referral to a BIP. Few domestic violence offenders are incarcerated directly after an arrest, and fewer still receive prison or jail terms following adjudication.[27]

The content of BIPs is generally cognitive-behavioral and gender-based cognitive-behavioral, as shaped by the "Duluth Model."[29] This approach focuses on the emotional makeup of men, the personality of the individual batterer and the sex-role attitudes of men, in general. (Other models used include "psychodynamics" and "anger management," but the Duluth Model of gender-based cognitive-behavioral change is the predominant approach.[27])

The supervision of offenders referred to BIPs is spotty, at best, and responses to offender noncompliance with attendance at BIPs is neither swift nor decisive.[27] Although many communities are moving to adopt a "coordinated community response" to the whole issue of domestic violence,[30] the actual "dose" of the intervention for batterers is still structured around arrest by police officers and referral to a BIP. The bulk of public policy attention on and public funding for domestic violence, especially funds flowing from the federal Violence Against Women Act (passed initially in 1993), is aimed at services and support for the immediate victims of intimate violence — women.

The typical intervention for children who are exposed to violence is a short or low-dose, *school-based* intervention. These interventions are commonly offered by either outside violence-prevention experts or by school-based counseling or student-assistance personnel. Here again, these interventions focus primarily on gender attitudes and cognitive restructuring. Their duration may be as brief as one session, or a limited series of sessions, perhaps with a "booster" session. Many of the school-based programs focus on teens — who are either in middle school or high school — with the goal of preventing later dating violence.[31] Therefore, many younger-age children are "missed" by such programs.

The one common attribute of these low-dose interventions is the paucity of evidence that they are actually effective at changing behavior.[23,27] While there are claims of success associated with such interventions,[32] there are few studies that use appropriate methods and measures that support such claims.[23,27]

Conclusion

It should not come as a surprise that few effective interventions are available to help and support children who are exposed to violence in the home. The knowledge base regarding this issue is thin: There are few empirical studies that bridge the child maltreatment and domestic violence silos and examine the scope of and impact on children who experience and/or are exposed to violence in their homes. In addition, it would appear that what passes for a knowledge base are largely common-sense assumptions or broadly painted portraits of what is assumed to happen to children who are exposed to family violence. The persistence of the "double whammy" notion of experience and exposure to violence, despite the lack of empirical support, is evidence of such a problem.

Our NFVSs support the contention that many children experience and are exposed to violence in their homes. However, the surveys also reveal that the consequences of experiencing and being exposed to violence depend on the gender *and* age of the child, *and* on the type of problem under examination.

The current crop of available programs and interventions is victim-driven, ideologically based and limited in dose and strength. Furthermore, there is little empirical evidence supporting the effectiveness of such programs. Even if the dose and/or strength of the interventions were increased marginally, it is unlikely to make a meaningful difference in terms of outcomes.

The data that my colleagues and I have discovered about children who experience and/or who are exposed to family violence suggest the following:

- There is a distinct need for more nuanced approaches to the issue of children's exposure to violence. Interventions should be problem-specific and should abandon the notion that exposure to family violence produces a robust outcome across behavioral domains.
- Interventions should be gender-specific. This suggestion is not new: Current interventions assume that boys react to exposure to family violence by acting out, and that girls react by internalizing their experiences. Our data do not support such rigid outcomes. However, it is clear that exposure to family violence produces different outcomes for boys than it does for girls. Perhaps most obviously, boys are affected primarily by "experiencing" this violence, while girls, especially teenage and latency-age girls, exhibit a "double whammy"-type response.
- Interventions need to be age-graded and developmentally appropriate. Exposure to family violence produces different behavioral impacts, depending on the age and the developmental status of the child.

One final note of caution: Current interventions for domestic violence are designed typically to effect change for both the offender *and* the victim. The desired outcome can be a change in attitudes or a change in behavior. Cognitive and behavioral changes are complicated, multistage processes that cannot be achieved by simply rolling out a program with edicts such as "Do it" or "Don't do it."[33] All those concerned about the costs and consequences of children's exposure to family violence — from parents and practitioners to policy makers — should avoid simple, short-term, low-dose, ideologically based solutions.

References

1. Brown BV, Bzostek S. *Violence in the Lives of Children.* Washington, DC: Child Trends; 2003.
2. Straus MA, Gelles RJ, Steinmetz S. *Behind Closed Doors: Violence in the American Family.* Garden City, NY: Sage Publications; 1988.
3. Straus MA. *Beating the Devil Out of Them: Corporal Punishment in American Families.* New York, NY: Lexington Books; 1994.
4. Gelles RJ. *Intimate Violence in Families.* 3rd ed. Thousand Oaks, Calif: Sage Publications; 1997.
5. Gelles RJ. *Contemporary Families: A Sociological View.* Thousand Oaks, Calif: Sage Publications; 1994.
6. US Dept of Health and Human Services. *Child Maltreatment 2001: Reports From the States to the National Center on Child Abuse and Neglect.* Washington, DC: US Dept of Health and Human Services, National Center on Child Abuse and Neglect; 2004.
7. US Dept of Health and Human Services. *Study of National Incidence and Prevalence of Child Abuse and Neglect: 1993: Study Findings.* Washington, DC: US Dept of Health and Human Services, National Center on Child Abuse and Neglect; 1996.
8. Gelles RJ, Straus MA. *Intimate Violence.* New York, NY: Touchstone Books; 1988.
9. Gelles RJ, Straus MA. Is violence towards children increasing? A comparison of 1975 and 1985 national survey rates. *Journal of Interpersonal Violence.* 1987;2:212-222.
10. Straus MA, Stewart JH. Corporal punishment by American parents: national data on prevalence, chronicity, severity, and duration, in relation to child and family characteristics. *Clinical Child and Family Psychology Review.* 1999;2:55-70.
11. Gallup Organization. *Disciplining Children in America: A Gallup Poll Report.* Princeton, NJ: Gallup Organization; 1995.
12. Straus MA. Children as witness to marital violence: a risk factor for lifelong problems among a nationally representative sample of American men and women. In: Schwartz DF, ed. *Children and Violence: Report of the Twenty-Third Ross Roundtable on Critical Approaches to Common Pediatric Problems.* Columbus, Ohio: Ross Laboratories; 1992:98-109.
13. Silverman A, Gelles RJ. The double whammy revisited: the impact of exposure to domestic violence and being a victim of parent to child violence. *The Indian Journal of Social Work.* 2001;62:305-327.
14. US Census Bureau. *Statistical Abstract of the United States: 1985.* 105th ed. Washington, DC: US Bureau of the Census; 1985.
15. Kempe CH, Schmitt BD. Neglect and abuse of children. In: Vaughan V, McKay R, eds. *Nelson Textbook of Pediatrics.* 10th ed. Philadelphia, Pa: WB Saunders Co; 1975:107-111.
16. Spinetta JJ, Rigler D. The child-abusing parent: a psychological review. *Psychological Bulletin.* 1972;77:296-304.
17. Widom CS. The cycle of violence. *Science.* 1989;244:160-166.

18. Kaufman J, Zigler E. Do abused children become abusive parents? *The American Journal of Orthopsychiatry.* 1987;57:186-192.
19. Kaufman J, Zigler E. The intergenerational transmission of abuse is overstated. In: Gelles RJ, Loseke DR, eds. *Current Controversies on Family Violence.* Thousand Oaks, Calif: Sage Publications; 1993:209-221.
20. Lemon NKD. The legal system's response to children exposed to domestic violence. *The Future of Children/Center for the Future of Children, the David and Lucile Packard Foundation.* 1999;9:67-83.
21. Hughes HM, Parkinson D, Vargo M. Witnessing spouse abuse and experiencing physical abuse: a "double whammy?" *Journal of Family Violence.* 1989;4:197-209.
22. Friedrich WN, Beilke RL, Urquiza AJ. Behavioral problems of young sexually abused boys. *Journal of Interpersonal Violence.* 1988;3:21-28.
23. Chalk R, King PA, eds. *Violence in Families: Assessing Prevention and Treatment Programs.* Washington, DC: The National Academies Press; 1998.
24. Gelles RJ. Child abuse as psychopathology: a sociological critique and reformulation. *The American Journal of Orthopsychiatry.* 1973;43:611-621.
25. Gelles RJ. *The Book of David: How Preserving Families Can Cost Children's Lives.* New York, NY: Basic Books; 1996.
26. Dobash RE. *Violence Against Wives: A Case Against the Patriarchy.* New York, NY: Free Press; 1979.
27. Gondolf EW. *Batterer Intervention Systems: Issues, Outcomes, and Recommendations.* Thousand Oaks, Calif: Sage Publications; 2002.
28. Cavanaugh MM, Gelles RJ. The utility of male domestic violence offender typologies: new directions for research, policy, and practice. *Journal of Interpersonal Violence.* 2005;20:155-166.
29. Pence EL, Shepard MF. An introduction: developing a coordinated community response. In: Shepard MF, Pence EL, eds. *Coordinating Community Responses to Domestic Violence: Lessons from Duluth and Beyond.* Thousand Oaks, Calif: Sage Publications; 1999:3-25.
30. Pence E, Paymar M. *Education Groups for Men Who Batter: The Duluth Model.* New York, NY: Springer Publishing; 1993.
31. Foshee VA, Linder GF, Bauman KE, et al. The Safe Dates Project: theoretical basis, evaluation design, and selected baseline findings. *American Journal of Preventive Medicine.* 1996;12(suppl):39-47.
32. Dutton DG. The outcome of court-mandated treatment for wife assault: a quasi-experimental evaluation. *Violence and Victims.* 1986;1:163-175.
33. Prochaska JO, Norcross JC, Diclemente CC. *Changing for Good: The Revolutionary Program That Explains the Six Stages of Change and Teaches You How to Free Yourself From Bad Habits.* New York, NY: Harper Collins; 1994.

Ecological Treatment for Parent-to-Child Violence

Cynthia Cupit Swenson, PhD
Lisa Saldana, PhD
Cathy Dodds Joyner, MEd
Scott W. Henggeler, PhD

Introduction

Parental violence towards a child increases the child's risk of developing serious mental health problems and, in the long run, engaging in violent crime and other antisocial behaviors. Maltreated children who experience severe emotional problems often require costly therapy and services, such as residential care and/or hospitalization, and eventually exact a heavy toll on themselves, their families and society, in general. Despite the multiple and often grave consequences that result from violence towards children, little is known about effective ways of preventing the violence, reducing its mental health impact and improving the functioning of abusive and/or at-risk families. To design effective interventions, clinicians should use as their guide existing child development literature and emerging findings on the links between children's physical factors and the multiple factors within the different systems with which the child interacts — parents, the family and the child's and family's social networks.

In this chapter, we outline an ecological conceptualization of and a treatment for parent-to-child violence. First, we present an empirical background of the mental health correlates of parent-to-child violence. Then we review the risk factors for child physical abuse in order to illustrate the need for an ecological treatment model. We describe recent work on applying an ecological treatment model and Multisystemic Therapy (MST) to parent-to-child violence.

The Effects of Child Physical Abuse: Serious Short- and Long-Term Mental Health Problems

There is no single consistent profile of symptoms for all children who experience physical abuse. Rather, the impact of physical abuse on mental health varies among children and among families, and occurs in multiple domains of functioning. Findings from multiple studies that examined the impact of child physical abuse across the developmental continuum have identified the potential for impaired short-term social and emotional functioning in 3 broad areas — externalizing,[1-22] internalizing[22-38] and cognitive problems.[16,38-49] These studies also identified the potential for impaired long-term functioning across a host of areas of maladaptation — from engaging in violent crime and antisocial behavior to substance abuse and suicide attempts (see Fig 1).[50]

Fig 1. Potential short- and long-term consequences of child physical abuse.[50]

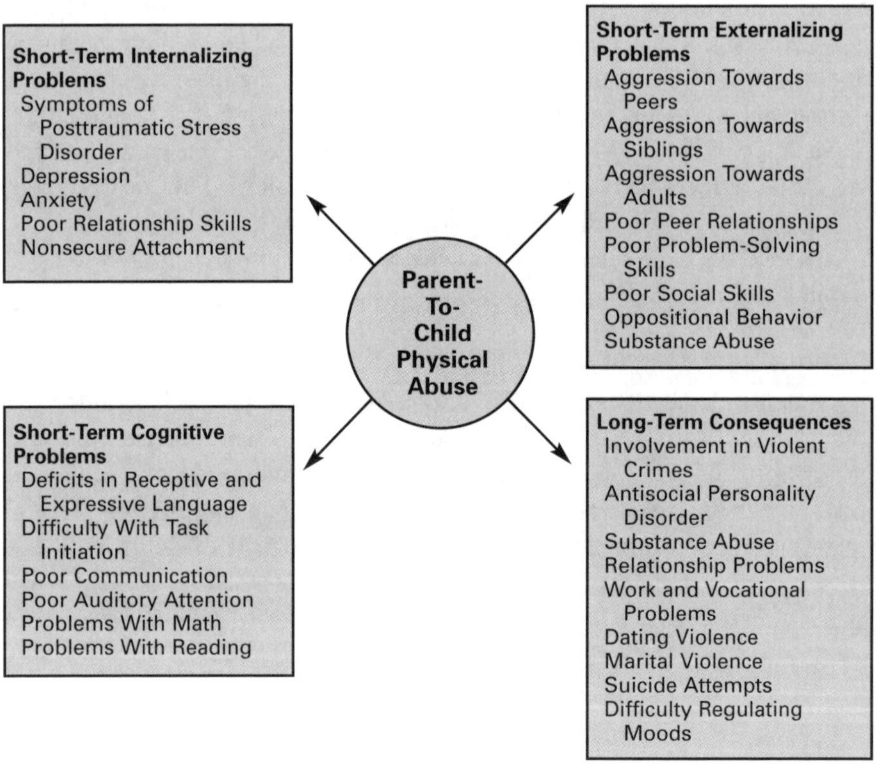

Short-term Functional Deficits Related to Child Physical Abuse

Externalizing problems

One of the most consistent findings in the literature is that physically abused children exhibit externalizing and aggressive behavior problems.[1-3] The aggression may be directed toward peers,[4-6] siblings[7] and/or adults[4,6,8] in both home and social/academic settings. Longitudinal data indicate that negative behaviors and negative affect can start as early as the toddler years and continue through preschool and early grade school years.[9,10]

Physically abused children may manifest externalizing behavior problems in their difficult relationships with peers. Empirical evidence shows that physically abused children are less socially competent than are their nonabused peers: For example, physically abused preschoolers often avoid peer interactions,[4] initiate fewer positive interactions with both peers and adults,[11] engage in less prosocial behaviors[6] and participate less frequently in parallel or group play[12] than do nonabused children. These problems with peers persist at least through early childhood.[9,10] Older physically abused children also engage less frequently in positive social interactions with both peers and adults.[7,13] Similarly, parents of physically abused children perceive their youngsters as being less socially involved, less socially skilled and less socially mature than their children's nonabused counterparts.[6,14-17] Beyond overt aggression and difficulty interacting with peers, other externalizing behavior problems include an increased propensity for violating rules,[18] oppositional behavior,[18] delinquency,[19] property offenses and arrests,[20] substance abuse[20-22] and cigarette smoking.[20-22]

Internalizing problems

Researchers who have assessed posttraumatic symptoms among physically abused children have found rates ranging from 0% to 50%[23-26] — and these symptoms may endure. Famularo and colleagues found a prevalence rate for posttraumatic stress disorder (PTSD) of 36% among physically abused children[27]; 33% still had symptoms of PTSD at the 2-year follow-up.[28] Across these studies, the majority of physically abused children were not diagnosed with PTSD, but rather reported a variety of symptoms of PTSD.[23-28] In addition, several studies indicated that child physical abuse is often associated with psychiatric diagnoses, such as depression,[29,30] agoraphobia[29] and anxiety disorders.[31,32] Child physical abuse has also been shown to contribute to lifetime disorders, such as dysthymia, when compounded by other risk factors.[22]

Internalizing problems are also evident in affected children's developmental deficits in their relationship skills. A significant body of research suggests that the maltreatment of infants and toddlers is associated with insecure attachment.[33,34] Among maltreated children, secure attachments may become insecure as the child matures.[35] Attachment problems affect an abused child in both the social and behavioral arenas. Nonsecure attachments with parents and/or caregivers in infancy are associated with poor social competence and increased aggression during the school years,[36,37] decreased readiness to learn in school[38] and an increased need for approval and/or attention seeking.[38]

Deficits in cognitive skills

Although early research documented intellectual deficits among physically abused children,[39,40] later studies did not find differences in the overall intellectual functioning of physically abused children compared with their nonabused peers.[42] Other studies reveal deficits in specific cognitive skills — including receptive language,[43] reading ability and expressive language skills,[44] initiation of tasks,[38,45] comprehension and abstraction abilities,[46] communication,[16] comprehension of social roles[47] and auditory attention and verbal fluency[46,48] — rather than in global cognitive functioning. Burke and colleagues[44] suggested that the physical aggression observed in physically abused children may, in part, result from an overreliance on physical forms of expression in the absence of adequate language skills. Academically, physically abused children perform lower on math and reading tests, and are more than twice as likely to repeat a grade as are their nonabused peers.[49] Physically abused children are also more likely to receive some type of discipline at school, including suspensions.[49]

The Long-Term Consequences of Child Physical Abuse

Moving beyond the childhood years, physical abuse as a youngster is a risk factor for mental health problems in adulthood. McCord,[51] for example, who followed 253 males from their early childhood over a 30-year period, found that the men who had been physically abused, rejected or neglected were more likely than the nonabused men to become juvenile delinquents and had higher rates of criminal convictions, mental illness and substance abuse in adulthood. In 2 other studies, Luntz and Widom[52] and Perez and Widom[53] followed 699 young adults and found that, compared with nonabused peers, individuals who were maltreated as children had higher rates of criminal offenses and antisocial personality disorders, and lower IQs and reading abilities. Retrospective data from clinical[54] and community samples[55,56] corroborate these findings: They indicate that, as adults, victims of child abuse are more likely than adults who do not have a history of abuse to have higher rates of substance abuse and psychiatric, interpersonal, vocational and antisocial behavior problems. A study by Malinosky-Rummell and Hansen showed that such victims are more likely to engage in dating violence, marital violence and suicidal attempts.[57]

Emerging research on the consequences of child abuse indicates that attachment problems may persist beyond infancy: For example, among adolescents, secure attachment is related positively to psychosocial adjustment.[58] In late adolescence and early adulthood, insecure attachment is associated with difficulties in managing conflicts with attachment figures and low confidence in regulating negative moods.[59]

As summarized, overwhelmingly, more than 2 decades of research on the impact of child physical abuse indicate that physically abused children often experience multiple mental health problems, which may place them at risk for *additional* abuse. Furthermore, child physical abuse increases the risk of serious mental health disorders in adulthood. To design effective interventions, clinicians must consider the potential for problems in multiple domains. Those researchers and clinicians designing interventions must also take into account risk factors other than those intrinsic to the child. These risk factors are discussed in the text that follows.

Risk Factors for Child Physical Abuse

Risk factors are those factors within the child and his/her ecology that correlate positively with the occurrence or recurrence of abuse. Based on descriptive reports and comparison studies, this section describes the child, parental, familial, social network and community characteristics that are associated with child physical abuse. Fig 2[50] presents a summary of the risk factors for child physical abuse across multiple systems.

Fig 2. Child, parental, familial, social network and community risk factors associated with parent-to-child physical abuse.[50]

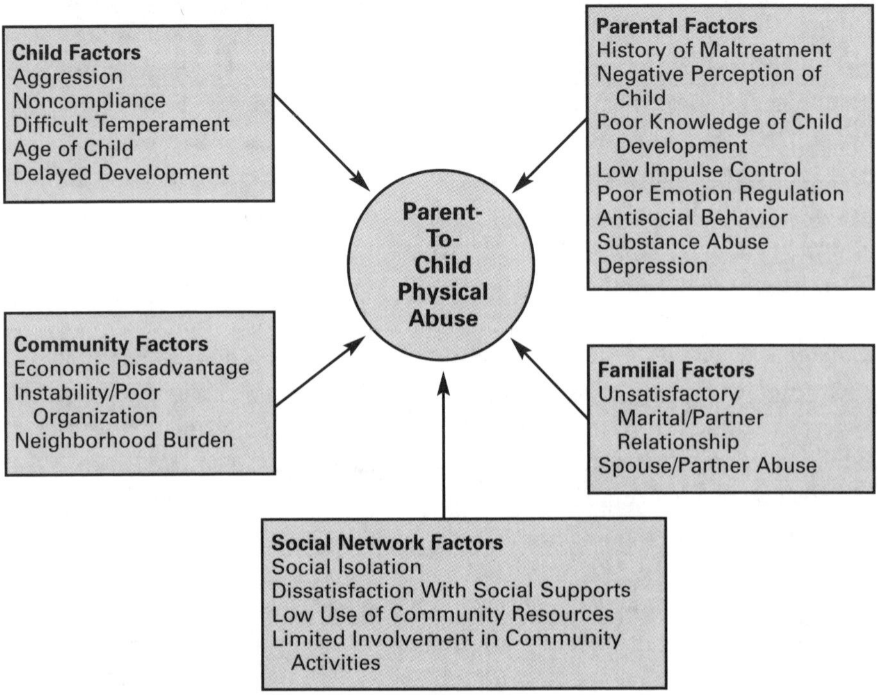

Child Risk Factors

Although children are not responsible for adults' abusive behavior, several child-based factors increase their risk of physical abuse. Primarily, noncompliant and aggressive behaviors increase a child's risk of being abused physically.[60] For infants, a difficult temperament, often manifested by prolonged crying, has been associated with physical abuse.[61] Younger and developmentally delayed children are victims of physical abuse more often than are older or nondelayed children.[62,63]

Parental Risk Factors

The characteristics of parents that correlate positively with child physical abuse are varied and cover multiple domains, and they may relate to historical events in the parents' lives that affect their current functioning.

- **History of childhood abuse.** A review by Kaufman and Zigler, published in 1987, estimated that approximately 30% of abusive parents were abused as children.[64] Therefore, while a history of child abuse may increase the risk of individuals abusing their own child, most abused children do not grow up to be abusers themselves. The specific mechanism(s) by which exposure to abuse and/or harsh punishment in childhood influences the later expression of abusive behavior is still unknown.[65,66]

- **Cognitive problems.** Empirical studies have described several cognitive problems in parents who abuse their children physically. These problems relate primarily to the parents' view of the child. One of these cognitive problems is parental attributional biases: Abusive parents tend to perceive their children in a more negative light than do nonabusive parents.[67,68] Studies with high-risk parents suggest the presence of cognitive rigidity, more critical evaluation and attributions of child noncompliance that implicate the child's negative intentions.[69-71] Parents may also report distortions in their beliefs about their children's motives. An abusive parent may see malicious intent where there is none: For example, if a child is injured, abusive parents may perceive the injury as an attempt to make them feel bad or manipulated. They may also perceive the child as responsible for certain events, the parents' welfare or other personal circumstances.[72,73] Abusers may also take responsibility for their own successes, but attribute the responsibility for their failures to the child.[74,75] Parents' negative perceptions of their children may lead the parents to be less accepting of and less empathic towards their children.[76] The biased perceptions and abuse become a vicious cycle: Blaming the child for the parents' behavior increases the risk of the parent abusing the child again and again.[74]

  In addition to attributional biases, abusive parents tend to harbor unrealistically high expectations of their children's behavior,[77] which may result in frustration with and eventually aggression toward the child. Some abusive parents consider physical discipline an appropriate form of parenting, which may contribute to their use of harsh discipline strategies[78] and a greater acceptance of physical punishment than do nonabusive parents.[79]

- **Emotion regulation problems.** Harsh parenting is associated with a variety of negative affective states, including irritability, sadness and anxiety,[78] as well as explosiveness, hostility, anger and the use of threats.[80,81] Abusive parents often engage in heightened emotion-focused coping, reflecting their reactivity to stressful circumstances.[82]

  Laboratory data support the view that some abusive parents show more adverse physiological and psychological reactions to various stressful stimuli[83] — real and/or perceived. However, the relationship between stress-induced parental emotional states and parental aggression is unclear. The heightened emotional states may be catalysts for aggression towards the child or they may result from the abusive activity itself.

- **Behavioral problems.** Several behavioral patterns are common among physically abusive parents. Impulse control problems may result in inappropriate actions, such as frequent negative or critical comments,[68] physical coercion or threats,[18] power assertion[84] or direct aggressive management practices.[70] On the other hand, behavioral deficits may take the form of more positive behaviors, such as attunement to the child,[85] positive affect and social behavior,[85] and physical affection[85] and problem-solving,[77,86] as well as prosocial control techniques.[87] Parents may also have deficits in basic parental management skills, such as a lack of monitoring or responding inappropriately to their children's behaviors.[88] Poor parenting skills or a limited knowledge of disciplinary alternatives can contribute to the use of harsh physical punishment.[88]

- **Psychiatric disorders.** The psychiatric disorders identified most frequently among physically abusive parents are depression,[68] substance abuse[68,89-92] and PTSD.[68,89-92] Clearly, such disorders may be barriers to effective parental functioning. Parental substance abuse, in particular, may decrease a parent's involvement in family activities and increase their intolerance for improper behavior by their child.[90,92,93] In addition, when a parent has a psychiatric disorder or a substance abuse problem, there is a greater likelihood that his/her child will be placed in foster care.[90,92,93]

- **Biological factors.** Research suggests that abusive parents exhibit hyperarousal to stressful child-related and non–child-related stimuli.[94,95] What is not clear is whether this hyperarousal appears in affected adults prior to any exposure to child stressors and whether it is associated with cognitive, affective or behavioral reactions to abusive behavior.

Familial Risk Factors

Although less is known about the familial risk factors that contribute to parental child abuse, several common characteristics have emerged in published studies.

- **Volatile home environment.** Observational studies have documented heightened aggressive and/or coercive behaviors among physically abusive families: Interactions among family members may be characterized by critical, hostile and/or verbally abusive behaviors.[96] In addition, hostile interactions are common between abusive parents and between abusive partners.[97,98]

- **Limited psychosocial resources.** In physically abusive families, there is often limited family cohesion and a low level of psychosocial support.[99] Limited family cohesion is associated with the potential for parental physical abuse.[100] In part, the low level of cohesion may relate to the lack of positive interactions among family members.[101]

- **General family stressors.** Employment disruptions, geographical moves, changes in financial status and other forms of instability are common among families that exhibit abuse.[102] The presence of numerous child and parent stressors correlates highly with parent-to-child violence.[103] This is especially true when family violence is present.[104,105] At a basic level, limited financial resources (ie, limited income, unemployment, inadequate housing, large family size, single parenthood) correlate positively with physical abuse.[68,106] Poverty alone is a salient correlate and predictor of child physical abuse.[68,106]

Social Network Risk Factors

Physically abusive families are often described as "isolated" and/or "lonely."[83] Affected parents and children alike may have limited contact with friends and/or family, or may be alienated completely from both. Published reports state that physically abusive families express general dissatisfaction with their social supports,[107,108] which likely contributes to the sense of isolation. Compounding the problem, abusive families tend not to use the resources available to them in their communities.[109] Parents who have limited social supports may be more susceptible to the negative effects of stress and family problems, and less bolstered by the positive influences of those within their social network.

Community Risk Factors

Studies that encompass many different regions of the United States have found the following consistent community risk factors for child maltreatment:

- **Limited finances and economic disadvantage.** Economically disadvantaged communities tend to exhibit higher rates of child maltreatment.[110-112] As noted by Emery and Laumann-Billings,[102] disadvantaged communities may have limited or nonexistent social services.
- **Instability, isolation and disorganization.** Communities with high rates of child maltreatment tend to be unstable, isolated and poorly organized.[111] In some of these neighborhoods, the instability is due to the high turnover of residents.[113] When neighborhood turnover is high, the likelihood of implementing an organizational framework and internal controls is reduced.[113]
- **Neighborhood burden.** Coulton, Korbin and Su[114] examined the relationship between child abuse and neighborhood structural variables — including poverty, child-care burden and instability. Both poverty and the burden of child care increased the potential for child maltreatment significantly.

Summary of Risk Factors

At present, there is no known single factor — or group of factors — that causes child abuse. Instead, an increased risk of child abuse is the result of a complex interaction among multiple factors within the child, parent, family, social network and community. The set of factors that determines whether a particular child in a particular family will be physically abused varies according to the characteristics of the family and the family's ecology. Therefore, *all* of the risk factors in *each* of the systems discussed previously must be considered when intervening to prevent or eliminate parent-to-child violence.

Implications for Treatment: Multiple Consequences and Correlates

The multiple, potential mental health consequences of child physical abuse (Fig 1)[50] and the risk factors in the multiple systems that make up the child's and family's ecology (Fig 2)[50] pose the following implications for the design and delivery of effective interventions:

- Given that mental health problems may occur across or within multiple domains, a thorough assessment of the youth's behavioral and cognitive functioning will help determine a baseline for key problem areas.
- The effects of physical abuse on the child may differ across various developmental periods. Therefore, therapists must be prepared to understand the various manifestations of behavioral and psychological problems and intervene in ways that are developmentally appropriate for the child and family.
- The clinician will likely find child, parental and familial problems in various domains. To address all of the key problems that increase the risk of child abuse, treatment should be comprehensive and include the child, parent(s) and family.
- Risk factors vary by family. Therefore, treatment must be individualized to match the needs of the youth and family. Treatment cannot be "one size fits all."

Summary of Treatment Implications

In sum, the multifaceted etiology of child physical abuse demands an equally multifaceted and comprehensive treatment that focuses on multiple domains of functioning: MST is such an intervention. MST is an ecologically based treatment model that addresses the youth's entire ecology. It was developed originally to treat deeply entrenched antisocial behavior in youth.[115] Recent research is continuing to examine the use of MST for the treatment of physically abused children and their families.[116] Its use in the arena of child physical abuse is warranted for the following reasons:

- Like delinquency, child physical abuse is related to numerous factors within multiple systems.
- Families who must be supervised by Child Protective Services (CPS) typically have multiple, serious needs and are overburdened by interacting with several different treatment providers.
- The majority of families in which child abuse is present either fail to engage in treatment or drop out before its completion.

The MST Model

The Theoretical Foundation

Theoretically, MST is rooted in systems theory and social ecological models of behavior. Both theories view behavior as "multidetermined" and driven largely by the relationships that the child has with others in his or her natural environment. Based primarily on the work of Bronfenbrenner,[117] Haley[118] and Minuchin,[119] the theoretical framework of MST assumes that children and adolescents are embedded in multiple systems that have direct and indirect influences on their behavior, and these influences are reciprocal and bidirectional.

Scientific Support for MST With Antisocial Youth and Their Families

Across 3 randomized, controlled trials of violent and chronic juvenile offenders, MST produced decreases of 25% to 70% in long-term rates of rearrest, and decreases of 47% to 64% in long-term rates of days in out-of-home placements.[120-122] These outcomes have resulted in considerable cost savings, bolstering the use of MST. The Washington State Institute for Public Policy concluded that MST saved $31,661 in placement and juvenile justice costs per participant.[123] Further savings from the costs to potential victims of these offenders increased this figure to $131,918 per participant. The capacity of MST to reduce adolescent conduct problems has been demonstrated in several other populations of youth who have serious clinical problems.[124,125]

Clinical Features of Standard MST

To facilitate replication studies and the implementation of MST programs in community settings, researchers and clinicians have developed, and described extensively, the following standardized components of MST:

- **A set of principles that guide the formulation of clinical interventions.** The clinical practice of MST follows 9 principles[126] (Table 1). Several studies have shown that positive outcomes for youth are associated significantly with therapists' adherence to these 9 principles (see upcoming text).

- **Family-friendly engagement process.** The MST therapist and clinical team are responsible for engaging families and achieving desired outcomes.[127] As the first step in treatment, the therapist must discover how to engage the family and others in treatment to achieve the targeted outcome(s). Families may be reluctant initially to collaborate with the therapist, especially when they are under the supervision of CPS: They may cancel appointments or may not return phone calls. There are, however, many perfectly valid reasons why a family may not be willing to engage in treatment: For example, family members may not trust the system providing the therapy or they may be concerned that the therapist is "collaborating" with CPS to remove the child/children from the family. One of the therapist's first tasks is to address these issues with the family.

  Several aspects of MST are designed specifically to promote family engagement in treatment:

  - MST therapists focus on the family's strengths rather than their deficits. Therefore, attribution of blame to parents or other family members for the child's behavior is not part of the process.

Table 1. The 9 Treatment Principles of Multisystemic Therapy (MST)[126]

Principle 1:	The primary purpose of assessment is to understand the fit between the identified problems and their broader systemic context.
Principle 2:	Therapeutic contacts emphasize the positive and use systemic strengths as levers for change.
Principle 3:	Interventions are designed to promote responsible behavior and decrease irresponsible behavior among family members.
Principle 4:	Interventions are present-focused and action-oriented, targeting specific and well-defined problems.
Principle 5:	Interventions target sequences of behavior within and between multiple systems that maintain the identified problems.
Principle 6:	Interventions are developmentally appropriate and fit the developmental needs of the youth.
Principle 7:	Interventions are designed to require daily or weekly effort by family members.
Principle 8:	Intervention effectiveness is evaluated continuously from multiple perspectives with providers assuming accountability for overcoming barriers to successful outcomes.
Principle 9:	Interventions are designed to promote treatment generalization and long-term maintenance of therapeutic change by empowering caregivers to address family members' needs across multiple systemic contexts.

Reprinted with permission from *Multisystemic Therapy and Neighborhood Partnerships: Reducing Adolescent Violence and Substance Abuse.* Copyright 2004. The Guilford Press.

- The home-based model of service delivery used in MST facilitates engagement by overcoming common barriers to getting services to clients, including lack of transportation or fear of accessing care in an unfamiliar setting. Families are often more comfortable on their own "turf" than they are in a clinic setting, and they may be more open to having a therapist come to their home instead of having to navigate through traffic or new places.

- Treatment is a collaborative process that focuses on the problems that families have identified as important to them.
- Most therapists do not "give up" on a family that is making limited progress. Rather, they assess the situation and seek to understand the family's barriers to engagement or progress. Then they implement new strategies to overcome these barriers.
- Engagement is viewed as an ongoing process that continues throughout the course of treatment, rather than as a perfunctory task that can be completed quickly. The therapist monitors the family's level of engagement continuously and takes corrective actions when engagement is low or waning. Engagement is a necessary, but not sufficient, condition for achieving positive clinical outcomes.

• **Structured analytical process used to prioritize interventions.** The MST analytical process provides a structured guide for treatment[128] (Fig 3). After identifying the problem behaviors based on information received from individuals in various systems (ie, caregivers, youth, teachers, CPS workers and other vested parties), the therapist consolidates the targets for change and obtains a baseline measure of these behaviors. Next, the therapist recruits the key individuals in the child's natural ecology and they become the treatment team. Through in-depth interviews, each team member provides his/her perspectives on the targeted problem behaviors, the strengths of the family and each system, and the changes that will be necessary to achieve success. The therapist uses this information to develop the overarching goals of treatment in a way that promotes ownership by all key participants.

The overarching goals define the scope and end point of treatment with MST. These goals must be concrete, measurable and realistic for the treatment's time frame. All interventions must relate to at least one of the overarching goals. When these goals are reached, treatment is complete.

After identifying the goals of treatment, the therapist prioritizes the necessary interactions and relationship changes by examining how the problem behaviors *fit* within the context of the youth's natural ecology: For example, if the child is not following the parents' rules, the therapist uses the input from each of the systems to record on a "fit circle" the possible factors driving the problem behavior (eg, the flouting of a rule). The therapist may then determine that the child's noncompliance is associated with, for example, one or more of the following "fit factors":

Fig 3. The MST analytical process.[128]

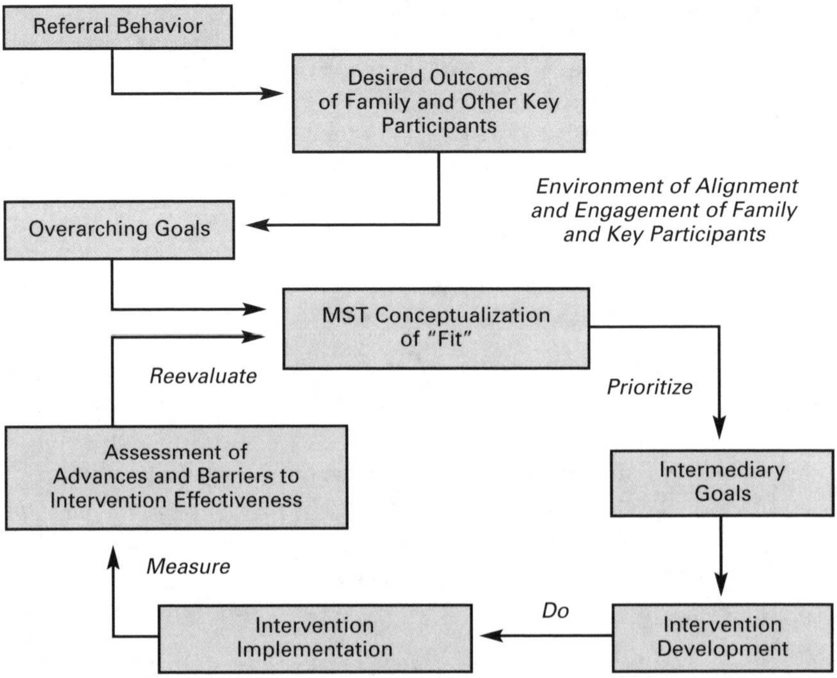

Reprinted with permission from *Multisystemic Therapy and Neighborhood Partnerships: Reducing Adolescent Violence and Substance Abuse.* Copyright 2004. The Guilford Press.

- The parent has limited parenting skills.
- Interactions between the parent and child often escalate.
- The parent is depressed and, as a result, rarely monitors the child's behavior.

After the therapist has identified the fit factors, the entire clinical team determines those factors that appear to be the primary drivers of the behavior problems. Initially, the treatment targets these factors for change, and these changes are defined as "intermediary goals": For example, the clinical team may determine that the lack of parental rules or of specific consequences for inappropriate behaviors is the primary factor driving the problem. Therefore, therapeutic attention would focus on working with the family to establish rules and consequences for not adhering to the rules. This type of change in parental management of the child's noncompliance is viewed as one of the intermediary goals — a change that will lead ultimately to the overarching treatment goal. If the child becomes compliant through more effective parental management of the behavior, it may not be necessary to attend to the other fit factors.

Throughout the intervention, the therapist and team members compare the intended outcomes with the actual outcomes and measure the successes achieved. If sufficient success is not achieved within a given time frame, the clinical team and the family will seek to identify the barriers to reaching the treatment goals. This newly arrived at information is then compared with or added to the current understanding of how the behaviors *"fit"* within the natural ecology, and the iterative process of identifying fit factors, prioritizing needed changes and intervening and evaluating begins anew. This structured analytic process continues until the overarching goals of therapy are achieved. Throughout treatment, the therapist helps the family to address any problems as independently as possible and to build a support system to help maintain the changes that have been achieved.

- **Evidence-based treatment techniques that are integrated into the MST conceptual framework.** MST incorporates interventions that have empirical support, such as the cognitive–behavioral therapies, behavioral therapies, pragmatic family therapies and certain pharmacological interventions (eg, for attention deficit-hyperactivity disorder). However, there are several differences between using these techniques within MST and using them alone. First, within MST, the child's ecology — *not* the individual child or the family — is the client. The evidence-based treatments to be used in MST have focused historically on a limited aspect of the youth's social ecology — for example, individual cognitive behavioral therapy for the treatment of anger management. In contrast, MST integrates these treatments into a broad-based ecological framework that addresses a range of pertinent factors across the family, peer group, school and community contexts. Second, because MST views caregivers as playing a critical role in achieving favorable long-term outcomes, interventions are delivered primarily by the caregivers whenever possible: For example, cognitive–behavior therapy used for improving a youth's management of his anger might be taught to the father by the therapist, and the father would then teach these skills to his son. Third, in stark contrast to how the vast majority of evidence-based interventions are delivered in the field, interventions using MST are supported by a strong, outcome-oriented quality assurance system that aims to enhance intervention fidelity and facilitate the attainment of desired clinical outcomes.

- **Home-based delivery of services that enables the provision of intensive therapy.** In all of the MST research studies and among all of the dissemination sites of MST in the United States and abroad, services are delivered in the home or in locations that are convenient to the affected families. The home-based model removes barriers to service access and increases the capacity of interventions to alter the youth's ecology. The key characteristics of the service delivery of MST include the following:
  - Low caseloads of 3 to 6 families allow clinicians to provide very personalized, intensive services to each family (2 hours to 15 hours per week, titrated to need).
  - Therapists work within a team of 3 to 4 practitioners; however, each clinician has his/her own caseload.
  - Treatment sessions may occur daily or several times per week; sessions decrease in frequency as the family progresses.
  - Treatment is time-limited and generally lasts for 4 months to 6 months, depending on the seriousness of the problems and the effectiveness of the interventions.
  - Treatment is delivered in the family's natural environment: in their home, in their community or in other places convenient to them.
  - Treatment is delivered at times convenient to the family; therefore, therapists work a flexible schedule.
  - Therapists are available to clients 24 hours per day, 7 days per week, generally through an on-call system.

  Through this home-based, service-delivery system, MST provides very intensive clinical services that are designed to keep children with the family unit, thereby preventing out-of-home placements. Such intensive, expensive services can be cost-effective when targeted to youth who are at high risk of out-of-home placement.[123]

- **Highly supportive supervision process.** MST clinical supervisors interact face-to-face with therapists, on average, 2 hours to 4 hours each week and are available 24 hours per day, 7 days per week on an on-call basis.

In addition, the clinical supervisor consults with therapists, as needed, and even attends therapy sessions if there are safety concerns or if clinical skill building is required.

The sole purpose of MST clinical supervision is to help therapists achieve the desired clinical outcomes with their client families. MST clinical supervision accomplishes the following:

- provides therapists with an understanding of the MST model
- facilitates therapists' adherence to the 9 treatment principles
- helps therapists determine how to engage families and key individuals from other systems
- helps therapists implement evidence-based techniques
- helps therapists identify barriers to the success of interventions

As specified in *The MST Supervisory Manual*,[129] the clinical supervisor is responsible for building the therapist's capacity to be effective. This is accomplished by determining the barriers to low adherence to the treatment principles of MST, when evident, and developing strategies to overcome those barriers, including providing additional learning experiences, reviewing and offering feedback on therapy sessions and/or accompanying the therapist during family sessions.

Weekly supervisory sessions are structured and goal oriented. Supervision is provided in a group format, which assures that each therapist is familiar with every case. This case familiarity is important since the therapists must develop an on-call schedule that requires that each periodically assumes responsibility for crisis response during nights, weekends and therapist vacations. Likewise, therapists have usually met each others' client families, which increases the families' and therapists' comfort levels in handling crises at a time when the primary therapist is unavailable.

- **Stringent quality assurance process to promote treatment fidelity.** Several published studies[122,130-132] have demonstrated a significant association between therapist fidelity to the treatment principles of MST and outcomes for affected youth and families. In light of these findings, the field has devoted considerable attention to quality assurance mechanisms aimed at enhancing treatment fidelity. The quality assurance system includes the following: an orientation training week; weekly on-site MST supervision; weekly telephone consultation with an expert in MST;

quarterly "booster" training on needed skills, as identified by the team; feedback on adherence ratings from parents and fellow therapists; and, during MST clinical trials, feedback via expert ratings of audiotaped therapy sessions.

With the exception of MST treatment that is provided within the context of research programs in clinical trials, all components of the quality assurance system are provided by MST Services (http://www.mstservices.com), which owns the exclusive license for MST technology and intellectual property through the Medical University of South Carolina.

Applying MST to the Problem of Parent-to-Child Physical Abuse

In an ongoing randomized clinical trial,[50] researchers at the Medical University of South Carolina are applying MST in cases of child physical abuse to address the following gaps in the scientific literature:

- Only a few recent studies have included comparison groups.
- The majority of recent studies did not use random assignment.
- Only a few studies have measured recidivism or the reincidence of abuse.
- Only a few studies have collected follow-up data.
- Little is known about the efficacy of treatments for physically abused adolescents.
- Virtually nothing is known about the effectiveness of treatments for physically abused adolescents.

This study, known as PEACE, Betta Fuh Fambly — the Project Empowering Adults, Children and their Ecology, for the Family (in the Gullah language; an English-based creole language spoken by African Americans inhabiting the sea islands and coastal areas of South Carolina, Georgia and northeastern Florida) — is a 5-year clinical trial funded by the National Institute of Mental Health. Participants include adolescents ages 10 years to 17 years who are referred by CPS because of physical abuse by a parent or caregiver. The study is being conducted in "the real world" of a community mental health center — the Charleston/Dorchester Community Mental Health Center.

PEACE, Betta Fuh Fambly, is following a 2-by-5 design: 2 groups with 5 assessments (at baseline, and at 2 months, 4 months, 10 months and 16 months). Investigators have assigned 86 families randomly to either MST or parent group therapy using Systematic Training for Effective Parenting of Teens (STEP-TEEN)[133] plus current community services. Assessments measure functioning across multiple systems: the child (eg, using the Children's Depression Inventory[134]); the parent(s) (eg, using the Conflict Tactics Scale[135]); the family (eg, using the Family Adaptability and Cohesion Evaluation Scale [3rd edition][136]); reabuse rates based on CPS records; cost; and service utilization.

PEACE: Adaptations to Standard MST

Since MST was developed and validated originally using families and the youth who exhibited antisocial behavior, the PEACE study required adaptations of the model to meet the needs of the participants. The current study standardized the following 9 adaptations:

- family safety planning
- functional analysis of the use of force or physical discipline
- treatment for PTSD
- treatment for anger management
- treatment for substance abuse
- family communication training
- "clarification" of the abuse
- inclusion of a psychiatrist
- involving CPS in treatment

Family safety planning. Although safety is always a critical issue when working with families that have mental health needs, it is of particular importance when counseling abusive families. The foremost goal of treatment is to maintain the physical safety of the youth and other family members. In the PEACE study, therapists conduct safety planning during the initial contact — and in subsequent sessions — with families. The safety plan includes a written "contract" developed by the family with the help of the therapist. The plan draws on the resources of the family, the extended family and friends and neighbors to assist during times of crises.

Functional analysis of the use of force or physical discipline. An integral part of standard MST is the use of the analytical process to determine how multiple factors contribute to symptoms — as well as the appropriate points of intervention. Building on this, functional analyses[50] are used in the PEACE study to evaluate the circumstances leading up to incidents of abuse (sometimes as distally as the day before), what occurred at the time of the abuse and the consequences following the incidents. The MST therapist completes functional analyses throughout the treatment process whenever there are events that threaten the safety of the family members or that constitute conflict.

Treatment for PTSD. One of the many lessons learned during the PEACE study is the critical importance of evaluating and treating the mental and physical health needs of the parents/caregivers of abused youth. In particular, PTSD appears to influence strongly a caregiver's capacity to parent effectively: Across families in which PTSD is identified in caregivers, MST therapists use cognitive–behavioral techniques, including exposure[137,138] and cognitive restructuring,[139,140] to reduce anxiety and assist in the resolution of traumatic events.

Treatment for anger management. Often, abusive parents *and* children who have been abused physically have difficulties with anger management. Using a cognitive–behavioral approach to treatment,[141,142] therapists in the PEACE study assess caregivers and youth participants for deficits in anger management and provide interventions when necessary. This protocol assumes that anger occurs in response to stress or provocation, and that the options for coping that are available during the time of stress need to be modified.

Treatment for substance abuse. The Community Reinforcement Approach (CRA), an empirically validated method of treating substance abuse that combines cognitive–behavioral techniques and an incentive program, is being used in the PEACE study.[143,144] CRA has been used across several MST programs when substance abuse was identified in either the youth or caregivers.

Family communication training. As part of its overall goal, the PEACE study trains parents and adolescents to communicate more effectively to solve problems.[145] The training protocol, which applies cognitive and behavioral techniques to problematic parent-adolescent interactions, helps the family understand when a situation may become conflictual and how to respond in a proactive manner using problem-solving skills.

"Clarification" of the abuse. Parents who abuse their children physically and blame the child for their actions are likely to repeat the abuse.[74] Conducting a "clarification" is a method for understanding the parent's thinking about an incident, intervening to elucidate for the parent the maladaptive nature of his/her thinking and subsequently helping the parent accept responsibility for the abusive actions and apologize to the child and the family. In the PEACE project, the clarification is conducted by having the abusive parent write a letter to the child and the family. This exercise spans at least a few therapeutic sessions — as the letter goes through several drafts — giving the therapist an opportunity to understand and correct any distortions the parent may have regarding the child and his/her responsibility for the abuse. The process culminates in a family meeting during which the responsibility for the abusive action is clarified verbally.

Inclusion of a psychiatrist. The PEACE study has taught us that maltreated children often have severe emotional problems that require the care of a psychiatrist — in a manner that is supportive of the MST model. In addition, many of the parents/caregivers have been proven to need medication management to stabilize them prior to the implementation of interventions that focus on them. The integration of evidence-based psychiatric interventions is now a *required* adaptation of MST when working with maltreating families.

Involving CPS in treatment. Consistent with the standard MST model, the PEACE study implements interventions within each of the critical systems that surround a child. For maltreated youth, one of the most visible systems is CPS. When a child is referred to the PEACE project, by definition he/she has been assigned to a CPS caseworker. The relationship that a family has with CPS may influence greatly their engagement in treatment and, conversely, their engagement in treatment may influence greatly the family's relationship with CPS. By involving the CPS caseworker in treatment, the MST therapist is in a position to help facilitate the development of a working relationship between the 2 parties that is most beneficial to the family.

Conclusions

Every aspect of parent-to-child violence is a complex problem. When the needs of abusive families are dealt with in standard, 1-hour-per-week, office-based therapy, only the surface issues are scratched. Many families inevitably receive no services whatsoever because they terminate treatment.

The long-term consequences of child physical abuse are too long-lasting and too grave not to venture beyond standard therapies to apply intensive treatments in an attempt to prevent adolescent and adulthood PTSD, violent crime, substance abuse, depression and an ongoing cycle of family violence.

PEACE, Betta Fuh Fambly, uses the guidance of existing scientific literature on the impact of abuse, the correlates of abuse and empirically supported treatments, and applies them through a model of MST to address the multiple, serious needs of abusive families. To address the needs of these families as completely as possible, the study made adaptations to the standard model of MST for juvenile delinquency: These adaptations include standardizing empirically supported treatment techniques for problems that are common to physically abusive families.

While this model may not be needed for all families who experience parent-to-child violence, families in which physical abuse is entrenched deeply may benefit from this type of intensive work that focuses on eliminating the violence and enabling the family to live together *in peace.*

Acknowledgment

Preparation of this manuscript was supported by grant R01MH60663-01 from the National Institute of Mental Health.

References

1. Conaway LP, Hansen DJ. Social behavior of physically abused and neglected children: a critical review. *Clinical Psychology Review.* 1989;9:627-652.
2. Kolko DJ. Individual cognitive behavioral treatment and family therapy for physically abused children and their offending parents: a comparison of clinical outcomes. *Child Maltreatment.* 1996;1:322-342.
3. National Research Council Panel on Research on Child Abuse and Neglect. *Understanding Child Abuse and Neglect.* Washington, DC: National Academy Press; 1993.
4. George C, Main M. Social interactions of young abused children: approach, avoidance, and aggression. *Child Development.* 1979;50:306-318.
5. Haskett ME, Kistner JA. Social interactions and peer perceptions of young physically abused children. *Child Development.* 1991;62:979-990.
6. Hoffman-Plotkin D, Twentyman CT. A multimodal assessment of behavioral and cognitive deficits in abused and neglected preschoolers. *Child Development.* 1984;55:794-802.
7. Burgess RL, Conger RD. Family interaction in abusive, neglectful, and normal families. *Child Development.* 1978;49:1163-1173.
8. Reidy TJ. The aggressive characteristics of abused and neglected children. *Journal of Clinical Psychology.* 1977;33:1140-1145.

9. Egeland B, Sroufe LA, Erickson M. The developmental consequence of different patterns of maltreatment. *Child Abuse & Neglect.* 1983;7:459-469.
10. Egeland B. A longitudinal study of high risk families: issues and findings. In: Starr RH Jr, Wolfe DA, eds. *The Effects of Child Abuse and Neglect: Issues and Research.* New York, NY: The Guilford Press; 1991:33-56.
11. Howes C, Espinosa MP. The consequences of child abuse for the formation of relationships with peers. *Child Abuse & Neglect.* 1985;9:397-404.
12. Alessandria SM. Play and social behavior in maltreated preschoolers. *Development and Psychopathology.* 1991;3:191-205.
13. Kaufman J, Cicchetti D. Effects of maltreatment on school-age children's socioemotional development: assessments in a day-camp setting. *Developmental Psychology.* 1989;25:516-524.
14. Kravic JN. Behavior problems and social competence of clinic-referred abused children. *Journal of Family Violence.* 1987;2:111-120.
15. Mash EJ, Johnston C, Kovitz K. A comparison of the mother-child interactions of physically abused and non-abused children during play and task situations. *Journal of Clinical Child Psychology.* 1983;12:337-346.
16. Perry MA, Doran LD, Wells EA. Developmental and behavioral characteristics of the physically abused child. *Journal of Clinical Child Psychology.* 1983;12:320-324.
17. Wolfe DA, Mosk MD. Behavioral comparisons of children from abusive and distressed families. *Journal of Consulting and Clinical Psychology.* 1983;51:702-708.
18. Trickett PK, Kuczynski L. Children's misbehaviors and parental discipline strategies in abusive and nonabusive families. *Developmental Psychology.* 1986;22:115-123.
19. Walker E, Downey G, Bergman A. The effects of parental psychopathology and maltreatment on child behavior: a test of the diathesis-stress model. *Child Development.* 1989;60:15-24.
20. Gelles RJ, Straus MA. The medical and psychological costs of family violence. In: Straus MA, Gelles RJ, eds. *Physical Violence in American Families: Risk Factors and Adaptations to Violence in 8,145 Families.* New Brunswick, NJ: Transaction Publishers; 1990:425-430.
21. Hotaling GT, Straus MA, Lincoln AJ. Intrafamily violence and crime and violence outside the family. In: Straus MA, Gelles RJ, eds. *Physical Violence in American Families: Risk Factors and Adaptations to Violence in 8,145 Families.* New Brunswick, NJ: Transaction Publishers; 1990:431-470.
22. Kaplan SJ, Pelcovitz D, Salzinger S, et al. Adolescent physical abuse: risk for adolescent psychiatric disorders. *The American Journal of Psychiatry.* 1998;155:954-959.
23. Deblinger E, McLeer SV, Atkins MS, Ralphe D, Foa E. Post-traumatic stress in sexually abused, physically abused, and nonabused children. *Child Abuse & Neglect.* 1989;13:403-408.
24. Famularo R, Fenton T, Kinscherff R. Child maltreatment and the development of posttraumatic stress disorder. *American Journal of Diseases in Children.* 1993;147:755-760.
25. Kiser LJ, Heston J, Millsap PA, Pruitt DB. Physical and sexual abuse in childhood: relationship with post-traumatic stress disorder. *Journal of the American Academy of Child and Adolescent Psychiatry.* 1991;30:776-783.
26. Pelcovitz D, Kaplan S, Goldenberg B, Mandel F, Lehane J, Guarrera J. Post-traumatic stress disorder in physically abused adolescents. *Journal of the American Academy of Child and Adolescent Psychiatry.* 1994;33:305-312.
27. Famularo R, Fenton T, Kinscherff R, Ayoub C, Barnum R. Maternal and child posttraumatic stress disorder in cases of child maltreatment. *Child Abuse & Neglect.* 1994;18:27-36.
28. Famularo R, Fenton T, Augustyn M, Zuckerman B. Persistence of pediatric post traumatic stress disorder after 2 years. *Child Abuse & Neglect.* 1996;20:1245-1248.
29. Flisher AJ, Kramer RA, Hoven CW, et al. Psychosocial characteristics of physically abused children and adolescents. *Journal of the American Academy of Child and Adolescent Psychiatry.* 1997;36:123-131.
30. Kazdin AE, Moser J, Colbus D, Bell R. Depressive symptoms among physically abused and psychiatrically disturbed children. *Journal of Abnormal Psychology.* 1985;94:298-307.

31. Kinard EM. Emotional development in physically abused children. *The American Journal of Orthopsychiatry.* 1980;50:686-696.
32. Kinard EM. Experiencing child abuse: effects on emotional adjustment. *The American Journal of Orthopsychiatry.* 1982;52:82-91.
33. Crittenden PM, Ainsworth MS. Child maltreatment and attachment theory. In: Cicchetti D, Carlson VK, eds. *Child Maltreatment: Theory and Research on the Causes and Consequences of Child Abuse and Neglect.* New York, NY: Cambridge University Press; 1989:432-463.
34. Carlson V, Cicchetti D, Barnett D, Braunwald KG. Finding order in disorganization: lessons from research on maltreated infants' attachments to their caregivers. In: Cicchetti D, Carlson VK, eds. *Child Maltreatment: Theory and Research on the Causes and Consequences of Child Abuse and Neglect.* New York, NY: Cambridge University Press; 1989:494-528.
35. Cicchetti D, Barnett D. Attachment organization in maltreated preschoolers. *Development and Psychopathology.* 1991;3:397-411.
36. Lamb ME, Nash A. Infant-mother attachment, sociability, and peer competence. In: Berndt TJ, Ladd GW, eds. *Peer Relationships in Child Development.* New York, NY: John Wiley & Sons; 1989: 219-245.
37. Mueller E, Silverman N. Peer relations in maltreated children. In: Cicchetti D, Carlson VK, eds. *Child Maltreatment: Theory and Research on the Causes and Consequences of Child Abuse and Neglect.* New York, NY: Cambridge University Press; 1989:529-578.
38. Aber JL, Allen JP. Effects of maltreatment on young children's socioemotional development: an attachment theory perspective. *Developmental Psychology.* 1987;23:406-414.
39. Kempe CH, Silverman FN, Steele BF, Droegemueller W, Silver HK. The battered-child syndrome. *JAMA: The Journal of the American Medical Association.* 1962;181:17-24.
40. Martin HP, Rodeheffer MA. The psychological impact of abuse on children. *Journal of Pediatric Psychology.* 1976;1:12-15.
41. Lynch MA, Roberts J. *The Consequences of Child Abuse.* London, England: Academic Press; 1982.
42. McFadyen RG, Kitson WJH. Language comprehension and expression among adolescents who have experienced childhood physical abuse. *Journal of Child Psychology and Psychiatry, and Allied Disciplines.* 1996;37:551-562.
43. Vondra JA, Barnett D, Cicchetti D. Perceived and actual competence among maltreated and comparison school children. *Development and Psychopathology.* 1989;1:237-255.
44. Burke AE, Crenshaw DA, Green J, Schlosser MA, Strocchia-Rivera L. Influence of verbal ability on the expression of aggression in physically abused children. *Journal of the American Academy of Child and Adolescent Psychiatry.* 1989;28:215-218.
45. Allen DM, Tarnowski KJ. Depressive characteristics of physically abused children. *Journal of Abnormal Child Psychology.* 1989;17:1-11.
46. Tarter RE, Hegedus AM, Winsten NE, Alterman AI. Neuropsychological, personality, and familial characteristics of physically abused delinquents. *Journal of the American Academy of Child Psychiatry.* 1984;23:668-674.
47. Barahal RM, Waterman J, Martin HP. The social cognitive development of abused children. *Journal of Consulting and Clinical Psychology.* 1981;49:508-516.
48. Tarter RE, Hegedus AM, Winsten NE, Alterman AI. Intellectual profiles and violent behavior in juvenile delinquents. *The Journal of Psychology.* 1985;119:125-128.
49. Eckenrode J, Laird M, Doris J. School performance and disciplinary problems among abused and neglected children. *Developmental Psychology.* 1993;29:53-62.
50. Kolko DJ, Swenson CC. *Assessing and Treating Physically Abused Children and Their Families: A Cognitive-Behavioral Approach.* Thousand Oaks, Calif: Sage Publications; 2002.
51. McCord J. A forty year perspective on effects of child abuse and neglect. *Child Abuse & Neglect.* 1983;7:265-270.
52. Luntz BK, Widom CS. Antisocial personality disorder in abused and neglected children grown up. *The American Journal of Psychiatry.* 1994;151:670-674.

53. Perez CM, Widom CS. Childhood victimization and long-term intellectual and academic outcomes. *Child Abuse & Neglect.* 1994;18:617-633.
54. Surrey J, Swett C Jr, Michaels A, Levin S. Reported history of physical and sexual abuse and severity of symptomatology in women psychiatric outpatients. *The American Journal of Orthopsychiatry.* 1990;60:412-417.
55. Duncan RD, Saunders BE, Kilpatrick DG, Hanson RS, Resnick HS. Childhood physical assault as a risk factor for PTSD, depression, and substance abuse: findings from a national survey. *The American Journal of Orthopsychiatry.* 1996;66:437-448.
56. Pollock VE, Briere J, Schneider L, Knop J, Mednick SA, Goodwin DW. Childhood antecedents of antisocial behavior: parental alcoholism and physical abusiveness. *The American Journal of Psychiatry.* 1990;147:1290-1293.
57. Malinosky-Rummell R, Hansen DJ. Long-term consequences of childhood physical abuse. *Psychological Bulletin.* 1993;114:68-79.
58. Noom MJ, Dekovic M, Meeus WHJ. Autonomy, attachment and psychosocial adjustment during adolescence: a double-edged sword? *Journal of Adolescence.* 1999;22:771-783.
59. Creasey G, Kershaw K, Boston A. Conflict management with friends and romantic partners: the role of attachment and negative mood regulation expectancies. *Journal of Youth and Adolescence.* 1999;28:523-543.
60. Belsky J. Etiology of child maltreatment: a developmental-ecological analysis. *Psychological Bulletin.* 1993;114:413-434.
61. Frodi AM. Contribution of infant characteristics to child abuse. *American Journal of Mental Deficiency.* 1981;85:341-349.
62. Ammerman RT, Van Hasselt VB, Hersen M, McGonigle JJ, Lubetsky MJ. Abuse and neglect in psychiatrically hospitalized multihandicapped children. *Child Abuse & Neglect.* 1989;13:335-343.
63. Diamond LJ, Jaudes PK. Child abuse in a cerebral-palsied population. *Developmental Medicine and Child Neurology.* 1983;25:169-174.
64. Kaufman J, Zigler E. Do abused children become abusive parents? *The American Journal of Orthopsychiatry.* 1987;57:186-192.
65. Cappell C, Heiner RB. The intergenerational transmission of family aggression. *Journal of Family Violence.* 1990;5:135-151.
66. Straus MA, Smith C. Family patterns and child abuse. In: Straus MA, Gelles RJ, eds. *Physical Violence in American Families: Risk Factors and Adaptations to Violence in 8,145 Families.* New Brunswick, NJ: Transaction Publishers; 1990:245-261.
67. Azar ST, Siegel BR. Behavioral treatment of child abuse. A developmental perspective. *Behavior Modification.* 1990;14:279-300.
68. Whipple EE, Webster-Stratton C. The role of parental stress in physically abusive families. *Child Abuse & Neglect.* 1991;15:279-291.
69. Dopke CA, Milner JS. Impact of child noncompliance on stress appraisals, attributions, and disciplinary choices in mothers at high and low risk for child physical abuse. *Child Abuse & Neglect.* 2000;24:493-504.
70. Caselles CE, Milner JS. Evaluations of child transgressions, disciplinary choices, and expected child compliance in a no-cry and a crying infant condition in physically abusive and comparison mothers. *Child Abuse & Neglect.* 2000;24:477-491.
71. Nayak MB, Milner JS. Neuropsychological functioning: comparison of mothers at high- and low-risk for child physical abuse. *Child Abuse & Neglect.* 1998;22:687-703.
72. Azar ST. The determinants of "maladaptive" parenting: validation of a social cognitive model. Poster presented at: New Directions in Child and Family Research: Shaping Head Start in the Nineties Conference; June 1991; Arlington, Va.
73. Azar ST. A cognitive behavioral approach to understanding and treating parents who physically abuse their children. In: Wolfe DA, McMahon RJ, Peters RD, eds. *Child Abuse: New Directions in Prevention and Treatment Across the Lifespan.* Thousand Oaks, Calif: Sage Publications; 1997:79-101. Banff Conference on Behavioral Science series, vol 4.

74. Bradley EJ, Peters RD. Physically abusive and nonabusive mothers' perceptions of parenting and child behavior. *The American Journal of Orthopsychiatry.* 1991;61:455-460.

75. Bugental DB, Mantyla SM, Lewis J. Parental attributions as moderators of affective communication to children at risk for physical abuse. In: Cicchetti D, Carlson VK, eds. *Child Maltreatment: Theory and Research on the Causes and Consequences of Child Abuse and Neglect.* New York, NY: Cambridge University Press; 1989:254-279.

76. Mash EJ, Johnston C. Determinants of parenting stress: illustrations from families of hyperactive children and families of physically abused children. *Journal of Clinical Psychology.* 1990;19:313-328.

77. Azar ST, Robinson DR, Hekimian E, Twentyman CT. Unrealistic expectations and problem-solving ability in maltreating and comparison mothers. *Journal of Consulting and Clinical Psychology.* 1984;52:687-691.

78. Simons RL, Whitbeck LB, Conger RD, Wu C. Intergenerational transmission of harsh parenting. *Developmental Psychology.* 1991;27:159-171.

79. Kelley ML, Grace N, Elliott SN. Acceptability of positive and punitive discipline methods: comparisons among abusive, potentially abusive, and nonabusive parents. *Child Abuse & Neglect.* 1990; 14:219-226.

80. Caspi A, Elder GH. Emergent family patterns: the intergenerational construction of problem behaviour and relationships. In: Hinde RA, Stevenson-Hinde J, eds. *Relationships With Families: Mutual Influences.* Oxford, England: Clarendon Press; 1988:218-240.

81. Patterson GR, DeBaryshe BD, Ramsey E. A developmental perspective on antisocial behavior. *The American Psychologist.* 1989;44:329-335.

82. Cantos AL, Neale JM, O'Leary KD, Gaines RW. Assessment of coping strategies of child abusing mothers. *Child Abuse & Neglect.* 1997;21:631-636.

83. Milner JS, Dopke C. Child physical abuse: review of offender characteristics. In: Wolfe DA, McMahon RJ, Peters RD, eds. *Child Abuse: New Directions in Prevention and Treatment Across the Lifespan.* Thousand Oaks, Calif: Sage Publications; 1997:27-54. Banff Conference on Behavioral Science series, vol 4.

84. Dolz L, Cerezo MA, Milner JS. Mother-child interactional patterns in high- and low-risk mothers. *Child Abuse & Neglect.* 1997;21:1149-1158.

85. Kavanagh KA, Youngblade L, Reid JB, Fagot BI. Interactions between children and abusive versus control parents. *Journal of Clinical Child Psychology.* 1988;17:137-142.

86. Hansen DJ, Pallotta GM, Tishelman AC, et al. Parental problem-solving skills and child behavior problems: a comparison of physically abusive, neglectful, clinic and community families. *Journal of Family Violence.* 1988;4:353-368.

87. Alessandria SM. Mother-child interactional correlates of maltreated and nonmaltreated children's play behavior. *Development and Psychopathology.* 1992;4:257-270.

88. Susman EJ, Trickett PK, Iannotti RJ, Hollenbeck BE, Zahn-Waxler C. Child-rearing patterns in depressed, abusive, and normal mothers. *The American Journal of Orthopsychiatry.* 1985;55:237-251.

89. Famularo R, Kinscherff R, Fenton T. Parental substance abuse and the nature of child maltreatment. *Child Abuse & Neglect.* 1992;16:475-483.

90. Famularo R, Kinscherff R, Fenton T. Psychiatric diagnoses of abusive mothers. A preliminary report. *The Journal of Nervous and Mental Disease.* 1992;180:658-661.

91. Kelleher K, Chaffin M, Hollenberg J, Fischer E. Alcohol and drug disorders among physically abusive and neglectful parents in a community-based sample. *American Journal of Public Health.* 1994;84: 1586-1590.

92. Murphy JM, Jellinek M, Quinn D, Smith G, Poitrast FG, Goshko M. Substance abuse and serious child mistreatment: prevalence, risk, and outcome in a court sample. *Child Abuse & Neglect.* 1991;15: 197-211.

93. Kelley SJ. Parenting stress and child maltreatment in drug-exposed children. *Child Abuse & Neglect.* 1992;16:317-328.

94. Casanova GM, Domanic J, McCanne TR, Milner JS. Physiological responses to non-child-related stressors in mothers at risk for child abuse. *Child Abuse & Neglect.* 1992;16:31-44.

95. McCanne TR, Milner JS. Physiological reactivity of physically abusive and at-risk subjects to child-related stimuli. In: Milner JS, ed. *Neuropsychology of Aggression.* Norwell, Mass: Kluwer Academic Publishers; 1991:147-166.

96. Claussen AH, Crittenden PM. Physical and psychological maltreatment: relations among types of maltreatment. *Child Abuse & Neglect.* 1991;15:5-18.

97. Fantuzzo JW, DePaola LM, Lambert L, Martino T, Anderson G, Sutton S. Effects of interparental violence on the psychological adjustment and competencies of young children. *Journal of Consulting and Clinical Psychology.* 1991;59:258-265.

98. Salzinger S, Feldman RS, Hammer M, Rosario M. Risk for physical child abuse and the personal consequences for its victims. *Criminal Justice and Behavior.* 1991;18:64-81.

99. Kolko DJ. Characteristics of child victims of physical violence: research findings and clinical implications. *Journal of Interpersonal Violence.* 1992;7:244-276.

100. Mollerstrom WW, Patchner MA, Milner JS. Family functioning and child abuse potential. *Journal of Clinical Psychology.* 1992;48:445-454.

101. Caliso JA, Milner JS. Childhood history of abuse and child abuse screening. *Child Abuse & Neglect.* 1992;16:647-659.

102. Emery RE, Laumann-Billings L. An overview of the nature, causes, and consequences of abusive family relationships. Toward differentiating maltreatment and violence. *The American Psychologist.* 1998;53:121-135.

103. Holden EW, Willis DJ, Foltz L. Child abuse potential and parenting stress: relationships in maltreating parents. *Psychological Assessment.* 1989;1:64-67.

104. Appel AE, Holden GW. The co-occurrence of spouse and physical child abuse: a review and appraisal. *Journal of Family Psychology: JFP: Journal of the Division of Family Psychology of the American Psychological Association (Division 43).* 1998;12:578-599.

105. Coohey C, Braun N. Toward an integrated framework for understanding child physical abuse. *Child Abuse & Neglect.* 1997;21:1081-1094.

106. Gillham B, Tanner G, Cheyne B, Freeman I, Rooney M, Lambie A. Unemployment rates, single parent density, and indices of child poverty: their relationship to different categories of child abuse and neglect. *Child Abuse & Neglect.* 1998;22:79-90.

107. Crittenden PM. Social networks, quality of childrearing and child development. *Child Development.* 1985;56:1299-1313.

108. Egeland B, Breitenbucher M, Rosenberg D. Prospective study of the significance of life stress in the etiology of child abuse. *Journal of Consulting and Clinical Psychology.* 1980;48:195-205.

109. Corse S, Schmid K, Trickett P. Social network characteristics of mothers in abusing and nonabusing families and their relationships to parenting beliefs. *Journal of Community Psychology.* 1990;18:44-59.

110. Zuravin SJ. The ecology of child abuse and neglect: review of the literature and presentation of data. *Violence and Victims.* 1989;4:101-120.

111. Coulton CJ, Korbin JE, Su M, Chow J. Community level factors and child maltreatment rates. *Child Development.* 1995;66:1262-1276.

112. Drake B, Pandey S. Understanding the relationship between neighborhood poverty and specific types of child maltreatment. *Child Abuse & Neglect.* 1996;20:1003-1018.

113. Bursik RJ Jr, Grasmick HG. *Neighborhoods and Crime: The Dimensions of Effective Community Control.* New York, NY: Lexington Books; 1992.

114. Coulton CJ, Korbin JE, Su M. Neighborhoods and child maltreatment: a multi-level study. *Child Abuse & Neglect.* 1999;23:1019-1040.

115. Henggeler SW, Borduin CM. *Family Therapy and Beyond: A Multisystemic Approach to Treating the Behavior Problems of Children and Adolescents.* Pacific Grove, Calif: Brooks/Cole; 1990.

116. Swenson C, Faldowski R, Saldana L. Mid-treatment outcomes of an effectiveness study: applying MST to child maltreatment. Brief symposium presented at: 17th Annual Research Conference of the Louis de la Parte Florida Mental Health Institute; February 28 – March 3, 2004; Tampa, Fla.

117. Bronfenbrenner U. *The Ecology of Human Development: Experiments by Nature and Design.* Cambridge, Mass: Harvard University Press; 1979.

118. Haley J. *Problem-Solving Therapy.* San Francisco, Calif: Jossey-Bass; 1976.

119. Minuchin S. *Families & Family Therapy.* Cambridge, Mass: Harvard University Press; 1974.

120. Borduin CM, Mann BJ, Cone LT, et al. Multisystemic treatment of serious juvenile offenders: long-term prevention of criminality and violence. *Journal of Consulting and Clinical Psychology.* 1995;63:569-578.

121. Henggeler SW, Melton GB, Smith LA. Family preservation using multisystemic therapy: an effective alternative to incarcerating serious juvenile offenders. *Journal of Consulting and Clinical Psychology.* 1992;60:953-961.

122. Henggeler SW, Melton GB, Brondino MJ, Scherer DG, Hanley JH. Multisystemic therapy with violent and chronic juvenile offenders and their families: the role of treatment fidelity in successful dissemination. *Journal of Consulting and Clinical Psychology.* 1997;65:821-833.

123. Aos S, Phipps P, Barnoski R, Lieb R. *The Comparative Costs and Benefits of Programs to Reduce Crime: Version 4.0.* Olympia, Wash: Washington State Institute for Public Policy; 2001.

124. Borduin CM, Schaeffer CM. Multisystemic treatment of juvenile sexual offenders: a progress report. *Journal of Psychology & Human Sexuality.* 2002;13:25-42.

125. Henggeler SW, Rowland MD, Randall J, et al. Home-based multisystemic therapy as an alternative to the hospitalization of youths in psychiatric crisis: clinical outcomes. *Journal of the American Academy of Child and Adolescent Psychiatry.* 1999;38:1331-1339.

126. Henggeler SW, Schoenwald SK, Borduin CM, Rowland MD, Cunningham PB. *Multisystemic Treatment of Antisocial Behavior in Children and Adolescents.* New York, NY: The Guilford Press; 1998.

127. Cunningham PB, Henggeler SW. Engaging multiproblem families in treatment: lessons learned throughout the development of multisystemic therapy. *Family Process.* 1999;38:265-281.

128. Swenson CC, Henggeler SW, Taylor IS, Addison OW. *Multisystemic Therapy and Neighborhood Partnerships: Reducing Adolescent Violence and Substance Abuse.* New York, NY: The Guilford Press; 2004.

129. Henggeler SW, Schoenwald SK. *The MST Supervisory Manual: Promoting Quality Assurance at the Clinical Level.* Charleston, SC: MST Institute; 1998.

130. Henggeler SW, Pickrel SG, Brondino MJ. Multisystemic treatment of substance-abusing and dependent delinquents: outcomes, treatment fidelity, and transportability. *Mental Health Services Research.* 1999;1:171-184.

131. Huey SJ Jr, Henggeler SW, Brondino MJ, Pickrel SG. Mechanisms of change in multisystemic therapy: reducing delinquent behavior through therapist adherence and improved family and peer functioning. *Journal of Consulting and Clinical Psychology.* 2000;68:451-467.

132. Schoenwald SK, Henggeler SW, Brondino MJ, Rowland MD. Multisystemic therapy: monitoring treatment fidelity. *Family Process.* 2000;39:83-103.

133. Dinkmeyer D Sr, McKay GD, McKay JL, Dinkmeyer D Jr. *Parenting Teenagers: Systematic Training for Effective Parenting of Teens.* Atascadero, Calif: Impact Publishers, Inc; 1998.

134. Kovacs M. *Children's Depression Inventory (CDI) Manual.* North Tonawanda, NY: Multi-Health Systems, Inc; 1981.

135. Straus MA. *Handbook for the Conflict Tactics Scales (CTS).* Durham, NH: Family Research Laboratory, University of New Hampshire; 2001.

136. Olson D, Portner J, Lavee Y. *FACES III.* Roseville, Minn: University of Minnesota, Department of Family Social Service; 1985.

137. Foa EB, Rothbaum BO, Riggs DS, Murdock TB. Treatment of posttraumatic stress disorder in rape victims: a comparison between cognitive-behavioral procedures and counseling. *Journal of Consulting and Clinical Psychology.* 1991;59:715-723.

138. Meadows EA, Foa EB. Intrusion, arousal, and avoidance: sexual trauma survivors. In: Follette VM, Ruzek JI, Abueg FR, eds. *Cognitive-Behavioral Therapies for Trauma.* New York, NY: The Guilford Press; 1998:100-123.

139. Resick PA, Schnicke MK. Cognitive processing therapy for sexual assault victims. *Journal of Consulting and Clinical Psychology.* 1992;60:748-756.

140. Resick PA, Schnicke MK. *Cognitive Processing Therapy for Rape Victims: A Treatment Manual.* New York, NY: The Guilford Press; 1993.

141. Feindler EL, Ecton RB. *Adolescent Anger Control: Cognitive-Behavioral Techniques.* New York, NY: Prentice Hall; 1986.

142. Novaco RW. Clinical problems of anger and its assessment and regulation through a stress coping skills approach. In: O'Donohue WT, Krasner L, eds. *Handbook of Psychological Skills Training: Clinical Techniques and Applications.* Boston, Mass: Allyn & Bacon; 1994:320-338.

143. Budney AJ, Higgins ST. *A Community Reinforcement Plus Vouchers Approach: Treating Cocaine Addiction.* Rockville, Md: National Institute on Drug Abuse; 1998. NIH publication 98-4309. Therapy Manuals for Drug Addiction, Manual 2.

144. Carroll KM. *A Cognitive-Behavioral Approach: Treating Cocaine Addiction.* Rockville, Md: National Institute on Drug Abuse; 1998. NIH publication 98-4308. Therapy Manuals for Drug Addiction, Manual 1.

145. Robin AL, Bedway M, Gilroy M. Problem solving communication training. In: Lecroy C, ed. *Handbook of Child and Adolescent Treatment Manuals.* New York, NY: Free Press; 1994:92-125.

School-Based Interventions for Children and Adolescents Exposed to Chronic Community Violence

Michele R. Cooley, MEd, PhD
Sharon F. Lambert, PhD

Introduction to Community Violence

Children and adolescents are exposed to community violence at alarmingly high rates. In fact, community violence — defined as deliberate acts intended to cause physical harm to a person or persons in the community[1] — has been designated a significant public health problem.[2] Although the *direct* victims of such violence are obvious, the *indirect* victims are far more numerous. They include bystanders and witnesses, family members, friends and acquaintances who know the victims and those who are cognizant of and/or anxious about the potential for community violence.[3,4]

Episodes of *chronic* community violence are distinguished from episodes of *acute* community violence in their likelihood of recurrence. Episodes of acute community violence are typically unlikely to recur[1] in the same setting and to the same individuals. The shootings at Columbine High School in Littleton, Colorado, in 1999 are an example of an episode of acute community violence. Conversely, chronic community violence involves *repeated* acts of violence over long periods of time in the same community that are widespread among settings and/or social groups. The consequences of chronic community violence impact significant portions of the community over a substantial period of time.[4]

Although a higher crime rate in a community increases the likelihood of *direct* exposure to violence, exposure to community violence occurs through a variety of modalities — including through the media, as a witness, through hearsay, as a victim and through war/terrorism — and extends beyond urban centers. Violence reported by the media has been researched for the longest period of time. However, in the United States, war/terrorism or "world violence" has received much recent research attention.

Consequences of Youth Exposure to Community Violence

The exposure of youth to community violence can cause adverse consequences to multiple domains of their adjustment,[5] including causing difficulties with emotional, behavioral and adaptive functioning, such as depression, anxiety, posttraumatic stress symptoms, aggression, poor academic functioning and achievement, substance abuse and health problems.[6-13]

Following is an excerpt from an interview conducted during the study published by Cooley-Quille and colleagues[6] in 2001, which illustrates how community violence is associated with posttraumatic stress disorder (PTSD):

> "'Michael' is a 13-year-old inner-city teen living with his mother and stepfather. Four years ago, Michael was walking home alone after playing ball with friends. He heard a man screaming and walked closer to investigate. Michael witnessed 2 men sawing the leg off of a third man. Extremely frightened, Michael ran home. He subsequently developed symptoms of PTSD, including nightmares, hypervigilance, foreshortened view of the future and increased startle response."

PTSD is the most widely recognized anxiety disorder that has physiological concomitants, although all anxiety disorders affect physiological, behavioral and cognitive response systems.[14] Consideration of *each* of these domains is essential to understanding the cause of PTSD[15] and other anxiety and internalizing symptoms. The symptoms of PTSD are physical and psychological manifestations of the link between community violence and anxiety. Their onset is necessarily preceded by an external stressor, and previous research supports the relationship between PTSD and youth exposure to community violence.[16,17] Exposure to the external trauma causes exaggerated neurotransmitter activity that is related to aggression,[18] hypersensitivity[18] and physiological and subjective hyperarousal.[19] Biological factors are involved, but they cannot explain solely why some individuals develop PTSD after an exposure to trauma, while others do not.[18]

Among youth, the adverse emotional and behavioral effects caused by repeated exposures to violence may play out in the settings in which they live and function: For example, some youth with externalizing problems, such as oppositional defiant or aggressive behavior, who have been exposed repeatedly to community violence may exhibit problem behaviors in the family and school settings.[20] Some may even become perpetrators of crime.[11]

Despite the significant potential adverse outcomes caused by repeated exposures to community violence, not all youth suffer severe negative consequences.[6] To the contrary, some children and adolescents possess intrinsic or ecological protective factors that may mitigate the emotional and behavioral problems associated with exposure to violence. Unfortunately, much of the available research has focused on identifying risk factors and adverse outcomes rather than on protective factors.[21]

Mental Health Services for Youth Exposed to Community Violence

The clinical response by mental health professionals to the epidemic of exposure to community violence among youth has been limited.[22] Most children who have been exposed to violence in their communities have not received formal mental health treatment or services of any kind[23,24]: For example, among a group of adolescents who received care in a primary care clinic, those victimized by violent crime did not seek medical or psychological intervention.[25] This is contrary to evidence that has shown that individuals who receive appropriate medical or psychological care suffer fewer consequences following exposure to violence.[26]

Even when affected youth receive mental health services, therapists may neglect to assess their exposure to community violence sufficiently and/or treat the related symptoms adequately. Therapists may not assess community violence in clinical settings routinely because they underestimate their clients' exposure or because they tend to focus on individual- and/or family-level processes rather than on contextual issues, such as pervasive violence in the community.[22] In sum, not assessing levels of exposure to community violence among youth is a substantial oversight when mental health and primary care providers work with children and adolescents who are at high risk for exposure. There *are* efficacious interventions — albeit few that have been published — designed to be utilized with this population.

Essential Components of Mental Health Interventions for Youth Exposed to Community Violence

Human ecology theory emphasizes the importance of understanding children in context — a critical component in the design of effective interventions.[27-29] Responding to cultural differences when intervening with youth is essential if we are to improve the delivery of mental health services.[30] Every community has unique cultural characteristics, strengths and needs: In addition to customizing interventions when working with specific populations, the process of eliciting the input of community residents is important prior to implementing intervention programs.[31]

Very few published interventions have been designed specifically for youth who have been exposed to community violence that also addressed the negative emotional and behavioral outcomes of that exposure. It is possible, however, to identify potential essential components of interventions that can be used with youth exposed to community violence by examining studies of related disorders: For example, several authors have investigated the efficacy of treating PTSD among youth exposed to trauma — although not necessarily community violence — including Farrell, Hains and Davies[32]; King and colleagues[33]; and March and associates.[34]

Building on this body of literature, Berman, Silverman and Kurtines[35] developed what they refer to as a "prototypical" intervention for youth exposed to community violence that targets their related symptoms of distress. A significant strength of this intervention is that it is a group cognitive-behavioral treatment program that was designed to be implemented by school counselors specifically as a school-based intervention. This program encompasses the following 3 primary components, all of which have been demonstrated to be efficacious in treating trauma-exposed and/or anxious youth[35]:

- The first component, *exposure-based behavioral exercises,* employs systematic exposure to the traumatic event or the traumatic cues. Exposure-based treatment elicits the memory of the feared event and provides the client with new information that is incompatible with the fear so that a new, more favorable memory is formed.[36] These exercises serve multiple purposes, including encouraging youth to express affect related to the traumatic event, and teaching them how to manage the emotions associated with the event.

- The second component revolves around enhancing affected youths' *coping skills.* Effective coping may buffer responses to stressful life events. In the case of chronic community violence, enhanced coping skills may prevent or reduce subsequent exposures to violence as youth learn ways to negotiate their environments and make safer choices effectively — despite living in violent and often hostile communities. Without the buffer of enhanced coping skills, continual exposure to violence may simultaneously impair the ability of affected children and adolescents to generate prosocial coping strategies and reinforce maladaptive coping responses, such as avoidance. Avoidance may actually serve to *maintain* fear or aggression, which then may adversely impact social and educational successes.
- The third component involves enhanced *social support,* which has been shown to ameliorate the adverse effects of stressful life events.[37] Within this program, youth are taught to identify perceived and actual sources of support — and subsequently engage these supports.

Clearly, these 3 components — exposure-based behavioral exercises, coping skills and social support — are essential for success in many types of treatment and preventive interventions for youth who have emotional and/or behavioral problems. Successful interventions for youth who have been exposed to chronic community violence must also take into consideration other factors, such as setting, culture and context.

Importance of School-Based Interventions for Youth Exposed to Chronic Community Violence

It is believed that the distractions that youth experience because of their chronic exposure to community violence disrupt their cognitive development.[3] Exposure to violence has been associated with attention deficits,[38,39] declines in cognitive performance[38-40] and declines in school achievement.[41] Some have theorized that these academic difficulties are the result of a reduced ability to concentrate because of distracting and intrusive thoughts about violent events that may accumulate over time and with repeated exposure.[3,42] Given the adverse impact of exposure to community violence on children's and adolescents' school-related functioning, school-based interventions are important to explore for several reasons:

- Low-income and urban youth who are at high risk for exposure to violence may be the least likely to seek (or be directed to) mental health services through traditional means of referral[35]: For example, they may be mandated through the court system to receive mental health services only after they have become perpetrators of violence themselves.
- Youth who have the greatest levels of exposure to community violence may also have the least access to mental health services.[35] Due to the high prevalence of exposure to violence among youth living in communities where violence is chronic, ongoing exposure may be considered "normal," therefore not something that warrants formal intervention.
- Youth may be exposed to violence in or around the school setting and experience feelings of distress.[43,44]

Providing mental health interventions on school premises is convenient for youth and for their caregivers: On-site healthcare services are readily available for those who may not otherwise have access to or utilize these services. Additional advantages of providing mental health interventions in school settings include the ready access to large groups of youth, support for programming by school administrators/staff and the creation of an environment that is conducive to learning.[45]

School-Based Interventions for Youth Exposed to Chronic Community Violence

Several recently developed school-based interventions are targeted specifically at the adverse emotional and behavioral outcomes associated with exposure to chronic community violence. Through a literature review of all published outcome studies of school-based interventions of this nature, we specifically identified 4 such interventions,[23,46-48] each of which is summarized in the following subsections. Each of these programs is implemented using a group format in school settings. The advantages of group mental health interventions include the following:

- They are time- and cost-efficient.
- They may facilitate discussions of traumatic events.
- They may help bring about discussions that can prove beneficial in normalizing experiences with and reactions to violence.[46,49]

The Neighborhood Club

The Neighborhood Club (NC)[23] is a supportive intervention designed to address the psychological consequences of exposure to chronic community violence among low-income, urban, 9-year-old to 12-year-old elementary school students. The program consists of 8, weekly, 1-hour sessions with activities that address 5 program goals:

- validating and normalizing emotional responses to violence
- regaining a sense of control over one's environment
- learning safety skills for coping with chronic community violence
- learning about grief and mourning processes
- reducing the effects of the symptoms of PTSD on school activities and other aspects of daily life

Each of the 8 sessions of the NC includes a component identified as contextually relevant for the affected youth. In session 1, "Introductions," group leaders — graduate psychology students who are assisted by undergraduate students — explain that the purpose of the group is to provide a safe place to talk about their neighborhoods, in both positive and negative ways. They also establish group ground rules. During session 2, "So Many Feelings," group members identify their feelings and discuss how to manage difficult feelings like anger and fear. In session 3, "Neighborhood Drawings," the children draw the things that they do and do not like about their neighborhoods in order to facilitate discussions about the positive and violent aspects of their neighborhoods. Drawings are an important tool because they allow children to communicate issues that they may not be able to express verbally.[23] The ultimate purposes of session 3 are to normalize feelings about chronic neighborhood violence and to discuss how to cope with fear. During session 4, "Skits and Safety Plans," the children learn about practical skills for coping with dangerous situations (eg, do not walk alone and drop to the ground if gunshots are heard) and feeling safer in their neighborhoods. The children rehearse these skills during role plays or by using skits with coaching from group leaders.

In session 5, "When Somebody Dies," the group addresses grief and mourning, as well as strategies for coping with loss. During session 6, "Gangs in the Neighborhood," group members discuss issues related to gang involvement, such as how the disadvantages outweigh the advantages, and how to respond when approached by gang members. Using role playing, they experiment with different strategies. In session 7, "Newspaper Review," the children review all of the previous sessions and create a newspaper that highlights their experiences while in the NC group, including features about NC activities or advice for coping with neighborhood problems. During the final group session, the "Goodbye Party," group members celebrate their accomplishments, distribute the printed NC newspaper and receive diplomas that celebrate their completion of the group's work.

Ten NCs had been conducted at the time that Ceballo[23] initially described this intervention. School principals and teachers referred children based on their knowledge of the children's family backgrounds and exposure to violence. Caucasian, African American and Hispanic students participated, with approximately equal numbers of boys and girls. Bilingual groups have been conducted in English and in Spanish.[50] Ceballo, Ramirez and Maltese[50] evaluated the NC by comparing pre- and posttest measures of depression and PTSD among 25 children who were randomly assigned to participate in the groups and 25 youngsters who served as wait-list controls. There were no significant differences between the groups at posttreatment.

According to Ceballo, Ramirez and Maltese[23,50] anecdotal reports from teachers and parents suggest that NC participants discussed their problems and concerns more openly after completing the group sessions. Program developers assert that a significant benefit of working with young children is that, in addition to ameliorating the current effects of exposure to violence, the program may have the following preventive effects for children living in environments that are actively affected by chronic violence:

- teaching active coping to deal with danger and existing symptoms
- promoting supportive connections with other youth who share similar experiences
- fostering a sense of control over particular aspects of their environment

Absorbing the benefits of each of these effects, in turn, may lessen the long-term consequences of exposure to violence. Further empirical evaluations, using randomized, controlled designs with longer follow-up periods than those published by Ceballo, Ramirez and Maltese,[50] should be conducted to determine the long-term effectiveness of the NC group intervention for children exposed to chronic community violence.

FRIENDS

Cooley, Boyd and Grados[46] examined the feasibility of "FRIENDS," an anxiety prevention intervention[51,52] developed in Australia for use with urban elementary school children exposed to community violence, in the United States. The acronym FRIENDS describes the content of the sessions: F = Feeling worried; R = Relax and feel good; I = Inner thoughts; E = Explore plans; N = Nice work, so reward yourself; D = Don't forget to practice; and S = Stay cool. The FRIENDS program is a cognitive-behavioral group intervention based on the "Coping Koala" anxiety-intervention program,[51] which was designed to teach children skills for coping with the behavioral, physiological and cognitive aspects of anxiety. The behavioral component of anxiety is targeted through activities, such as problem solving and graduated exposure to fears. The physiological component is addressed by increasing children's awareness of their physical sensations in response to stress and anxiety, and teaching them relaxation techniques. To address the cognitive component of anxiety, children learn how to use positive self-talk and self-rewards to create more realistic self and environmental evaluations, as well as to reward themselves for partial successes.

Since the FRIENDS intervention was developed in Australia and not designed specifically for youth who have been exposed to community violence, Cooley, Boyd and Grados[46] modified the intervention to make it relevant for the culture and context of inner-city American elementary school children: For example, during one of the original FRIENDS relaxation exercises, children were to imagine that they were baby kangaroos riding in their mothers' pouches. The joeys, who had to tuck themselves into tight balls to hide from a farmer who was pointing a gun at them, were instructed to "relax and stretch" once the threat of harm had passed. When this exercise was used in the United States, a group member questioned why the farmer would be shooting kangaroos. Group members discussed this issue, and the context of the session was altered so that it focused primarily on developing skills to use when faced with the threat of gun violence.

Participants for the pilot feasibility study were drawn from a public elementary school located in an inner-city, low-socioeconomic and very-high-crime neighborhood.[46] The preintervention screening included the following 4 phases, based on procedures outlined by Dadds and colleagues.[53] All fifth-grade students (n = 91) were eligible for the screening. The researchers obtained parental consent and child assent from 89% (n = 81) of the fifth-grade class.

- During the first phase, students completed the Revised Children's Manifest Anxiety Scale (RCMAS).[54]
- In phase 2, teachers selected a maximum of 3 students who displayed the highest level of anxiety and a maximum of 3 students who displayed the most aggressive and/or disruptive behavior.
- During the third phase, the researchers developed a list of eligible participants that included students who had at least "moderate" self-reported anxiety on the RCMAS or were included in the teacher selections of the most anxious children. Students were excluded if they were in special education classes or were selected by their teachers as highly aggressive and/or disruptive.
- In phase 4 of the selection process, the parents of the 37 children (46%) who met the phase 3 inclusion criteria were contacted to obtain permission for their children to participate in a psychiatric interview and the FRIENDS intervention, *if* they were subsequently selected. The researchers obtained parental consent for 11 (14%) of the eligible students. These 11 students then completed the Anxiety Disorders Interview Schedule for Children (ADIS-C),[55-57] and self-report measures of exposure to community violence (via the Children's Report of Exposure to Violence[1]), anxiety, depression and social skills. The researchers invited those students who had been exposed to community violence and who obtained a clinical severity rating on the ADIS-C of "mild-to-moderate anxiety disorder" to participate in the group. One student who suffered from clinically severe anxiety was referred to a community mental health center for treatment because the modified FRIENDS intervention — designed as a school-based *preventive* intervention rather than a *treatment* program — was targeted toward children who exhibited only mild-to-moderate symptoms and disorders of anxiety.

Ten students (8 females, 2 males) completed the 11-session FRIENDS intervention program. Sessions, held biweekly, were conducted by a group leader and a coleader. At postintervention, overall RCMAS scores were decreased significantly (preintervention M = 19.8; postintervention M = 10.8; $t = 6.84$, $P<.001$). Significant decreases were also evident in the following RCMAS subscales: physiological anxiety (preintervention M = 7.4; postintervention M = 3.2; $t = 6.50$, $P<.001$), worry/oversensitivity (preintervention M = 8.5; postintervention M = 5.3; $t = 4.07$, $P<.005$)

and social concerns/concentration difficulties (preintervention M = 4.1; postintervention M = 2.3; $t = 2.95$, $P<.05$). The students also reported significantly less test anxiety, on the Test Anxiety Scale for Children,[58] after the intervention (preintervention M = 14.6; postintervention M = 10.0; $t = 3.58$, $P<.01$).

From preintervention to postintervention, there was no evidence of a significant change in depressive symptoms on the Children's Depression Inventory (CDI),[59] in total anxiety as assessed by the Multidimensional Anxiety Scale for Children[60] or in social skills (*P*s>.10); although depressive symptoms and social skills were not direct targets of the FRIENDS intervention.[46]

This feasibility study provided additional information to the investigators about aspects of the FRIENDS intervention that required other cultural and contextual modifications to make it appropriate for use with inner-city American youth who have been exposed to chronic community violence. Further evaluations of the efficacy of the FRIENDS intervention are currently underway.

Trauma- and Grief-Focused Interventions

Saltzman and colleagues[47] described a trauma- and grief-focused, school-based intervention for adolescents exposed to chronic community violence. This program was adapted from interventions designed by the University of California at Los Angeles (UCLA) Trauma Psychiatry Service to address the needs of individuals (not only children and adolescents) exposed to trauma through natural disasters, community violence and war. The program is comprised of the following 4 components:

- a self-report assessment of the individual's exposure to community violence, and his/her degree of depression, grief and posttraumatic stress symptoms; students who reported significant exposure to violence and/or emotional distress were invited to continue in the program
- an individual screening interview to validate self-assessment results, identify impairment(s) in multiple domains (ie, home, school, peer relationships) and determine if the individual is eligible for a group-based intervention

- a detailed, individual, clinical interview to obtain information about experiences with trauma and loss, negative emotions, trauma reminders and psychosocial functioning; and to provide psychoeducation about trauma and bereavement
- trauma- and grief-focused group interventions based on 5 treatment foci — identification of the traumatic experiences; reminders of loss and trauma; the interaction between trauma and grief; adverse experiences following the trauma; and developmental outcomes — outlined by Pynoos, Steinberg and Wraith[61] and Layne and colleagues.[62] Group intervention consists of 20 semistructured sessions that address building group cohesion, developing coping skills, processing traumatic experiences and promoting adaptive grieving

A preliminary field trial of this program was conducted in a secondary school setting and reported in 2001.[47] A total of 812 students completed surveys regarding trauma exposure and distress. Twenty-six students (3.2%) who reported *significant* exposure to violence and/or emotional distress were invited to participate in one of 5 group psychotherapy programs; each group consisted of 5 to 7 participants. The majority of group participants, who were male (61%), ranged in age from 11 years to 14 years (M = 2.58). Group members were primarily Hispanic (68%); 28% were African American; 4% were Caucasian.

Following the psychotherapeutic intervention, Saltzman and colleagues[47] assessed the participants' symptoms of PTSD using the UCLA PTSD Reaction Index–Adolescent Version (RI–R).[63] For all group participants, the RI–R scores were reduced significantly (pretest M = 42.38; posttest M = 36.81; $t_{25} = 3.53$, $P<.01$) and grade point averages had improved significantly (pretest M = 2.02; posttest M = 2.29; $t_{25} = 4.19$, $P<.001$). Scores on the Grief Screening Scale[64] decreased only for those group members who had experienced traumatic losses (pretest M = 11.00; posttest M = 8.57; $t_7 = 3.38$, $P<.05$). Saltzman and colleagues[47] observed no significant changes in symptoms of depression.

Cognitive-Behavioral Intervention for Trauma in Schools

The Cognitive-Behavioral Intervention for Trauma in Schools (CBITS)[48] is a group-based program designed for multiethnic, inner-city school students. The intervention employs cognitive-behavioral techniques that have proven effective in patients with PTSD: It addresses the students' depression, anxiety and symptoms of PTSD that are the result of exposure to chronic community violence. The contents of the therapeutic sessions include the following:

- education about responses to trauma
- relaxation training
- identification of feelings
- linking thoughts with feelings
- combating erroneous negative thoughts
- constructing fear hierarchies
- imagined exposure to the feared event(s)
- being exposed to memories of trauma through writing and drawing
- social problem solving

Imagined exposure to the traumatic event(s) occurs first during an individual session (between session 3 and session 6), then through writing or drawing in the group interventions. Generalization of techniques is facilitated through homework assignments.[65]

As part of the Mental Health for Immigrants Program (MHIP) — a culturally sensitive, trauma-focused program developed for the immigrant student population in the Los Angeles, California, Unified School District — a pilot test of CBITS was conducted among a sample of Hispanic children exposed to community violence.[66] The MHIP youth intervention consisted of 8 sessions based on CBITS.[48] An optional component of the intervention, designed for parents, included 4, 2-hour sessions that complemented the youth program by teaching parents the techniques that their children were learning in the MHIP sessions in order to address the effects of the traumas they experienced. Additionally, teachers in participating schools were invited to an in-service training regarding the effects of trauma on children.[66]

The potential MHIP pilot-test participants, Hispanic immigrant students, were enrolled in the 3rd through 8th grades in Los Angeles-area public schools. Of the 11 schools that had a high immigrant enrollment that were invited to participate in the MHIP, 9 agreed to take part. Eligibility criteria for participation in the intervention group included being foreign-born, immigrating to the United States within the prior 3 years and speaking Spanish as their primary language. Of the 879 students who were screened, the 276 (31%) youngsters who reported experiencing exposure to violence and significant symptoms of depression and/or PTSD were invited to participate in the MHIP. The researchers obtained written parental consent and child assent for 229 of these students (83%). At the beginning of the school year, these students were assigned randomly to the intervention group or a wait list that acted as the control group.

A total of 198 students (152 intervention group; 46 wait-list controls) completed the program. Participants' mean age was 11 years, and two thirds of the participants were in middle school. At the 3-month follow-up, mean depression scores on the CDI[59] decreased significantly for children in the intervention group (baseline CDI M = 16.3; follow-up CDI M = 13.5; $t = 5.1$, $P < .001$), but remained virtually the same for children in the wait-list group (baseline CDI M = 16.3; follow-up CDI M = 16.2; $t = 0.1$, NS). Similarly, scores on the Child PTSD Symptom Scale (CPSS)[67] were significantly lower for children in the intervention group (baseline CPSS M = 18.8; follow-up CPSS M = 13.0; $t = 7.5$, $P < .001$), but were not significantly lower for children in the control group (baseline CPSS M = 18.1; follow-up CPSS M = 15.7; $t = 1.3$, NS). Multivariate analyses indicated that the intervention group had lower follow-up CDI scores and lower CPSS scores than did the wait-list group after controlling for baseline symptoms, age, gender, country of origin and parental demographical characteristics. Information regarding longer-term outcomes is not yet available.

Stein and colleagues[65] conducted a randomized, controlled trial to examine the effectiveness of the CBITS[48] on reducing symptoms of depression and PTSD, and improving psychosocial functioning and behavior in middle school students. The potential study participants, 769 students in the 6th grade, were enrolled in 2 middle schools located in a socioeconomically disadvantaged and primarily Hispanic area of Los Angeles. With written parental consent in hand, these students were screened for exposure to chronic community violence and symptoms of PTSD. Students were eligible to participate in the intervention only if they met *all* of the following criteria:

- exposure to 3 or more violent events
- symptoms of PTSD in the clinical range
- willingness to discuss their PTSD-related exposure in a group setting
- ability to participate actively in a group intervention because they were not too disruptive

One hundred twenty-six (79%) of the 159 eligible students participated in the 10-session CBITS. Students were randomly assigned to an early intervention group (n = 61) or to a delayed intervention group (n = 65) that completed the CBITS 3 months after the screening.

To assess the effects of the CBITS intervention, mean differences in outcomes for the early intervention group and the delayed intervention group were compared at 3 months and at 6 months, adjusting for baseline scores. In lieu of *P* values, the investigators reported adjusted mean differences between the intervention groups and a confidence interval. At the 3-month assessment, when the delayed intervention group had not yet received the CBITS, youth self-reports of the symptoms of PTSD on the CPSS[67] were significantly lower for children in the early intervention group (mean = 8.9) than they were for students in the delayed intervention group (mean = 15.5); (adjusted mean difference = –7.0; effect size = 1.08 SD). In addition, self-reports of depressive symptoms, as recorded on the CDI,[59] were also significantly lower for children in the early intervention group (mean = 9.4) than they were for students in the delayed intervention group (mean = 12.7); (adjusted mean difference = –3.4; effect size = 0.45 SD). Using the Pediatric Symptom Checklist,[68] parents of students in the early intervention group reported that their children exhibited significantly less psychosocial dysfunction (mean = 12.5) than parents did of children who were in the delayed intervention group (mean = 16.5); (adjusted mean difference = –6.4; effect size = 0.77 SD). There were no differences in teacher-reported acting-out problems, shy/anxious behavior or learning problems. At the 6-month assessment — when both groups had completed the CBITS — the intervention and wait-list groups did not differ in terms of youth-reported symptoms of PTSD or depression, parent-reported psychosocial functioning or teacher-reported behavior/learning problems.

Summary of School-Based Interventions

The school-based interventions described previously provide initial first steps for addressing the emotional and behavioral outcomes of the epidemic of exposure to chronic community violence among youth. These group interventions are an important means for increasing access to and utilization of mental health services for youth who are at risk and might not be identified otherwise. A review of these programs highlights the relevant targets that should be addressed with interventions that aim to assist youth exposed to chronic community violence. It also suggests areas to explore with future interventions.

Components of Successful Interventions for Youth Exposed to Chronic Community Violence

As discussed previously, in each of the 4 interventions reviewed, exposure-based exercises and efforts to develop coping skills were included, to some extent: In their review of the basic elements of interventions designed for youth exposed to chronic community violence, Berman, Silverman and Kurtines[35] outlined 3 key intervention strategies: using exposure-based exercises, helping clients develop coping skills and assisting with building social support systems. The FRIENDS program, as described by Cooley, Boyd and Grados,[46] includes graduated exposures to the trauma and enhancement of problem-solving skills. The randomized, controlled trial conducted by Stein and colleagues[65] also incorporated exposure-based exercises and the development of coping skills. They found that CBITS effectively reduced the symptoms of posttraumatic stress and depression among youth participating in the intervention. Similarly, the Trauma- and Grief-Focused Intervention[47] incorporated the processing of traumatic experiences and an enhancement of coping skills. Youth enrolled in this program reported fewer symptoms of posttraumatic stress after participating in the group. Although social support enhancement was not an explicit target of any of the 4 reviewed interventions, the utilization of social supports may be considered a type of adaptive coping strategy; and the group format inherent in each of these interventions may have fostered peer social support. As such, it appears that enhanced social support was included in the interventions we reviewed.

In addition to the 3 intervention components suggested by Berman, Silverman and Kurtines,[35] it is important that interventions designed for youth who are exposed to chronic community violence address the *perceived* as well as the actual threat of exposure to that violence.[69] Youth exposed to chronic community violence may face the continued threat of exposure because they reside in dangerous or high-crime environments. These youth often express concerns about their safety and the safety of significant others. Regardless of whether these fears are real or perceived, youth exposed to chronic community violence frequently experience significant adverse consequences, including emotional distress and externalizing behaviors (eg, aggression).[5] The NC intervention includes strategies for managing perceived and real threats: In fact, one full session is devoted solely to helping youth develop practical skills for coping with dangerous situations and feeling safe in their environments.[23] Similarly, Cooley, Boyd and Grados[46] adapted the Australian FRIENDS intervention in the United States to include a session on what to do when faced with gun violence.

Lastly, successful interventions for youth exposed to chronic community violence must take into account the diverse reactions of each youth. Individuals exposed to the same violent event may have very different responses to that event. Responses to exposure to chronic community violence have been shown to vary according to individual characteristics, such as coping style,[70] proximity to the violent event, whether the individual is the victim or perpetrator,[71,72] as well as perceptions of the exposure to violence.[20] In addition, youth of different ages and developmental levels are likely to manifest different reactions to chronic community violence and have different vulnerabilities to the same event.[5] Consequently, interventions designed for youth exposed to chronic community violence must incorporate strategies to accommodate individual differences in response to exposure.[5]

Areas to Explore in Future Interventions

The 4 interventions reviewed in this chapter focus primarily on the symptoms of distress among youth exposed to chronic community violence. Although 3 of the 4 interventions include pre- and postintervention outcome data, not all of the interventions incorporate randomized, controlled designs. Future follow-up efficacy trials should be conducted on each of the following studies: Ceballo[23]; Cooley, Boyd and Grados[46]; Saltzman and colleagues[47]; and Jaycox[48]; as well as the "prototypical" intervention described by Berman, Silverman and Kurtines.[35]

Externalizing behaviors, although recognized as a significant correlate and consequence of exposure to violence,[73] were not targeted specifically in any of the reviewed interventions. In fact, significant externalizing behavior problems were an *exclusion* criterion in some of the interventions. Results reported by Stein and colleagues[65] suggest that improvements in classroom behavior will not likely result from an intervention designed to address symptoms of distress. Specifically, participation in the CBITS program[66] did not result in significant reductions in classroom behavior problems. Interventions for youth are needed that target externalizing behaviors related to exposure to chronic community violence as well as for the co-occurring problems of distress and internalizing behavior.

Future research should also examine preventive interventions for youth *at risk* for exposure to chronic community violence: These should include universal interventions that teach skills for avoiding risk — even the types portrayed in the media — and enhancing effective coping in dangerous situations. Studies that focus on protective factors that mitigate adverse emotional, behavioral and academic outcomes associated with exposure to chronic community violence will facilitate the development of preventive interventions. Important among these protective factors are parental/caregiver and other social supports.

Lastly, there is a need for empirically tested interventions that specifically target youth exposed to chronic community violence. Evidence-based interventions in such situations are critical if we are to prevent or reduce the negative consequences of such exposure and promote healthy adjustment among those who have been exposed to chronic community violence.

References

1. Cooley MR, Turner SM, Beidel DC. Assessing community violence: The Children's Report of Exposure to Violence. *Journal of the American Academy of Child and Adolescent Psychiatry.* 1995;34:201-208.
2. Koop CE, Lundberg GB. Violence in America: a public health emergency. Time to bite the bullet back [published corrections appear in *JAMA: The Journal of the American Medical Association.* 1992;268:3074 and *JAMA: The Journal of the American Medical Association.* 1992;271:1404]. *JAMA: The Journal of the American Medical Association.* 1992;267:3075-3076.
3. Horn JL, Trickett PK. Community violence and child development: a review of research. In: Trickett PK, Schellenbach CJ, eds. *Violence Against Children in the Family and the Community.* Washington, DC: American Psychological Association; 1998:103-138.
4. Lorion RP. Exposure to urban violence: contamination of the school environment. In: Elliott DS, Hamburg BA, Williams KR, eds. *Violence in American Schools.* New York, NY: Cambridge University Press; 1998:293-311.

5. Berkowitz SJ. Children exposed to community violence: the rationale for early intervention. *Clinical Child and Family Psychology Review.* 2003;6:293-302.
6. Cooley-Quille M, Boyd RC, Frantz E, Walsh J. Emotional and behavioral impact of exposure to community violence in inner-city adolescents. *Journal of Child Clinical Psychology.* 2001;30:199-206.
7. DuRant RH, Cadenhead C, Pendergrast RA, Slavens G, Linder CW. Factors associated with the use of violence among urban black adolescents. *American Journal of Public Health.* 1994;84:612-617.
8. Fitzpatrick KM, Boldizar JP. The prevalence and consequences of exposure to violence among African-American youth. *Journal of the American Academy of Child and Adolescent Psychiatry.* 1993;32:424-430.
9. Fehon DC, Grilo CM, Lipschitz DS. Correlates of community violence exposure in hospitalized adolescents. *Comprehensive Psychiatry.* 2001;42:283-290.
10. Freeman LN, Mokros H, Poznanski EO. Violent events reported by normal urban school-aged children: characteristics and depression correlates. *Journal of the American Academy of Child and Adolescent Psychiatry.* 1993;32:419-423.
11. Gorman-Smith D, Tolan P. The role of exposure to community violence and developmental problems among inner-city youth. *Development and Psychopathology.* 1998;10:101-116.
12. Schwab-Stone ME, Ayers TS, Kasprow W, et al. No safe haven: a study of violence exposure in an urban community. *Journal of the American Academy of Child and Adolescent Psychiatry.* 1995;34:1343-1352.
13. Schwartz D, Gorman AH. Community violence exposure and children's academic functioning. *Journal of Educational Psychology.* 2003;95:163-173.
14. Kendall PC, Hammen C. *Abnormal Psychology: Understanding Human Progress; Understanding Human Problems.* Boston, Mass: Houghton Mifflin; 1995.
15. Jones JC, Barlow DH. The etiology of posttraumatic stress disorder. *Clinical Psychology Review.* 1990;10:299-328.
16. Pynoos RS, Frederick C, Nader K, et al. Life threat and posttraumatic stress in school-age children. *Archives of General Psychiatry.* 1987;44:1057-1063.
17. Schwarz ED, Kowalski JM. Malignant memories: PTSD in children and adults after a school shooting. *Journal of the American Academy of Child and Adolescent Psychiatry.* 1991;30:936-944.
18. Turner SM, Beidel DC, Cooley-Quille MR. *Social Effectiveness Therapy (SET): SET Therapist's Guide.* Toronto, Ontario, Canada: Multi-Health Systems; 1997.
19. Keane TM, Gerardi RJ, Lyons JA, Wolfe J. The interrelationship of substance abuse and PTSD: epidemiological and clinical considerations. In: Galanter M, ed. *Recent Developments in Alcoholism.* Vol 6. New York, NY: Plenum Press; 1988:27-48.
20. Hill HM, Madhere S. Exposure to community violence and African American children: a multidimensional model of risks and resources. *Journal of Community Psychology.* 1996;24:26-43.
21. Ceballo R, Ramirez C, Hearn KD, Maltese KL. Community violence and children's psychological well-being: does parental monitoring matter? *Journal of Clinical Child and Adolescent Psychology: The Official Journal for the Society of Clinical Child and Adolescent Psychology, American Psychological Association, Division 53.* 2003;32:586-592.
22. Guterman NB, Cameron M. Young clients' exposure to community violence: how much do their therapists know? *The American Journal of Orthopsychiatry.* 1999;69:382-391.
23. Ceballo R. The Neighborhood Club: a supportive intervention group for children exposed to urban violence. *The American Journal of Orthopsychiatry.* 2000;70:401-407.
24. Guterman NB, Hahm HC, Cameron M. Adolescent victimization and subsequent use of mental health counseling services. *The Journal of Adolescent Health: Official Publication of the Society for Adolescent Medicine.* 2002;30:336-345.
25. Gladstein J, Rusonis EJ, Heald FP. A comparison of inner-city and upper-middle class youths' exposure to violence. *The Journal of Adolescent Health: Official Publication of the Society for Adolescent Medicine.* 1992;13:275-280.
26. Pynoos RS, Nader K. Children's exposure to violence and traumatic death. *Psychiatric Annals.* 1990;20:334-344.

27. Bronfenbrenner U. *The Ecology of Human Development: Experiments By Nature and Design.* Cambridge, Mass: Harvard University Press; 1979.
28. Lerner R. *America's Youth in Crisis: Challenges and Options for Programs and Policies.* Thousand Oaks, Calif: Sage Publications; 1995.
29. Lewis JA, Lewis MD, Daniels JA, D'Andrea MJ. *Community Counseling: Empowerment Strategies for a Diverse Society.* Pacific Grove, Calif: Brooks-Cole; 1998.
30. Kazdin AE. Adolescent mental health. Prevention and treatment programs. *The American Psychologist.* 1993;48:127-141.
31. Reese LE, Vera EM, Thompson K, Reyes R. A qualitative investigation of perceptions of violence risk factors in low-income African American children. *Journal of Clinical Child Psychology.* 2001;30:161-171.
32. Farrell SP, Hains AA, Davies WH. Cognitive behavioral interventions for sexually abused children exhibiting PTSD symptomatology. *Behavior Therapy.* 1998;29:241-255.
33. King NJ, Tonge BJ, Mullen P, et al. Treating sexually abused children with posttraumatic stress symptoms: a randomized clinical trial. *Journal of the American Academy of Child and Adolescent Psychiatry.* 2000;39:1347-1355.
34. March JS, Amaya-Jackson L, Murray MC, Schulte A. Cognitive-behavioral psychotherapy for children and adolescents with posttraumatic stress disorder after a single-incident stressor. *Journal of the American Academy of Child and Adolescent Psychiatry.* 1998;37:585-593.
35. Berman SL, Silverman WK, Kurtines WM. Children's and adolescents' exposure to community violence, post-traumatic stress reactions, and treatment implications. *The Australasian Journal of Disaster and Trauma Studies* [serial online]. 2000;1. Available at: http://www.massey.ac.nz/%7Etrauma/issues/2000-1/berman.htm. Accessed January 14, 2004.
36. Foa EB, Kozak MJ. Emotional processing of fear: exposure to corrective information. *Psychological Bulletin.* 1986;99:20-35.
37. Cohen S, Wills TA. Stress, social support, and the buffering hypothesis. *Psychological Bulletin.* 1985; 98:310-357.
38. Saltzman WR. Exposure to community violence and the prediction of violent antisocial behavior in a multi-ethnic sample of adolescents. *Dissertation Abstracts International.* 1996;57:2223.
39. Singer MI, Anglin TM, Song LY, Lunghofer L. Adolescents' exposure to violence and associated symptoms of psychological trauma. *JAMA: The Journal of the American Medical Association.* 1995;273:477-482.
40. Henrich CC, Schwab-Stone M, Fanti K, Jones SM, Ruchkin V. The association of community violence exposure with middle-school achievement: a prospective study. *Journal of Applied Developmental Psychology.* 2004;25:327-348.
41. Bell CC, Jenkins EJ. Traumatic stress and children. *Journal of Health Care for the Poor and Underserved.* 1991;2:175-188.
42. Taylor RJ, Tucker MB, Chatters LM, Jayakody R. Recent demographic trends in African American family structure. In: Taylor RJ, Jackson JS, Chatters LM, eds. *Family Life in Black America.* Thousand Oaks, Calif: Sage Publications; 1997:14-62.
43. Pynoos RS, Nader K. Psychological first aid and treatment approaches to children exposed to community violence: research implications. *Journal of Traumatic Stress.* 1988;1:445-473.
44. Warner BS, Weist MD. Urban youth as witnesses to violence: beginning assessment and treatment efforts. *Journal of Youth and Adolescence.* 1996;25:361-377.
45. Catalano RF, Berglund ML, Ryan JAM, Lonczak HC, Hawkins JD. *Positive Youth Development in the United States: Research Findings on Evaluations of Positive Youth Development Programs.* Washington, DC: US Dept of Health and Human Services, National Institute of Child Health and Human Development, Administration for Children & Families; 1999.
46. Cooley MR, Boyd RC, Grados JJ. Feasibility of an anxiety preventive intervention for community violence-exposed African American children. *The Journal of Primary Prevention.* In press.

47. Saltzman WR, Pynoos RS, Layne CM, Steinberg AM, Aisenberg E. Trauma- and grief-focused intervention for adolescents exposed to community violence: results of a school-based screening and group treatment protocol. *Group Dynamics: Theory, Research, and Practice.* 2001;5:291-303.
48. Jaycox L. *CBITS: Cognitive–Behavioral Intervention for Trauma in Schools.* Longmont, Colo: Sopris West Educational Services; 2003.
49. Foy DW, Eriksson CB, Trice GA. Introduction to group interventions for trauma survivors. *Group Dynamics: Theory, Research, and Practice.* 2001;5:246-251.
50. Ceballo R, Ramirez C, Maltese KL. A bilingual "Neighborhood Club": intervening with children exposed to urban violence. *American Journal of Community Psychology.* In press.
51. Barrett PM, Lowry-Webster H, Holmes J. *The FRIENDS Program: Treatment Manual.* Queensland, Australia: Griffith Early Intervention Project; 1998.
52. Barrett PM. Evaluation of cognitive-behavioral group treatments for childhood anxiety disorders. *Journal of Clinical Child Psychology.* 1998;27:459-468.
53. Dadds MR, Spence SH, Holland DE, Barrett PM, Laurens KR. Prevention and early intervention for anxiety disorders: a controlled trial. *Journal of Consulting and Clinical Psychology.* 1997;65:627-635.
54. Reynolds CR, Richmond BO. What I think and feel: a revised measure of children's manifest anxiety. *Journal of Abnormal Child Psychology.* 1978;6:271-280.
55. Silverman WK. Diagnostic reliability of anxiety disorders in children using structured interviews. *Journal of Anxiety Disorders.* 1991;5:105-124.
56. Silverman WK, Albano AM. *Anxiety Disorders Interview Schedule for DSM-IV–Child Interview Schedule.* San Antonio, Tex: The Psychological Corporation; 1996.
57. Silverman WK, Nelles WB. The Anxiety Disorders Interview Schedule for Children. *Journal of the American Academy of Child and Adolescent Psychiatry.* 1988;27:772-778.
58. Sarason IG. Test anxiety, attention and the general problem of anxiety. In: Spielberger CD, Sarason IG, eds. *Stress and Anxiety.* Vol 1. Washington, DC: Hemisphere/Wiley; 1975:165-188.
59. Kovacs M. *Children's Depression Inventory (CDI).* New York, NY: Multi-Health Systems; 1992.
60. March JS, Parker JD, Sullivan K, Stallings P, Conners CK. The Multidimensional Anxiety Scale for Children (MASC): factor structure, reliability and validity. *Journal of the American Academy of Child and Adolescent Psychiatry.* 1997;36:554-565.
61. Pynoos RS, Steinberg AM, Wraith R. A developmental model of childhood traumatic stress. In: Cicchetti D, Cohen DJ, eds. *Risk, Disorder, and Adaptation.* New York, NY: Wiley; 1995:72-95. Cicchetti D, Cohen DJ, eds. *Developmental Psychopathology*; vol 2.
62. Layne CM, Pynoos RS, Saltzman WR, et al. Trauma/grief-focused group psychotherapy: school-based postwar intervention with traumatized Bosnian adolescents. *Group Dynamics: Theory, Research, and Practice.* 2001;5:277-290.
63. Rodriguez N, Steinberg AM, Pynoos RS. *UCLA PTSD Reaction Index–Adolescent Version.* Los Angeles, Calif: University of California at Los Angeles; 1999.
64. Layne CM, Steinberg A, Savjak M, Pynoos RS. *Grief Screening Scale.* Los Angeles, Calif: University of California at Los Angeles; 1998.
65. Stein BD, Jaycox LH, Kataoka SH, et al. A mental health intervention for schoolchildren exposed to violence: a randomized controlled trial. *JAMA: The Journal of the American Medical Association.* 2003;290:603-611.
66. Kataoka SH, Stein BD, Jaycox LH, et al. A school-based mental health program for traumatized Latino immigrant children. *Journal of the American Academy of Child and Adolescent Psychiatry.* 2003;42:311-318.
67. Foa EB, Johnson KM, Feeny NC, Treadwell KR. The Child PTSD Symptom Scale: a preliminary examination of its psychometric properties. *Journal of Clinical Child Psychology.* 2001;30:376-384.
68. Jellinek MS, Murphy JM, Robinson J, Feins A, Lamb S, Fenton T. Pediatric Symptom Checklist: screening school-age children for psychosocial dysfunction. *The Journal of Pediatrics.* 1988;112: 201-209.

69. Aisenberg E, Mennen FE. Children exposed to community violence: issues for assessment and treatment. *Child & Adolescent Social Work Journal: C&A.* 2000;17:341-360.

70. Dempsey M, Overstreet S, Moely B. "Approach" and "avoidance" coping and PTSD symptoms in inner-city youth. *Current Psychology: Developmental, Learning, Personality, Social.* 2000;19:28-45.

71. Marans S, Cohen DJ. Children and inner-city violence: strategies for intervention. In: Leavitt LA, Fox NA, eds. *The Psychological Effects of War and Violence on Children.* Hillsdale, NJ: Lawrence Erlbaum Associates; 1993:281-301.

72. Martinez P, Richters JE. The NIMH community violence project: II. Children's distress symptoms associated with violence exposure. *Psychiatry.* 1993;56:22-35.

73. Lynch M. Consequences of children's exposure to community violence. *Clinical Child and Family Psychology Review.* 2003;6:265-274.

Section 4: Social and Economic Implications: Outcomes for Both the Individual Child and Society

Abstracts from Section 4: Social and Economic Implications: Outcomes for Both the Individual Child and Society

The Second Mouse's Agenda: A Comprehensive Model for Preventing and Reducing Violence in the Lives of School-Age Children

Philip B. Uninsky, JD

The Partnership for Results is a not-for-profit agency dedicated to promoting community-wide collaborations that foster the healthy development of children from infancy through secondary school. The Partnership brings social and political science into practical service through a variety of strategies — creation of a new form of local governance; implementation of a continuum of evidence-based programs; and the development of interagency assessment tools and databases. Independent evaluations have demonstrated that the preventive and early intervention activities introduced by the Partnership have lowered the levels of juvenile delinquency and physical aggression substantially, and have reduced the use of residential treatment programs by the child welfare and juvenile justice systems significantly. The Partnership has also succeeded in involving all public agencies that have child-caring functions — education, mental health, human services, health care and law enforcement — in coordinating their program implementation activities, integrating their service planning and ensuring their sustainability.

Residential Mobility Interventions as Treatments for the Sequelae of Neighborhood Violence

Greg J. Duncan, PhD
Elizabeth Clark-Kauffman, PhD
Emily K. Snell, PhD

Despite recent reductions in neighborhood crime and poverty, children and adults in many unsafe neighborhoods are still traumatized by witnessing and/or living in constant fear of violence. In this chapter, after reviewing the evidence on neighborhood violence and its effects on mental health, we focus on the promise of residential mobility intervention programs to reduce neighborhood violence-related mental health problems. Most of our attention is devoted to the Moving to Opportunity (MTO) residential mobility program, which randomly assigns families the opportunity to move from public housing in high-poverty urban neighborhoods to low-poverty neighborhoods. An evaluation of adult and child outcomes, 4 years to 7 years postbaseline, revealed substantial program-based improvements in adults' perceptions of neighborhood safety and victimization, as well as in their mental health. The impact of the violence experienced by children was much smaller than that for adults, and it was also smaller for boys than for girls. The improvements in mental health were confined to the girls. Evidence suggests that problem behaviors exhibited by boys may actually have worsened as the result of their families participating in the MTO program offer to move to low-poverty neighborhoods.

The Second Mouse's Agenda: A Comprehensive Model for Preventing and Reducing Violence in the Lives of School-Age Children

Philip B. Uninsky, JD

Introduction and Overview

The Partnership for Results (the "Partnership") is a not-for-profit agency formed in 1999 to administer a Safe Schools/Healthy Students (SS/HS) grant from the US Department of Education (USDOE), the US Department of Health and Human Services and the US Department of Justice (USDOJ). Its principal mission has been to develop a model for implementing evidence-based programs (EBPs) to accomplish the following:

- reduce juvenile violence and destructive risk taking
- prevent and reduce the exposure of children and youth to violence
- mitigate academic underachievement and failure

The Partnership has concentrated its efforts on Auburn, NY, a small city of approximately 30,000 residents, and several nearby communities in rural Cayuga County, NY. These communities exhibit many of the signs of distress that afflict other regions of the United States that are losing their industrial base and are in economic decline, including high levels of physically aggressive behavior and substance abuse among youth, and high rates of domestic violence.

As with any ambitious service delivery initiative, the Partnership has had to overcome several impediments, primarily agency territoriality, implementer resistance to change and the common tendency of high-quality programs to regress to a predictable mean. Part of the agenda developed by the Partnership is to establish an effective, durable and replicable structure for overcoming these impediments. In addition, the Partnership has worked to address the following 2 significant and still unresolved questions in the field of prevention and early intervention for at-risk children and families:

- What results can be gained by implementing a *continuum* of proven programs?
- What mechanisms must be implemented to overcome the obstacles to interagency collaboration?

Although concerns about program efficacy and accountability have created heightened interest in EBPs, little is known about the consequences of introducing them simultaneously across all of the service systems that care for children — education, health care, mental health care, substance abuse, child welfare, family court and law enforcement. In fact, it is quite rare for communities to implement more than a handful of EBPs in their repertoire of prevention and early intervention programs. This reluctance is the result of several factors, including the following:

- the extent to which categorical funding streams are linked to discrete service modalities
- the continuing elaboration of the regulatory framework for mandated services and procedural requirements
- a disinclination on the part of public authorities to invest in prevention during times of economic retrenchment
- the reluctance of organizational decision makers to encumber their agencies with the administrative and fiscal burdens associated with implementing EBPs

Given these barriers, it is evident why few communities have implemented a broad spectrum of EBPs along the proven principles of public health programming. To do so would entail developing a continuum of prevention and early intervention programs that operate, to the maximum extent possible, in natural settings, such as day care centers, schools and households, and that serve, across a broad range of needs, children of all ages and their families.

The development of such a continuum of services certainly has its proponents among many policy makers and researchers. There is good reason to believe that such an approach could have a substantial, positive effect on the social, emotional and academic development of children throughout the community. Indeed, it is quite possible that the cumulative outcome of these coexisting programs might exceed the sum of the impact of each individual program.[1,2] However, in the absence of concrete guidance from research and practice, when the Partnership began its activities in 1999, it was still unknown whether the simultaneous implementation of many EBPs could occur while consistently meeting or exceeding the results predicted by the validating research for each program.

Educational, human services and law enforcement agencies have generally acknowledged the need to act collaboratively when providing services for at-risk children and their families, but they have typically failed to do so on any kind of ongoing basis. To a large extent, this failure is due to structural problems: Each part of the service delivery system, both public and private, operates in a discrete, single-discipline "silo." Categorical funding streams from the federal and state governments are linked to programmatic and reporting requirements that tend to channel clients through system-specific, single-discipline assessments and treatments. The capacity to exchange client information across disciplines is limited by a complex web of critically important state and federal laws and regulations intended to protect confidentiality.

In most communities, moreover, the service delivery system is created in an ad hoc and piecemeal manner. It is the product of stakeholders competing for narrowly defined vested interests and responding to intermittent crises. In the absence of an interagency framework that allows for coordination, at-risk children and their families are compelled to navigate a fragmented system, accessing services by cycling through various entry points — from family court to social service agencies to the special education system. As a result, diagnoses are narrowly framed, interventions tend to be discontinuous and services offered are often incomplete.

This state of affairs — the absence of *substantive* interagency collaboration — certainly prevailed in Cayuga County when the Partnership initiated its activities. At least in theory, a resolution of this problem could be achieved if public agencies jointly developed a structure of interorganizational coordination; one that involved, at a minimum, the following elements[3-7]:

- multisystem service planning and service delivery
- flexibility in allocating funds
- a system for sharing information that protects clients' privacy and rights

What is not clear in the burgeoning literature on local governance is how to turn theory into practice.

The Partnership Model: Offering a Continuum of Services

There is considerable evidence that the model developed by the Partnership, described in the following pages, overcomes the common obstacles to system reform. It also implements a continuum of evidence-based interventions that coexist well and are supported effectively by substantive interagency collaboration. Using a variety of blended funding techniques, all of the initiatives developed by the Partnership have been sustained by public agencies for a significant period of time beyond the end of the initial 3 years of funding under the SS/HS award, many of them indefinitely. This is a clear indication that the project has been accepted by the community, in general, and by public agencies, in particular, as a legitimate approach for reducing violence and substance abuse, and for improving the quality and reach of services for children and their families.

The Partnership developed a systematic approach to comprehensive assessment and service integration that has been adopted by public and private human services agencies, as well as by school districts and law enforcement agencies in Cayuga County. Independent evaluators have found that the continuum of EBPs set in motion by the Partnership were implemented rapidly, reaching their eligible populations effectively and operating with high degrees of fidelity to the program's models and principles.[8,9] These programs are producing results that consistently meet or exceed those predicted by research, as reported by the Partnership,[10] the Children's Institute (Rochester, NY, unpublished data, 2002, 2003), the National Center for Children, Families and Communities (Boulder, Colo, unpublished data, March 2003) and by the Every Person Influences Children (EPIC) National Center for Parenting and Character Education (Buffalo, NY, unpublished data, 2002).

The Partnership model and its programs address many of the external and internal factors that interfere with positive social, emotional and academic child development, including community and school violence, problems in the home, racial and ethnic conflicts, substance abuse, poverty, poor health and disabilities. Independent analyses of archival data and survey data indicate that the following changes have taken place in the target area focused on by the Partnership — Auburn, NY, and surrounding Cayuga County:

- Students are more likely to perceive schools as "safe places."[11]
- Substance abuse rates are declining.[11]

- Standardized test scores, at least in the elementary schools, are increasing.[11]
- In-school violence rates are falling dramatically.[10*]
- Juvenile arrest rates are declining[12†] and delinquency levels are dropping (Cayuga County [NY] Attorney's Office, unpublished data, 1999–2003).[‡]

The approach that the Partnership took to accomplish these results is perhaps best characterized by a bit of folk wisdom: "The early bird may get the worm, *but the second mouse gets the cheese.*" The agenda of the Partnership belongs to that careful, observant and living rodent, adopting only those practices, programs and organizational principles that, to the fullest extent possible, are already borne out by experience. Part of the strategy of the Partnership entails the use of a very restrictive definition of EBPs[13] — as noted in legislation proposed in New York State to replicate the Partnership model — that insists on high-quality, independent evaluations and evidence of prior successful replication in a similar community. With these goals in mind, the Partnership adopted the following definition of EBPs with an eye toward maximizing successful replication: "[An EBP is] a program whose evaluation, which has been completed by an independent agency with demonstrated expertise in evaluation, yields statistically significant data demonstrating the program's effectiveness in accomplishing its intended purposes, and which has been replicated in another community with an effectiveness that is comparable to that indicated in the evaluation."[13]

Whenever possible, the Partnership also gives priority to EBPs developed and operating in New York State. Such programs perform well within the state's regulatory structure and, when they are school-based, are more likely to

*MAGI Educational Services, the independent evaluator of the Partnership, compared the average number of serious, school-based incidents of physical aggression for the 2 years prior to Partnership initiation of program activities in the city of Auburn, NY (1999 and 2000), with the number of incidents during the first 2 years of program activities and found that there was a significant reduction in violence over time: 54% in the 5 elementary schools, 83% in the 2 middle schools and 31% in the city's high school. In addition, there was a 96% reduction in school bomb threats and a 68% decline in urgent calls to the police made by the schools.

†The most recent county-level data published by the New York State Council on Children and Families indicates that, from 1999 to 2001, there was a 48% decline in the arrests of youth ages 13 years to 15 years in Cayuga County, NY.

‡Comparing the 2 years prior to program implementation (1999 and 2000) with the first 3 years of Partnership program activities (2001 to 2003), there was a 20% decline in the number of petitions before the family court for juvenile delinquency and a 32% decline in the number of charged juvenile delinquency offenses.

conform to its learning standards. In addition, proximity of the parent agency to the project assures more timely access to vital technical assistance, which, among other matters, helps assure fidelity to the EBP model.

The organizational structure and guiding principles of the Partnership, however, cannot be gleaned merely from historical experience. Its agenda — the "second mouse's" — is a deliberate exercise in applying social science and political science to practical service by adopting procedures that are well grounded in research and implemented only after thorough review by practitioners. In particular, the Partnership embraces clearly delineated lessons emerging from research in a wide range of fields, including the following:

- the critical role an active system of local governance and collaborative decision making among public institutions plays in integrating, improving and sustaining service[2-7]
- the impact of a "systems-of-care" approach to the delivery of human services[14-18]
- the understanding that violent, truant and other destructive risk-taking behaviors have complex etiologies that require comprehensive strategies in order to be reduced substantially[19-22]
- the relative efficacy and cost-efficiency of preventive and early intervention programs[23-29]
- the role that fidelity to EBP practices and procedures plays in engendering positive program outcomes[30-36]
- the use of management information systems to improve the quality of strategic planning, interagency service delivery and program accountability[37-39]

An Overview of the Partnership Model

The Partnership model, as depicted in Figure 1, integrates 8 governing principles, the first of which is the development of a comprehensive and multidisciplinary screening and assessment process.[40] (Note: Fig 1 and the other figures noted in this chapter belong to and are copyrighted by the Partnership for Results, Inc., and can be found at various links on its Web site: http://www.partnershipforresults.org/.) As a growing body of research indicates, children confronting multiple risks are more likely than other youth to engage in violence, struggle in school and participate in a wide range of

***Fig 1. The 8 governing principles of the Partnership model.*[40]**

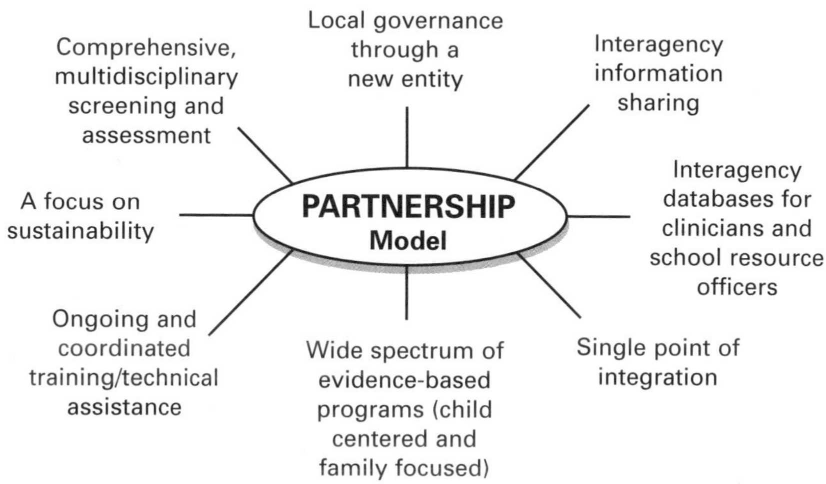

destructive risk-taking behaviors, including truancy, delinquency, substance abuse and gang participation[41-44]: For example, a 1999 study of juvenile delinquents placed in detention facilities in New York State found that more than 95% faced 4 or more significant personal and environmental risk factors.[45] Services for this population, once they have become habitual offenders, are proving ineffective: 75% are rearrested within 36 months of release, and the majority of these arrests are for violent felony offenses.[45] Interventions with multiply at-risk children that occur at earlier stages of the onset of destructive risk-taking behavior are demonstrably more effective and cost-efficient than are the more intensive, restrictive alternatives.[46,47]

The Assessment Process

To provide intervention services in an integrated and timely manner, it is essential that certain conditions be met. An assessment process should comprehensively identify those risks most clearly related to the development of violent and destructive risk-taking behaviors. Such an assessment should also serve to improve the ability of qualified professionals to diagnose problems and strengths accurately in an interdisciplinary manner.

In 2000 and 2001, the Partnership convened an interdisciplinary expert panel of clinicians and psychometricians to identify effective instruments for the assessment of possibly at-risk adolescents. A review of more than 80 age-appropriate and validated instruments revealed that there is a paucity of sufficiently comprehensive interdisciplinary tools that address risk. Remarkably, few of the instruments reviewed were attuned to the early onset of problems, and efforts to combine instruments would have resulted in measurement tools that were unduly intrusive or exigent for clients. As a result, the expert panel, supported by a team of evaluators, developed a 2-tiered assessment process. The first stage of this interdisciplinary assessment process is the "Observation Checklist,"[48] which screens for the early onset of symptoms related to mental illness, substance abuse, exposure to violence and cognitive disabilities. These behavioral warning signs, expressed in lay terms, focus on both internalizing and externalizing behaviors. Completed by classroom teachers, the Observation Checklist serves the dual role of educating school personnel and ensuring early and narrowly targeted referrals of multiply at-risk adolescents for intensive assessment.

The Adolescent Well-Being Assessment Tool, or Well-BAT as it is commonly known, is the instrument used in the second stage of the interdisciplinary screening and assessment process. (An excerpt of the Well-BAT, including the roster of advisors involved in its development, is available at http://www.partnershipforresults.org/pdfs/Well-Being_Assessment_Excer.pdf.[48]) Completed by a mental health clinician, with parental or caretaker consent, the Well-BAT provides a systematic overview of the early onset of problems associated with mental illness, substance abuse, exposure to violence and learning disabilities across the principal contexts — individual, family, school and community — of the youth being assessed. The 37 rubrics that comprise the Well-BAT are completed using multiple sources of information: interviews with teachers, youth and family members; clinical observations; and a wide array of collateral information derived from such sources as school records, child welfare investigations, prior mental health and substance abuse assessments and medical reports. Several of the rubrics are scored with the aid of 2 standardized self-report measurement instruments: the Personal Experience Screening Questionnaire,[49,50] which is structured to identify substance abuse short of dependence, and the Youth-Pediatric Symptom Checklist,[51] which assesses the severity of internalizing and externalizing problems. Independent evaluations of the Well-BAT indicate that it meets a high standard of discriminant validity, contrasting groups validity and overall reliability.[48] These reports also concluded that the Well-BAT provides high levels of internal consistency, stability over time and interrater reliability.

When completed, the Well-BAT provides a foundation for the development of comprehensive integrated service plans, particularly for the child or adolescent who can benefit from early preventive and intervention services, both therapeutic and nontherapeutic in nature. The Well-BAT is an instrument that permits clinicians, who have appropriate and ongoing training, to extend their observations beyond their usual discipline-specific parameters. To use the Well-BAT successfully, however, the following systems must first be in place:

- a method to gather collateral information used in the Well-BAT that incorporates legal protections safeguarding confidentiality
- a process for addressing concerns among law enforcement, education, mental health and other agencies that the information they generate will not be used inappropriately or misunderstood when shared
- a system for maximizing accountability regarding use of the Well-BAT, the development of comprehensive service plans and the routine review of outcomes

Moreover, successful use of the Well-BAT requires a sustained effort at agency coordination, so that clinicians working in a broad range of environments — from schools to foster care — can receive training and ongoing technical assistance in the use of the instrument. In other words, as practiced by the Partnership, comprehensive assessments presume a change in local governance.

A Change in Local Governance

Both the Articles of Incorporation and the Memorandum of Understanding (MOU) drawn up by the Partnership in 2000 expressed a commitment to accomplish the following:

- promote comprehensive, interagency service planning
- facilitate the implementation, to the maximum extent possible, of a continuum of outcome-based EBPs
- collectively sustain effective programs

The Partnership operates as a quasi-governmental entity. Its Board of Directors is comprised of public agency leaders from city and county governments in the areas of education, law enforcement and human services. Current board members include the superintendents of the Auburn Enlarged City School District and the Cayuga-Onondaga Board of Cooperative Educational Services, a judge of the Auburn City Court, the Chief of Police of the City of Auburn, a representative of the Cayuga County Attorney's Office (which serves as the presentment agency for delinquency petitions) and the commissioners of the Cayuga County mental health, social services and health departments.

Very early in the life of the Partnership, board members made a distinct transition from perceiving the Partnership as yet another coalition having grand designs but promising few accomplishments to understanding it to be an agency that required their very active participation and collaboration.[10] This was due partly to the fact that the founding corporate documents included a clearly articulated process of system reform linked to measurable goals and objectives, rather than the vague mission statement common to these kinds of documents. In addition, because the directors of the Partnership are members of a board rather than a coalition or working group, they have a collective fiduciary responsibility to ensure that the corporate funds of the Partnership are expended in keeping with the agency's mission. This requirement encouraged a high level of involvement, even if it was rooted initially in a history of interagency territoriality and related concerns about gaining access to newly available federal funds.

Early successes reinforced active participation by agency leaders in this new form of local governance. Many EBPs, if implemented properly and rapidly, result in substantial short-term positive behavioral and economic benefits, such as gains in basic educational skills and shorter stays in high-cost restrictive programs. Two examples of such early success for the Partnership were Opportunity for Academic Success in School (OASIS) and Intensive Supervision Conditional Discharge (ISCD). OASIS is an intensive, summer, educational-enrichment program for younger children (those entering grades 1 through 4) that is validated by the New York State Sharing Success Program.[52] In each of the early years of implementation (2000–2003), Partnership analyses of OASIS pre- and posttesting data indicated average gains of at least 29% in math skills and 30% in English language skills among participants. ISCD is a therapeutic, community-based alternative to incarceration for adjudicated delinquents.[53-55] Using practices and procedures articulated by the juvenile intensive supervision model, ISCD clinicians and case managers were able to maintain program compliance for more than 75% of participants, with less than 35% of participants rearrested 1 year after program completion — a rate far below that of youth placed in detention facilities.[45]

In addition, the 3-year federal grant for the SS/HS initiative, which was awarded to the Auburn Enlarged City School District in late 1999, provided the Partnership with the financial resources to employ a central staff to support program development. This staff possessed expertise in the development of training curricula, child and family law, information technology and program funding. As a freestanding, quasi-governmental agency, the Partnership also has the flexibility to assemble a specialized team of independent contractors who can provide targeted technical assistance services in areas such as psychometrics and assessment instrument development, database programming and specialized training in evaluation and therapeutic techniques. In sum, the Partnership promotes affiliation and, ultimately, greater collaboration by externalizing the costs of systems change. It does so by alleviating the burdens of implementation, which include negotiating with the parent agencies for EBPs, training implementers and collecting and analyzing data that are critical to maintaining fidelity to program models.

Within 1 year of its establishment, the Partnership became a legitimate form of local governance for public agencies in Cayuga County that have responsibilities for the welfare of children and families. Policy making regarding the interconnected issues of violence, destructive risk taking and academic achievement moved from a single-agency, system-specific orientation to one of multisystem planning and coordination. The emphases on meeting state and federal requirements and program standards expanded to an even greater emphasis on achieving particular program outcomes. In addition, the commitment of agencies to sustaining — and even expanding — this locally developed continuum of performance-based preventive and early intervention programs resulted in the development of many new revenue sharing and flexible funding arrangements.

A critical component of the emerging role of the Partnership as a legitimate entity of local governance was that it became the locus of service integration for children with multiple problems and their families. Public agencies rely on Partnership staff to provide training and ongoing technical assistance for the Well-BAT to clinicians working in educational, child welfare, mental health, substance abuse and juvenile justice settings. A team of attorneys from the Partnership and the public sector developed an MOU to encourage the routine provision of client-specific information required for comprehensive assessment and integrated service planning. Following a review of the legal, procedural and practical barriers limiting information sharing, the Partnership developed a Waiver of Confidentiality and Consent-to-Treatment for parents that protects clients' rights and encourages parents to participate in the assessment and treatment process. Presently incorporated into the interagency MOU, the following are the conditions of the Waiver:

- It is revocable at any time.
- It expires on a specific date.
- It is written in clear, accessible language.
- It permits the signatory to limit the range of information provided.
- It affirms the rights of parents and clients to have a deliberative voice in developing the treatment plan.
- It guarantees that any information will be used *only* for the purposes of assessment and treatment.
- It states that the information will not be redisclosed without obtaining subsequent permission and, in that circumstance, will be used only for the purposes of treatment and service planning.

Clinicians are obligated legally to present the Waiver to parents in person, providing an opportunity for clinicians to explain the advantages of parental involvement in a comprehensive assessment and service integration model. This face-to-face technique for collecting data from the Well-BAT has proved noncontroversial: In fact, Partnership records indicate that fewer than 1% of parents refused to participate among the more than 355 referrals made for comprehensive assessment from October 2000 through December 2003 in Cayuga County.

The public agencies also designated the Partnership as the sole repository for the multidisciplinary database. The prohibition on redisclosure without parental permission, the limitation that the data collected be used only for assessment and treatment and the location of the data in a secure, neutral site help address the concerns of families, clients and public agencies that the information collected might be used inappropriately. The security of the data is reinforced by policies that limit access to clients' data *only* to their clinicians and supervisors, a Partnership resource coordinator (who assists the clinical staff with developing integrated service plans) and a data manager who plays a critical role in maintaining the high quality of program delivery. In sum, the Partnership has become a single point of service integration for multiply at-risk children and their families.

Building a Data Management System

Given the volume of information collected by the Partnership — from referrals, assessments, family demographics and educational and treatment histories to service plans and outcome data — it was clear from the outset that a high-quality and dependable data management system was needed. Without such a system, it would be difficult for clinicians to maintain program integrity and accountability, particularly when working with complex cases. Under the model of service integration established by the Partnership, clinicians performing assessments using the Well-BAT function both as counselors and case managers who help assure that an intervention is truly comprehensive. They do so by routinely identifying additional, complementary therapeutic and nontherapeutic services for clients and their families. Using only paper files, clinicians would be unable to link accurate, synchronous views of clients' strengths and weaknesses with optimal treatment plans — and therefore the process of tracking counseling, case management and outcome data would become unduly burdensome.

Over a period of 2 years, the Partnership developed and refined an interagency database known as CHARI — Children At-Risk Interagency database. Used by clinicians, CHARI is a repository for all pertinent client data that is updated continuously. With menus that can be drawn down easily, and with logic checks, internal clocks and systematic reminders for required data updates, CHARI improves the consistency, accuracy and timeliness of client information. Beyond facilitating service integration, CHARI also functions as a single point of accountability, permitting program administrators and clinical supervisors, with the support of a data manager, to accomplish the following tasks:

- ensure that programmatic milestones are met
- monitor assessment and data collection practices
- supervise the formulation and implementation of treatment plans
- discern patterns in the efficacy of services

Interviews with clinicians and supervisory staff indicate that CHARI, in conjunction with the Well-BAT, helps improve the results of preventive and early treatment interventions in complex cases by minimizing service redundancies, preventing the phenomenon of clients cycling through the system repeatedly and improving service continuity and the coordination of service delivery. (This is anecdotal evidence based on interviews and focus groups conducted by the independent evaluator of the Partnership, which has been reported to the Executive Director of the Partnership.) Evaluators of the Partnership have not yet measured the extent to which CHARI and Well-BAT improve outcomes. Given the unique configuration of the Partnership model and the extent of change wrought in the service delivery system, a before-and-after comparison may prove to be a problematic exercise. However, one indication of the positive impact of CHARI and Well-BAT is evident in the school-based Partnership counseling program — the Mobile Outreach Services Team (MOST). In a review of MOST, an independent evaluator concluded that its "...comprehensive approach to assessment, individual program design and service delivery [resulted, for cases open at least 180 days, in] nearly two-thirds of treatment goals [having] been judged as making progress, with one in five goals having been achieved."[10]

Partnership EBPs: Selection and Efficacy

The Partnership implemented a broad spectrum of EBPs, creating a continuum of prevention and early intervention programs that operates in natural settings and serves a broad range of needs for children of all ages. Following a comprehensive review of the strengths and weaknesses of the human service, educational and law enforcement systems, the Partnership staff selected appropriate EBPs, which they accomplished in consultation with Partnership board members and representatives of parent groups, community-based organizations and other constituencies. Beyond the intrinsic efficacy of a particular EBP and the extent to which it addressed an unmet need in the community, the selection criteria for the programs included the following:

- the sustainability of the EBP, either through expanding staff capacity or by accessing recurring funding streams
- the degree to which the program complemented existing initiatives

- for school-based programs, the extent to which the EBPs conformed to New York State learning standards and were perceived as minimally intrusive by teachers, particularly those preparing students for testing

In-depth descriptions of the programs implemented, along with their validation materials, are available at the Partnership Web site — http://www.partnershipforresults.org/programs.

The continuum of EBPs functions in the following areas:

- school-based violence prevention curricula — Second Step, Educational Karate, Building Relationships in Greater Harmony Together
- school-based, community-oriented policing and law-related education — School Resource Officers
- educational enrichment — after-school programs, OASIS, vocational education
- home visitation by nurses — Nurse-Family Partnership
- parenting skills — EPIC, Guiding Good Choices (GGC)
- child care and school-based assessment and counseling — Therapeutic Day Care, MOST
- preventive mental health services — Primary Mental Health Program
- family therapy and related initiatives — Functional Family Therapy, Family Group Conferencing (FGC), Multisystemic Intensive Foster Care
- therapeutic alternatives to incarceration — ISCD

All of the EBPs were implemented in less than 1 year, except for one; the newly initiated parenting skills and substance abuse prevention program (GGC). Today, all of these programs are operating at capacity *and* with a high degree of fidelity to their program models and principles. As noted previously, these programs are producing results that consistently meet or exceed those predicted by research, with the expected outcome that levels of violence, substance abuse and delinquency are dropping significantly.[8-12] An effective and simultaneous implementation of such a broad spectrum of programs is the product of a system of local governance truly committed to implementing a comprehensive, integrated service delivery system.

Fig 2. The Partnership: school-based programs.[56]

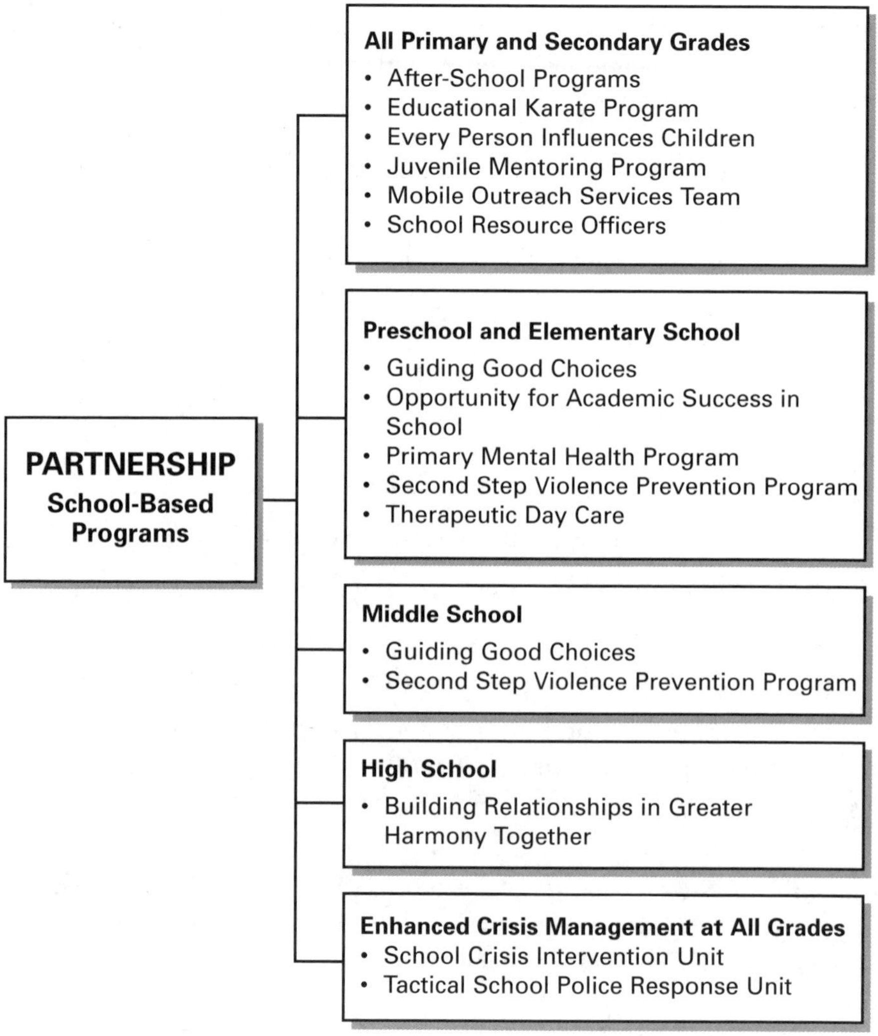

From the outset, the public agencies ensured that staff members involved in EBPs were available for training programs. These training sessions were organized on a recurring basis, providing opportunities for the Partnership to address barriers to implementation as they arose. Given their collective commitment to performance-based programming and their Board of Directors

Fig 3. The Partnership: community-based programs.[57]

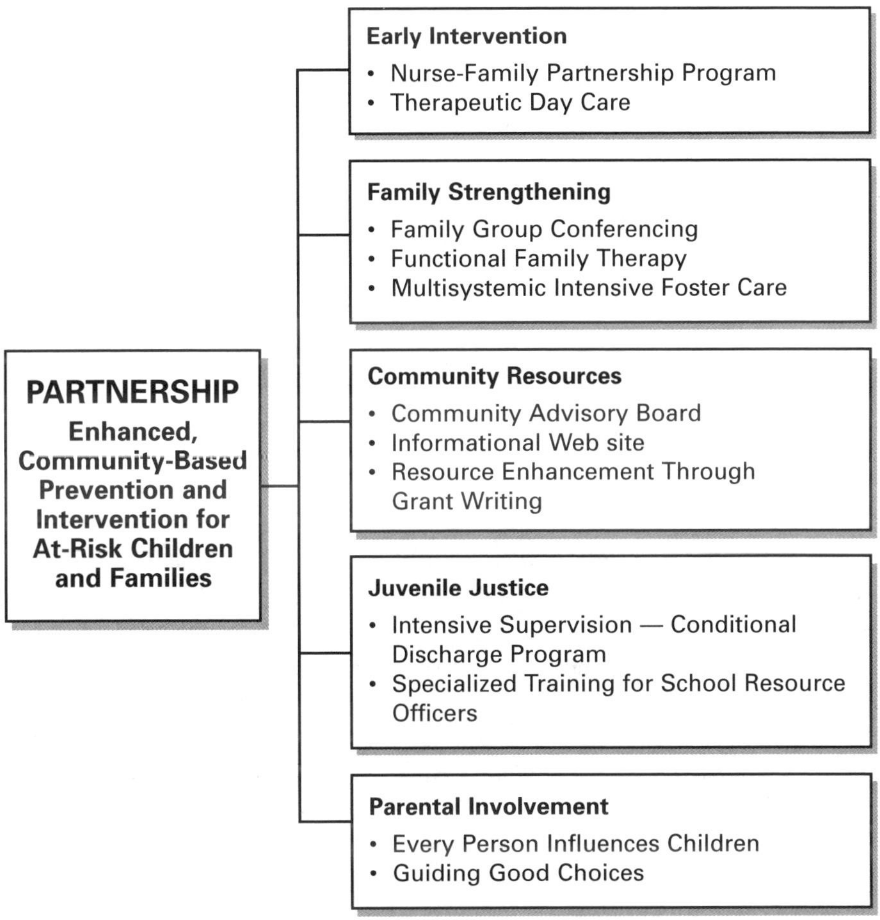

fiduciary responsibilities, directors of public agencies have taken great pains to ensure that the programs of the Partnership maintain their fidelity to EBP practices and principles. They do so by frequently providing the Partnership with data about the programs, as well as opportunities to survey those staff members who are involved with the implementation of the programs. With this information, the Partnership is able to prevent program "slippage," or the steady regression to the mean of local practices prior to implementation of the EBPs.

It has become evident that one aspect of fidelity to an EBP — providing the service to those children and families who can benefit most from the program — will likely result in high levels of program efficacy. The Partnership model has maximized the accuracy of client-program linkage in several ways, including the following:

- Staff members who are implementing the programs are involved in training sessions for programs other than their own, thereby increasing their knowledge of the eligibility criteria for other programs.
- The comprehensive assessment and service integration system implemented by the Partnership is designed to achieve precise referrals for clients who have complex problems.
- The sheer number of EBPs "on the ground" in Cayuga County promotes specialization: Therefore, programs are not pressured, as they so often are, to stretch the boundaries of client eligibility.

Program efficacy is also a function of staff commitment to the EBP. As an agency of governance, the Partnership, at the board level, has been particularly effective in formulating solutions to the obstacles to implementation that are so often encountered. These solutions include, but are by no means limited to, restructuring agency referral protocols, developing workable mechanisms for consulting the staff about program improvements and motivating recalcitrant supervisors. The motivation level of EBP implementers is affected by a program's potential for *sustainability*. It is not uncommon, and certainly not unjustifiable, for service providers to view grant-driven demonstration programs as transient in nature. In Cayuga County, by contrast, it has been rare for Partnership programs to sit on the cusp of losing their funding. Indeed, all of the implemented initiatives were sustained for several years beyond the SS/HS funding — and many will be sustained indefinitely.

Sustaining Partnership Programs

For the Partnership, sustainability is principally a matter of program design, persistent advocacy and fundraising, coupled with the capacity and willingness of participating public agencies to interweave — or "braid" — their funding streams. Selecting an EBP for implementation takes into account, among other criteria, whether the EBP can be financed by a recurring funding stream or by a strategic expansion of staff capacity. On occasion, an EBP is a potential alternative to an ongoing program whose results are perceived by public agencies as disappointing. In such instances, one strategy is to pilot a limited implementation for purposes of comparison, creating the opportunity to demonstrate the advantages of the EBP to staff and administrators and preparing the way for a funded program transformation without staff displacement. This occurred in the case of OASIS, a validated summer educational enrichment program that was piloted with 30 students, which is now the Auburn Enlarged City School District's elementary summer program, funded principally through Title I — a federal program that provides funding for academic programs that target socially and economically disadvantaged students.

If implemented effectively, certain EBPs provide both a therapeutic impact and a significant economic benefit for the locality, which can prove to be critical criteria for identifying an applicable and ongoing revenue source to assure sustainability. This is certainly the case for secondary prevention programs that address the needs of children who are delinquent and at risk of placement in juvenile detention or who are abused or neglected and at risk of placement in foster care or in a residential treatment center. The Partnership has implemented 3 such programs — FGC and 2 multisystemic programs — and all are being sustained with county expenditures that are being matched by an ongoing state preventive-services funding stream. For all 3 programs, the transition to this blended funding stream occurred while the community was in the midst of serious economic retrenchment. Despite these circumstances, public agency directors on the board of the Partnership were successful in persuading legislators to appropriate the county's share of funding for these programs by demonstrating that the program's effectiveness was accompanied by significant short-term savings. An independent cost-benefit analysis demonstrated, for example, that the ISCD program for adjudicated delinquents saved the county more than $214,000 in placement costs annually (Fagliarone Group CPAs, Auburn, NY, unpublished data, July 2003).

Sustaining curricular initiatives, such as Second Step (the violence prevention program), can be a relatively straightforward matter. Once the program is implemented successfully, the Partnership combines turnkey training of motivated staff members on each school campus with dedicated support for ongoing training opportunities provided by the school district. For many programs, however, achieving sustainability involves a more complex strategy, with the public agencies blending grants and other short-term revenues with longer-term funding streams. The following provide several examples:

- MOST, a school-based assessment, counseling and service integration program implemented by the Partnership, which is funded principally with a combination of Medicaid reimbursements, a formula-driven state mental health allocation made to the county (known as Community Reinvestment) and a portion of a 5-year grant from the USDOJ
- management and continuing development of the CHARI database, which is supported by proceeds from a Partnership campaign of social entrepreneurship and by portions of several grants involving programs that utilize CHARI
- Partnership after-school programs, which serve the multiple purposes of educational enrichment and the prevention of violence and substance abuse, while providing opportunities for counseling in a natural setting, all of which are supported by blending recurring funds from the New York State Education Department (through the Extended School Day/Violence Prevention Program), the US Department of Agriculture (through the Child and Adult Care Food Program), The After-School Corporation (a NY-based foundation that is a national leader in moving after-school programs to use proven practices and procedures; see http://www.tascorp.org/) and the USDOE (through Title I), as well as by multiyear grants

These flexible funding strategies demonstrate the ongoing commitment of this quasi-governmental agency to maintaining a comprehensive local approach to prevention and early intervention.

Conclusion

The Partnership for Results has succeeded in developing a comprehensive, integrated system of services for at-risk children and their families by following a deliberate, experience-driven agenda that is similar to that of the "second mouse." It has brought social science and political science into the world of service delivery. By implementing a continuum of EBPs that maintain a high level of fidelity to their program models, this intervention produces results that consistently meet or exceed those predicted by research. The challenges of interagency information sharing, service planning and resource allocation have been addressed effectively and locally by a quasi-governmental entity. At least in one community — Cayuga County, NY — the Partnership model appears to be overcoming the obstacles that often stand in the way of delivering services that promote the positive social, emotional and academic development of at-risk children.

References

1. Center for Mental Health Services. *The CMHS Approach to Enhancing Youth Resilience and Preventing Youth Violence in Schools and Communities.* Rockville, Md: US Dept of Health and Human Services, Substance Abuse and Mental Health Services Administration, Center for Mental Health Services; 1999. Publication KEN01-0105.
2. Office of Juvenile Justice and Delinquency Prevention. *Guide for Implementing the Comprehensive Strategy for Serious, Violent, and Chronic Juvenile Offenders.* Washington, DC: US Dept of Justice, Office of Justice Programs, Office of Juvenile Justice and Delinquency Prevention; May 1995. Publication NCJ 153681.
3. Center for the Study of Social Policy. *Changing Governance to Achieve Better Results for Children and Families.* Washington, DC: Center for the Study of Social Policy; December 1995.
4. Edwards RW, Jumper-Thurman P, Plested BA, Oetting ER, Swanson L. Community readiness: research to practice. *Journal of Community Psychology.* 2000;28:291-307.
5. Glisson C, Hemmelgarn A. The effects of organizational climate and interorganizational coordination on the quality and outcomes of children's service systems. *Child Abuse & Neglect.* 1998;22:401-421.
6. Ragan M, Nathan RP. *Welfare Reform and the Development of Comprehensive Human Service Systems.* Paper presented at: Conference of the American Political Science Association; August 2002; Boston, Mass.
7. White JA, Wehlage G. Community collaboration: If it is such a good idea, why is it so hard to do? *Educational Evaluation and Policy Analysis.* 1995;17:23-38.
8. Partnership for Results. Early evaluation findings reveal broad and deep implementation of Partnership programs and services. "The Partnership": Cayuga County Safe Schools/Healthy Students Partnership: Key Findings from the Independent Evaluation; MAGI Educational Services; March 8, 2001. Available at: http://www.partnershipforresults.org/eval_initiative.html. Accessed January 15, 2004.
9. Partnership for Results. Partnership significantly expands capacity to provide programs and services to students and families. "The Partnership": Cayuga County Safe Schools/Healthy Students Partnership: Key Findings from the Independent Evaluation; MAGI Educational Services; November 2002. Available at: http://www.partnershipforresults.org/eval_initiative.html. Accessed January 15, 2004.
10. Partnership for Results. The Partnership has significantly enhanced the delivery of needed programs & services and improved the outcomes of targeted students. "The Partnership": Cayuga County Safe Schools/Healthy Students Partnership: Key Findings from the Independent Evaluation; MAGI Educational Services; December 2002. Available at: http://www.partnershipforresults.org/eval_initiative.html. Accessed January 15, 2004.
11. Partnership for Results. Thoughtful intervention & prevention in Partnership schools positively impacts the learning environment & student risk behaviors. "The Partnership": Cayuga County Safe Schools/Healthy Students Partnership: Key Findings from the Independent Evaluation; MAGI Educational Services. January 2003. Available at: http://www.partnershipforresults.org/eval_initiative.html. Accessed January 15, 2004.
12. New York State Kids' Well-being Indicators Clearinghouse. Access data: KWIC region profile: Cayuga County: citizenship. Available at: http://nyskwic.org/access_data/region_profile.cfm?countyID=36011&go22.x=11&go22.y=8). Accessed January 15, 2004.

13. *New York Local Interagency Violence Prevention and Services Integration Act of 2003.* New York State Assembly No. 6790; New York State Senate No. 4530; §996-a(3); 2003. Proposed legislation.
14. Stroul BA, Friedman RE. *System of Care for Children and Youth with Severe Emotional Disturbances.* Washington, DC: Georgetown University Center for Child and Human Development; 1994.
15. Bickman L, Noser K, Summerfelt WT. Long-term effects of a system of care on children and adolescents. *The Journal of Behavioral Health Services & Research.* 1999;26:185-202.
16. Farmer EMZ. Issues confronting effective services in systems of care. *Children an d Youth Services Review.* 2000;22:627-650.
17. Kagan SL, Neville PR. *Integrating Services for Children and Families: Understanding the Past to Shape the Future.* New Haven, Conn: Yale University Press; 1994.
18. Manteuffel B, Stephens RL, Santiago R. Overview of the national evaluation of the Comprehensive Community Mental Health Services for Children and Their Families Program and summary of current findings. *Children's Services: Social Policy, Research, and Practice.* 2002;5:3-20.
19. Farrington DP. Early developmental prevention of juvenile delinquency. *Criminal Behaviour and Mental Health.* 1994;4:209-227.
20. Farrington DP, Welsh BC. Delinquency prevention using family-based interventions. *Children & Society.* 1999;13:287-303.
21. Hawkins JD, Herrenkohl T, Farrington DP, Brewer D, Catalano RF, Harachi TW. A review of predictors of youth violence. In: Loeber R, Farrington DP, eds. *Serious & Violent Juvenile Offenders: Risk Factors and Successful Interventions.* Thousand Oaks, Calif: Sage Publications; 1998:106-146.
22. Loeber R. The natural history of juvenile conduct problems, substance abuse, and delinquency: evidence of developmental progression. *Advances in Clinical Psychology.* 1987;11:73-124.
23. Brewer DD, Hawkins JD, Catalano RF, Neckerman HJ. Preventing serious, violent, and chronic juvenile offending: a review of evaluations of selected strategies in childhood, adolescence, and the community. In: Howell JC, Krisberg B, Hawkins JD, Wilson JJ, eds. *A Sourcebook: Serious, Violent, & Chronic Juvenile Offenders.* Thousand Oaks, Calif: Sage Publications; 1995:61-141.
24. Brooks TR, Pettit M. *Early Intervention: Crafting a Community Response to Child Abuse and Violence.* Washington, DC: Child Welfare League of America; 1997.
25. Cohen MA. The monetary value of saving a high-risk youth. *Journal of Quantitative Criminology.* 1998;14:5-33.
26. Howitt PS, Moore EA. The efficacy of intensive early intervention: an evaluation of the Oakland County Probate Court Early Offender Program. *Juvenile and Family Court Journal.* 1991;42:25-36.
27. Karoly LA, Greenwood PW, Everingham SS, et al. *Investing in Our Children: What We Know and Don't Know About the Costs and Benefits of Early Childhood Interventions.* Santa Monica, Calif: Rand Corporation; 1998.
28. Loeber R, Farrington DP. Never too early, never too late: risk factors and successful interventions for serious and violent juvenile offenders. *Studies on Crime and Crime Prevention.* 1998;71:7-30.
29. Office of Juvenile Justice and Delinquency Prevention. *Delinquency Prevention Works.* Washington, DC: US Dept of Justice, Office of Justice Programs, Office of Juvenile Justice and Delinquency Prevention; November 1995. Publication NCJ 155006.
30. Blakely CH, Mayer JP, Gottschalk RG. The fidelity-adaptation debate: implications for the implementation of public sector social programs. *American Journal of Community Psychology.* 1987;15:253-268.
31. Bond GR, Evans L, Salyers MP, Williams J, Kim HW. Measurement of fidelity in psychiatric rehabilitation. *Mental Health Services Research.* 2000;2:75-87.
32. Gresham FM, Gansle KA, Noell GH, Cohen S, Rosenblum S. Treatment integrity of school-based behavioral intervention studies: 1980-1990. *School Psychology Review.* 1993;22:254-272.
33. Jerrell JM, Ridgely MS. Impact of robustness of program implementation on outcomes of clients in dual diagnosis programs. *Psychiatric Services (Washington, DC).* 1999;50:109-112.
34. McHugo GJ, Drake RE, Teague GB, Xie H. Fidelity to assertive community treatment and client outcomes in the New Hampshire dual disorders study. *Psychiatric Services (Washington, DC).* 1999;50:818-824.

35. McGrew JH, Bond GR, Dietzen L, Salyers M. Measuring the fidelity of implementation of a mental health program model. *Journal of Consulting and Clinical Psychology.* 1994;62:670-678.

36. Teague GB, Bond GR, Drake RE. Program fidelity in assertive community treatment: development and use of a measure. *The American Journal of Orthopsychiatry.* 1998;68:216-232.

37. Baker F, O'Brien G. Intersystems relations and coordination of human service organizations. *American Journal of Public Health.* 1971;61:130-137.

38. Kettner PM. *Achieving Excellence in the Management of Human Service Organizations.* Upper Saddle River, NJ: Allyn & Bacon; 2002.

39. Woodbridge M, Huang L. Interagency MIS: higher order data connections. *Data Matters: An Evaluation Newsletter* [serial online]. Spring 2001;4:1. Available at: http://64.233.161.104/search?q=cache:FA6_NqvfQ_gJ:gucchd.georgetown.edu/files/products_publications/datamatters4.pdf+Data+Matters:++An+Evaluation+Newsletter+2001&hl=en. Accessed January 15, 2004.

40. About us. Partnership for Results Web site. Available at: http://www.partnershipforresults.org/about_us.html. Accessed January 15, 2004.

41. Brier N. Predicting antisocial behavior in youngsters displaying poor academic achievement: a review of risk factors. *Journal of Developmental and Behavioral Pediatrics: JDBP.* 1995;16:271-276.

42. Elliott DS, Huizinga D, Menard S. *Multiple Problem Youth: Delinquency, Substance Use, and Mental Health Problems.* New York, NY: Springer-Verlag; 1989.

43. Fagan J, Pabon E. Contributions of delinquency and substance use to school dropout among inner-city youths. *Youth & Society.* 1990;21:306-354.

44. Hawkins JD, Herrenkohl TI, Farrington DP, et al. Predictors of youth violence. *OJJDP Juvenile Justice Bulletin.* Washington, DC: US Dept of Justice, Office of Justice Programs, Office of Juvenile Justice and Delinquency Prevention; April 2000. Publication NCJ 179065.

45. Frederick B. *Factors Contributing to Recidivism Among Youth Placed With the New York State Division for Youth.* Albany, NY: New York State Division of Criminal Justice Services, Office of Justice Systems Analysis, Bureau of Research and Evaluation; August 1999.

46. Aos S, Phipps P, Barnoski R, Lieb R. *The Comparative Costs and Benefits of Programs to Reduce Crime.* Olympia, Wash: Washington State Institute for Public Policy; May 2001.

47. Dryfoos JG. *Adolescents At Risk: Prevalence and Prevention.* New York, NY: Oxford University Press; 1990.

48. DeMasi ME, Kelsh TJ, Tierney CC. *The Adolescent Well-Being Assessment Instrument: An Interdisciplinary Approach.* Albany, NY: Capital Assessments, Inc; 2003. Partnership for Results Web site. Available at: http://www.partnershipforresults.org/pdfs/Well-Being_Assessment_Excer.pdf. Accessed January 15, 2004.

49. George MS, Skinner HA. Assessment. In: Annis HM, Davis CS, eds. *Drug Use by Adolescents: Identification, Assessment and Intervention.* Toronto, Ontario, Canada: Alcoholism and Drug Addiction Foundation; 1991:85-108.

50. Winters KC. Development of an adolescent alcohol and other drug abuse screening scale: Personal Experience Screening Questionnaire. *Addictive Behaviors.* 1992;17:479-490.

51. Pagano ME, Cassidy LJ, Little M, Murphy JM, Jellinek MS. Identifying psychosocial dysfunction in school-age children: the Pediatric Symptom Checklist as a self-report measure. *Psychology in the Schools.* 2000;37:91-106.

52. OASIS (Opportunity for Academic Success In School). Sharing Success Web site. Available at: http://www.sharingsuccess.org/code/eptw/profiles/42.html. Accessed January 15, 2004.

53. Barton WH, Butts JA. Viable options: intensive supervision programs for juvenile delinquents. *Crime & Delinquency.* 1990;36:238-250.

54. Krisberg B, Neuenfeldt D, Wiebush R, Rodriguez O. *Juvenile Justice: An Assessment.* Washington, DC: US Dept of Justice, Office of Justice Programs, Office of Juvenile Justice and Delinquency Prevention; 1994. Publication NCJ 150064.

55. Wiebush RG. Juvenile intensive supervision: the impact on felony offenders diverted from institutional placement. *Crime & Delinquency.* 1993;39:68-89.

56. School-based & after school programs for children and families: school-based graphic overview. Partnership for Results Web site. Available at: http://www.partnershipforresults.org/programs.html#. Accessed January 15, 2004.

57. Enhanced, community-based prevention & intervention for at-risk children & families: community-based graphic overview. Partnership for Results Web site. Available at: http://www.partnershipforresults.org/programs.html#. Accessed January 15, 2004.

Residential Mobility Interventions as Treatments for the Sequelae of Neighborhood Violence

Greg J. Duncan, PhD
Elizabeth Clark-Kauffman, PhD
Emily K. Snell, PhD

Introduction and Overview

The statistics on neighborhood violence and children's mental health tell a grim story.[1-3] In a national study, more than 33% of girls and close to 50% of boys between the ages of 12 years and 17 years reported witnessing violence.[4] From studies of poor urban neighborhoods, estimates of the prevalence of witnessing violence by youth are much higher.[5,6] As we illustrate in this chapter, using chilling personal accounts, qualitative studies of families living in public housing in high-crime neighborhoods corroborate these statistics.

For children, the evidence we review suggests that witnessing neighborhood violence is associated with a host of adverse mental health consequences, including depression,[7,8] anxiety[7-10] and posttraumatic stress disorder (PTSD),[7,8] as well as poor school performance[7,11] and aggression.[7,11,12] However, the *independent* contribution of neighborhood violence has been established in these studies only rarely. Because families living in violent neighborhoods are more likely to experience socioeconomic[13,14] and other disadvantageous family conditions,[15] as well as to exhibit partner and/or parent-child violence,[15] it is far from clear whether poor child outcomes are the product of family-specific or neighborhood-specific characteristics. Moreover, because children, especially adolescent children, have considerable input into selecting their peer groups and community activities, it is also unclear whether improvements in community conditions will translate into large reductions in the levels of neighborhood violence they may witness and/or perpetuate.

This chapter reviews the available evidence regarding the trends in violence and the links between neighborhood violence and children's mental health. However, our primary focus is the potential of residential mobility intervention programs to improve the health and well-being of children *and* adults.

Several noteworthy residential mobility programs developed over the past 30 years have provided opportunities for families living in crime-ridden, inner-city neighborhoods to move to safer and more affluent neighborhoods.[16,17] In the case of the Chicago-based Gautreaux program,[17,18] which was in operation between 1976 and 1997, and then again beginning in 2002, families received financial assistance and counseling to facilitate their moves to wealthier, less-segregated neighborhoods.

In the mid-1990s, the Moving to Opportunity (MTO) program[16] provided similar opportunities to families living in 5 US cities — Baltimore (Md), Boston (Mass), Chicago (Ill), Los Angeles (Calif), and New York City (NY). The MTO program defined qualifying neighborhoods *solely* on the basis of income rather than on income *and* race/ethnicity. MTO featured the random assignment of families as well as an in-depth evaluation that included surveys about the mental and physical health of the children and the adults that were conducted 4 years to 7 years after their assignment to a qualifying neighborhood. Data from this evaluation provide convincing evidence of the positive impact on both children and their families of moving to safer, more affluent neighborhoods.

Qualitative studies of families enrolled in both the MTO program[16] and the 2002 Gautreaux program[18] provide detailed accounts of families whose experiences are consistent with the quantitative evidence emerging from these studies. Kling, Liebman and Katz, who conducted open-ended interviews with several MTO participants living in Boston, discovered that nearly all participants viewed the crime and violence in their neighborhoods of origin as the most important reasons for enrolling in the program.[19]

Popkin, Harris and Cunningham conducted open-ended interviews with adults and youth in all 5 MTO cities 5 years into the demonstration program. They found that adults who moved because of their participation in the program had experienced some positive changes, particularly increases in neighborhood safety[20]: For example, among families randomly assigned to the MTO program who moved to low-poverty neighborhoods, adults stressed the increase in safety and the contrast between neighbors in their new communities and those in public housing. Results for adolescents were more mixed: Although adolescents who moved also noted improvements in neighborhood quality, they reported increased suspensions and disciplinary infractions in their new schools. Older teens were more likely to retain ties to their former neighborhoods, sometimes even moving back to them. Qualitative interviews are underway currently in Baltimore and Chicago (under the direction of Kling and Edin) with a larger sample of MTO participants as this chapter goes to press. Qualitative interviews (under the direction of Edin) are also underway with families involved in the 2002 Gautreaux residential mobility program.[18]

Throughout this chapter we present glimpses from 2 qualitative interviews (using the pseudonyms Diane and Stephen) that provide more detail about the families involved in the MTO[16] and Gautreaux[18] programs. These cases were chosen to illustrate some of the issues we raise in this chapter and were drawn from ongoing research projects involving participants in the Gautreaux[18] and MTO[16] programs. We begin with Diane, a married African American mother of 2 in her mid-20s who signed up to participate in the 2002 Gautreaux residential mobility program[18]:

Diane: A Case Study from the 2002 Gautreaux Program[18]

Diane was eager to move from her public housing development located on the south side of Chicago. She felt strongly that her neighborhood was a very poor environment for her children; Jordan, age 7 years, and Tiara, age 4 years. During the last year alone there had been 3 shooting incidents near Jordan's school and after-school center. Recently, Jordan mentioned to Diane that he wanted to take a gun to school to protect himself. This comment, as well as other behaviors and attitudes he had been exhibiting, concerned her greatly.

Diane said: *"I have to be hard on my son because I don't want him to follow the same path [as I did]. That's why it's important for me to move out of the neighborhood I'm in. Because if this is what you're around, this is what you're gonna know. And I see what he's learning: He comes home saying…even gang stuff. And I feel strongly — when it comes to that — because of what I've been through.… He told his teacher… She asked him what do he want to be [when he grows up].… He told her, 'I wanna be a killer.' Now, that's not my son.… [But] he feel like he have to have somebody to defend himself. I guess he listen to them [the other children at school] talking about the gang: 'Get in this gang.' And he is only in second grade. So, I have to get him out of [here].… He was like, 'Mom, I wanna be a killer.'"*

(continued later in this chapter)

The experiences of the 4200 families who participated in the MTO experiment[16] — and, to a lesser extent, the families who participated in the 2002 Gautreaux program[18] — are the focus of this chapter. We begin with a review of the relevant literature, which is followed by an overview of the MTO program and its key results. The final section of the chapter is devoted to interpreting the results of the MTO program, with the goal of providing evidence that could be used to develop effective neighborhood-based interventions to address children's mental health sequelae associated with living in violent neighborhoods.

Neighborhood Violence and Mental Health: Background Data

American children and adolescents, particularly those living in high-poverty urban areas, are exposed to and affected by disturbingly high levels of violence in their communities.[1,2] Exposure to community violence has been established as a risk factor for poor physical and socioemotional development in children and adolescents.[15,21] Although the United States has experienced a general decline in violence since the mid-1990s,[1,22] homicide rates and firearm-related deaths among American youth are still higher than those for the same-age youth in any other industrialized nation.[1-3]

The rate of community crime increased dramatically during the 1980s and early 1990s. From 1985 to 1991, the homicide rate among youth ages 15 years to 19 years increased 154%, surpassing that of all other age groups.[23] This trend reversed during the mid-1990s, and by 1999 arrest rates for violent crimes had fallen below their 1993 levels.[22,24] However, Rosenberg and Mercy estimated that reported homicide rates reflect only a very small fraction (ie, 1%) of the nonfatal violence witnessed and/or experienced by today's youth.[25]

These declines in reported violence have paralleled decreases in both the number of people living in poverty and the levels of concentrated neighborhood poverty.[13,26] The number of people living in neighborhoods that had poverty rates of 40% or higher decreased by 24% between the 1990 and 2000 censuses,[13] and this decline occurred in all racial groups. However, another analysis of census data demonstrated that the number of children living in "severely distressed" neighborhoods — characterized by high poverty rates, high percentages of female-headed households and high percentages of unemployed working-age males and high school dropouts — increased by 18% during the 1990s.[26] These severely distressed neighborhoods, which are found most commonly in urban metropolitan areas, represent communities that offer limited resources for children and adolescents.

Trends in violent crime in the 5 MTO cities closely paralleled the trends in national crime during the 1980s, with all 5 cities experiencing increases in their annual rates of murder — but not all experienced declines during the 1990s (see Fig 1).[27] Homicides in Los Angeles decreased by 30% between 1991 and 1996,[28] the decline in homicides in New York City was nearly

Fig 1. Number of murders/year in 5 US cities, 1985 to 2003. [27]

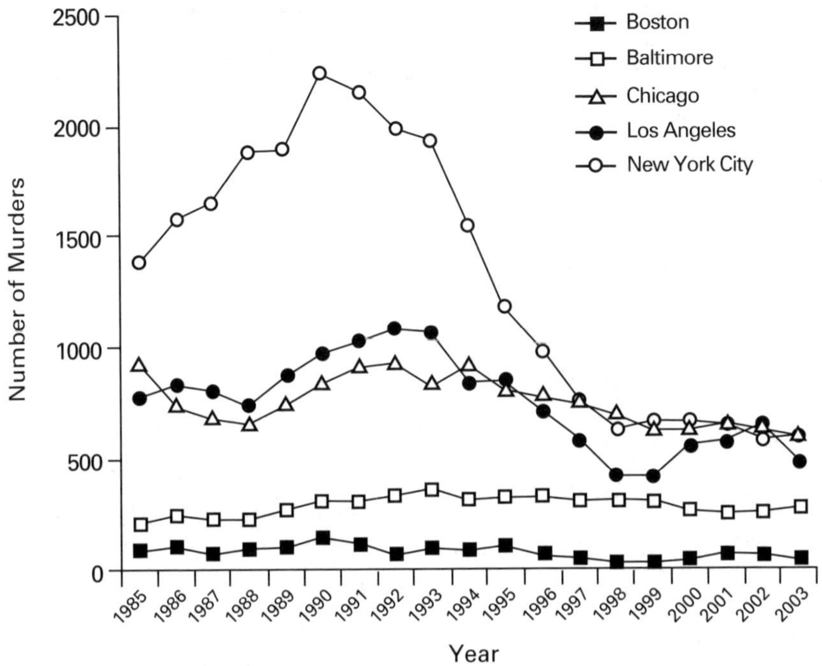

Note: Data from the Bureau of Justice Statistics, compiled from FBI Uniform Crime Reports.
Source: Federal Bureau of Investigation Web site. Uniform Crime Reports: Crime in the United States — 2003. Available at: http://www.fbi.gov/ucr/03cius.htm. Accessed April 26, 2005.

75%[29] and homicides in Chicago dropped, as well.[30] In contrast, the rate of homicide by firearms in Baltimore actually increased by 40% during the early 1990s.[31]

The national arrest rate for youth who committed violent crimes,[32] as shown in Fig 2, reflects the widely reported[33,34] trends of increases in violence during the late 1980s,[35] followed by decreases in violence since the mid-1990s.[35] Self-reports of violent behavior among adolescents declined during the 1990s, as well: For example, according to the Youth Risk Behavior Survey, between 1991 and 1997, the percentage of students who carried a weapon decreased 30%, the percentage of students injured in a physical fight decreased 20%

Fig 2. Violent crime arrest rates for youth ages 15 years to 20 years, 1970 to 2003.[32]

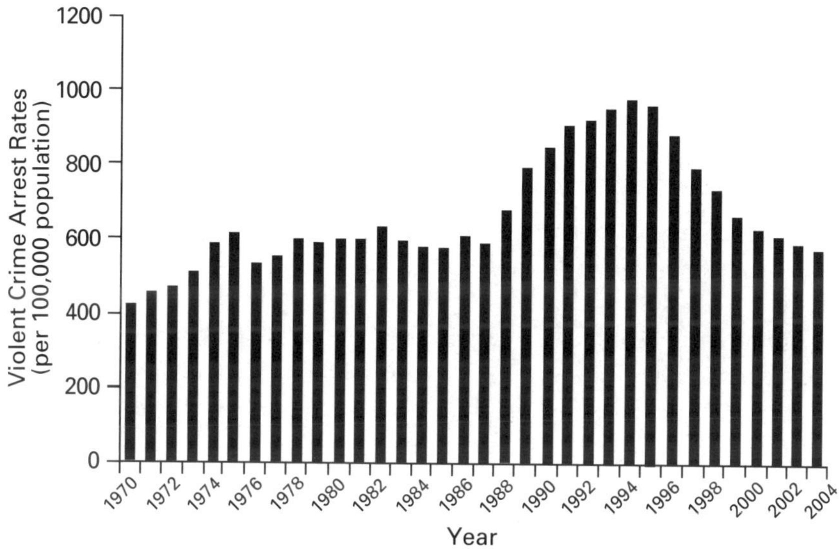

Source: Bureau of Justice Statistics Web site. Data for analysis — crime & justice electronic data abstracts: spreadsheets. National data. Available at: http://www.ojp.usdoj.gov/bjs/data/arrests.wk1. Accessed April 26, 2005.

and the percentage of students involved in a physical fight decreased 14%.[36] Brener and colleagues also reported significant improvements in school safety during the 1990s.[36] The percentage of students who carried a weapon on school property decreased 28%, while the percentage of students who were involved in a physical fight on school property declined 9%.[36]

Still, rates of exposure to violence remain alarmingly high among many groups of young people. Youth living in neighborhoods characterized by low socioeconomic status (SES) reported higher levels of hazards, such as crime, violence, drug use and graffiti, than did youth living in high SES neighborhoods.[6] In lower SES neighborhoods, exposure to violence is more prevalent among boys than among girls: A study using cross-sectional convenience samples from low SES neighborhoods reported recently that 87% of boys and 70% of girls had witnessed a violent act, while 63% of boys but only

33% of girls had been the actual victim of a violent act.[37] Although it has also been reported that students are less likely to be injured, attacked or killed at school than they are at home or anywhere else in the community,[7] results from qualitative interviews suggest that many boys are especially concerned about becoming victims of school violence.[7,38] Lastly, significant ethnic disparities persist with respect to exposure to violence with nationally representative studies reporting that African American adolescents are victimized at higher rates than are white and Hispanic adolescents.[4] National data show that severe injuries caused by firearms are the most common cause of death among African American males between the ages of 10 years and 34 years.[3] These facts highlight the levels of violence that children and adolescents still witness and experience in American cities today.

Community-based studies have shown that parents' reports of their children's exposure to community violence are routinely lower than are their children's self-reports.[39,40] In addition, children's reports of their exposure to violence predict levels of behavior problems more accurately, even after controlling for their parents' reports of their children's exposure to violence.[39,40] Behavior problems exhibited in early childhood are of significant concern because antisocial behavior that carries over into late childhood and early adolescence is the strongest predictor of committing violence in later adolescence.[41]

A growing body of literature suggests that, indeed, there may be important short- and long-term consequences of childhood exposure to community violence. A community-based, cross-sectional study of youth in Los Angeles found that those youth who perceived greater levels of threats in their neighborhoods were more likely to experience symptoms of depression, anxiety, oppositional defiant disorder and conduct disorder.[42] Other investigators have reported associations between childhood exposure to violence and a vast array of adverse health consequences, including depression,[7,8] social withdrawal,[7] anxiety,[7-10] PTSD,[7,8,10] sleep disturbances,[7-10] poor school performance,[7,11] participating in behaviors that harm others and/or their property,[7,11] having negative beliefs and attitudes towards others,[7] and aggressiveness.[7,11,12] A cross-sectional study found links between childhood exposure to community violence and childhood behavior problems, even after controlling for SES and family aggression.[15] A study of elementary school children in the Chicago Public Schools found that exposure to community violence increased the incidences of a child's violent behavior as well as his/her beliefs about the prevalence of aggression.[21] A longitudinal community sample of adolescents in neighborhoods in Baltimore found that the self-reported fear of crime was related to anxiety and depression over time.[14] In addition, investigators have found that both boys and girls who reported witnessing community violence displayed greater levels of delinquent behavior[4] and PTSD.[4,12] Furthermore, the impact of witnessing violence can vary with age: Younger children who have been exposed to community violence are more likely to report symptoms of PTSD than are children who are over the age of 12 years.[7]

Several mostly cross-sectional studies have also found connections between neighborhood conditions and parenting behaviors. Parents in unsafe neighborhoods are less likely to have outside sources of social support and are less likely to provide their children with supervision[10,14,43-46]: For example, a cross-sectional study of children living in high-crime neighborhoods in Boston found that there were independent effects of maternal exposure to community violence and family violence on maternal distress, which, in turn, related to parenting style.[15]

Buka and Earls have conceptualized violent behavior as the result of poor physical and emotional development, as well as of unfavorable family, peer and societal influences at several points in life.[41] Unfortunately, much of the existing literature on children's exposure to violence focuses exclusively on either exposure to family violence[47] or exposure to neighborhood violence.[15] Many studies use cross-sectional, community-based samples that do not focus specifically on community violence.[15,48] Other studies hypothesize that a child's reaction to exposure to community violence would be similar to his/her reaction to parental abuse or exposure to family violence.[10,15] We have found only a few studies that have investigated the impact of both family-level and community-level violence on children's outcomes: For example, a study of high school students in 3 cities (Cleveland, Ohio; a small city in northeast Ohio; and Denver, Colorado) found that witnessing violence at home, being a victim of a mugging, or witnessing threats, knifings or shootings all contributed to a student's level of reported anxiety, stress and depression.[44] Thus, it is clear that there is a need for research that establishes the distinct contributions of community-based violence and/or home-based violence to child outcomes.

Residential Mobility Programs: Interventions for Neighborhood Violence

What can be done to alleviate the ills caused by neighborhood violence? Interventions directed at reducing crime are the first and most obvious possibility. Earlier in this chapter we documented the declining crime rates in several large US cities,[27] although there is little consensus about the reasons for this decline.[29,49-51]

Ridding the nation of its most crime-infested public housing has become a popular approach to combating neighborhood violence. Through the US federal government's HOPE VI program, created in 1993, 72,000 public housing units have been demolished or been slated for demolition, and mixed-income housing and voucher subsidies have been actively promoted. Since 1993, the US Department of Housing and Urban Development (HUD) has awarded nearly $5 billion through HOPE VI for housing redevelopment and client services. HOPE VI plans to replace 95,100 units: Approximately half (48,800 units) will be new public housing units for low-income residents, while the remainder will be targeted to higher-income residents. These units will include those that will have lower subsidies for moderate-income households as well as those that will have no subsidies in order to serve market-rate renters and home buyers.[52] As of 2004, 49,828 units had been demolished, and 21,000 new units had been created.[53]

A longer-standing US federal government policy approach to solving the problem of crime-infested public housing developments has been housing mobility programs, such as the "Section 8" tenant-based rental subsidy programs provided by HUD. These Section 8 programs — now called "Housing Choice Vouchers" — provide low-income families with a financial subsidy when they move to a private-market apartment or house that meets the specific requirements of the program.

Currently, approximately 2.1 million vouchers are given to low-income families, which is up from only 162,000 vouchers in 1977.[54,55] These housing vouchers hold the following appeal for political conservatives *and* liberals:

- They rely on the private sector, rather than on the government, to provide housing services to the poor.
- They improve the housing quality for low-income families.
- They provide low-income families with more choices about where to live.

Yet, the increased residential mobility that housing vouchers have allowed poor families is controversial because many residents of working- and middle-class neighborhoods fear that the arrival of low-income neighbors will lower property values and increase their own children's social problems.

How successful have these programs been at enabling affected children and adults to escape neighborhood violence and enjoy improvements in their mental and physical health? A high-quality, experimental evaluation was designed to answer these questions: In 1994, HUD began the MTO program, which randomly assigned low-income families living in public housing within high-poverty neighborhoods in the 5 major US metropolitan cities mentioned previously to one of 3 research groups:

- Families in the *control group* received no special assistance, but they were eligible for all federal programs other than Section 8.
- A *Section 8 group* received conventional Section 8 private-market housing subsidies without any constraints on relocation choices.
- An *experimental group* received Section 8-type housing vouchers that they could redeem only by moving to low-poverty census tracts (that had poverty rates lower than 10%).

The experimental group also received substantial counseling from local non-profit agencies and search assistance to help voucher recipients find and lease units in qualifying neighborhoods. Housing-related counseling included teaching search skills, making home visits, taking clients on tours of low-poverty areas and negotiating with brokers and landlords. Counseling was also provided in such areas as budget and household management, job development and parenting.[56] The randomized experimental design of the MTO program enabled us to identify the causal impacts of offering families the financial resources to move to new neighborhoods, combined, in the case of the experimental group, with counseling assistance and relocation constraints.

Families in both the experimental and Section 8 groups were required to sign 1-year leases. Those who moved before the initial lease expired lost their eligibility for their financial subsidies, while families who wished to relocate after the first year were free to do so without restriction and were allowed to keep their subsidies. Thus, MTO required experimental-group movers to live in low-poverty areas only for the first year after the move. All moves occurred between 1994 and 1998. In the fall of 2003, an evaluation was published of experimental and control group differences 4 years to 7 years after baseline.[16] In this chapter, although we present some of our own analyses of those data, for the most part we venture to summarize the results of the study by Orr and colleagues.[16]

Findings From the MTO Study

MTO Sample at Baseline

Scattered across public housing projects within the 5 study cities, the 4200 families in the MTO evaluation were similar in many respects, yet quite diverse in others.[16] (For a discussion, see Appendix C in Orr, et al.[16]) Similarities included the fact that the vast majority of families were headed by women (92%), had no member employed (72%) and relied on welfare income (62%). Virtually all of the participants from Baltimore and Chicago were African American, while roughly equal percentages of participants from Boston, New York City and Los Angeles were Hispanic and African American. Most families were very poor: Household incomes averaged $9300 for a median of 3 children.

When asked about their primary reasons for moving, more than 80% of families ranked "getting away from drugs and gangs" as either their first or second most important motivation. Violence-related reasons were the primary motivators for moving among participants from all 5 study cities. Better schools and bigger or better apartments were the first or second choice of approximately 50% of the respondents.

Neighborhood Conditions Before and After the Moves

According to the 1990 US census, the neighborhoods (ie, census tracts) in which MTO participants resided when they signed up for the program had an overall poverty rate of 56% — well above the 40% threshold that Wilson[57] and Massey and Denton[58,59] have used to define neighborhoods of concentrated poverty. The economic boom of the 1990s dropped the average overall poverty rate in these same neighborhoods to 49%. The racial and ethnic isolation[58,59] (defined by the percentage of neighborhood residents who belong to minority groups) of these origin neighborhoods held steady at 91% between 1990 and 2000.

Table 1, which provides our calculations based on the data from the MTO experiment,[16] shows neighborhood conditions at the time of follow-up, 4 years to 7 years after baseline. For control-group families, we present results for the entire group, as well as for the 2 subsets of control-group families who either moved or did not move during the period between baseline and the follow-up. Perhaps surprisingly, 70% (n = 917) of control-group families moved at least once during the study period. However, you will recall that control-group families who volunteered for the MTO opportunity did so with the specific goal of gaining help with a move, and they were free to move at any point without either financial or counseling resources to facilitate their moves. In fact, all low-income families moved at surprisingly high rates. Table 1 shows that control-group families who moved at least once settled in neighborhoods that had considerably lower poverty rates (34%) than did control-group families who did not move (51% poverty level).

To focus attention on the moves to low-poverty areas, we have disregarded the Section 8 treatment group (results detailed in Orr, et al[16]) and concentrate exclusively on the experimental-group families, all of whom were offered the opportunity to move to neighborhoods that had poverty rates of less than 10%. In Table 1, we present the results for the entire experimental group offered the assistance (n = 1729), for the subset that moved under the terms of the program (n = 820) and for the even smaller subset that moved under the terms of the program and continued to reside in the housing units in which they were first placed (n = 261). Superscript daggers adjacent to figures in Table 1 indicate instances where experimental-group means differed significantly from control-group means (P<.05).

Table 1 documents the substantial impact of the MTO program on participants' neighborhood poverty rates. Taken as a whole, the neighborhood poverty rate of all families assigned to the experimental group was 31%, which was significantly lower than the average 39% neighborhood poverty rate among the control-group families. As might be expected, the mean neighborhood poverty rate (22%) was lower still for experimental-group families who moved under the terms of the program. At the time of follow-up, experimental-group families who continued to reside in the housing units in which they were first placed enjoyed the lowest neighborhood poverty rate of all — 13%. The higher poverty rate in the neighborhoods of the larger set of experimental-group families who moved several times, compared with the

*Table 1. Neighborhood Conditions at Follow-up in the Moving to Opportunity (MTO) Experiment[16]**

Parameter	All Control-group Families	Control-group Families Who Stayed in Place
Observations	1310	393
Neighborhood poverty rate in 2000	39%	51%
Neighborhood minority rate in 2000	88%	94%
Respondent feels unsafe or very unsafe		
– On the streets near home at night	45%	61%
– On the streets near home during day	25%	36%
During the last 6 months, respondent or member of respondent's household		
– Had purse snatched	7%	7%
– Was beaten/assaulted	10%	10%
– Experienced break-in	8%	8%
– Experienced one or more crimes	21%	24%
Social capital		
– Respondent thinks it is likely or very likely neighbors would react if they saw children skipping school/hanging out on street	37%	29%

*Note: Authors' calculations based on data from MTO experiment.
†$P<.05$ (experimental-group means vs control-group means)

rate in the neighborhoods of the subset of experimental-group families who moved only once, shows that the subsequent mobility of experimental-group families undid some of the advantages of their initial moves.

Table 1 also documents the surprisingly small differences in neighborhood racial/ethnic composition among all groups. Only in the case of the experimental-group families, who did not subsequently move after their program

Control-group Families Who Self-moved	All Experimental-group Families	Experimental-group Families Who Moved	Experimental-group Families Who Moved Only Once
917	1729	820	261
34%	31%†	22%†	13%†
85%	85%†	81%†	68%†
38%	31%†	15%†	21%†
20%	16%†	5%†	7%†
7%	6%	4%	4%
9%	7%†	4%†	4%†
8%	8%	9%	7%
20%	17%†	12%†	12%†
40%	47%†	60%†	52%†

placements, were fewer than 81% of their neighbors either African American or Hispanic. This is in sharp contrast with the results of the Gautreaux program, where participants' neighborhoods at placement averaged 28% African American and were still only 48% African American some 15 years after the initial moves.[60] The MTO families who were randomly assigned to the experimental group were given Housing Choice Vouchers that were usable only in census tracts that had less than 10% of the population living below the poverty line.[16] All 5 of the MTO cities had ethnic neighborhoods that met this "less-than-10%" poverty criterion, and experimental-group families tended to opt to move to them. This reflects some combination of preferences on the part of MTO families and the willingness of landlords to rent to MTO families in these neighborhoods.

Police departments do not publish crime data for small geographical areas. Therefore, it is virtually impossible for us to describe crime rates in the specific neighborhoods in which participants of the MTO program resided. As such, surveys of participants provided the crime-related data shown in Table 1. At follow-up, 45% of MTO families in the control group and 31% of families in the experimental group reported feeling either unsafe or very unsafe on the streets near their homes at night. During the day, 25% of families in the control group and 16% of families in the experimental group reported the same feelings ($P<.05$). Similar improvements were found among other indicators of neighborhood safety within the experimental-group families (see chapter 3 in Orr, et al[16]): For example, in several instances, victimization rates for experimental-group families were significantly lower than for control-group families.

The neighborhoods of families in the experimental group were also richer in "collective efficacy,"[61] with 60% of adults indicating that it was likely that neighbors would do something about misbehaving youth (Table 1). Less than 40% of adults in the control group reported the same probability. Interestingly, this higher "social capital" did not translate into larger or more diverse friendship networks for experimental-group families (see data in chapter 3 in Orr, et al[16]; however, data not shown in Table 1).

Overall, the MTO intervention proved very successful at addressing the neighborhood crime problems that sparked most adult participants' interest in the program.

Parent Mental and Physical Health

The follow-up survey provided several measures of the mental and physical health of program participants. Using data from chapter 4 in Orr and colleagues,[16] Table 2 highlights some of the experimental- versus control-group differences.

The most comprehensive mental health measure in the MTO study was a measure of depression using the Composite International Diagnostic Interview-Short Form (CIDI-SF) "Major Depressive Episode" scale.[62] At the follow-up

Table 2. Parent Mental and Physical Health Measures in the MTO Experiment[16]

	Control-group Mean	Experimental-group Mean Minus Control-group Mean*
Mental Health		
Was depressed during past year (including boundary cases)	22	–4†
Felt psychological distress during past month	33	–3†
Felt calm and peaceful at least most of the time during past month	47	–6†
Had anxiety‡ during past year	39	NS§
Physical Health		
In fair or poor health	33	NS
Had asthma or wheezing attack during past year	21	NS
Is obese (body mass index [BMI] ≥30)	47	–5†

Note: Data from Exhibit 4.2 in Orr, et al.[16]
*Represents Intent-to-Treat effects, which are mean differences between all members of the experimental and control groups, adjusted by multiple regression for differences in baseline characteristics.
†$P<.05$.
‡Parent experienced either "a period lasting one month or longer when most of the time he or she felt worried, tense or anxious" or "a time when he or she worried a lot more than most people would in his or her situation."
§Not significant.

interview, 22% of adults in the control group reported experiencing at least one depressive episode during the 12 months prior to the interview. In contrast, 18% of adults in the experimental group reported the same. Because only 47% of the experimental-group families moved under the terms of the MTO program, we made some additional assumptions and used these data to estimate the impacts for those who did move. In the case of episodes of depression, the estimated impact of the MTO treatment on those adults who moved was 8%. In other words, moving to a neighborhood that had a higher SES and a lower crime rate resulted in 8% fewer cases of depressive episodes among adults in the experimental group than among adults in the control group. This rate of impact on depression compares favorably with medical trials of best-practice depression care.[63,64]

Differences in mental health were evident among other measures, as well. On an index of "psychological distress,"[16] the fraction of 6 mental health items that adults reported experiencing during the previous month (eg, "so sad nothing could cheer you up"; "nervous"; "everything was an effort") was significantly higher among adults in the control group than among adults in the experimental group. There was also a significant difference between the 2 study groups in the number of adults who reported feeling "calm and peaceful" during the previous 30 days — favoring the experimental group. While differences in the occurrence of anxiety during the previous 12 months also favored those adults in the experimental group, the treatment impacts proved not statistically significant.[16]

The effect of safer neighborhoods on parent mental health is seen readily among participants in the 2002 Gautreaux program.[18] Diane, the mother of 2 children whom we introduced previously in this chapter, had difficulty raising her 7-year-old son in her neighborhood of origin. Under the Gautreaux program, Diane, her children and her new husband Harold moved to a suburb of Chicago, more than 30 miles from her original neighborhood. The following tells of Diane's experience of moving to this new, safer neighborhood:

Diane: A Case Study from the 2002 Gautreaux Program[18] (continued)

Diane is much happier in her new neighborhood. Her sense of personal safety has increased markedly and she feels better about her children's safety. When asked how she would describe her new neighborhood to a friend back in the city (Chicago), she said:

"I'd tell them it's nice. It's almost like living in the country [laughing]. But it's nice and it's quiet. And it's good because the children…they're not only playing with just black children. It's a mix, you know, so that's what I like most about it. My kids don't have a problem with going out and playing. They're not running in saying, 'He beat me up.' We don't have a problem with them going out playing, and then I don't have to literally sit there and watch them. I keep checking on them because that's just me, but they can honestly go out and play and I really have no worries. So, I'd tell them it's a WONDERFUL neighborhood. It's wonderful."

(continued later in this chapter)

Residential mobility provided few significant benefits to parents' overall physical health — in contrast with mental health — as measured by respondents' self-assessment of overall health and asthma symptoms (Table 2) and by reported limits on activity or blood pressure levels (results not shown). The only notable exception was in reported obesity, which was significantly lower among adults in the experimental group than among adults in the control group. Given the high rate of obesity in this sample (47% of adults in the control group reported heights and weights that produced body mass indexes [BMIs] greater than 30), this outcome is likely to have important positive consequences for participants.

Children's Exposure to Violence

All school-age children spend substantial portions of their day away from home, with adolescents having the greatest latitude to choose where and with whom they spend their time. Drawn from chapter 3 in Orr and colleagues,[16] Table 3 summarizes the results from an extensive battery of questions regarding children's exposure to violence that were asked of youth who were between the ages of 8 years and 19 years.

Table 3. Children's (Ages 8y to 19y) Exposure to Violence and Victimization in the MTO Experiment[16]

	Control-group Mean	Experimental-group Mean Minus Control-group Mean*
Reports existence of gangs in neighborhood or school		
All youth	54	–6†
Girls	52	–7†
Boys	56	NS‡
Saw people selling or using illegal drugs in neighborhood at least once/week during past month		
All youth	35	–5†
Girls	37	–10†
Boys	34	NS
Heard gunshots in neighborhood at least once/week during past month		
All youth	12	–3†
Girls	11	NS
Boys	13	–4†
Saw someone shoot or stab another person during past year		
All youth	13	NS
Girls	12	NS
Boys	14	NS
Someone pulled a knife or gun on child during past year		
All youth	9	NS
Girls	6	NS
Boys	12	NS
Someone cut, shot, or stabbed child during past year		
All youth	4	NS
Girls	3	NS
Boys	5	NS

Note: Data from exhibit 5.5 in Orr, et al.[16]

*Represents Intent-to-Treat effects, which are the mean differences between all members of the experimental and control groups, adjusted by multiple regression for differences in baseline characteristics.

† $P<.05$.

‡ Not significant.

In the MTO program, disappointingly few significant effects emerged regarding children's exposure to violence: For example, although children in families assigned to the experimental group were significantly less likely to report the presence of gangs in their new neighborhoods or schools, hear gunshots recently in their new neighborhoods or report witnessing drug sales, there were no statistically significant decreases in their reports of witnessing shootings or stabbings or being threatened or injured by a knife or gun. What is evident in these data is the failure of better neighborhoods (as measured by census-based poverty and other demographic characteristics and by parents' reports of neighborhood safety) to translate into uniformly safer neighborhoods for children. We now speculate as to why this might be the case.

Children's Mental Health, Physical Health and Behavior

Given the minimal improvements in neighborhood and school violence reported by children in the MTO experimental group, it seems reasonable to expect that residential mobility programs would have a limited impact on children's mental and physical health. Based on chapter 5 in Orr and colleagues,[16] Table 4 documents one of the most *unexpected* patterns of results for the MTO program — the beneficial impacts on mental health for girls, but null to detrimental effects for boys.

The interviews conducted with the study youth included several mental health measures, responses to which were reported directly by the children who were between the ages of 12 years and 19 years at the time of the follow-up interview. Parents reported the mental health of their children who were ages 5 years to 11 years. Girls in the experimental group reported significantly fewer symptoms of psychological distress during the previous month than did their control-group counterparts. In the case of lifetime generalized anxiety disorder (as first developed for the Adolescent Supplement to the National Co-morbidity Survey Replication[16,65]), a significantly smaller proportion of girls in the experimental-group families reported such a condition. Reports of lifetime depression were also lower among experimental-group girls, relative to control-group girls, but they did not reach a level of significance. When considered with the previously reported results for women who moved, these results suggest that the moves to better neighborhoods appear to have similarly beneficial effects on the mental health of mothers and their daughters.

Table 4. Children's Mental and Physical Health and Behavior Problems in the MTO Experiment[16]

	Control-group Mean	Experimental-group Mean Minus Control-group Mean*
Mental Health		
Youth's level of psychological distress during past month†		
All youth, ages 12 years-19 years	26	NS
Girls, ages 12 years-19 years	30	–5‡
Boys, ages 12 years-19 years	21	NS
Youth reports of lifetime depression		
All youth, ages 12 years-19 years	7	NS
Girls, ages 12 years-19 years	10	NS
Boys, ages 12 years-19 years	3	NS
Youth reports of lifetime generalized anxiety disorder		
All youth, ages 12 years-19 years	7	NS
Girls, ages 12 years-19 years	9	–4‡
Boys, ages 12 years-19 years	4	NS
Parental reports of child behavior problems§		
All youth, ages 5 years-11 years	29	NS
Girls, ages 5 years-11 years	25	NS
Boys, ages 5 years-11 years	33	+4‡
Youth reports of behavior problems		
All youth, ages 12 years-19 years	34	+4‡
Girls, ages 12 years-19 years	35	NS
Boys, ages 12 years-19 years	34	+8‡
Physical Health		
Parental reports that child had asthma or wheezing attack during past year		
All youth, ages 5 years-11 years	15	NS
Girls, ages 5 years-11 years	12	NS
Boys, ages 5 years-11 years	18	NS
Youth reports of asthma or wheezing attack during past year		
All youth, ages 12 years-19 years	16	NS
Girls, ages 12 years-19 years	19	NS
Boys, ages 12 years-19 years	13	NS

(continued)

Table 4. Children's Mental and Physical Health and Behavior Problems in the MTO Experiment[16] (continued)

	Control-group Mean	Experimental-group Mean Minus Control-group Mean*
Parental reports that child had injury requiring medical attention during past year		
All youth, ages 5 years-11 years	7	NS
Girls, ages 5 years-11 years	5	NS
Boys, ages 5 years-11 years	10	NS
Youth reports of injury requiring medical attention during past year		
All youth, ages 12 years-19 years	12	NS
Girls, ages 12 years-19 years	11	NS
Boys, ages 12 years-19 years	14	NS
Youth's BMI is at 95th percentile or higher		
All youth, ages 12 years-19 years	17	NS
Girls ages, 12 years-19 years	16	NS
Boys ages, 12 years-19 years	17	NS

Notes: Mental health data from Exhibit 4.5 in Orr, et al.[16] Parental reports of child behavior problems from exhibit 5.1 in Orr, et al.[16] Youth reports of behavior problems from exhibit 5.2 in Orr, et al.[16] Physical health data from exhibits 4.3 and 4.4 in Orr, et al.[16]

*Represents Intent-to-Treat effects, which are the mean differences between all members of the experimental and control groups, adjusted by multiple regression for differences in baseline characteristics.

†Fraction of 6 distress items that the youth reported sometimes feeling or often feeling during the past 30 days. The 6 distress items were feeling nervous, hopeless, restless or fidgety, so depressed nothing could cheer you up, everything was an effort, and worthless.

‡$P<.05$.

§Fraction of 11 behavior problems sometimes true or often true of child or youth. The 11 behavior problems were the following: difficulty concentrating; cheating or lying; bullying or being cruel or mean to others; disobedient at home; difficulty getting along with other children; restless or overactive; strong temper; withdrawn; hanging around with kids who get into trouble; disobedient at school; and trouble getting along with teachers.

In contrast, experimental-group boys showed *none* of these mental health benefits, relative to control-group boys. The findings actually indicate worse mental health for boys in the experimental group, although the differences were not statistically significant. Boys in the experimental-group families exhibited significantly worse behavior, according to both self-reports and parents' reports. Items in the behavior problem index[66] included the following:

- being "disobedient at home or school"
- being "withdrawn" or "bullying"
- being "cruel to others"

In the case of youth reports, the differences between experimental- and control-group boys in exhibiting these problem behaviors were quite large. Administrative data on arrests showed that experimental-group boys (ages 15 years to 19 years at follow-up) were significantly more likely to be arrested for crimes to property (but not for other crimes) than were control-group boys (see exhibit 5.3 in Orr, et al[16]; results not shown in Table 4).

Mirroring the improvements in mental health, the behavior of female youth was generally more positive for those in the experimental group than for those in the control group. For the set of results included in chapter 5 of Orr and colleagues,[16] the data show significantly less risky behavior (eg, cigarette smoking and marijuana use) among experimental-group girls, relative to their control-group counterparts.

In terms of physical health, the favorable BMI results exhibited for parents (Table 2) were not evident for either the boys or the girls. There were also no significant differences in parent or youth reports of asthma symptoms or injury rates. Not shown in Table 4 are the null results for the parent-reported measure of their children's general health.

Understanding the Results of the MTO Experiment

The MTO program provides a dramatic test of the consequences of moving from high-crime, high-poverty neighborhoods to much safer, more affluent locales.[16] The experimental evaluation shows several favorable impacts on families, although the results are not universally positive. Despite subsequent mobility, families originally placed in low-poverty neighborhoods still resided in much safer and more affluent neighborhoods 4 years to 7 years later. This appeared to translate into important improvements in the mental health and physical health of the mothers and thus enabled them to achieve the goals that brought them into the program.

The puzzle is why these moves produced smaller and less-consistent improvements for the female youth and, in fact, may have worsened the problem behaviors of the male youth. Investigators involved in the MTO evaluation devoted considerable effort to understanding the mediating processes, which are outlined in the following text, that might account for the observed variable impacts of the MTO program: For example, experimental-group families undertook steps that undid some of the possible advantages of moving to middle-class neighborhoods. As discussed previously, subsequent moves by the experimental-group families placed them in neighborhoods that were considerably less affluent than were their original placement neighborhoods. Moreover, the previous section in this chapter documented that although experimental-group families moved to more affluent areas, most did not move to racially or ethnically integrated neighborhoods. Quite simply, cultural and racial discrimination may limit the availability of high-quality public services in minority neighborhoods. It appears that it may take a program like Gautreaux[17] — which defined target neighborhoods in terms of poverty *and* race — to induce *permanent* moves to neighborhoods that are both more affluent and more culturally and racially integrated.

The quality of the schools attended by children in the experimental group did not improve as much as might be expected. In chapter 6 of Orr and colleagues,[16] the investigators show that the children in the experimental group who moved in conjunction with the MTO program attended schools that ranked in only the 25th percentile, based on student test scores.[16] While this is significantly ($P<.05$) higher than the 17th percentile ranking of the schools attended by children in the control group, it certainly does not appear that the MTO program resulted in many children in the experimental group attending high-quality schools. When the youth in both groups were asked to characterize the climate in and the resources of their schools, virtually no experimental-/control-group differences were found (see chapter 6 in Orr, et al[16]). Evidence from a qualitative study of families in the MTO program suggests that the "school choice" built into many urban school systems offered parents the option of sending their children to schools close to their neighborhoods of origin — near where many of their relatives still lived — and many parents took advantage of this opportunity.[20] Perhaps they did so because they were more comfortable with their children's original schools or schools in neighborhoods with which they were familiar.

Also, it appears that the children's own choices of peers and activities maintained (for girls) or undid (for boys) some of the potential advantages of the safer and more affluent neighborhoods. Adolescent girls, but not boys, in the experimental group were significantly more likely than their control-group counterparts to participate in sports teams, engage in structured after-school activities and attend school regularly (see Appendix E in Orr, et al[16]). In contrast, adolescent boys, but not girls, in the experimental group were more likely than their control-group counterparts to have friends who sold or used illegal drugs.

To illustrate what might be occurring with these adolescent males, consider the situation with Stephen, an African American male who lived in a housing project in the near south side of Chicago for most of his early childhood. Stephen's family, which was assigned to the MTO experimental group in Chicago, moved in conjunction with the program. He was 18 years of age when he recounted what it was like to grow up in his housing-project neighborhood — and what had happened since then:

Stephen: A Case Study from the MTO Program[16]

"I've seen a lot of stuff I shouldn't have seen; like people getting jumped on, and a lot of violence and stuff.... Being in a project, you know there's going to be shooting. I heard drive-by shootings at night, while I was sleeping. I slept on the floor a lot — me and my sister [to avoid being shot]."

Stephen, who had seen much violence in his life, described numerous incidents of observing or hearing about violent incidents, but he was also actively involved in violence himself. Much of his elementary school years were spent, as he explained, creating and maintaining a high level of respect among other children, which was accomplished only through fighting. His MTO-related move did little to change this pattern. He continued to fight at his original neighborhood school:

"In my third-grade summer school, I got into a fight with the teacher because I was at a point where I was like, 'If you ain't my momma, you ain't got nothing to say to me. You can't tell me what to do.' That was my whole attitude then."

(continued on next page)

Stephen: A Case Study from the MTO Program[16] (continued)

Stephen then fought at his initial MTO school:

"I got into a lot of fights, but it's like that didn't affect me at school or nothing because I never got suspended."

Stephen continued to fight at his post–MTO-move school:

"[Fighting] was something I was known for by the teachers and the principals. I got there in my fifth-grade year. By my seventh-grade year, I done fight almost every male from sixth grade on up to eighth. . . . I fought like every male in the school, except basically like 5 of them."

Stephen emphasized that he fought for respect. Although there were some students in his school who were involved in gangs, such groups were not the issue for him. As he saw it, if you were harassed or jumped at school, you had to defend or avenge yourself; otherwise you looked "soft" and you would be attacked again.

(continued later in this chapter)

Although Stephen moved to better neighborhoods through the MTO program, his behavior appeared to have changed little, if at all, in his new schools.

Furthermore, it appears that the advantages of safer, more affluent neighborhoods failed to translate into the kinds of family advantages that might have promoted the children's well-being: Adults who moved in conjunction with the MTO program remained similar to their control-group counterparts in terms of their employment status, welfare dependence, family income and parenting practices, as well as in their connections to their children's schools and the parents of their children's friends. A concern with much of the non-experimental literature regarding neighborhood influences is that it is often difficult to distinguish "neighborhood effects" from "family influences."[67] Perhaps something similar is operating within the MTO program: Perhaps truly effective policies may require *both* neighborhood *and* family changes.

Here again, Diane's case proves instructive: Although her family's move to a safer suburban neighborhood appeared to have solved many neighborhood-related problems, it may have actually aggravated family-related issues:

Diane: A Case Study of the 2002 Gautreaux Program[18]

(continued)

Diane's move created stress and conflict in her relationship with her new husband, Harold, who could not find steady work in the new neighborhood, and money problems plagued the family.

This stress proved upsetting to her son, Jordan, whose biological father was in jail for homicide. Jordan had always found it difficult to contend with his father's absence from his life. However, Jordan had grown to love and view Harold as his new dad. Thus, Harold's disagreements with Diane were particularly stressful for him. One evening, Diane found Jordan in the bathtub under water, appearing to try to drown himself. In addition, Jordan's teachers at his new school noticed changes in his behavior as well.

The marital stress escalated into an episode of domestic violence. As Diane explained:

"It was like a money thing, you know. All the bills was on me because he had been back and forth with the temp service. The man [at the temporary employment service] would like give him jobs, tell him, 'Oh yeah, this is permanent,' and it would be for 2 weeks. Well, we got all these bills that need to be paid. And, I guess I was stressed out. He was stressed out. And so we got into it one day....He like choked me, so it scared me."

Diane called the police, Harold was arrested and she dropped the charges only when Harold agreed to participate in an anger management program. Although this incident seemed to end on a positive note for Diane and Harold — Harold was going to counseling, the couple was attending marital therapy and they were currently happy in their marriage — Harold's arrest proved very upsetting for Jordan. When Jordan came home from school that day to discover that Harold was in jail, he took it very hard.

(continued on next page)

Diane: A Case Study of the 2002 Gautreaux Program[18] (continued)

As Diane related: "*He was like, 'I'm going to kill myself and I don't want to live anymore. We don't have a real family.' He was like, 'You know my real father is in jail. How could you send Harold to jail? You're not going to stop me this time. You're not going to be able to find me, and I'm going to put a LOT of water [in the tub].'*"

Neighborhood violence and other social ills may indeed contribute to the mental health problems of children growing up in impoverished, high-crime communities. But evidence from the MTO program discussed in this chapter suggests that dramatic changes in neighborhood quality may *not* produce corresponding reductions in the levels of violence experienced by children and adolescents. Girls, however, appeared to be more responsive than were the boys to neighborhood-based opportunities. Girls were also more likely to enjoy the mental health benefits that these improved opportunities can provide.

Nevertheless, other kinds of changes may matter more for boys. The following changes certainly did in the case of Stephen:

Stephen: A Case Study from the MTO Program[16] (continued)

Upon graduation from elementary school — 5 years after his family's initial move through the MTO program — everything changed for Stephen. As he explained:

"*After eighth grade, that whole fighting thing and all that stuff stopped. I don't really hang with nobody. I don't hang with nobody.*"

Two major events occurred in his life at this time. First, Stephen and his mother decided that it would be better if he did not attend the local high school. This high school, Stephen explained, was so violent that he

"*. . . would probably be in jail right now, because that's all they do is fight.*"

(continued on next page)

Stephen: A Case Study from the MTO Program[16] (continued)

Instead, he completed a correspondence course from home, thereby earning his high school diploma. Second, around this same time, Stephen became more involved in the large church that his mother attended. Stephen was asked by a youth pastor to join the church-affiliated rap club, although he was neither a believer nor very involved in the church at that time. This rap group evolved into a step-fraternity — an historical African American fraternal organization that focused on dance and music. Today, at age 18, Stephen's faith is strong, and he participates in this group on most days of the week. He has also "graduated" to a level of responsibility as a student leader at the church.

Currently, Stephen is largely disconnected from his previous networks. All of his friends are from the church. None are from the local neighborhood. In addition, he stays off the neighborhood streets, as he is likely to be stopped by the police, which used to happen to him at least once a month.

In Stephen's case, the pivotal factor behind his switch to a positive trajectory was not a direct effect of his MTO move. In fact, the violence he experienced at the local schools in his MTO-qualifying neighborhood appears to have been just as great as the violence he experienced in the schools in his prior neighborhood.

Conclusion

Overall, the results to date from evaluations of the MTO residential mobility program show that such programs are not likely to be cure-alls for the mental health problems associated with living in high-crime neighborhoods. Moves to low-crime, more affluent neighborhoods do, indeed, appear to improve the mental health of adults and, to a lesser extent, the mental health of female youth. Conversely, for boys, there appear to be no such positive mental health impacts. If anything, we have seen negative impacts on their behavior. It is possible, of course, that this picture will change during the planned 10-year follow-up of MTO participants. For now, however, it appears that an intervention that is focused exclusively on neighborhood — rather than also on child, family and school factors — is unable to solve the myriad health and behavioral problems of children growing up in violent urban neighborhoods.

Acknowledgments

Support for the Moving to Opportunity research presented in this chapter was provided by grants from the National Science Foundation (SBE-9876337 and BCS-0091854), the National Institute of Child Health & Human Development and the National Institute of Mental Health (R01-HD40404 and R01-HD40444), the US Department of Housing and Urban Development, the MacArthur Foundation, the Robert Wood Johnson Foundation, the Russell Sage Foundation, the Smith Richardson Foundation, the Spencer Foundation and the W.T. Grant Foundation. Support for the Gautreaux evaluation work was provided by the MacArthur Foundation, the Ford Foundation, the Foundation for Child Development and the Family and Child Well-being Research Network of the National Institute of Child Health & Human Development (2 U01 HD30947-07). We are grateful to Dorothy Duncan and Jeffrey Kling for their helpful comments.

References

1. Rates of homicide, suicide, and firearm-related death among children — 26 industrialized countries. *MMWR. Morbidity and Mortality Weekly Report.* 1997;46:101-105.
2. American Academy of Pediatrics: Committee on Injury and Poison Prevention. Firearm-related injuries affecting the pediatric population. *Pediatrics.* 2000;105:888-895.
3. Nonfatal and fatal firearm-related injuries — United States, 1993–1997. *JAMA: The Journal of the American Medical Association.* 2000;283:47-48.
4. Kilpatrick DG, Saunders BE, Smith DW. *Child and Adolescent Victimization in America: Prevalence and Implications.* Washington, DC: US Dept of Justice, National Institute of Justice; 2002. Publication NCJ 186167.
5. Purugganan OH, Stein RE, Silver EJ, Benenson BS. Exposure to violence among urban school-aged children: is it only on television? *Pediatrics.* 2000;106(suppl):949–953.
6. Campbell C, Schwartz DF. Prevalence and impact of exposure to interpersonal violence among suburban and urban middle school students. *Pediatrics.* 1996;98:396-402 [published erratum appears in *Pediatrics.* 1997;99:A40].
7. Garbarino J, Bradshaw CP, Vorrasi JA. Mitigating the effects of gun violence on children and youth. *The Future of Children/Center for the Future of Children, the David and Lucile Packard Foundation.* 2002;12:73-85.
8. Kendall-Tackett K. The health effects of childhood abuse: four pathways by which abuse can influence health. *Child Abuse & Neglect.* 2002;26:715-729.
9. Pynoos RS, Frederick C, Nader K, et al. Life threat and posttraumatic stress in school-age children. *Archives of General Psychiatry.* 1987;44:1057-1063.
10. Osofsky JD. The effects of exposure to violence on young children. *The American Psychologist.* 1995;50:782-788.
11. Dyson JL. The effect of family violence on children's academic performance and behavior. *Journal of the National Medical Association.* 1990;82:17-22.
12. Singer MI, Miller DB, Guo S, Flannery DJ, Frierson T, Slovak K. Contributors to violent behavior among elementary and middle school children. *Pediatrics.* 1999;104:878-884.

13. Jargowsky P. *Stunning Progress, Hidden Problems: Declines in Concentrated Poverty in the 1990s* [audiotape and videotape]. Washington, DC: The Brookings Institution and Living Cities; May 19, 2003.
14. Wandersman A, Nation M. Urban neighborhoods and mental health. Psychological contributions to understanding toxicity, resilience, and interventions. *The American Psychologist.* 1998;53:647-656.
15. Linares LO, Heeren T, Bronfman E, Zuckerman B, Augustyn M, Tronick E. A mediational model for the impact of exposure to community violence on early child behavior problems. *Child Development.* 2001;72:639-652.
16. Orr L, Feins JD, Jacob R, et al. *Moving to Opportunity for Fair Housing Demonstration Program: Interim Impacts Evaluation.* Washington, DC: US Dept of Housing and Urban Development, Office of Policy Development & Research; September 2003.
17. Rubinowitz LS, Rosenbaum JE. *Crossing the Class and Color Lines: From Public Housing to White Suburbia.* Chicago, Ill: University of Chicago Press; 2000.
18. Pashup J, Edin K, Duncan GJ, Burke K. *2005 Residential Mobility Program: Participation from the Client's Perspective: Findings from Gautreaux Two.* Evanston, Ill: Institute for Policy Research, Northwestern University; 2005.
19. Kling JR, Liebman JB, Katz LF. *Bullets Don't Got No Name: Consequences of Fear in the Ghetto.* Evanston, Ill: Northwestern University/University of Chicago, Joint Center for Poverty Research; 2001. JCPR Working Paper 225.
20. Popkin SJ, Harris LE, Cunningham MK. *Families in Transition: A Qualitative Analysis of the MTO Experience.* Washington, DC: The Urban Institute; 2001.
21. Guerra NG, Huesmann LR, Spindler A. Community violence exposure, social cognition, and aggression among urban elementary school children. *Child Development.* 2003;74:1561-1576.
22. Office of the Surgeon General. *Youth Violence: A Report of the Surgeon General.* Rockville, Md: US Dept of Health and Human Services, US Public Health Service, Office of the Surgeon General; 2001.
23. Buka SL, Stichick TL, Birdthistle I, Earls FJ. Youth exposure to violence: prevalence, risks, and consequences. *The American Journal of Orthopsychiatry.* 2001;71:298-310.
24. Cole TB, Flanagin A. What can we do about violence? *JAMA: The Journal of the American Medical Association.* 1999;282:481-483.
25. Rosenberg ML, Mercy JA. Homicide: epidemiologic analysis at the national level. *Bulletin of the New York Academy of Medicine.* 1986;62:376-399.
26. O'Hare W, Mather M. *The Growing Number of Kids in Severely Distressed Neighborhoods: Evidence from the 2000 Census.* Baltimore, Md: The Annie E. Casey Foundation: October 2003.
27. Federal Bureau of Investigation. Uniform Crime Reports: Crime in the United States — 2003. Available at: http://www.fbi.gov/ucr/03cius.htm. Accessed April 26, 2005.
28. Curry GD, Maxson CL, Howell JC. *Youth Gang Homicides in the 1990's.* Washington, DC: US Dept of Justice, Office of Justice Programs, Office of Juvenile Justice and Delinquency Prevention; March 2001. Publication NCJ 186816.
29. Corman H, Mocan N. *Carrots, Sticks and Broken Windows.* Cambridge, Mass: National Bureau of Economic Research; July 2002. NBER Working Paper w9061.
30. Skogan WG, Steiner L, Hartnett SM, et al. *Community Policing in Chicago, Years Eight and Nine: An Evaluation of Chicago's Alternative Policing Strategy and Information Technology Initiative.* Evanston, Ill: Institute for Policy Research, Northwestern University; December 2002.
31. Bureau of Justice Statistics. Homicide trends and characteristics. Available at: http://bjsdata.ojp.usdoj.gov/dataonline/Search/Homicide/Homicide.cfm. Accessed April 26, 2005.
32. Bureau of Justice Statistics. Data for analysis — crime & justice electronic data abstracts: spreadsheets. National data. Available at: http://www.ojp.usdoj.gov/bjs/data/arrests.wk1. Accessed April 26, 2005.
33. Associated Press. Crimes of violence are up 5% in U.S. *The New York Times.* April 9, 1990; sect A:17.
34. Malcolm AH. More Americans are killing each other. *The New York Times.* December 31, 1989; sect 1, pt 1:20.
35. Federal Bureau of Investigation. Data for analysis - crime & justice electronic data abstracts; spreadsheets; national data. Available at: http://www.ojp.usdoj.gov/ bjs/dtdata.htm#National. Accessed April 26, 2005.

36. Brener ND, Simon TR, Krug EG, Lowry R. Recent trends in violence-related behaviors among high school students in the United States. *JAMA: The Journal of the American Medical Association.* 1999;282:440-446.
37. Purugganan OH, Stein RE, Silver EJ, Benenson BS. Exposure to violence and psychosocial adjustment among urban school-aged children. *Journal of Developmental and Behavioral Pediatrics: JDBP.* 2003;24:424-430.
38. Pollack WS. *Real Boys' Voices.* New York, NY: Random House; 2000.
39. Kuo M, Mohler B, Raudenbush SL, Earls FJ. Assessing exposure to violence using multiple informants: application of hierarchical linear model. *Journal of Child Psychology and Psychiatry, and Allied Disciplines.* 2000;41:1049-1056.
40. Augustyn M, Frank DA, Posner M, Zuckerman B. Children who witness violence, and parent report of children's behavior. *Archives of Pediatrics & Adolescent Medicine.* 2002;156:800-803.
41. Buka S, Earls F. Early determinants of delinquency and violence. *Health Affairs (Project Hope).* 1993;12:46-64.
42. Aneshensel CS, Sucoff CA. The neighborhood context of adolescent mental health. *Journal of Health and Social Behavior.* 1996;37:293-310.
43. Sampson RJ, Laub JH. Urban poverty and the family context of delinquency: a new look at structure and process in a classic study. *Child Development.* 1994;65(2, special number):523-540.
44. Singer MI, Anglin TM, Song LY, Lunghofer L. Adolescents' exposure to violence and associated symptoms of psychological trauma. *JAMA: The Journal of the American Medical Association.* 1995;273: 477-482.
45. Pettit GS, Bates JE, Dodge KA, Meece DW. The impact of after-school peer contact on early adolescent externalizing problems is moderated by parental monitoring, perceived neighborhood safety, and prior adjustment. *Child Development.* 1999;70:768-778.
46. Ceballo R, McLoyd VC. Social support and parenting in poor, dangerous neighborhoods. *Child Development.* 2002;73:1310-1321.
47. Carter LS, Weithorn LA, Behrman RE. Domestic violence and children: analysis and recommendations. *The Future of Children/Center for the Future of Children; the David and Lucile Packard Foundation.* 1999;9;4-20.
48. Veenema TG. Children's exposure to community violence. *Journal of Nursing Scholarship: An Official Publication of Sigma Theta Tau International Honor Society of Nursing/Sigma Theta Tau.* 2001;33: 167-173.
49. Cook PJ, Laub JH. *After the Epidemic: Recent Trends in Youth Violence in the United States.* Cambridge, Mass: National Bureau of Economic Research; October 2001. NBER Working Paper w8571.
50. Donohue JJ, Levitt SD. The impact of legalized abortion on crime. *The Quarterly Journal of Economics.* 2001;116:379-420.
51. Joyce T. *Did Legalized Abortion Lower Crime?* Cambridge, Mass: National Bureau of Economic Research; June 2001. NBER Working Paper w8319.
52. Popkin SJ, Katz B, Cunningham MK, Brown KD, Gustafson J, Turner MA. *A Decade of HOPE VI: Research Findings and Policy Challenges.* Washington, DC: Urban Institute Press; 2004.
53. Kingsley GT, Abravanel MD, Cunningham M, et al. *Lessons From HOPE VI for the Future of Public Housing.* Washington, DC: Urban Institute Press; 2004.
54. US Dept of Housing and Urban Development. *Section 8 Tenant-Based Housing Assistance: A Look Back After 30 Years.* Washington, DC: US Dept of Housing and Urban Development, HUD User; March 2000.
55. Center on Budget and Policy Priorities. *Introduction to the Housing Voucher Program.* Washington, DC: Center on Budget and Policy Priorities; May 15, 2003. Publication 051403.doc.
56. Feins JD, McInnis D, Popkin SJ. *Counseling in the Moving to Opportunity Demonstration Program.* Cambridge, Mass: Abt Associates; October 1997.
57. Wilson WJ. *The Truly Disadvantaged: The Inner City, the Underclass, and Public Policy.* Chicago, Ill: University of Chicago Press; 1987.

58. Massey DS, Denton NA. The dimensions of residential segregation. *Social Forces.* 1988; 67:281-315.

59. Massey DS, Denton NA. *American Apartheid: Segregation and the Making of the Underclass.* Cambridge, Mass: Harvard University Press; 1993.

60. Keels M, Duncan G, DeLuca S, Mendenhall R, Rosenbaum JE. *Fifteen Years Later: Can Residential Mobility Programs Provide a Permanent Escape From Neighborhood Segregation, Crime, and Poverty?* Evanston, Ill: Northwestern University/University of Chicago, Joint Center for Poverty Research; 2003. JCPR Working Paper 330.

61. Sampson RJ, Raudenbush SW, Earls F. Neighborhoods and violent crime: a multilevel study of collective efficacy. *Science.* 1997;277:918-924.

62. Kessler RC, Andrews G, Mroczek D, et al. The World Health Organization Composite International Diagnostic Interview Short Form (CIDI-SF). *International Journal of Methods in Psychiatric Research.* 1998;7:171-185.

63. Wells KB, Sherbourne C, Schoenbaum M, et al. Impact of disseminating quality improvement programs for depression in managed primary care: a randomized controlled trial. *JAMA: The Journal of the American Medical Association.* 2000;283:212-220.

64. Katon W, Russo J, Frank E, et al. Predictors of nonresponse to treatment in primary care patients with dysthymia. *General Hospital Psychiatry.* 2002;24:20-27.

65. Harvard School of Medicine. National Cormorbidity Survey: instruments. Available at: http://www.hcp.med.harvard.edu/ncs/instruments.php. Accessed April 26, 2005.

66. Zill N, Peterson JL. Marital disruption, parent-child relationships, and behavior problems in children. *Journal of Marriage and the Family.* 1986;48:295-307.

67. Duncan GJ, Raudenbush SW. Neighborhoods and adolescent development: how can we determine the links? In: Booth A, Crouter AC, eds. *Does It Take a Village? Community Effects on Children, Adolescents, and Families.* Hillsdale, NJ: Lawrence Earlbaum Associates; 2001:105-136.

Section 5: Natural and Man Made Disasters: Unique Interventions for Children in Violent Situations

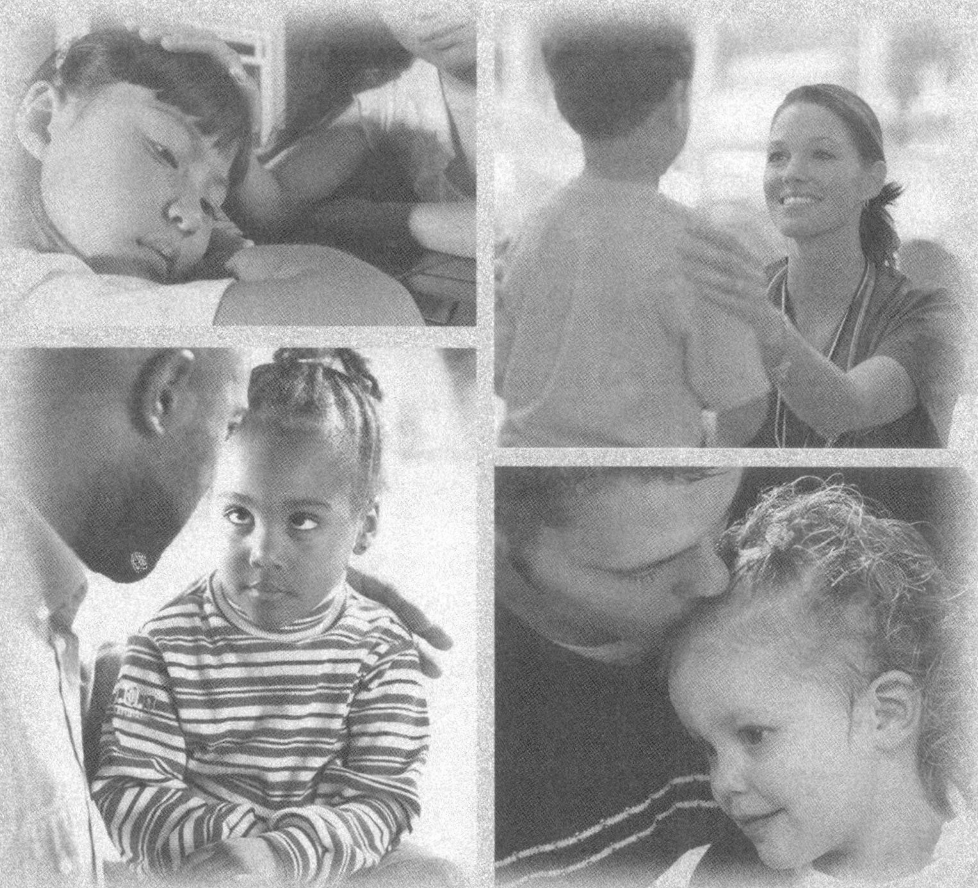

Abstracts from Section 5: Natural and Man Made Disasters: Unique Interventions for Children in Violent Situations

Social and Economic Impact on Children Exposed to Violence in Cambodia, and a Model for Action

Sochua Mu Leiper, MSW

Cambodia is a nation still undergoing reconstruction after almost 30 years of war, genocide and armed conflicts. Extreme poverty and the breakdown of the social fabric continue to expose children to physical and sexual violence. Interventions by the government and the international community have focused largely on prevention of childhood disease. However, efforts to prevent abuse, neglect and violence — which are the main causes of rape, homelessness, child labor and child prostitution — are nearly nonexistent. Cambodia's successful recovery from the ravages of war depends on good governance. Investing in children is the moral responsibility of every citizen.

Child-Oriented Systemic Interventions in a Community Exposed to Disaster: The Tel Aviv Model

Nathaniel Laor, MD, PhD
Leo Wolmer, MA
Smadar Spirman, MA
Ze'ev Wiener, MD

Disasters, whether natural or instigated by human beings, inflict acute and extensive damage on property and lives, and may exert an ongoing and disruptive impact on the livelihoods and basic daily routines of individuals and communities. Disasters may serve as catalysts for a variety of social processes, among them competition for resources and leadership, sociopolitical instability and a general state of anger and discomfort within the affected society. To help entire communities contain the effects of a traumatic event—that is, to cope with the losses and return to a normal routine as quickly as possible—medical and healthcare professionals must embrace a systemic, socially oriented perspective. In the field of emergency child mental health, associated professionals must also be able to work across and within various public and private systems, including the medical educational and community service systems.

In this chapter, we will discuss the following:

- A theory of disaster based on ecological systems theory and on principles borrowed from the fields of public health, preventive medicine, community welfare, education and urban planning
- The weaknesses and vulnerabilities of a free-market (ie, liberal, low-control) mental health system, using Israel as a case study
- The "Tel Aviv Model" as an example of a comprehensive, child-oriented disaster-preparedness and resilience program

Mobilizing Trauma Resources for Children

William W. Harris, PhD
Frank W. Putnam, MD
John A. Fairbank, PhD

Childhood trauma is a major, worldwide public health problem. For many children, the unaddressed consequences of trauma will affect them adversely for their entire lives, affect the lives of those around them and ultimately affect the lives of their own children. Systematic and large-scale public health screenings of children for trauma-related symptoms and behavioral problems offer significant opportunities and critical challenges. Since trauma comes in many different forms for children of various ages, genders and cultures, there is no simple, universal, highly accurate screening measure. Therefore, screening approaches should identify children who have a constellation of risk factors that are associated highly with traumatic antecedents. In this chapter, we discuss measures that can serve as starting points for child trauma pilot screening programs, and the ethical issues related to screening. We offer an asset-focused public health approach to childhood trauma and a 5-pronged model of observation, analysis, experimentation, implementation and evaluation that can be adopted by trauma experts to address this worldwide public health emergency.

Social and Economic Impact on Children Exposed to Violence in Cambodia, and a Model for Action

Sochua Mu Leiper, MSW
Minister of Women's and Veterans' Affairs
Royal Government of Cambodia

Introduction

Social and Political Context: War, Genocide and Armed Conflict

The Vietnam War, which spread from Vietnam to Cambodia and Laos from the 1960s to the mid-1970s, affected the social, political and economic structures of the 3 countries that formed French Indochina. Cambodia was, however, the nation devastated most deeply by the Vietnam War, as the Pol Pot regime of the Khmer Rouge/Communists prolonged the years of conflict. The brutal Pol Pot regime, which ruled Cambodia from 1975 to 1979, systematically killed more than 2 million people. Beginning in 1980, different political factions continued the armed conflict with the non-Communist Cambodians; this lasted until the signing of the Paris Peace Agreement in 1992. Subsequently, the United Nations (UN) conducted and funded general elections in Cambodia in 1993. The UN operations, which were undertaken to restore peace and stability in the region prior to these elections, proved to be very expensive.

The 2 decades of war, genocide and armed conflict ruined Cambodia by depleting the country of its human, natural and financial resources. Not a single Cambodian family was left untouched by the painful realities of separation and death. The Khmer Rouge was responsible for systematic killings, famine, diseases and the forced movements of the country's people from the big cities to small rural villages where they worked as farmers. The leaders of the Khmer Rouge discouraged any practice of religion, forced everyone to dress alike and took control of all the businesses and farms. Of the more than 2 million Cambodians killed, many were former government officials and educated people.

The devastating consequences of the prolonged years of war and unrest left Cambodia with one of the lowest human development records in the world — ranking 148th out of 173 countries worldwide.[1]

The reconstruction of Cambodia, which began after 1993, continues to be a great challenge to the ruling government despite the period of relative stability in the past decade. In 2003, the cost for reconstruction and development programs was estimated at $563 million US, 75% of which was covered by international assistance programs.[2] The Cambodian national budget is limited primarily to paying the salaries of civil servants and to providing very basic human services, that are too insignificant to make a difference to the 36% of the population who live with fewer than 3 full meals each day.[2]

Although much of the country's infrastructure — roads, buildings and bridges — has been rebuilt or repaired, the social reconstruction of Cambodia is another matter. It has been slow and often is at risk of not being sustained when necessary funding is terminated by donors worldwide. The social and cultural values, norms, support systems and even communities and leaders, which once provided security and safety for the people no longer remain the same and, in fact, many no longer exist.

The crumbling of these traditional support systems continues to expose the family unit and the community to daily risks, dangers and violence. The high level of violence inside and outside the home is one of the most powerful threats to the people of Cambodia. Violence is even more of a reality for the women and children of Cambodia, very commonly the most vulnerable and most neglected members of the community. (See Tables 1 and 2 for the health and education indicators for female children and adults, as tabulated in 2000 by the Ministry of Planning of Cambodia.)

Table 1. ***Cambodia at a Glance: Health Indicators***[3]

Indicator	Value
Maternal mortality	437/100,000 live births
Infant mortality	95/1000 live births
Total fertility rate among women 15 years to 49 years of age	4%
Life expectancy for women	58 y
Percentage of GDP* spent on healthcare	10.9%
Ratio of citizens to physicians	6808:1
Ratio of citizens to healthcare workers	598:1

*Gross domestic product

Table 2. ***Cambodia at a Glance: Education Indicators***[3]

Indicator	Value
Percentage of population >20 years of age	55%
Employment among girls 6 years to 11 years of age	84%
School enrollment among girls 12 years to 17 years of age	16%
Female literacy rate	41%
Percentage of national budget spent on education	18.2%

Consequences of Armed Conflicts on Children

Child Labor

According to the *1998 Population Census of Cambodia*, the total population of the country was approximately 11.5 million.[4] Children 14 years of age and younger represented 42.8% of the total population. More than 36% of the total population lived below the poverty line, or were making less than 50 cents per day.[2] Based on these statistics, I estimate that at least 1 million (approximately 20%) Cambodian children eat fewer than 3 meals per day. Therefore, stunting of growth and malnutrition among Cambodian children are serious problems.[3]

The high rate of poverty in Cambodia explains why child labor is so common and such a serious problem in this country. A large number of households headed by a single parent (25%) and poor educational facilities are other factors that encourage the supply of child laborers. A 1996 survey of child labor[5] in Cambodia estimated that 15.9% of children between the ages of 5 years and 17 years worked to contribute to their families' incomes, although to this author this figure seems quite low. Among children ages 5 years to 14 years, this figure dropped to 9.2%. Nearly 26% of the children who worked reported that they first started working before the age of 9 years — and as early as the age of 5 years.[5]

More than 90% of working children in Cambodia live in the rural areas of the country.[5] Although a smaller number of children — estimated at 6000 — work in the large towns and cities, they do so at particularly high risks.[5] They are the street children, garbage collectors, porters and beggars. Life on the streets exposes these children to crimes, police harassment, drugs and sexual exploitation.

Forty percent of working children in Cambodia work more than 40 hours per week.[5] Malnutrition, illnesses, infections and injuries are reported twice as frequently by working children as by nonworking children.[5] Long hours coupled with dangerous equipment at work increase the risk of accidents and/or injuries to these children.

Changes in Sociocultural Patterns and Relations

Even today, Cambodia remains at an interface: The Cambodian national government is rebuilding its communities and reconstructing the nation.[6] The rebuilding of the country's communities is vital for the reestablishment of a basic and fundamental foundation for children's growth and well-being. For the approximately 1 million Cambodian children living below the poverty line, the reweaving of a social fabric that includes the family support system and a functional and reliable community has the capacity to spare them from chronic exposure to abuse and violence.

As an independent nation, Cambodia has not yet regained the spirit it lost during the years of destruction caused by war and genocide. At the grassroots level, Cambodian villagers are now less willing to take initiative and express their opinions because they fear reprisals by and repercussions from the village chiefs. Family members also now trust each other less because the social fabric has been worn thin by political, economic, social and cultural change. Because of the daily struggle to make ends meet, individual members of the community are forced to focus on their own survival rather than on the collective survival and spirit of the community. As economic pressures increase, the catalysts for family conflicts may be rooted in simple jealousy or caused by a significant problem, such as a loss of the family's land.

The absence of many male heads of households — again, due to deaths caused by war and genocide — puts an additional burden on the female heads of households and/or the eldest members of the families.[7] The primary reasons that approximately 50% of females drop out of school by the age of 10 years include poverty (the need to be employed to earn money for the benefit of the family), the need to complete household chores and the culturally based necessity to provide a space in school for their brothers.[5]

Economic and health problems that plague Cambodian families often cause them to lose their land and incur significant debt. Ultimately, this forces them to abandon their children when they can no longer afford to care for them, or to place their children in bondage as domestic servants in order to repay a debt. The subordinate position of Cambodian children in the family, relative to their older family members, shapes their early acceptance of family duties, and their expectancy of abuse and even violence. These children are taught at a young age to remain silent; self-expression by youngsters is generally forbidden. Even pain must be endured in total silence. Children are taught to refrain from questioning adults when they are given orders. Challenging any adult or any older member of the family or community is considered disrespectful.

HIV/AIDS: A New Cause of Separation and Loss for Children

The widespread infection of HIV/AIDS is a relatively new cause for separation from family and loss for the children of Cambodia. Although the prevalence rate of HIV/AIDS has declined from 3.9% in 1997 to 2.8% in 2001, Cambodia is still the country in its region that is most affected by HIV.[8] The infection rate among pregnant women in Cambodia, which stands at 2.3%, is of great concern to the government and international aid workers.[8] For infants and children, HIV/AIDS poses a new challenge to the family structure. More than 200,000 Cambodian children are orphans because of AIDS,[8] and their future remains uncertain because any kind of community response is limited by a lack of financial resources and social services, as well as by discrimination.

Government-funded programs and counseling designed to assist adults and children with handling the loss, grief and separation issues attendant with AIDS and other issues are almost nonexistent. Less than 15 Cambodian psychologists have been trained in such counseling for adults. Programs that meet the needs of children, with few exceptions, remain limited to helping them access basic shelter, food and security in times of loss or separation. In addition, because of the cultural belief that limits the self-expression of children, government support for counseling programs is unlikely to be a priority in the near future.

Violence Against Children

The daily international media coverage of violence against Cambodian children — including rape, sexual exploitation, incest and domestic violence — highlights the dangers these children face.

Cambodia is known to be involved in human trafficking, primarily for sexual exploitation. Amazingly, a full 40% of the victims are estimated by non-government (human rights) organizations to be children under the age of 16 years.[9] The human tragedy of trafficking cannot be denied, and the chance that these young victims will ever return to a "normal" life is, sadly, very slim.

The following are the main reasons for the boom in human trafficking[9]:

- poverty
- social upheaval
- limited educational opportunities
- poor enforcement of the laws against human trafficking
- a culture of violence and impunity
- corruption in the law enforcement system
- a weak judiciary system
- cultural values that legitimize human trafficking

The direct role of parents and/or guardians in the sale of children is a legacy of war and the culture of violence that still exists in Cambodia today.[9]

In mid-1995, women's groups in Cambodia initiated a movement to address the serious issue of domestic violence. Subsequently, a survey of domestic violence,[2] conducted in 1996 by the Ministry of Planning of the Royal Government of Cambodia, showed that 1 of every 6 women in Cambodia had been a victim of domestic violence. Although no study has looked at the issue of children and domestic violence in Cambodia, incidences of neglect and abuse brought about as a result of domestic conflict are well-reported by social service organizations and women's groups.

Based on the results of the survey,[2] the Ministry of Women's and Veterans' Affairs drafted a law designed to prevent domestic violence, which was submitted to the Cambodian Parliament in 2003. The draft law received a wide range of support but, at the same time, received strong criticism and opposition from the more conservative members of the Parliament: They viewed the draft law as too liberal, giving too much freedom to victims of domestic violence, including children.

The draft law provides a legal mechanism with which to prevent domestic violence and to respond to the needs of victims. As proposed, the law recognizes the full rights of children, giving them the power to be represented in court, to request protection by law enforcement and to request an adult or an organization to apply for a court order to protect them from the perpetrator(s), even if the perpetrator(s) is/are the victim's own parents or members of their immediate family. The draft law, if passed, will be the first and only law in Cambodia to specifically spell out the responsibilities and roles of the local authorities and police to provide immediate protection to victims and to define the victims' rights for specific services. To ensure immediate action and protection, the proposed law gives the police and prosecutors the duty to investigate, as well as the right to enter the alleged perpetrator's abode, to seize weapons and to arrest the perpetrator(s). This more streamlined process would shorten existing police and legal procedures, which currently limit victims' access to both justice and protection.

The Cambodian Constitution prohibits violence against children, and includes special provisions for children to receive care and services from their parents and/or the state. Cambodia is also a signatory to UNICEF's "Convention on the Rights of the Child." Yet, meeting children's basic needs and protecting them against violence have not been high priorities on the Cambodian government's agenda. The draft law on domestic violence will have to wait until a new government is formed, following Parliamentary Elections, before further discussions can resume.

In 2002, a local human rights organization — the Association de Droits de l'Hommes au Cambodgeor; ADHOC — conducted the first-ever survey regarding rape in Cambodia.[10] The survey yielded important data that explain the causes of rape, specifically the rape of children.[10] Of the 313 cases of rape reported in the survey, 65% of the victims were under the age of 18 years. According to ADHOC, only 33% of all rape cases were reported to the police. Some of the results of the survey are shown in the following tables:

***Table 3. Relationship of Perpetrator to Victim of Rape*[10]**

Perpetrator	Percentage*
Neighbor	53.4
Father/stepfather/grandfather	15.4
Cousin	9.3
Unrelated	7.3
Policeman/soldier	6.2
Family member sharing same residence	3.1
Employer	1.2
Other	1.0
Total	100

*Percentages as provided in report. Total of percentages does not equal 100%.

***Table 4. Perpetrator-Reported Reasons for Rape of Young Girls*[10]**

Reason	Percentage†
Easy to persuade	20.0
Love	20.0
Alcohol or drug influenced	14.5
Revenge	12.4
Other	12.0
After viewing pornographic movies	6.5
Easy to pay off to avoid lawsuit	4.6
Felt the need to rape	4.0
Not knowing it is a crime	2.0

†Percentages as provided in report. Total of percentages does not equal 100%.

Nearly 44% of reported rape cases were resolved in court, 28% were settled out of court, 19% were never resolved and 9% were dropped because of lack of evidence.[10] The average time of day of the rapes, which occurred most commonly during the daylight hours, indicates the vulnerability and exposure of young children to this violent act. The large number of unreported cases of rape and the use of money as a means of settlement reveal that children's safety and rights are often ignored, and certainly not protected. Court officials in Cambodia admit openly to negligence or a lack of knowledge regarding the gathering of evidence of rape, especially when the alleged victim is a child. Victims commonly report a great sense of guilt and sadness when the perpetrator is known to them, as if the crime committed were their fault.[10] The shame of being raped by a trusted member of one's family, and the guilt and fear associated with denouncing the person and the crime are 2 key reasons why a significant number of rape cases go unreported.

The paucity of interventions made on behalf of children who are victims of rape are a major concern that requires immediate action. Clearly, the raping of children is on the increase in Cambodia. The unabashed cultural belief that children have no feelings leaves them isolated as victims and further traumatized by this act of violence.

The Culture of Impunity

The level of impunity in Cambodia, a stark remnant of the country's decades of war and genocide, leaves victims of violence fearful of seeking justice. The police are so poorly paid by the government that they cannot adequately support their families, and therefore, instead of investigating an alleged crime, they do not hesitate to simply ask alleged perpetrators to pay a compensation to the victim of a crime or to the family of the victim (from which they themselves may receive a portion), even though violence of any form is considered a crime in Cambodia. The corruption of court officials is even more difficult to limit because the court functions as an independent institution under the direct supervision of the Supreme Council of Magistracy. The Supreme Council is chaired by the Monarch (King), who, as the Head of State, has only ceremonial power. In addition, interestingly and amazingly, the Supreme Council has not met even once since it was formed in 1993. Furthermore, Cambodian judges are affiliated most frequently with the current ruling party, which often interferes in the decisions of the court. This situation often leaves cases of abuse, violence and other crimes completely unresolved.

Most cases of violence against children in Cambodia go unreported, with the exception sometimes of sexual exploitation. However, organizations working to defend the rights of children are too few to assist in all cases. Therefore, fewer than 25% of cases of sexual exploitation of children are reported and resolved within the court setting.[10] Although recommendations have been made to the government to establish a special court for children's cases, the lack of experts in the field of children's rights in Cambodia, coupled with the weakness of the Ministry of Justice to promote or draft legislation, have left the issue unconsidered at the highest level.

The Changing Scene in Cambodia for Child Victims of Violence

"SITH KOMAR": An Acknowledgment of Children's Rights

Although the social and psychological scars and sufferings of the people of Cambodia caused by war and genocide run deep — and the people continue to live with the legacy of this violent past — the relatively recent efforts of international and domestic organizations working at the community level to address the needs and protection of the nation's children are beginning to show signs of success. "SITH KOMAR," or "Children's Rights," for example, a UNICEF-based program designed to mobilize community participation and resources for the benefit of the full protection of children's rights, deserves recognition. It is a nationwide, long-term program that has received the full support of the Cambodian government.

The first step taken by SITH KOMAR — and other such organizations — in their approach to the poor situation of children in Cambodia is to better understand the lives of these children through *their* eyes and *their* words. This approach shatters the cultural norm in Cambodia that has labeled children as unable to think for themselves. Various studies[11] conducted on the coping mechanisms of children living under extremely difficult circumstances — such as on the streets, in squatter areas and/or in those areas most affected by land mines — have revealed the following about these children:

- *They trust, cooperate with and care for each other:* Children living under extreme circumstances make many sacrifices, including their own comfort, in order to keep their family unit together. Assisting each other forms a safety net that children have the strength and desire to build.

- *They are able to recognize, access and make use of effective resources:* Children on the streets share information with each other about resources available in the community.
- *They are able to assess their present conditions, plan for the future and overcome daily challenges:* Abandoned children assess and plan new situations as a group in order to earn an income and look for better shelter.
- *They create, identify and negotiate options:* Abandoned children work together to create new options for daily survival. In times of illness, these skills are very important.
- *They avoid and resolve household and community conflicts:* Abandoned children tend not to respond to provocation, and they deliberately minimize their interactions with other people in order to minimize their exposure to violence and risks.

The second step taken by these organizations has been to support the rebuilding of the family unit and the community spirit because they are the base for immediate and long-term stability and peace for the children. The children who participated in the UNESCO consultations with youth in 1998 perceived a halt to the killings and peace as a prerequisite for any other initiatives.[12]

Mith Samlanh (Friends): A Recommended Model of Action for Children Living With Violence

"Mith Samlanh," or "Friends" in the Cambodian language, is a unique organization that works with the country's street children who are the victims of violence to help them change their lives and proactively work to change the lives of other children in similar situations. With the broad goal to reintegrate these street children back into the general society, Mith Samlanh sponsors the following activities:

- **An Outreach Program:** Managed by trained social workers and physicians working together as teams, the program provides special drop-in centers that children can access easily. In these drop-in centers, children are not threatened by local authorities simply because they are all seemingly unwanted members of the society. An important feature of these centers is that they provide the children with the opportunity to continue working — but with a measure of security and safety. On average, 3000 children use the centers each month. Children as young as 12 years of age seek shelter in these drop-ins because they have no other immediate relatives to live with. Activities provided at the centers include literacy and math classes, hygiene and nutrition counseling, and the provision of information about HIV/AIDS, reproductive health and substance abuse.

- **Peer Education:** This program recruits and trains "peer educators," who work with and live with the street children right on the streets. These "peer educators" are trained primarily to act as safety agents. They mainly provide accurate information about drug abuse, reproductive health, HIV/AIDS and links to community resources.

The successes of these 2 preventive activities are illustrated in the following firsthand story:

> *"Within only 2 years, Mith Samlanh completely changed my life. In 1998, my father died, leaving my mother to support 5 children. My mother remarried twice and died 2 years later. I then lived with my stepfather, who was a very cruel man. He forced me to beg, took away my money and beat me. I tried to escape, failed and was punished severely. I succeeded in escaping the second time. I made friends on the streets. We worked together and lived together. I started sniffing glue and slowly began using amphetamines. Then, I met 'Friends' social workers, began to come to the drop-in centers and got involved in their activities. I started taking a vocation skills course, stopped taking drugs and can now begin thinking about a new life."*

- **Transitional House:** This program provides a place for street children to rest and reside for a longer period of time. They are engaged in the daily routine of a family-like atmosphere. Children at "The House" must attend school or vocational training classes during the daytime. Counseling, sports and cultural activities keep these children occupied the rest of the time. The House can accommodate up to 250 children at a time.

A resident of the Transitional House described his life as follows:

> *"When I first heard about Transitional House, I was busy working and enjoying life and did not need it. Later, when things were worse, [when life on the streets became dangerous] I finally decided to go there. I felt safe, welcomed and invited. I was among other children and peers. I felt equal to them. Now I have a place there. I should have thought about going to the House a long time ago."*

- **The Boarding House:** Also known as "The Hotel," it is located in the heart of the capital city of Phnom Penh. Children who work at night but need a place to stay during the daytime can rent space for a small fee. A wide range of activities, peer education and counseling are available to the children, who range in age from 13 years to 18 years. The Boarding House charges "guests" less than 25 cents per day in US currency.

A pleased resident describes her encounter with The Boarding House:

"I come from a poor family in a rural area. My parents cannot read or write. Floods and [then] drought came to my village, and my siblings and I stopped going to school. My parents quarreled every day and were sometimes very violent. I escaped and came to the city by oxcart. I survived life in the city for the first week, working and living at the railway station. I met some other children who showed me to The Boarding House. When there, I plan my life with the staff, but my struggle for a better future is still ongoing…"

- **Education Center:** The purpose of this center is to allow street children and otherwise poor children, who are unable to afford public school or cannot attend because they work, to receive an education. This transitional program prepares children for the public school system. Dance, culture, play and art therapy are part of the program. Approximately 200 children are enrolled in the Education Center at any one time.

The Education Center made 2 "students" very happy:

"'Children, today we will have an award ceremony at Club Friends,' my teacher said. 'We sent your drawings to be judged. Some of you won prizes. Among the world's winners, 2 Cambodian children from The Education Center were at the top of the list.'"

- **The Training Center:** This center teaches income-producing skills to street children, which helps boost their self-esteem. Training is offered in car repair, welding, catering, business management and sewing. Family and community reintegration are also aims of this program. The Training Center serves 300 children each day.

This training helps other siblings, as well:

"I first heard of Friends when my brother's leg was cut by broken glass when we were working in the public rubbish dump. He was bleeding badly and was helped by a 'Friends' staff member who was also working in the public rubbish dump. She saved my brother's life and enrolled me in The Training Center program. I am about to graduate from the cooking class and hope to be placed in a restaurant. Now I can have a future together with my brother."

- **Family Reconciliation and Reintegration Program:** In this program, the "Friends" team works initially with the child to trace the child's family background and the child's reason for leaving home. The team from the child's home province follows up and locates the family. When successful, the reintegration begins and is monitored continually by program staff. A maximum of 50 children are reunited and reintegrated every month.

The dream of a street child comes true when the family is located, when the last tears are shed and when the sense of belonging to a family or community is finally restored. The comprehensive range of programs and activities provided by "Friends" is costly and requires the ongoing training of social workers — as well as an open mind to social change. The rights of the children and the hopes for their futures should be the main foci, even at the cost of challenging longtime traditions.

Conclusion

Cambodia is a nation still under reconstruction following decades of war, genocide and armed conflict. Extreme poverty, the breakdown of the social fabric, the existing culture of impunity and a weak legal system continue to expose the people, especially children, to the risks of abuse, neglect and violence.

The rebuilding of a sense of community is most vital for the reestablishment of a basic foundation for children's growth and well-being. For the many Cambodian children living below the poverty line, it is this rebuilding of communities — which includes the family support system — that will spare them from chronic exposure to abuse and violence.

In situations of extreme poverty, such as those that exist in Cambodia today, children as young as 5 years of age must contribute to the daily incomes of their families. The forced economic contribution made by children through physical labor and/or sexual exploitation exposes them to many risks and denies them their fundamental rights to a life free of fear, want and hunger. It also denies them access to education and health care. The primary school and secondary school dropout rates among children — girls in particular — are serious factors to be considered carefully by the government, and will have a direct impact on human capital and eventually limit the skills of the

Cambodian labor force. The poor health of the country's children affects their readiness for education. Their constant state of hunger and weakness affects their overall growth and will ultimately become a significant expense for the country when ongoing care and intervention are required.

The approaches taken by international and domestic organizations to respond to the immense needs of Cambodian children must include the fortification of family and community life, for it is in these settings that children receive the kind of security that they cannot get from therapy. New legislation to protect the rights of children and a commitment to judicial reform are also needed. Perpetrators of violence against Cambodian youth must be brought to a just court and the victims must be given justice. These are essential if the children of Cambodia are to regain control of their lives.

The unfettered actions of children on behalf of other children have proven to be the most effective. We must listen to the voices of the children and give them the space and the right to participate in the reconstruction of Cambodia. This is a model that will help bring about national healing and ensure a brighter future for Cambodia's children.

References

1. United Nations Development Programme. *Human Development Report 1993: People's Participation.* New York, NY: Oxford University Press; 1993.
2. Ministry of Planning of Cambodia. *Socioeconomic Survey of Cambodia 1996.* Mandaluyong City, Manila, Philippines: Asian Development Bank; 1996.
3. National Institute of Statistics - Cambodia. *Cambodia Demographic and Health Survey 2000 (CDHS 2000).* Phnom Penh, Cambodia: Ministry of Planning, National Institute of Statistics - Cambodia; 2000.
4. National Institute of Statistics - Cambodia. *1998 Population Census of Cambodia: Key Statistics.* Phnom Penh, Cambodia: Ministry of Planning, National Institute of Statistics - Cambodia; 1998.
5. Sophear M. *Child Labour in Cambodia: An Overview.* Geneva, Switzerland: The International Labour Organization; April 18, 1997.
6. Nee M, Healy J. Towards restoring life: Cambodian villages. Paper presented at: The NGO Forum on Cambodia; 1995; Phnom Penh, Cambodia.
7. Boyden J, Gibbs S. *Vulnerability and Resilience: Perception and Responses to Psycho-Social Distress in Cambodia.* Oxford, England: The International NGO Training and Research Centre; 1996.
8. National AIDS Authority. *Building a Better Understanding of the Situation and Response to HIV/AIDS in Cambodia.* Phnom Penh, Cambodia; Ministry of Health, National AIDS Authority; 2001.
9. Cambodian Women's Development Agency. *Selling Noodles: The Trafficking in Women and Children in Cambodia.* Phnom Penh, Cambodia: Cambodian Women's Development Agency; 1996.
10. ADHOC: Cambodia Human Rights and Development Association. *Survey on Rape.* Phnom Penh, Cambodia; 2002.

11. American Friends Service Committee, Socio-Cultural Vulnerability and Coping Strategies (SCVCS) Research Project. *Bins of Gold: Livelihoods of Young People in the Tonle Bassac Squatter Area, Phnom Penh.* Phnom Penh, Cambodia; 2002. Vulnerable People's Responses to Adversity and Change; SCVCS report No. 6.
12. Cambodian National Commission for UNESCO. *Open Window Towards the Future: Contribution of Cambodian Youth to the Definition of National Priorities.* North West, Cambodia: Cambodian National Commission for UNESCO; 1998.

Child-Oriented Systemic Interventions in a Community Exposed to Disaster: The Tel Aviv Model

Nathaniel Laor, MD, PhD
Leo Wolmer, MA
Smadar Spirman, MA
Ze'ev Wiener, MD

Introduction

Disasters, whether natural or instigated by human beings, usually occur suddenly and unexpectedly, leaving extensive damage, loss and widespread human suffering in their wake. They inflict acute and extensive harm on property and lives, and may exert an ongoing and disruptive impact upon the livelihoods and basic daily routines of affected individuals and communities. Without question, disasters can have far-reaching consequences: For example, the September 11, 2001, attack on the World Trade Center buildings in New York City (NY) caused the death and injury of thousands of people and resulted in massive economic losses.

Dense population, extreme climates, poverty and limited industrial and economic development are all correlated positively with higher mortality rates in the wake of a disaster.[1] The ability to cope with disasters is usually further hampered by limited community and educational resources. Even if the event itself is brief, its impact upon individuals and society can persist for many years. Since disasters typically occur on a large scale, they disrupt not only the daily lives of individuals, but also the functioning of their entire social network.[2] Stated simply, disasters affect the involved community's infrastructure, resulting in the following:

- an inability to meet residents' basic needs
- widespread unemployment
- major risks to health

Disasters may also generate a variety of sociopolitical challenges, as well, including general sociopolitical instability, a competition for resources and leadership, and a general state of anger and discomfort within the affected society. Moreover, extensive destruction may lead to the displacement of large population groups.

Mental health interventions for relief, revitalization and reactivation can benefit diverse social institutions — such as families, schools and local governments in many different geographical settings — even if these interventions were developed originally for Western countries and are implemented cross-culturally.[3,4] However, our own experience has shown that the healthcare professionals in charge of these interventions must agree on the endorsement of a systemic, community-oriented perspective — and the primary institutions within the community must collaborate *in advance of* disasters to prepare intervention protocols. Unfortunately, such a perspective is rarely found, even in Israel, although it does support a public system for the delivery of mental health care.

In particular, mental health professionals working in the aftermath of a disaster must be willing and able to understand the problems at hand and work within both the mental health and healthcare systems, while they collaborate *simultaneously* with colleagues from a wide range of fields (eg, education, welfare, medicine, police). Furthermore, these professionals must have the ability and authority to confront immediate practical problems, such as resource allocation, and muster powers of endurance to sustain their efforts and those of their teams in order to manage longer-term problems without succumbing to burnout or secondary traumatization.

In the area of child mental health, the difficulties are compounded because professionals must work across various public and private systems, including the healthcare system, the educational system and the community service system. Nonetheless, most position papers and guidelines for organizing emergency mental health services remain almost entirely oblivious to disaster preparedness, as well as to the specific local and municipal systems within which emergency child mental health services should be implemented.[5,6]

A Theory of Disaster

The Dimension of Time

It is possible to distinguish the impact of disasters on individuals and on communities according to the following 4 stages[7]:

- The *predisaster stage* is characterized by signs that warn of an impending event that may induce a sense of uncertainty and insecurity among the area's citizens. Not all disasters, however, are preceded by such warning signs: Therefore, this stage does not always occur.
- In most cases, the *first stage* of a disaster is the event itself.
- The *second stage* of a disaster, which engenders massive structural and functional damage, as well as regression within society, follows immediately after and is sometimes indivisible from the first stage. During this stage of a disaster, the flood of resources entering the affected area and the widespread attention given by local, national and international media generate initial optimism in survivors. However, these survivors soon sense the seemingly insurmountable tasks placed upon the area's bureaucracy, and feelings of optimism are overwhelmed by an awareness of reality, disillusionment and feelings of abandonment and injustice. This second stage, which is characterized by its upheaval, lasts approximately 18 months to 36 months, after which the community begins to stabilize.
- During the *third stage* of a disaster, survivors begin to face the sociocultural losses that may threaten their collective ideology and identity.[8] The Holocaust, as well as the nuclear bombings of Hiroshima and Nagasaki, are examples of mass disasters that have had profound, long-term consequences on the identities of nations. These sociocultural losses, which are often overlooked by disaster managers and decision-makers, may not surface until months or years after a disaster, or they may be present from the very first stage of the disaster.

Implementing Child-Oriented Systemic Interventions Following a Disaster

Mental health professionals working in a disaster area are confronted with numerous clinical disorders in the affected population, including posttraumatic stress, anxiety, dissociation, depression and grief. When intervening following a disaster, whether with children or adults, there are several principles that should guide their efforts:

- **Assess risks early and reach out to as many people as possible, using screening tools that are quick and easy to use, reliable and sensitive.**[9,10] Since almost every affected individual exhibits some form of pathology after a disaster, the possibility of identifying false-positive or false-negative cases can be reduced easily by employing responsible professional parameters and by keeping the criteria quite narrow for identifying the most at-risk individuals.[11,12] To improve the identification of children at risk, this assessment should also review all risk and vulnerability factors, particularly past functioning (eg, exposure to previous trauma and mental health problems) and disaster-related events (eg, witnessing dreadful images and experiencing displacement and personal losses), as well as posttraumatic, dissociative and grief symptoms.[13]
- **Implement systematic, broad-scale community outreach programs within 1 month to 3 months postdisaster.** Adult *and* young survivors of disasters are often reluctant to seek professional help[14,15]: Therefore, outreach programs become necessary in order to identify at-risk individuals who can then be directed to the appropriate treatment. Such outreach programs should incorporate clinical triage protocols that match risk groups with intervention programs.[16-19]
- **Assure that clinicians remain sensitive to their working environment.** Psychological interventions following disasters require an integrative approach because such events affect children, families, communities and, indeed, the entire socioeconomic and cultural matrix of the disaster zone.[20] Clinical evaluations must be subordinate to social considerations: Therefore, mental health clinicians will need to collaborate with the healthcare delivery system in order to achieve the desired results. Pynoos, Goenjian and Steinberg[21] believe that it is the responsibility of disaster mental health professionals to mediate and facilitate the adaptation of government and social institutions, school communities and intervention teams to the emerging needs of adults and children in the aftermath of a

disaster. Mental health professionals can identify these needs by examining population screening data and subsequently determining the appropriate allocation of institutional responsibilities and resources.

- **As quickly as possible, redifferentiate the roles of the professionals — psychiatrists, psychologists, social workers, child caretakers and educators — who are called upon to care for the basic needs of survivors.** One of the primary effects of a disaster is the loss of "role differentiation"; that is, the disappearance of boundaries among the traditionally differentiated roles of these professionals.[22] This primary regression must be counteracted by a process of planned role redifferentiation, which takes into consideration the unique roles and the distinctive contributions of these professionals at the later stages of a disaster.
- **Rehabilitate survivors within their most natural institutional environment.** Based on ecological principles,[21,22] a responsible intervention program should link the mental health system to the survivor's relevant environment in order to create an "eco-niche" within which rehabilitation can take place. Toward this end, child mental health professionals must work hand in hand with area professionals from other involved services (eg, health, education and welfare). We believe that local educators, nurses, community workers and other similar professionals are suited properly to serve as mediators of such interventions for children because they occupy central positions within the community institutions that constitute the normal social matrix of the family and the child. These community institutions (eg, schools, primary care clinics and community centers) could also serve as social reactivation centers within which communities provide large-scale interventions. The institutions themselves are thereby rehabilitated, as well. Mental health workers who work across their professional boundaries and endorse the ecological approach must develop a curiosity about new domains. They must also be ready to educate other professionals and be educated by the professionals simultaneously in these other domains.

Planning Disaster Intervention Programs

Since the effects of a mass disaster are extensive, mental health professionals must be prepared to coordinate with already-established authorities the intervention programs they intend to implement for individuals, families, neighborhoods and communities. Schools, community centers, primary care centers and well-baby clinics, whether still intact or in the process of being reconstituted, are ideal settings in which to initiate early interventions.[23-26] Local teachers, nurses and community workers — who have well-developed relationships with area children and parents — can play important educational and therapeutic roles.[27] However, these local mediators themselves have suffered trauma, and they may need symptomatic relief, training in disaster-related interventions and an opportunity to reclaim their original roles.

Following a disaster, survivors experience several transitions,[22] which must be considered when designing and implementing programs intended to help survivors cope with the "disaster syndrome." These transitions cover various dimensions:

- **Time** — Survivors move from a state in which time is frozen on the past experience to a creative, future orientation.
- **Vitality** — Survivors progress from a fixation on death and loss to a reinvolvement with life and revitalization.
- **Self-efficacy** — Survivors evolve from passive submission through feelings of grief, shame and anger, and finally to a reengagement of personal strengths.
- **Attachment** — Survivors move from being withdrawn and alienated to being involved once again with their environment, family and society.
- **Identity** — Survivors' views of the world evolve from mythological and magical perspectives on disaster and their fate to a revised sociocultural identity based on themselves as authors contributing to the historical events and taking responsibility for their development.

During the postdisaster period, mental health professionals must be prepared to manage the following:

- identify and respond to needs that have emerged because of changes in societal institutions
- help other professionals in relevant fields reassume their roles, and provide the tools for them to do so
- define or redefine their own place within "the system"

Continuous support from and supervision by mental health professionals during the course of postdisaster intervention may effectively decrease survivors' ambivalence and resistance to interventions that are often perceived as foreign and intrusive.[16,18] In the particular case of child mental health professionals, *successful* interventions will require that they collaborate with relevant individuals within existing systems to create an integrated child and adolescent emergency care team. This emergency care team becomes a hub of professionals interested in the well-being of children and families whose task is to accomplish the following:

- negotiate and integrate the various dimensions of reality that were shattered by the disaster
- delegate professional authority and responsibility to each of its members
- ultimately, confront and manage the long-term effects of the disaster and the sociocultural losses that threaten the existing collective ideology and identity of the community[8]

Through empowerment — which is *critically important* — individuals and communities can eliminate their helplessness. Empowerment enables them to accomplish the following[28]:

- recover their dignity and self-esteem
- enhance their critical self-awareness
- regain control over resources and objectives
- recover their senses of personal and collective responsibilities

To be empowered means that *individuals* (children and adults) become able to identify their specific needs and discover hidden leadership qualities, while *communities* gain greater senses of interdependence, cohesion and cooperation. The process of becoming empowered is of particular importance to displaced populations because it allows newly formed communities to achieve greater control over their natural and social environments.

The Mental Health System: Its Weaknesses and Vulnerabilities

Most position papers on organizing emergency mental health services deal primarily with large-scale considerations and guidelines for interventions in the aftermath of a disaster.[5,6] They focus specifically on medical and psychological interventions to alleviate children's suffering after trauma — but provide little discussion about disaster preparedness, particularly at the local and municipal contexts within which emergency child mental health services must be implemented. As a result, professionals who care for children under disaster conditions may find themselves at a loss as to how to make the range of expertise that is available within a community accessible to the actual victims. This bewilderment may be especially evident during times of imminent worldwide terrorist attacks.

In a free-market system, the various agencies involved in the care and treatment of children who become the victims of a disaster typically have few ties to each other. Furthermore, since they are geared toward needs that arise in times of routine events, they are often ill-equipped to mobilize on a mass scale or provide the skilled manpower necessary for handling disaster victims properly.[22]

The following overview of the Israeli system of disaster preparedness, with particular interest given to the district of Tel Aviv, describes the shortcomings that were present, until recently, and highlights the need for the implementation of disaster preparedness mechanisms in order for a community to deal effectively with disaster — and to care for the most vulnerable within it, especially the children.

Israel: A Case Study of Disaster Preparedness

In Israel, the middle level of command and service in the area of mental health consists of district psychiatrists who are responsible for coordinating mental health services within their districts, which usually encompass several municipalities and local governments: For example, the Tel Aviv district, with its population of more than 1.15 million, consists of 13 municipalities. During times of calm, the role of these district psychiatrists is limited primarily to the application of the mental health laws concerning enforced hospitalization. During emergencies, when collaboration among municipalities becomes mandatory, the district psychiatrists *regulate* and *coordinate* all mental health services within the district. However, the *actual command* of community interventions still rests with the local governments.

This split between the regulation and coordination of mental health services and the command of community mental health interventions may prove dysfunctional during times of stress, such as in the midst of a disaster. During periods of calm, the districts' loosely organized mental health system enjoys relative stability. However, in times of emergency, the system may disintegrate. Of course, under conditions of extreme stress or continuous strain, disintegration can be expected of any ostensibly pluralistic, liberal system that is characterized by minimal control, regulation and integration.

A brief review of the sectors of the Tel Aviv mental health system and its local environment reveals its vulnerabilities in times of emergency:

- **Emergency Civil Services:** From the outset of a major disaster, the local government, as part of the Interior Ministry's Emergency Civil Services, is responsible for the protection of the entire community. The only exception to the local government's authority is the area's soldiers, who are the responsibility of the Home Front Command of the Israeli army. Currently, there are no regulations that integrate emergency child mental health services under the authority of the local government. Some of the child mental health services are rendered by health maintenance organizations (HMOs), others are provided within the school system, while still others are provided by government agencies. The individual municipalities do not have departments of mental health, and, therefore, even in times of emergency, rely on a loose coordination of these services provided by the district psychiatrists.
- **The Army or Home Front Command:** During an emergency, this military body provides meager mental health services. It functions in a capacity that strictly assesses population needs and subsequently responds using primarily the resources of local governments and municipalities. The Department of Mental Health within the army's Medical Corps shares responsibility with the local governments for assessing and treating reserve soldiers returning to the community.

- **Local Governments and Municipalities:** These civilian bodies provide few mental health services. They do, however, have emergency response teams that can spring into action when a disaster occurs. These municipal emergency teams, which consist of professionals from social work, counseling psychology, education, medicine and nursing, provide immediate and direct interventions at the site of the incident. However, generally, these professionals are equipped neither organizationally nor professionally to cope with the overall mental health challenges posed by a major disaster. Similarly, the Israeli Public Health System, which deals routinely with preventive medicine, is meagerly equipped to deal with community emergencies.
- **Mental Health Service Providers:** The community mental health system is comprised of service providers; some are privatized (HMO-based), while others are governmental. This system functions with little governmental or regional regulation, coordination or integration. Few of the providers offer psychological trauma centers.
- **Treatment Institutions:** Providing treatment to the victims of major disasters and mental trauma falls under the jurisdiction of several public entities, including municipal emergency response teams, hospitals, community clinics and the rehabilitation departments of the National Insurance Institute and the Ministry of Defense.
- **Primary Care Clinics:** These facilities have a specific role only when a biological disaster occurs (eg, involvement in immunizations, distribution of preventive medications, primary diagnoses and interventions), but not for other types of major disasters. These clinics, which are part of the nation's HMO systems, are coordinated by district physicians in times of emergency.
- **Rescue Teams:** The local emergency system also provides rescue teams — police, ambulance services and fire brigades — all of which operate in a loosely coordinated fashion with the community mental health system, and, therefore, receive insufficient support.

- **Volunteers:** Individual volunteers and nongovernmental organizations are also involved in any disaster relief effort. They are coordinated by a special division within the municipality's headquarters.

Obviously, being so segmented, the integration of all of these institutions and services may become unmanageable during and after a disaster — child mental health care, in particular, because of the lack of regulations and the extreme vulnerability of children.

In the following section, we describe the Tel Aviv Model and how it applies to disaster events that involve children.

The Tel Aviv Model

The upheaval caused by disasters challenges our basic assumptions regarding privatization and urbanization. Following a disaster, communities must have access to large-scale interventions that benefit all affected residents, without discrimination or segregation by socioeconomic class. However, as is evident from the previous summary, community resources for dealing with major disasters are typically meager and unstable.

Its Structure

The Tel Aviv Model,[7,22] on the other hand, creates a headquarters for the provision of mental health services within a community — the Mental Health Emergency Headquarters — that is accountable for integrating and operating all mental health services within its area of responsibility (as defined by the local government), as well as for providing appropriate training to mental health professionals. In other words, during a disaster, the Mental Health Emergency Headquarters integrates municipal, national, military and HMO systems into a single operational framework whose goal is to serve the entire community.

For an integrated emergency response system to function properly in unstable times, it must be established securely *before* an emergency situation arises. Therefore, Preparedness and Resilience Community Centers must first be established. In Tel Aviv, these centers were implemented in conjunction with 4 existing institutions that work with infants, children and adolescents: primary care clinics, well-baby clinics, schools (under the auspices of school psychologists and counselors) and the army. Before we embark on a formal description of the Tel Aviv Model, we present an example of its activation in the early days of the current wave of terrorist attacks on Tel Aviv.

The Model in Action

On June 1, 2001, a terrorist's suicide bomb exploded at the entrance of a youth club, resulting in the deaths of 21 adolescents and causing injuries to 120 more. Most of the dead and wounded attended a specific school in Tel Aviv. An emergency intervention was initiated at the site immediately with the deployment of intervention teams, which consisted of social workers supported by school psychologists. The victims who were transported to area hospitals by the rescue teams were followed subsequently by liaison professionals who provided home visits, and, when necessary, referred victims to Regional Trauma Centers (RTCs) to receive continued care.

Within the affected school, we implemented a comprehensive school reactivation program that included school administrators, teachers and students. Our teams successfully integrated professionals from the Ministry of Education (school counselors), the municipality (school psychologists and social workers) and the Donald J. Cohen and Irving B. Harris Center for Trauma and Disaster Intervention of the Association for Children at Risk (clinical psychologists, social workers and psychiatrists). For several weeks following the bombing, a field station comprised of mental health professionals operated within the school in order to facilitate outreach to children at risk (eg, witnesses of the bombing and friends of the casualties) and to reduce the possible stigma of referral to a mental health clinic. School psychologists were responsible for the long-term follow-up with the students, as well as for their referral to a trauma center, if necessary.

In addition, we initiated a process whereby all victims and their families were recognized by the Institute for Social Security and received the appropriate assistance — financial and treatment services — as established by law. The Welfare Department within the municipality, in joint cooperation with the Cohen–Harris Center, recognized the affected families as a "community," and initiated with them a long-term healing process that included periodic gatherings, annual commemorations, professional interventions (ie, group, family and individual) and recreational activities.

The Emergency Mental Health System Under the Tel Aviv Model

As soon as rescue teams complete their initial tasks following an emergency, municipal intervention teams arrive on the scene immediately to conduct screenings and refer at-risk victims to RTCs. The intervention teams are multidisciplinary: Each is comprised of social workers, psychologists, educators, physicians, nurses and professional support workers, such as ambulance attendants and members of the fire brigade. These intervention teams provide immediate physical and emotional assistance at the disaster site and/or at evacuation centers, if evacuation is deemed necessary. They are also responsible for the screening of each member of the affected families — children and adults — as well as the screening of the family as a functional unit.

The Liaison Unit of the Emergency Headquarters refers victims to the RTCs and provides home visits for victims. Information about the casualties is transferred from the hospitals and from the National Institute for Forensic Medicine's (NIFM's) Victim Identification Facility to the Family Notification Unit. Teams within this unit, which include a member of the city council, a member of the clergy, a physician or paramedic, social workers and a police officer, notify the families of the deceased and assist with funeral arrangements. The NIFM's Victim Identification Facility also functions as a liaison for the intervention teams working with families who need to identify the remains of their loved ones *and* for the special mental health teams working with the families and the pathologists in the victim identification process.

The RTCs integrate primary care, well-baby care, education (schools and kindergartens) and social services. Each center is comprised of 3 multidisciplinary professional units:

- **Screening and Evaluation Unit:** Performs intakes 24 hours a day, every day, for evaluations prior to treatment, and it provides assessments of disabilities. Once victims return to their communities, this unit dispatches teams to monitor them. The teams collect data on the levels of harm evident within the population and develop tools to assess individual, group and community interventions. If necessary, victims return to the RTC for follow-up.

- **Treatment Unit:** Specializes in various short- and long-term treatment programs for individuals, groups and families.
- **Community Intervention Unit:** Serves in the community as the primary liaison for the emergency and treatment teams.

The Regional Trauma Centers are also involved in community preparedness and resilience. In this capacity, their role is to design and develop community preparedness, intervention and rehabilitation programs that meet the unique needs of infants, children and adolescents, as well as the elderly, disabled, chronically ill and other special population groups, including new immigrants, foreigners and minorities. These programs actually operate through community institutions, such as the schools, well-baby clinics, primary care clinics, mental health clinics, old-age homes and community centers.

Interventions are also integrated among emergency organizations, such as the Israeli Red Cross (aka, Magen David Adom), the Victim Identification Facility, the Burial Society, the security forces (ie, army and police) and public nonprofit organizations. Representatives of the medical organizations (eg, primary care, nursing and mental health) are trained in mental health techniques and procedures — for use in emergencies and major disasters — by the municipal intervention teams of the RTCs in cooperation and coordination with the Emergency Mental Health Headquarters (EMHH) and the primary care system. This "Preparedness and Resilience Program" of the RTCs supports the existing mental health system through the planned and organized use of volunteers and activists, thereby enhancing both community resilience and rehabilitation.

The EMHH is responsible for pooling resources, integrating systems beyond the level of the local government and training and providing continuing education to the professionals, paraprofessionals and support teams involved in all of the emergency interventions. The EMHH is also responsible for researching and forecasting various disaster scenarios — and for preparing accordingly. A special program, "Who Will Help the Helper?" provides support and guidance to all of the various interdisciplinary workers. During and shortly after the acute stage of the emergency, the EMHH operates a Hotline Service that provides emotional first aid over the telephone in the form of brief, focused assistance.

What we have outlined thus far is the response to a *civil* emergency. Since the Israeli Defense Forces consist primarily of reserve soldiers, military emergencies may require a civilian response in their second stage. Intervention protocols have been developed and applied for cases in which military and civilian professionals work together in the community to facilitate the smooth transition from traumatic military service back to normal social routines. (unpublished data, 2005)

The role of the Local Government Emergency Headquarters (LGEH) is to formulate strategic organizational and professional principles for use in emergency situations in which the population is harmed or at risk of being harmed. The LGEH consists of representatives of the following:

- organizations from within the local government (eg, welfare services, education, public health, tourism, security and emergency services)
- organizations outside the local government (eg, the mental health command, community medical clinics [HMOs], the army [Home Front Command and the Mental Health Department of the Medical Corps], the Ministries of Health, Education and Welfare, the National Insurance Institute, the Religious Council and various volunteer organizations)

The ability to successfully integrate the various systems involved in emergency preparedness and operations, particularly those that are not under the auspices of the local government, but operate within the city (eg, HMOs, military and mental health), requires the leadership of a flexible public structure — ready to assume this enormous responsibility and spearhead the process of designing and planning programs, generating and allocating resources, implementing programs, training professionals and assessing the disaster and its aftermath. In Tel Aviv, this leadership challenge has been met by the Cohen–Harris Center.

Recently, the Cohen–Harris Center established the School for the Study of Trauma, Preparedness and Community Resilience that serves the Tel Aviv metropolitan area. At this school, representatives from all disciplines and systems are trained together to assume leadership roles and understand the emergency protocols discussed in this chapter.

Conclusion

The Tel Aviv Model has successfully integrated existing institutions and professionals from numerous fields to create a comprehensive matrix within which a community can prepare adequately for and handle the chaos, stress and severe mental health consequences of large-scale disasters. This model provides evidence that a system that is developed and established securely during everyday, nonemergency times will withstand the upheaval engendered by disaster *and* provide the services necessary to empower both individual victims and the community as a whole.

In modern society, although privatization is generally considered to be a positive virtue, disaster preparedness highlights its dangers: When the resources of a society are coordinated loosely, they may leave vulnerable populations without access to any protection or treatment resources whatsoever. The Tel Aviv Model takes all of this into account and has created a matrix that allows a community to prepare for disaster adequately, take action when necessary and treat any at-risk population efficiently.

Disaster preparedness and resilience-building should permeate all systems of community care and serve as the focal point around which to integrate them operationally. A focus on the care of children serves as a working hypothesis for and an active reminder of the need for system integration. The Tel Aviv Model described in this chapter proposes the use of system mediators to bridge community gaps and promote preparedness, resilience and rehabilitation. The model is also relevant in times of calm: It facilitates coping with the current challenges to the social fabric, such as the process of privatization, urban alienation, violence and massive immigration — as well as the recent continuous threat of terrorism. Endorsing the model's philosophy may enable leaders of all types to convey and implement a vision of hope within their communities for the sake of the next generation — the children.

References

1. Ursano RJ, Fullerton CS, McCaughey BG. Trauma and disaster. In: Ursano RJ, McCaughey BG, Fullerton CS, eds. *Individual and Community Responses to Trauma and Disaster: The Structure of Human Chaos.* Cambridge, England: Cambridge University Press; 1995:3-27.
2. World Health Organization. *Psychosocial Guidelines for Preparedness and Intervention in Disaster.* Geneva, Switzerland: World Health Organization; 1991. Publication MNH/PSF/91.3.
3. Galante R, Foa D. An epidemiological study of psychic trauma and treatment effectiveness after a natural disaster. *Journal of the American Academy of Child Psychiatry.* 1986;25:357-363.

4. Goenjian AK, Karayan I, Pynoos RS, et al. Outcome of psychotherapy among early adolescents after trauma. *The American Journal of Psychiatry.* 1997;154:536-542.
5. DeWolfe DJ. *Field Manual for Mental Health and Human Service Workers in Major Disasters.* Washington, DC: US Dept of Health and Human Services, Substance Abuse and Mental Health Services Administration, Center for Mental Health Services. DHHS Publication No. ADM 90-537. Available at: http://www.mentalhealth.org/publications/allpubs/ADM90-537/Default.asp. Accessed June 15, 2002.
6. Young BH, Ford JD, Ruzek JI, Friedman MJ, Gusman FD. *Disaster Mental Health Services: A Guidebook for Clinicians and Administrators.* White River Junction, Vt: National Center for PTSD. Available at: http://www.ncptsd.org/publications/disaster/index.html. Accessed July 10, 2003.
7. Laor N. The role of mental health professionals after mass disasters. Paper presented at: The Promised Childhood Congress; April 30, 2001; Tel-Aviv, Israel.
8. Danieli Y. *International Handbook of Multigenerational Legacies of Trauma.* New York, NY: Kluwer Academic Publishers; 1998. Plenum Series on Stress and Coping.
9. Cochrane A, Holland W. Validation of screening procedures. *British Medical Journal (Clinical Research Ed.).* 1969;27:3-8.
10. Ohan JL, Myers K, Collett BR. Ten-year review of rating scales. IV: scales assessing trauma and its effects. *Journal of the American Academy of Child and Adolescent Psychiatry.* 2002;41:1401-1422.
11. Lonigan CJ, Phillips BM, Richey JA. Posttraumatic stress disorder in children: diagnosis, assessment, and associated features. *Child and Adolescent Psychiatric Clinics of North America.* 2003;12:171-194.
12. Green BL. Assessing levels of psychological impairment following disaster: consideration of actual and methodological dimensions. *The Journal of Nervous and Mental Disease.* 1982;170:544-552.
13. Laor N, Wolmer L, Kora M, Yucel D, Spirman S, Yazgan Y. Posttraumatic, dissociative and grief symptoms in Turkish children exposed to the 1999 earthquakes. *The Journal of Nervous and Mental Disease.* 2002;190:824-832.
14. Norwood AE, Ursano RJ, Fullerton CS. Disaster psychiatry: principles and practice. *The Psychiatric Quarterly.* 2000;71:207-226.
15. Schwarz ED, Kowalski JM. Malignant memories. Reluctance to utilize mental health services after a disaster. *The Journal of Nervous and Mental Disease.* 1992;180:767-772.
16. Lindy JD, Grace MC, Green BL. Survivors: outreach to a reluctant population. *The American Journal of Orthopsychiatry.* 1981;51:468-478.
17. Saltzman WR, Layne CM, Steinberg AM, Arslanagic B, Pynoos RS. Developing a culturally and ecologically sound intervention program for youth exposed to war and terrorism. *Child and Adolescent Psychiatric Clinics of North America.* 2003;12:319-342.
18. Austin LS, Godleski LS. Therapeutic approaches for survivors of disaster. *The Psychiatric Clinics of North America.* 1999;22:897-910.
19. Pfefferbaum B, Nixon SJ, Tucker PM, et al. Posttraumatic stress responses in bereaved children after the Oklahoma City bombing. *Journal of the American Academy of Child and Adolescent Psychiatry.* 1999;38:1372-1379.
20. Goenjian A. A mental health relief programme in Armenia after the 1988 earthquake. Implementation and clinical observations. *The British Journal of Psychiatry: The Journal of Mental Science.* 1993;163:230-239.
21. Pynoos RS, Goenjian AK, Steinberg AM. A public mental health approach to the postdisaster treatment of children and adolescents. *Child and Adolescent Psychiatric Clinics of North America.* 1998;7:195-210.
22. Laor N, Wolmer L, Spirman S, Wiener Z. Facing war, terrorism, and disaster: toward a child-oriented comprehensive emergency care system. *Child and Adolescent Psychiatric Clinics of North America.* 2003;12:343-361.
23. Klingman A. School-based interventions following a disaster. In: Saylor CF, ed. *Children and Disasters.* New York, NY: Kluwer Academic Publishers; 1993:187-210. Issues in Clinical Child Psychology.

24. Pynoos RS, Nader K. Psychological first aid and treatment approach to children exposed to community violence: research implications. *Journal of Traumatic Stress.* 1988;1:445-473.

25. Smith P, Dyregrov A, Yule W, Gupta L, Perrin S, Gjestad R. *Children and Disasters: Teaching Recovery Techniques.* Bergen, Norway: Children and War Foundation; 1999.

26. Wolmer L, Laor N, Yazgan Y. School reactivation programs after disaster: could teachers serve as clinical mediators? *Child and Adolescent Psychiatric Clinics of North America.* 2003;12:363-381.

27. Vernberg EM, Vogel JM. Interventions with children after disasters. *Journal of Clinical Child Psychology.* 1993;22:485-498.

28. Rappaport J. Terms of empowerment/exemplars of prevention: toward a theory for community psychology. *American Journal of Community Psychology.* 1987;15:121-148.

Mobilizing Trauma Resources for Children

William W. Harris, PhD
Frank W. Putnam, MD
John A. Fairbank, PhD

Introduction

Childhood trauma is a major, worldwide public health problem. For many children, the unaddressed consequences of trauma will affect them adversely for their entire lives, affect the lives of those around them and ultimately affect the lives of their own children. The effects of childhood trauma can be pervasive, reducing school readiness and performance, diminishing cognitive abilities, causing or increasing substance abuse, and causing crippling mental disorders and costly physical health problems. Rapid identification of children who have been traumatized could lead to earlier interventions and thereby limit the negative sequelae for victims. Early interventions will reduce the enormous costs of trauma for both victims and society.

Incidence of Childhood Trauma

Children face a high risk of experiencing serious trauma: For example, more than 25% of the children in the Great Smoky Mountains Study (GSMS), a longitudinal trial of the mental health of children living in the western counties of North Carolina, experienced at least one traumatic event by the age of 16 years.[1] These traumatic experiences included the following:

- traumatic loss of a loved one
- exposure to life-threatening accidents, fires and natural disasters
- maltreatment by caregivers
- other forms of serious violence and victimization

A recent study of children in grades 4 through 12 in New York City (NYC, NY) found that 64% had experienced at least one significant traumatic event prior to the September 11, 2001, attack on the World Trade Centers.[2] Indeed, the number of children in the United States who have been the victims of serious interpersonal violence is shockingly high: In 1997, the National Survey of Adolescents in the United States, sponsored by the National Institute of Justice, reported that nearly 4 million adolescents ages 12 years to 17 years experienced a serious physical assault during their lifetime.[3] This nationally representative survey of American teenagers also found that 9 million youth had witnessed serious violence during their lifetime.

While a precise figure of the number of children maltreated by caregivers each year does not exist, the number of children nationwide who have experienced abuse, neglect and/or exposure to domestic violence is estimated to exceed 3 million.[4-6] The Child Maltreatment Report (CMR) prepared by the National Child Abuse and Neglect Data System (under the auspices of the US Department of Health and Human Services' [USDHHS] National Center on Child Abuse and Neglect) aggregates child protection reports annually from all 50 states: In 2000, the CMR estimated that approximately 879,000 children were victims of child abuse and neglect[7] — a victimization rate of 12.2 per 1000 children. Among these victims, 63% suffered some form of neglect, 19% were physically abused and 10% were sexually abused. Many of these children suffered multiple forms of abuse and neglect, but, for reporting purposes, were included in only one category. General population surveys yield rates of child abuse and neglect that are 2 to 3 times higher than in official child abuse reports, and there is a significant overlap (estimated to be 30% to 60%) between families where there is child abuse and families that experience domestic violence.[8]

Consequences of Trauma

As a group, traumatized children manifest significantly higher rates of behavioral and emotional problems and academic failure than do nonabused children: Common problems include depression, anxiety, aggression, conduct disorder, sexualized behaviors, eating disorders, somatization and substance abuse.[9] Although the relative contribution of abuse and neglect versus family environment and genetic factors to these psychopathologies has been debated, recent studies of children who are twins confirm a significant causal relationship between child abuse and major psychopathology.[10] These behavioral and emotional deficits predispose children to negative adolescent trajectories that include early drop-out from school, substance abuse and promiscuity, and they contribute significantly to adverse adult outcomes, such as depression, posttraumatic stress disorder (PTSD), substance abuse, poor medical health and low occupational attainment.[11] Among groups of twins where one twin has experienced child abuse and the other twin has not, the abused twins exhibit significantly higher rates of depression, attempted suicide, conduct disorder, alcohol dependence, nicotine dependence and sexual promiscuity.[9,12,13] Although the research base on emotional abuse, neglect and exposure to domestic violence is not as extensive as it is for child abuse, the findings are similar.[14]

Abused and neglected children also perform more poorly in school than do nonabused children.[15-18] Cognitive deficits — which are perhaps abuse related — may trigger the emergence of behavioral difficulties in some abused children[19,20]: For example, children who are having difficulties learning may act out or be inattentive. These behavioral problems may lead to rejection by peers and teachers, thereby decreasing opportunities for positive instruction, classroom participation and supportive feedback.[21,22] In fact, a longitudinal study of sexually abused girls by Trickett, McBride-Chang and Putnam found that teachers who were blinded to the abuse status of these children rated the maltreated girls as significantly less likeable than matched control girls who were not abused.[23]

Studies have also identified the significant effects of child abuse and neglect on IQ scores and language ability.[17-24] Children with maltreatment-related PTSD showed significant impairments on attention tasks, abstract reasoning and executive functioning when compared with matched healthy children.[25] A population-based sample of more than 1000 pairs of twins found that exposure to domestic violence accounted for approximately 4% of the variation in child IQ and was associated with an average decrease in IQ of 8 points.[26] This is comparable to the average decrease of 3 to 4 IQ points caused by significant exposure to lead.[27,28]

What Constitutes Trauma?

While children experience many types of trauma, the most common forms occur typically at the hands of their parents and/or caregivers.[29] Neglect and physical and sexual abuse are often found in combination with emotional abuse and exposure to domestic violence.[5] In addition, many neglected and/or abused children live in unstable, crime-ridden neighborhoods, and therefore are also exposed to violence in their schools and communities.[30]

Researchers seeking to understand the effects of trauma on child development often draw distinctions between "acute" (or single-incident) trauma and "chronic" (or repetitive) trauma, sometimes referred to as Type I trauma and Type II trauma, respectively. Single episodes of serious accidental trauma can cause significant problems for a child. However, in a stable and supportive caregiving environment, symptoms often resolve, so that the rate of serious long-term complications, such as PTSD, is relatively low.

Chronic trauma, which involves either sustained or repetitive traumatic experiences, occurs typically in an environment where there is minimal adult support or healthy caregiving. Children exposed to chronic trauma generally have significantly worse outcomes than do those children who are exposed to acute accidental traumas.[31] In addition, the ongoing failure of parents or caregivers to protect the child is experienced as betrayal and contributes further to the adversity of the experience. When trauma is inflicted on a child deliberately by a parent or caregiver, as is often the case in child abuse, the intentional quality of that experience exacerbates its severity.

How Does Trauma Affect Children?

Research has identified a set of critical developmental processes, both psychological and biological, that traumatic experiences affect.[32] These processes, often conceptualized as developmental threads, run the course of the child's development and set the pattern for adult life. They broadly shape individuals' capacity to self-regulate in the face of stress, their sense of self and their ability to relate to others. The age and gender of the child, the number and types of traumas, the duration of the experience(s), the presence or absence of supportive adults and other factors influence developmental outcomes in ways that are presently only partially understood.[33] However, it is well established that significant trauma disrupts normal development in ways that are detrimental to many areas of adult functioning and often leads to costly emotional and physical problems that could be avoided or minimized by earlier intervention.[34]

The capacity for "emotional regulation" is one of the major casualties of significant early-life trauma. Traumatized individuals often suffer significant mood swings, anger, irritability and profound depression. Numerous studies have established that individuals who have a history of child abuse suffer from major depression at nearly 3 times the rate of nonabused individuals.[33] Serious problems with the modulation of mood and the regulation of anger can greatly complicate a child's ability to perform in school and to develop healthy peer relations — and may lead to situations that result in injury to self or others.[32] Similarly, the ability to regulate attention is often compromised in traumatized children. Problems with concentration, sometimes due to the symptoms of PTSD, such as hyperarousal or hypervigilance, may also impair school performance.[35]

The social development of the traumatized child is further compromised by significant problems with self-esteem and sense of identity. One of the most devastating effects of child abuse is that abused children often hate themselves and express these feelings through self-destructive behaviors. Indeed, studies have established that a history of child abuse increases suicide attempts by as much as 12-fold.[11,33] A process that runs parallel to the abused child's problems with self-esteem is his/her extreme difficulty in forming healthy social relationships with peers and partners. Disruptions in attachment — the fundamental parent/caregiver-child bond — are believed to be responsible for the difficulty in developing trusting, reciprocal relationships. Difficulties with modulation of anger and mood further compromise the ability to form healthy social relationships.

Lastly, research is finding that traumatic experiences, such as sexual abuse, can actually affect the development of the brain and impair important neuroendocrine systems.[36-43] The areas of the brain affected appear to be those associated with the regulation of emotion, as well as those affecting learning and memory.[36-38] Other brain regions associated with the control of impulses and reasoning, problem solving and judgment are also impaired and, therefore, have less influence on an individual's behavior.[36-38] Major hormonal systems, such as the hypothalamic-pituitary-adrenal axis, which plays a crucial biological role in buffering the physical effects of stress, are significantly dysregulated in victims of childhood trauma.[39-43] In addition, the sympathetic nervous system — often referred to as the "fight-or-flight" system — has been found to be hyperactive in traumatized individuals, leading to increased arousal and hypervigilance.[42] This hyperactivity of the fight-or-flight system probably contributes to hyperarousal, poor concentration and increased irritability, all of which take a toll on school and social success.

Protective Factors and Resiliency

By studying children in various adverse situations, developmental psychologists have identified several "protective factors" that are associated with increased resistance to stress.[34] Protective factors are individual or environmental characteristics that predict or are correlated with positive outcomes for children.[34] The most important of these protective factors[34] include the following:

- intelligence
- the capacity for emotional regulation
- the presence of social supports provided by caring, competent adults
- a positive belief about oneself
- belief in the safety and fairness of the situation
- a motivation to act effectively on one's environment

Traumatic experiences, including child abuse and neglect, may seriously undermine these protective factors, even to the point of reducing IQ significantly, which may be the single most important protective factor.[26]

Even co-occurring multiple protective factors can be overwhelmed by significant levels of trauma. The Adverse Childhood Experiences (ACE) study, a decade-long collaboration between Dr. Robert Anda of the Centers for Disease Control and Prevention and Dr. Vincent Felitti of the Kaiser Permanente Department of Preventive Medicine, examined the cumulative effects of multiple adverse childhood experiences on physical and mental health.[11] Using a simple 0-to-6 scoring system, which counts the numbers and types of ACEs that occur before the age of 18 years, the study has repeatedly found that ACEs are correlated positively with physical and psychological problems in children: As the number of ACEs increases, there is a graded increase in the number of physical and psychological problems.[11] Compared with subjects who have no ACEs, individuals who have 4 or more ACEs are at a significantly greater risk for a broad range of serious health problems. The ACE study provides clear evidence that multiple traumas and/or chronic trauma can overwhelm the psychological and physical well-being of all but the most resilient of children.

Trauma as a Risk Factor

Generally, "risk" refers to an increased probability of negative outcomes occurring among members of a group who share one or more characteristics.[34] The factors that *predict* or are *correlated positively with* these negative outcomes — either in terms of symptoms or of a failure to achieve one's potential — are termed "risk factors." Risk factors can be genetic, individual or environmental, and they interact with protective factors in complex ways. Risk factors often co-occur, particularly in highly traumatizing environments. In combination, they are more predictive than they are in isolation. Studies of risk and resiliency in children include trials of broad and cumulative risks, trials of stressful life events and trials of acute trauma and chronic adversity.[10,11]

Studies have identified childhood trauma and adversity as major risk factors for many serious adult mental and physical health problems. Depression is at least 3 times more prevalent in victims of child abuse than it is in the general population.[33] Depression, one of the leading public health problems worldwide, is estimated to have cost the United States approximately $44 billion in lost worker productivity in 2003.[44] The ACE study found that children who have 4 or more ACEs have an increased risk of four- to 12-fold for alcoholism, drug abuse and suicide attempts, and two- to fourfold for smoking, poor general health, sexual promiscuity and sexually transmitted diseases.[11] These children were also more likely to be physically inactive and/or severely obese. Trauma, through its effect on health-risk behaviors, such as smoking and obesity, contributes to multiple health problems, including heart disease, cancer and liver disease.[11] Similar results have been obtained in several other studies, including trials of twins that controlled for genetic factors.[10,45,46]

Childhood trauma is not a risk factor that is confined merely to one generation: The children of victims of child abuse and neglect are at a significantly increased risk of being victimized themselves.[47,48] The cumulative costs of child abuse and neglect, particularly when aggregated across generations, far outweigh the costs of prevention and early intervention programs.[49]

Assessment and Evaluation Strategies and Issues

Systematic and large-scale public health screenings of children for the detection of trauma-related symptoms and behavioral problems offer critical opportunities and significant challenges. Public health screenings generally involve the administration of a test or a selective examination to individuals who are not overtly symptomatic for the purpose of classifying them with respect to a condition of interest. In some instances, the individual may be asymptomatic (eg, using a Pap smear to detect early cervical cancer), while in other instances, the individual may be symptomatic, but the underlying disorder has not been identified (eg, screening for depression). Generally, screening tests are not definitive, and further diagnostic evaluation is required for individuals who test positive. However, screening has played a critical role in public health for many years and, in many cases, has become a routine part of standard medical care.

Public health screening always involves a complicated trade-off among several issues that must be considered for each condition. A disorder is considered appropriate for screening if it meets all of the following criteria[50]:

- It must be serious.
- Early treatment must make a significant difference in outcome.
- The prevalence of the disorder must be sufficiently high among the population screened.
- The ultimate costs of the outcomes associated with the disorder must be high enough to offset the costs associated with screening, further evaluation and treatment.

Universal Versus Targeted Screening for Traumatized Children

Universal screening involves testing an entire population or as much of that population as can be reached readily. Universal screening of adults for hypertension can be justified because high blood pressure is a serious condition resulting in significant mortality.[51] In addition, its prevalence is high: It has been estimated that up to 25% of all adults in the United States have some degree of hypertension.[52] Universal screening for phenylketonuria, a rare (one in 15,000 live births) congenital absence of a liver enzyme, is also justified because the resulting, irreversible, severe mental retardation can be prevented when detected by a simple, accurate, inexpensive, one-time test. However, when a condition is relatively rare, and/or the test to detect the condition is not entirely accurate or is very expensive, screening must be focused on a high-risk population in order to be feasible and justifiable.

Although the prevalence of trauma among children is high in the United States, it is not evenly distributed across the population. Certain groups of children have dramatically higher rates of trauma and/or exposure to violence and would benefit from early detection and intervention. The following are considered high-risk groups:

- children who are known to have been abused and/or neglected (most of whom receive little or no intervention for the trauma)[53]
- children in foster care; 70% to 80% of children are placed in foster care because their parents and/or caregivers have abused them or their siblings[54,55]
- children who witness domestic violence and/or the violent death of a parent, caregiver, sibling or friend[56]
- children who are victims of catastrophic accidents or mass casualty events, such as those associated with school violence, terrorism or natural disasters[57]
- children in the juvenile justice system[58]
- refugee children from countries that have had or are having major armed conflicts and/or civil disturbances[59]
- children who require psychiatric hospitalization for certain symptoms or behavioral problems (eg, suicide attempts and running away)

Because trauma presents in many different forms for children of different ages, genders and cultures, there is no simple, universal, highly accurate screening measure. Moreover, it is not feasible for many of the service systems now working with these children to definitively establish whether specific traumatic events have occurred. Therefore, screening approaches for trauma should aim to identify children who have a constellation of risk factors, such as poverty, homelessness, multiple births during adolescence and other vulnerabilities and behavioral problems that are highly associated with traumatic antecedents: The latter include symptoms of PTSD (which vary with age[60]), sexualized behaviors, certain fears and aggressive behaviors.

In order to screen very young children, parents, guardians and/or other involved adults would need to participate in the screening process. Older children and adolescents could complete their own self-report measures. Positive screens would require a comprehensive follow-up evaluation conducted by a professional familiar with the manifestations of childhood trauma.

Assessing Screening Tools

The *validity* of a screening tool is measured by how well it does what it is supposed to do — which is to ascertain whether individuals are positive or negative for a particular disorder. The *effectiveness* of a tool is quantified by calculating the following 3 elements:

- sensitivity — the probability of testing positive if the disorder is truly present
- specificity — the probability of testing negative when the disease is truly absent
- positive and negative predictive value — positive predictive value is the probability that a person who tests positive actually has the disorder; negative predictive value is the probability that a person who tests negative is truly free of the disorder

While the ideal test is highly sensitive *and* highly specific, in practice there is a trade-off when developing a screening tool that involves systematically weighing the probability of having false-positives and false-negatives. Ultimately, the feasibility of a screening program depends on its acceptability, its cost-effectiveness and the "yield" of cases. The yield is often quantified by calculating the predictive values of the test. Before any screening program can be instituted on a large scale, it is necessary to establish these parameters for the given measure in the population being screened.

Candidate Screening Measures for Childhood Trauma

Much work remains to be done before the populations who are at high risk for trauma-related negative outcomes can be effectively screened. However, several childhood trauma measures have been developed that can serve as starting points for pilot screening programs[61,62]: One example is a simple screening measure reported on in *JAMA: the Journal of the American Medical Association* — the Screening Tool for Early Predictors of PTSD, which predicts PTSD in children who were seriously injured in accidents or burned in fires.[63] Using 12 questions — 4 directed at the child, 4 completed by the parent or caregiver and 4 answered with information gleaned from the child's medical record — it is possible to predict subsequent symptoms of PTSD with good accuracy. The sensitivity of the measure for predicting posttraumatic stress at 3 months postinjury was 0.88 for children and 0.96 for parents/caregivers, with negative predictive values of 0.95 for children and 0.99 for parents/caregivers.

Other trauma-focused behavioral measures, such as the Trauma Symptom Checklist-Child, are well along in their development and validation processes and could be widely deployed in the near future.[61] In addition, widely used general behavioral measures, such as the Child Behavioral Checklist (CBCL), could be calibrated as trauma screening measures based on analyses of samples collected previously from traumatized children[64]: For example, in the GSMS, Costello and colleagues successfully used items from the "Externalizing Problems Scale" of the CBCL to screen a general population of children living in western North Carolina.[65] Subsequently, the investigators conducted detailed interviews with all children who scored above a predetermined cutoff point — the top 25% of the CBCL scale's total scores.

The National Child Traumatic Stress Network (NCTSN), which is sponsored by the Substance Abuse and Mental Health Services Administration of the USDHHS, is comprised of more than 50 centers nationwide that provide treatment and services to traumatized children and their families. Located in 32 states and the District of Columbia (DC), the NCTSN is well-situated to undertake the validation of these and other measures across a wide range of age groups, service sectors, cultural settings and types of trauma, including exposures to mass casualty events.[66]

Ethical Issues in the Assessment of Traumatized Children

One of the major — but often unacknowledged — reasons that children are not actively screened for trauma is that all 50 states and DC already have mandatory reporting laws that require certain persons (who vary by state, but usually include physicians and teachers, and often include law enforcement personnel, social workers, child care providers and mental health professionals) to report any and all suspicions of child abuse or neglect to the proper authorities. There are legal repercussions if they knowingly fail to do so.[67] Unfortunately, rather than placing themselves in an awkward situation — where they must make formal reports of suspicions of child abuse — many professionals who fall under these mandated reporting requirements choose not to inquire about traumatic experiences, especially child abuse and neglect. In addition, researchers conducting surveys of mental health issues in children may deliberately choose not to inquire about trauma in order to avoid the obligation of mandatory reporting. Therefore, given the current environment, any widespread screening program intended to detect trauma in children must have an established and well-vetted protocol for handling suspicions of child abuse and neglect.

False-positive screens are yet another significant concern. Virtually all screening measures will misidentify some individuals as having a particular condition, when, in fact, they do not. Reporting a false-positive trauma screen to child welfare authorities could initiate a very stressful investigation and conceivably cause harm to the child and/or family. This risk must be balanced against the need to protect children from the further harm that could result if the proper report were not made for a case that is true-positive. One way to minimize such false-positive risks is to use multiple evaluation measures that are administered serially. Employing multiple evaluations tends to increase the specificity of the screen because a series of measures that prove positive is more likely to represent a true disorder. The threshold for mandated reporting can then be set at a much higher level than that which is based on a single screening measure.

On a cautionary note, it is generally considered unethical to screen for a medical or psychological disorder if there is no effective, evidence-based intervention known to treat the disorder. When such an intervention exists, a secondary concern is whether that intervention is truly available to and accessible by the population being screened. The creation of a systematic, large-scale screening program to identify traumatized children must proceed in concert with deployment of evidence-based interventions that are readily accessible to the populations of children being screened. The NCTSN is perhaps the best-positioned organization to couple trauma screening across multiple systems serving children with effective therapeutic interventions in the same communities.

An Asset-Focused Public Health Approach to Childhood Trauma

Epidemiological evidence has shown that in the United States there are sufficiently large numbers of undiagnosed and/or untreated children who have been affected by trauma to warrant significant public concern — both for affected children and society at-large.[10,11] Indeed, we consider the situation to be a serious public health emergency that warrants the following actions in order to mobilize vital resources for these children and their families:

- *Accumulate and aggregate the various epidemiological studies pertaining to traumatized children.* While these studies often provide point-in-time counts of the number of teen pregnancies, reported cases of child abuse, incarcerated juveniles and/or the incidents of domestic violence involving children, they rarely acknowledge the frequent overlaps among these categories: That is, many of the children accounted for in one category also appear in several other categories.
- *Systematically identify, study and facilitate the development of relationships and partnerships among trauma service providers and agencies that have preexisting relationships with and responsibilities for these children and their families.* These partnerships will allow researchers and clinicians to identify and serve affected children in a more timely and effective manner.
- *Move beyond the boundaries of traditional trauma agencies and programs into the schools, juvenile detention facilities, substance abuse treatment programs for adolescents, shelters and other residential settings where traumatized children live, work and play — and establish a systematic program for screening, diagnosing and treating them.*
- *Assess the unmet needs for services and match those identified needs with the capacity to deliver the required services.* This process requires a clear-headed approach that identifies the available mental health assets and the entities that have the capacity to deliver these assets to the locations where needs exist. At this stage, it is likely that we will find a mismatch

between needs and assets. If this is the case, a separate analysis must be undertaken to determine how to address this situation. A critical part of the analysis will include understanding insurance program funding and training requirements for partner agencies and primary trauma paraprofessional service providers.

- *Identify, examine, experiment with, develop and implement best-practice strategies and protocols for reaching and helping as many of these affected children and families as possible.* This will require a long-term commitment by individuals in the trauma field working in partnership with policy makers, elected officials and their staffs.
- *Evaluate continuously all of the outlined efforts with regard to program quality, effectiveness and other outcomes.* Continuing to learn and being open to outcome research is important, but it is not necessary to wait for the "perfect" research answers to begin this challenge: As Voltaire noted, "the best is the enemy of the good."[68]
- *Convene a group of policy and political analysts to explore the opportunities for and the barriers to securing the necessary government supports for the actions described here.* Some policies can be affected by state and federal regulations. Other policies, particularly those concerning funding streams, will require legislative action.
- *Initiate a public education project to highlight child trauma as a significant public health emergency.* Policy analysts, elected officials and their staffs and the public at-large must be cognizant of child trauma and neglect, and the effects on these children of experiencing directly and being exposed to various traumatic events. They must understand that there are significant personal and societal consequences associated with the failure to acknowledge and address this public health emergency. Furthermore, it is imperative for them to understand that the timely diagnosis and provision of appropriate mental health services can make real and measurably positive differences in the lives of these children and their families, their developmental trajectories and, ultimately, for society.
- *Become more vigilant about identifying and acting upon opportunities to prevent childhood traumatic events from occurring in the first place.* Professionals in the trauma field have learned a great deal about preventing teen pregnancy, decreasing the incidence of chronic domestic violence,

intervening successfully — if rarely — in cases of alcohol and substance abuse and more. Any new frontal attack on this public health emergency will require an active, dynamic prevention component.

Adopting a 5-Pronged Model to Preventing and Treating Childhood Trauma

If the action plan in the preceding section seems overly ambitious or unrealistic, consider the recent experience with crime reduction in NYC. A transit police officer observed that some crime "posses" frequented certain places at specific times and acted in predictable ways to victimize the public. The transit police had not considered the mismatch between their law enforcement assets and the predictable times and locations of crimes. When their crime-fighting assets were mapped out and matched to the most probable crime locations and times, a dramatic reduction in crime ensued.[69]

We believe that a similar model of observation, analysis, experimentation, implementation and evaluation can be adopted by those in the field of trauma to address the public health emergency of childhood trauma. The idea of moving resources from where they are currently located to problem areas in order to be more efficient in the delivery of services to specific populations is not new. Indeed, over the last 15 years, professionals in the field of trauma have implemented this approach. Working in partnership with other professional fields, they have achieved some important successes, 4 examples of which follow.

Legal Partners Aid Underprivileged Parents — Boston, Massachusetts

In 1989, Boston City Hospital pediatrician Dr. Barry Zuckerman and his colleagues noticed an alarming increase in the number of women delivering babies who had crack cocaine in their systems. Historically, the standard procedure to address this problem had been to refer the mothers to a substance abuse counseling program. Unfortunately, "referring out" became a self-fulfilling prophecy: These mothers rarely succeeded in getting the substance abuse services they needed so desperately, although they did manage to bring their newborns to the Boston City Hospital Pediatric Primary Care Clinic for care.

Noticing this, Dr. Zuckerman formed a partnership with a local substance abuse program. He brought counselors directly on-site at the Pediatric Primary Care Clinic to serve the mothers in this familiar setting. His reasoning was clear: Mothers loved and cared about the health of their babies. Obviously, these mothers had a vested interest in bringing their babies into the clinic for care. On-site substance abuse counselors used the pediatric visit as an opportunity to provide critically needed substance abuse counseling to the mothers.

Noting the success of this effort, Dr. Zuckerman and his colleagues subsequently formed additional partnerships, bringing more services into the pediatric setting, including early literacy training for mothers and early childhood education (eg, the successful national program, "Reach Out and Read," which currently serves more than 1.5 million children at 1800 pediatric sites nationally).[70] They also brought public interest lawyers into the hospital's Primary Care Clinic to help underprivileged new mothers and fathers assure their access to food, safety, housing, health care, mental health care, social services and other goods and services that they were legally entitled to receive. This model of situating lawyers where they can serve clients directly is being replicated in several locations around the country (B. Zuckerman, MD, personal communication). Dr. Zuckerman and colleagues also introduced "Healthy Steps" into the Primary Care Clinic. "Healthy Steps" is a program that includes an on-site child development specialist who, as part of the pediatric team, provides information and support for parents to promote their children's development. In each of these cases, professionals from other fields were brought to the pediatric site where the current and future clients — children and their families — had either a preexisting or a potential relationship.

Community Policing Model — New Haven, Connecticut

In the early 1990s, Dr. Steven Marans, a psychoanalyst, and his colleagues at the Yale (University) Child Study Center (YCSC) created the Child Development-Community Policing (CD-CP) program in partnership with the New Haven (Conn) Department of Police Service (NHDPS). (Read more about the CD-CP in Dr. Marans' chapter in this publication.) The CD-CP came into existence after the NHDPS had already implemented a model of community policing that assigned officers to permanent neighborhood beats and emphasized the development of close, problem-solving relationships with the citizens of these communities. Because of the high rates of community violence that were fueled by the explosion in the crack-cocaine drug market, then Chief of Police Nick Pastore also wanted to focus on ways officers might be of greater help to children and families affected by the violence around them — in their homes, schools and neighborhoods. For help, he turned to Dr. Donald Cohen, MD, former director of the YCSC, as well as to Dr. Marans and other colleagues at the YCSC. Former Chief Pastore recounted the following experience that demonstrated the opportunity and the great need for help in addressing these issues:

> The NHDPS was called to a crime scene where a woman had been stabbed to death. As he was leaving the scene, Chief Pastore noticed several young children who had witnessed the woman's murder. He recognized that ignoring these children — leaving them alone and unaided in dealing with their traumatic experience — was unacceptable. He also realized that his police officers alone could not help the many children and families caught up in the scenes of violence that the police responded to on a daily basis. Fortunately, Chief Pastore found ready, potential partners at the YCSC, where Dr. Cohen and his colleagues recognized the limits of their clinic-based approaches to identifying and providing help to the many psychological casualties of violent trauma.

The CD-CP now trains police officers in principles of child development, human functioning and trauma as they apply to policing strategies and responses. Simultaneously, the program trains clinicians in policing practices as they apply to acute and follow-up trauma interventions (that are community- and clinic-based) as well as in forensic work and crisis consultation. Clinicians at YCSC are on-call 24/7 to respond immediately — on the scene to police calls for domestic violence and other crises that involve children and families. The CD-CP conducts weekly case conferences that include senior police personnel and YCSC clinicians, as well as other partners from the schools, child protective services and the juvenile courts. During these conferences, participants discuss and develop coordinated strategies for responding to current cases of domestic violence that involve children. The CD-CP program has now been replicated in 14 communities nationwide, and a pilot program designed to develop a similar effort with fire departments is in its initial stages.[71,72]

Court and Child Trauma Project Work Hand in Hand — San Francisco, California

Dr. Alicia Lieberman, a developmental clinical psychologist, directs the Child Trauma Research Project at the University of California at San Francisco. This project works in partnership with the San Francisco Unified Family Court. When domestic violence crimes are brought to the attention of the court, young children who have witnessed and/or experienced violence are referred to Dr. Lieberman's program. Dr. Lieberman and her colleagues subsequently develop a trauma treatment program for the mother and child. (See Dr. Lieberman's chapter in this publication.)

Violence Intervention Program — Miami/Dade County, Florida

The Violence Intervention Program for Children and Families, a program that is similar to the project headed by Dr. Lieberman, is directed by Dr. Joy Osofsky, a professor of pediatrics and psychiatry at the Louisiana State University Health Sciences Center (LSUHSC), working in collaboration with Judge Cindy Lederman, Administrative Judge of the 11th Circuit Juvenile Court in Miami/Dade County, Florida. The seed for this program was planted when Dr. Osofsky and Judge Lederman served on the National Research Council Committee, which evaluated family violence intervention programs. Both ventured to learn about the other's expertise: Dr. Osofsky initiated consultations with Judge Lederman on domestic violence cases, and Judge Lederman became a Fellow of the National Center for Infants, Toddlers and Families. Today, when children and families involved in cases of domestic violence and/or trauma appear before Judge Lederman, she calls upon the trauma professionals at the LSUHSC — her partners — to assist in the disposition of the cases. (See Dr. Osofsky's and Judge Lederman's chapter in this publication.)

These programs are examples of trauma professionals forming partnerships with other organizations and disciplines to bring additional perspectives, resources and services to at-risk children and their families. Not coincidentally, each of these programs has a current relationship with the NCTSN. Several other members of the NCTSN are also involved in a variety of partnerships that are tangential to, but not directly involved in, the field of trauma. The NCTSN is in an excellent position to serve as a unifying entity for professionals and caregivers to facilitate the extended reach of services to traumatized children and families wherever they are located.

There are other examples of successful child trauma service programs that have been located in the same settings as the clients served, including Head Start and other early childhood programs administered by the USDHHS and the individual 50 states and DC. In many of these programs, trauma professionals train other adults — such as teachers, peer counselors and/or caregivers who encounter traumatized families and children — on-site.

Partnering to Reach At-Risk Populations

The practice of establishing programs in the same settings where the population of those who need services are situated has been referred to as "co-location," "one-stop shopping" and "wraparound service programs." Providing comprehensive services at a single site underpins the organizational structures of programs such as Head Start and Early Head Start.

However, all such programs have not been implemented successfully: For example, collocating pregnancy health programs and mental health programs in schools has often been blocked because some individuals have objected to the distribution of birth control (including condoms) and the provision of abortion counseling. In addition, when service providers undertook efforts to join data banks from police departments and/or welfare agencies with departments of children and youth services, they were stymied by technological difficulties as well as by client privacy issues.

We acknowledge these difficulties and are not suggesting that mobilizing trauma resources for children is a simple task. But we emphasize that past experiences and current activities show that it is possible for trauma professionals and trauma programs to undertake these partnerships successfully. Public health approaches to screening and assessing the extent of trauma in specific populations have been undertaken with success in Hawaii[73] and in NYC following the terrorist attacks of September 11, 2001.[2] Efforts are currently underway elsewhere to expand and broaden these diagnostic approaches: For example, over the last few years, Manhattan (NYC) Community Board 7 has used a Geographic Information System to create a comprehensive map of services in their neighborhood (which includes more than 200,000 residents of the West Side of NYC's Central Park), overlaying governmental, nonprofit and business functions (D. Harris, member of Manhattan Community Board 7 and President of the Children's Research and Education Institute, personal communication). Mapping poverty and other risk factors by census tracts is a commonly accepted practice. Preparing dynamic maps of where children are throughout the day, week and year by age and caregiving institution has also been suggested.[74]

Collaborative efforts underway in Israel among the country's defense forces, Department of Mental Health and several other agencies present promising models of developing relationships and partnerships among agencies and clinicians to mobilize and deliver trauma resources to needy populations on a real-time basis. We have much to learn from our Israeli colleagues who are addressing mental health preparedness in the face of ongoing war and terrorism. (See Dr. Laor's chapter in this publication.)

Legislating and Funding Mental Health Parity

While there is a deep frustration today regarding the accessibility and availability of mental health/trauma services for many traumatized children and their families, the US Congress has promised to again consider enacting a Mental Health Parity law. If enacted, this law would establish, among other things, important new regulations that would require enhanced access to services for these traumatized children and their families.

Historically, the US Congress has been organized according to strict, separate jurisdictional powers, such that funding decisions are made across many different committees and subcommittees. This fragmented approach results in several different committees addressing problems faced by *some* children, at *some* times, in *some* places — as if children had separate parts and were not whole people living in a context of family and community. The challenge for policy makers working in this fractured jurisdictional environment is prodigious.

Nevertheless, the fractured reality of many US congressional committees that have distinctly separate powers can also be considered an opportunity for trauma professionals. During most years, authorizing original legislation, as well as legislation that reauthorizes existing spending authority, is considered to address some of the problems that face these children and families, and this legislation can become a vehicle for improvements in the provision of trauma resources and services.

The newly established US Department of Homeland Security has huge resources within its domain. However, it has yet to be determined how much money will be devoted to children's mental health services associated with acts of terrorism. How will preparedness, prevention and trauma service opportunities be addressed during, for example, an "Orange Alert"? While this department is organized as a new federal entity, it has become quite clear that state and local government agencies and programs will play critically important roles and will be called upon to help children and families in the event of natural and/or man-made disasters. Will the trauma field be "at the table" when these responses are being designed? Will the trauma field have a role in advising how these limited resources are allocated?

Conclusions

Our children are increasingly becoming the collateral damage of a violent society. We understand fully the potentially adverse consequences of failing to identify, assess and treat those in need. The public health emergency of traumatized children and their families presents a unique opportunity and responsibility for the trauma community to organize and mobilize a coordinated effort to confront and change this unacceptable situation.

As trauma professionals, we *must* become more aggressive in considering "the best interests of the child." We must forge and nurture new partnerships with other colleagues, disciplines and organizations that are responsible for and often serve traumatized children on a daily basis. Through these partnerships, we can identify problems at an earlier stage and bring to bear appropriate resources more rapidly.

Partnerships with pediatricians are vital. These colleagues often see traumatized children in the regular course of events — as they present with physical, emotional and/or comorbid conditions. Pediatricians are uniquely attuned to the developmental stages of children and to the potential for negative sequelae if problems are left unaddressed. A working partnership between pediatricians and trauma professionals could have important and positive ramifications for affected children and their families.

While small, forward steps are possible and indicated, we must always keep the larger picture in mind. We must organize ourselves with a new sense of urgency and determination in order to address the problem fully. It is up to us to educate our governmental officials — local, state and federal — as well as the public at-large so that they understand how significantly trauma affects children and families. It is important that as a society we understand that there will be potential serious and very negative short- and long-term consequences if traumatized children and their families are left unserved. It is equally important that policy makers, healthcare professionals and the public understand that if needed services are provided, we can help many of these children and families — and the payoff will extend far beyond just these individuals.

Actions to Take

We recommend 2 parallel approaches to address the problem of childhood trauma. The first approach — which is outlined in the bulleted points that follow — is incremental, in the sense that it builds upon existing relationships and services. The formal and informal networks and partnerships that are already in existence can take some of these steps immediately. Individuals and/or organizations and programs can do the same. The following list is only suggestive. It is by no means all-inclusive, and the order in which recommendations are presented does not indicate their priority.

- We must take an inventory of existing partnerships among trauma professionals and organizations, child and family assistance agencies, trauma-related associations and government programs. Sharing this inventory broadly may spark ideas for creating important new relationships and partnerships.

- We also must identify all of the membership associations for trauma professionals, as well as all of the conferences they attend regularly. These associations include the International Society for Traumatic Stress Studies, the Children's Defense Fund and the American Professional Society on the Abuse of Children. Charting the membership composition of these associations, as well as their attendance data, will help us determine how to expand their reach and extend their learning and teaching opportunities. Some associations may wish to invite other associations to share research, present papers and/or collaborate at conferences or meetings. The resulting cross-fertilization could produce valuable ideas and opportunities.

- More can and should be done to actively embed our research, calls for papers, presentations, etc, in/on others' Web sites and E-mail list-serves. By doing so, the trauma field could reach literally millions of additional people outside the field with offers of useful information. By embedding ourselves in other partners' electronic and print communications environments, we can take advantage of their preexisting relationships with their clients, and thereby extend the reach for trauma services to additional children. The National Resource Center of the NCTSN, which is the Network's coordinating center, is well-positioned to take on this assertive, proactive role to extend the reach of Web-based information and knowledge about the scope, impact and effects of treating childhood traumatic stress. The NCTSN can work with other organizations and associations to implement reciprocal links between its Web site and their Web sites.

There are many more incremental approaches that we can also pursue. It is vital to begin to take some of these steps *now*, and share information actively with a focus on doing a better job of serving traumatized children and their families.

Nevertheless, an incremental approach to the future often presents individuals and organizations with what appear to be insurmountable barriers that discourage change, innovation and creativity. Therefore, although an incremental approach is necessary, it is not sufficient. A "deductive" approach is also called for — one that requires us to lay out a vision of the *gold standard* for trauma knowledge and services 10 years down the road — and the barriers that must be surmounted in order to reach that vision.

As clinicians and researchers, we often limit ourselves to enumerating future research needs. While acknowledging these future needs is essential, we must not stop there. The issues associated with broad-based screening and assessment presented in this chapter are meant to be instructive. We must weigh carefully the mandatory reporting requirements, as well as the potential for false-positive/false-negative results. But we must move forward with experimental approaches for screening and assessing discrete populations — incarcerated children, for example, or children and parents who sign informed consent documents vetted thoroughly through institutional review boards — to see if, indeed, we can identify, assess and treat more children than we serve currently.

Other questions that we must address as we fashion a future for trauma prevention and intervention include the following: What methods of reimbursement are needed to sustain a *gold standard* trauma field in the future? What role will be played by a mental health parity bill? How will limited resources — both private and public — be allocated to the problems? Who will make these decisions? What studies already exist that demonstrate the costs of providing some services to some children — and what are the benefits of doing so? What additional studies are required? Who will undertake and fund these additional studies?

Any analysis of unmet needs in populations of traumatized children will quickly reveal the following:

- We need more trained trauma professionals and trauma paraprofessionals.
- We must develop partnerships between and among child-serving agencies.
- We must increase the size and scope of programs serving traumatized children and their families.

Longer-range planning considerations should address the gap in capacity between available trauma personnel assets and the actual needs in the field. A strong effort to broaden and deepen the talent pool of trauma professionals is of the highest priority. Moreover, training programs for future generations of trauma professionals and trauma paraprofessionals should reflect the cultural diversity of the children and families served, as well as that of the professionals who serve them. A major goal of the NCTSN is to bring about such a fundamental change in the nature and availability of opportunities for training so that trauma professionals are better prepared to help traumatized children and their families.

Lastly, we must identify the leaders who will take the field of trauma into the future. How will they organize? What existing and new partnerships will be required to bring together such a group charged with planning for the future? What organization(s) will oversee the effort: the Institute of Medicine, the National Academy of Sciences, the National Institutes of Health or private foundations?

Final Thoughts

We believe strongly that we can do an even better job in the future of mobilizing trauma resources for children — a better job of identifying, a better job of treating and a better job of helping traumatized children and their families. We know that this work is vitally important to each and every child, and that we can often succeed in helping children gain a more secure claim on their futures. However, to achieve this goal, we also know that we must do a much better job of communicating with the policy makers and the political and advocacy communities — and especially with the public at-large. All of these constituencies must become more aware that trauma matters. They must understand that left unaddressed and/or untreated, trauma can have multiple deleterious effects on children and their families.

The public health approach to childhood trauma that we have outlined in this chapter carries with it the potential for a more hope-filled future for our children. As clinicians, researchers and advocates for traumatized children, our role is to serve as mediators for providing these children with the help they need to reach their full potential as healthy and productive citizens.

Acknowledgment

Authors' Note: *We gratefully acknowledge and appreciate the support and leadership of our colleagues in the National Child Traumatic Stress Network (NCTSN). The NCTSN is supported by grants from the Center for Mental Health Services and the Substance Abuse and Mental Health Services Administration of the US Department of Health and Human Services. Additionally, we gratefully acknowledge the contributions of Ellen Gerrity, PhD, and David Harris, MSEd, to the development of this paper.*

References

1. Costello EJ, Erkanli A, Fairbank JA, Angold A. The prevalence of potentially traumatic events in childhood and adolescence. *Journal of Traumatic Stress.* 2002;15:99-112.
2. Applied Research and Consulting LLC, Columbia University Mailman School of Public Health, New York State Psychiatric Institute. Effects of the World Trade Center attack on NYC public school students: initial report to the New York City Board of Education. NYC Department of Education Web site. Available at: http://www.nycenet.edu/offices/spss/wtc_needs/firstrep.pdf. Accessed February 18, 2005.

3. Kilpatrick D, Saunders B. Prevalence and consequences of child victimization: research preview. Washington, DC: US Dept of Justice, National Institute of Justice; April 1997.

4. Carter LS, Weithorn LA, Behrman RE. Domestic violence and children: analysis and recommendations. *The Future of Children/Center for the Future of Children, the David and Lucile Packard Foundation.* 1999;9:4-20.

5. Fantuzzo JW, Mohr WK. Prevalence and effects of child exposure to domestic violence. *The Future of Children/Center for the Future of Children, the David and Lucile Packard Foundation.* 1999;9:21-32.

6. Osofsky JD. The impact of violence on children. *The Future of Children/Center for the Future of Children, the David and Lucile Packard Foundation.* 1999;9:33-49.

7. Administration for Children & Families. Child maltreatment 2000: 11 years of reporting. Washington, DC: US Dept of Health & Human Services, Administration for Children and Families, Administration on Children, Youth and Families, Children's Bureau. 2002. Available at: http://www.acf.hhs.gov/programs/cb/publications/cmreports.htm. Accessed January 15, 2004.

8. Edleson JL. The overlap between child maltreatment and woman battering. *Violence Against Women.* 1999;5:134-154.

9. MacMillan HL, Munn C. The sequelae of child maltreatment. *Current Opinion in Psychiatry.* 2001;14:325-331.

10. Kendler KS, Bulik CM, Silberg J, Hettema JM, Myers J, Prescott CA. Childhood sexual abuse and adult psychiatric and substance abuse disorders in women: an epidemiological and cotwin control analysis. *Archives of General Psychiatry.* 2000;57:953-959.

11. Felitti VJ, Anda RF, Nordenberg D, et al. Relationship of childhood abuse and household dysfunction to many of the leading causes of death in adults. The Adverse Childhood Experiences (ACE) Study. *American Journal of Preventive Medicine.* 1998;14:245-258.

12. Nelson EC, Heath AC, Madden PA, et al. Association between self-reported childhood sexual abuse and adverse psychosocial outcomes: results from a twin study. *Archives of General Psychiatry.* 2002;59:139-145.

13. Paolucci EO, Genuis ML, Violato C. A meta-analysis of the published research on the effects of child sexual abuse. *The Journal of Psychology.* 2001;135:17-36.

14. Erickson MF, Egeland B. Child neglect. In: Myers JEB, Berliner L, Briere J, Hendrix CT, Jenny C, Reid TA, eds. *The APSAC Handbook on Child Maltreatment.* 2nd ed. Thousand Oaks, Calif: Sage Publications; 2002:3-20.

15. Veltman MWM, Browne KD. Three decades of child maltreatment research: implications for the school years. *Trauma, Violence, & Abuse.* 2001;2:215-239.

16. Leither J, Johnson M. Child maltreatment and school performance. *American Journal of Education.* 1994;102:154-189.

17. Shonk SM, Cicchetti D. Maltreatment, competency deficits, and risk for academic and behavioral maladjustment. *Developmental Psychology.* 2001;37:3-17.

18. Lansford JE, Dodge KA, Pettit GS, Bates JE, Crozier J, Kaplow J. A 12-year prospective study of the long-term effects of early child physical maltreatment on psychological, behavioral, and academic problems in adolescence. *Archives of Pediatrics & Adolescent Medicine.* 2002;156:824-830.

19. Hinshaw SP. Externalizing behavior problems and academic underachievement in childhood and adolescence: causal relationships and underlying mechanisms. *Psychological Bulletin.* 1992;111:127-155.

20. Arnold D. Co-occurrence of externalizing behavior problems and emergent academic difficulties in high-risk boys: a preliminary evaluation of patterns and mechanisms. *Applied Developmental Psychology.* 1997;18:317-330.

21. Kupersmidt JB, Coie JD. Preadolescent peer status, aggression, and school adjustment as predictors of externalizing problems in adolescence. *Child Development.* 1990;61:1350-1362.

22. McEvoy A, Welker R. Antisocial behavior, academic failure, and school climate: a critical review. *Journal of Emotional and Behavioral Disorders.* 2000;8:130-140.

23. Trickett P, McBride-Chang C, Putnam F. The classroom performance and behavior of sexually abused females. *Development and Psychopathology.* 1994;6:183-194.

24. Eckenrode J, Laird M, Doris J. School performance and disciplinary problems among abused and neglected children. *Developmental Psychology.* 1993;29:53-62.
25. Beers SR, De Bellis MD. Neuropsychological function in children with maltreatment-related posttraumatic stress disorder. *The American Journal of Psychiatry.* 2002;159:483-486.
26. Koenen KC, Moffitt TE, Caspi A, Taylor A, Purcell S. Domestic violence is associated with environmental suppression of IQ in young children. *Development and Psychopathology.* 2003;15:297-311.
27. Needleman H. Lead poisoning. *Annual Review of Medicine.* 2004;55:209-222.
28. Wasserman GA, Factor-Litvak P, Liu X, et al. The relationship between blood lead, bone lead and child intelligence. *Neuropsychology, Development and Cognition. Section C, Child Neuropsychology: A Journal on Normal and Abnormal Development in Childhood and Adolescence.* 2003;9:22-34.
29. US Dept of Health and Human Services. *Child Maltreatment, 2002.* Washington, DC: US Dept of Health and Human Services, Administration on Children, Youth and Families; 2004.
30. Crouch JL, Hanson RF, Saunders BE, Kilpatrick DG, Resnick HS. Income, race/ethnicity, and exposure to violence in youth: results from the National Survey of Adolescents. *Journal of Community Psychology.* 2000;28:625-641.
31. Pine DS, Cohen JA. Trauma in children and adolescents: risk and treatment of psychiatric sequelae. *Biological Psychiatry.* 2002;51:519-531.
32. Pynoos RS, Steinberg AM, Piacentini JC. A developmental psychopathology model of childhood traumatic stress and intersection with anxiety disorders. *Biological Psychiatry.* 1999;46:1542-1554.
33. Putnam FW. Ten-year research update review: child sexual abuse. *Journal of the American Academy of Child and Adolescent Psychiatry.* 2003;42:269-278.
34. Masten AS, Coatsworth JD. Competence, resilience, and psychopathology. In: Cicchetti D, Cohen DJ, eds. *Developmental Psychopathology: Risk, Disorder, and Adaptation.* Vol 2. New York, NY: John Wiley & Sons; 1995:715-752.
35. Cicchetti D, Lynch M. Toward an ecological/transactional model of community violence and child maltreatment: consequences for children's development. *Psychiatry.* 1993;56:96-118.
36. De Bellis MD, Keshavan MS, Clark DB, et al. A.E. Bennett Research Award. Developmental traumatology. Part II: Brain development. *Biological Psychiatry.* 1999;45:1271-1284.
37. De Bellis MD, Keshavan MS, Frustaci K, et al. Superior temporal gyrus volumes in maltreated children and adolescents with PTSD. *Biological Psychiatry.* 2002;51:544-552.
38. De Bellis MD, Keshavan MS, Shifflett H, et al. Brain structures in pediatric maltreatment-related posttraumatic stress disorder: a sociodemographically matched study. *Biological Psychiatry.* 2002;52:1066-1078.
39. De Bellis MD, Lefter L, Trickett PK, Putnam FW Jr. Urinary catecholamine excretion in sexually abused girls. *Journal of the American Academy of Child and Adolescent Psychiatry.* 1994;33:320-327.
40. De Bellis M, Putnam F. The psychobiology of childhood maltreatment. *Child and Adolescent Psychiatric Clinics of North America.* 1994;3:1-16.
41. De Bellis MD, Chrousos GP, Dorn LD, et al. Hypothalamic-pituitary-adrenal axis dysregulation in sexually abused girls. *The Journal of Clinical Endocrinology and Metabolism.* 1994;78:249-255.
42. De Bellis MD, Baum AS, Birmaher B, Ryan ND. Urinary catecholamine excretion in childhood overanxious and posttraumatic stress disorders. *Annals of the New York Academy of Sciences.* 1997;821:451-455.
43. De Bellis MD, Baum AS, Birmaher B, et al. A.E. Bennett Research Award. Developmental traumatology. Part I: Biological stress systems. *Biological Psychiatry.* 1999;45:1259-1270.
44. Stewart WF, Ricci JA, Chee E, Hahn SR, Morganstein D. Cost of lost productive work time among US workers with depression. *JAMA: The Journal of the American Medical Association.* 2003;289:3135-3144.
45. True WR, Rice J, Eisen SA, et al. A twin study of genetic and environmental contributions to liability for posttraumatic stress symptoms. *Archives of General Psychiatry.* 1993;50:257-264.

46. Dinwiddie S, Heath AC, Dunne MP, et al. Early sexual abuse and lifetime psychopathology: a co-twin-control study. *Psychological Medicine.* 2000;30:41-52.

47. Vogel ML. Gender as a factor in the transgenerational transmission of trauma. *Women & Therapy: A Feminist Quarterly.* 1994;15:35-47.

48. Ney PG. Transgenerational triangles of abuse: a model of family violence. In: Viano EC, ed. *Intimate Violence: Interdisciplinary Perspectives.* New York, NY: Hemisphere Publishing; 1992:15-25.

49. Fromm S. Total estimated cost of child abuse and neglect in the United States: statistical evidence. Prevent Child Abuse America, Web site. Available at: http://www.preventchildabuse.org/learn_more/research_docs/cost_analysis.pdf. Accessed February 17, 2005.

50. Harris RP, Helfand M, Woolf SH, et al. Current methods of the US Preventive Services Task Force: a review of the process. *American Journal of Preventive Medicine.* 2001;20(suppl 3):21-35.

51. US Preventive Services Task Force. Screening for high blood pressure: recommendations and rationale. Agency for Healthcare Research and Quality. Web site. Available at: http://www.ahrq.gov/clinic/3rduspstf/highbloodsc/hibloodrr.htm. Accessed February 17, 2005.

52. Burt VL, Whelton P, Roccella EJ, et al. Prevalance of hypertension in the US adult population. Results from the Third National Health and Nutrition Examination Survey, 1988-1991. *Hypertension.* 1995;25:305-313.

53. Burns BJ, Phillips SD, Wagner HR, et al. Mental health need and access to mental health services by youths involved with child welfare: a national survey. *Journal of the American Academy of Child and Adolescent Psychiatry.* 2004;43:960-970.

54. Marx L, Benoit M, Kamradt B. Foster children in the child welfare system. In: Pumariega AJ, Winters NC, eds. *The Handbook of Child and Adolescent Systems of Care: The New Community Psychiatry.* San Francisco, Calif: Jossey-Bass; 2003:332-350.

55. Putnam FW, Liss MB, Landsverk J. Ethical issues in maltreatment research with children and adolescents. In: Hoagwood K, Jensen PS, Fisher CB, eds. *Ethical Issues in Mental Health Research With Children and Adolescents.* Hillsdale, NY: Lawrence Earlbaum Associates; 1996:113-132.

56. Carter L, Kay SJ, George JL, King P. Treating children exposed to domestic violence. *Journal of Emotional Abuse.* 2003;3:183-202.

57. Norris FH, Friedman MJ, Watson PJ. 60,000 disaster victims speak: Part II. Summary and implications of the disaster mental health research. *Psychiatry.* 2002;65;240-260.

58. Abram KM, Teplin LA, Charles DR, Longworth SL, McClelland GM, Dulcan MK. Posttraumatic stress disorder and trauma in youth in juvenile detention. *Archives of General Psychiatry.* 2004;61: 403-410.

59. Shaw JA. Children exposed to war/terrorism. *Clinical Child and Family Psychology Review.* 2003;6: 237-246.

60. Scheeringa MS, Zeanah CH, Myers L, Putnam FW. New findings on alternative criteria for PTSD in preschool children. *Journal of the American Academy of Child and Adolescent Psychiatry.* 2003;42: 561-570.

61. Briere J. *Trauma Symptom Checklist for Children™ (TSCC™): Professional Manual.* Odessa, Fla: Psychological Assessment Resources; 1996.

62. Steinberg AM, Brymer MJ, Decker KB, Pynoos RS. The University of California at Los Angeles Post-traumatic Stress Disorder Reaction Index. *Current Psychiatry Reports.* 2004;6:96-100.

63. Winston FK, Kassam-Adams N, Garcia-Espana F, Ittenbach R, Cnaan A. Screening for risk of persistent posttraumatic stress in injured children and their parents. *JAMA: The Journal of the American Medical Association.* 2003;290:643-649.

64. Achenbach TM. *Child Behavior Checklist: Manual/4-18 and 1991 Profile.* Burlington, Vt: University of Vermont; 1991.

65. Costello EJ, Angold A, Burns BJ, et al. The Great Smoky Mountains Study of Youth. Goals, design, methods, and the prevalence of DSM-III-R disorders. *Archives of General Psychiatry.* 1996;53: 1129-1136.

66. Steinberg A. Disaster mental health assessment strategies for children and adolescents. Paper presented at: NIMH/SAMHSA/NCPTSD Roundtable Meeting on Assessment and Screening Following Disasters and Mass Violence; August 26-27, 2003; Bethesda, Md.

67. National Clearinghouse on Child Abuse and Neglect Information. Mandatory reporters of child abuse and neglect: 2003 child abuse and neglect state statute series statutes-at-a-glance. Available at: http://nccanch.acf.hhs.gov/general/legal/statutes/manda.pdf. Accessed February 17, 2005.

68. Voltaire. Available at: http://en.wikiquote.org/wiki/Voltaire. Accessed February 18, 2005.

69. Gladwell M. *The Tipping Point: How Little Things Can Make a Big Difference.* New York: Back Bay Books/Little, Brown and Company; 2000.

70. High PC, LaGasse L, Becker S, Ahlgren I, Gardner A. Literacy promotion in primary care pediatrics: can we make a difference? *Pediatrics.* 2000;105(4,pt 2):927-934.

71. Marans S. Psychoanalysis on the beat: children, police and urban trauma. In: Solnit AJ, Neubauer PB, Abrams S, Dowling AS, eds. *The Psychoanalytic Study of the Child.* Vol 51. New Haven, Conn: Yale University Press; 1996:522-541.

72. Marans S, Murphy R, Berkowitz S. Police-mental health responses to children exposed to violence: the Child Development-Community Policing Program. In: Lewis M, ed. *Child and Adolescent Psychiatry: A Comprehensive Textbook.* 3rd ed. Baltimore, Md: Lippincott Williams and Wilkins; 2002:1406-1416.

73. Chemtob CM, Nakashima JP, Hamada RS. Psychosocial intervention for postdisaster trauma symptoms in elementary school children: a controlled community field study. *Archives of Pediatrics & Adolescent Medicine.* 2002;156:211-216.

74. Harris WW. Time frames. *New Directions for Youth Development.* Summer 2003:119-126.

Section 6: Summary

Speaking With One Voice and Collaborating on Behalf of Traumatized Children

Alicia F. Lieberman, PhD

This book offers a multifaceted look at a multidimensional problem: the destructive psychological and sociological consequences of children's exposure to violence. The participants in the Pediatric Round Table on which this book is based represent a variety of disciplines — among them pediatrics, psychology, psychiatry, sociology, social work, the judicial system, public policy and government. Many of the contributors work at the interface of various disciplines and service systems, creating models of collaboration that aim at fostering integrative approaches to service access and successful intervention. Taken together, the chapters in this publication illustrate the broad scope and creative vision of the work being done on behalf of children exposed to violence; the limitations of our knowledge; the insufficiency of our preventive and palliative actions to date; and the magnitude of the challenge to improve the lives of traumatized children.

The consensus that emerged from the Pediatric Round Table is that any effort to address the sequelae resulting from children's exposure to violence must be a collaboration among clinical practice, research and public policy that focuses on the child in the context of his or her family and community. Although easy to articulate, this goal is difficult to implement because each of these areas — clinical practice, research and public policy — differs significantly from the others in its priorities and methodology, creating an "interdisciplinary culture gap" that interferes with communication, the assimilation of new knowledge and its practical application to intervention programs. The exchanges that followed each authors' presentations made clear that, despite the prevailing good will and collegiality among the participants, individual thinking *and* group process were influenced by often implicit assumptions about the value of different approaches. In this regard, the Pediatric Round Table was a microcosm of the interactions that routinely occur in the "outside world" whenever members of different disciplines congregate to exchange ideas and plan a course of action.

The following bullet points summarize the prevailing assumptions in the field of exposure to violence by children and youth:

- Researchers strive to build an empirically-grounded knowledge base that informs intervention programs, giving precedence to promising interventions that emerge from randomized controlled trials.
- Clinicians, on the other hand, value flexibility in responding to clients' individual needs and cultural characteristics, stressing that the accumulated experience derived from clinical practice with many traumatized children and families constitutes a legitimate knowledge base to guide decision-making and program development.
- Representatives of public policy and government emphasize the urgency of distilling the essence of what we know, transcending disciplinary and theoretical biases and converting knowledge into action to improve public health and the lives of suffering children and their families.

Compounding these *interdisciplinary* strains is the *intradisciplinary* tendency to specialize in one type of exposure to violence to the exclusion of all others. Optimally, clinicians with these different perspectives can make significant contributions to a *comprehensive* understanding of the effects of children's exposure to violence and foster the development of a multifaceted approach to prevention and treatment. In reality however, as Richard J. Gelles, PhD, points out, the wide range of perspectives often contributes to the maintenance of rigid conceptual silos within the profession that interferes with efforts to work across disciplines, service systems and types of trauma. For example, there is a persistent and harmful divide separating the researchers, clinicians and policy makers who focus on domestic violence from those who specialize in child abuse. In spite of the substantial overlap in the incidence of domestic violence and child abuse, both groups frequently fail to understand and acknowledge the interconnectedness of the developmental disruption and sequelae associated with children's exposure to violence of any kind.

In addition, the different points of views represented by clinical practice, research and public policy also have important practical implications. One of the key factors influencing politicians' funding decisions is their perception of the credibility of the individuals and groups bearing the many and often competing messages they receive. As a result, it is imperative to speak about the needs of traumatized children in ways that do justice to the importance of this topic in the public domain. We ask ourselves: Is there a unified message that researchers and clinicians working with children who have been exposed to violence can deliver to promote the creation and maintenance of urgently needed prevention and intervention programs? The consensus that emerged from this Pediatric Round Table is that we cannot wait to take action toward this end. Even in the absence of sufficient research or sufficient funding, and resources to launch the scope of services needed, it is urgent to take the necessary steps to improve access to services and raise the standard of treatment for children exposed to violence.

Research on exposure to violence by children and youth has played a pivotal role in documenting the profound and long-term negative impact of different forms of violence on children's physical, emotional, social and cognitive development. In fact, the chapters in this book begin with a review of the significant body of research supporting this conclusion. The cumulative weight of the studies that are cited conclusively dispels the popular but mistaken idea that children's cognitive immaturity and developmental resilience make them inherently resistant to or resilient in the face of trauma. The research evidence on children's exposure to violence is consistent with the empirical findings from the field of developmental psychopathology that the timing, frequency and intensity of adverse experiences are associated with the magnitude of negative developmental outcomes.[1-3] For example, abused and neglected children living in violent neighborhoods were found to fare far worse than maltreated children living in less violent communities, attesting to the compounding effects of family and community violence.[4] Similarly, there is evidence that children who are subjected to physical abuse and also witness domestic violence experience more developmental, emotional, social and cognitive problems than do children who are exposed to only 1 of these 2 stressors.[5]

Over the last 20 years, we have witnessed major advances in the understanding of causality in atypical child development, including the complex influences of risk and protective factors and the heterogeneity of individual responses to exposure to violence. The very same risk factors may lead to different outcomes for different individuals (a process known as multifinality) while, conversely, differing risk factors and trajectories may lead individuals to similar mental health problems (a process known as equifinality).[6,7] This diversity of outcomes has shifted the attention of research to the concept of *pathways,* deemphasizing linear connections between individual risk factors and developmental outcomes and, instead, placing an emphasis on the factors that initiate and maintain an individual on a particular developmental course that may result subsequently in particular outcomes.[8] The implications for children who are exposed to violence are clear: The evidence from research indicates that early and protracted exposure to violence of different types in the absence of protective factors — such as emotionally supportive relationships and environments — results in pervasive mental health problems in a variety of developmental domains. In their chapter, Robert S. Pynoos, MD, MPH, and Alan M. Steinberg, PhD, point out that their research and that of others comfirm that the dose of the exposure is emerging as an important factor in predicting the impact of any one traumatic event.[9]

In this book, Victor G. Carrión, MD, presents evidence that the impact of children's exposure to interpersonal violence is not restricted to behavioral domains alone; it extends to the physiology and anatomy of the brain as well. Presently, we do not know the extent to which changes in brain structure and physiology are reversible, for whom and under what conditions. However, the finding that exposure to violence sculpts the brain in ways that increase the likelihood of maladaptive responses to normative environmental demands and stress conditions adds urgency to the need for clinical interventions that promote a return to normal developmental progression.

The Clinical Arena: Reaching Toward Best Practices

In the clinical arena, there is growing consensus on the characteristics of best practice for the treatment of posttraumatic stress in children and adolescents. Pynoos and Alicia F. Lieberman, PhD, and others identify the following key parameters[10]:

- an overarching developmental perspective that guides efforts to restore developmental momentum to the child's functioning
- the inclusion of parents as partners in the child's treatment
- the engagement of the child's and family's ecological contexts and service systems to bolster accurate appraisals of danger and enact protective interventions
- the use of methods that are culturally compatible with the child's and the family's values
- the creation of a trauma narrative as an organizing theme of the treatment in order to give meaning to the trauma and to place it in the larger context of the child's age-appropriate expectations, interests and activities

Michele R. Cooley, MEd, PhD; Joy D. Osofsky, PhD; Judge Cindy S. Lederman; Cynthia Cupit Swenson, PhD; Lieberman and other authors describe groundbreaking clinical programs to achieve ecological validity by offering treatment in a variety of developmentally and culturally appropriate settings, such as the home, childcare centers, family resource centers and schools, and by incorporating systematic collaboration with one or more service systems, including pediatrics,[11] the police, the legal system,[12,13] child protective services,[14] schools and a multisystemic approach. A perspective on collaboration with law enforcement is provided by Steven Marans, PhD, while Sochua Mu Leiper, MSW, explores the need for a multisystemic approach in Cambodia. A consistent thread among these diverse approaches is the importance of a therapeutic focus on the child's most salient and age-appropriate relationships for the following purposes:

- generating or restoring the child's trust in parental competence to protect
- promoting reciprocity and social competence in the child's relationships with parents, peers and authority figures
- fostering the child's sense of community belonging to stimulate adherence to societal norms

Across treatment approaches, this therapeutic focus aims at providing a counterbalance to the shattering of the child's developmentally appropriate expectations of protection by parents, teachers, authority figures and the community at large as the result of the violence.

As Pynoos and Steinberg point out, the experience of violence destroys not only trust in interpersonal relationships but also emotional engagement in the social contract. Leiper tells us that this rupture takes on cataclysmic dimensions in countries ravaged by war, terrorism and politically motivated massacres. In these circumstances, the entire social fabric — including public institutions, governmental policies and cultural values — must be coordinated and focused on prevention, protection and intervention. In Cambodia, a "culture of impunity" is the legacy of decades of war and genocide, and the resulting cultural dislocation, widespread extreme poverty, demoralization and despair. In the context of reconstructing Cambodia, children's survival needs are the country's top mental health priority, and these needs are so immediate that they stretch the scarce resources that are available through the government and through international aid. Emerging efforts to create an infrastructure to protect young victims of violence and sexual exploitation — the true victims of the "culture of impunity" — take the form of programs that provide for children's basic needs, including food, health care, transitional housing and training in income-producing skills.

In Israel, another country facing ongoing terrorism and war, the picture is very different. Unlike Cambodia, Israel has sturdy democratic institutions, high educational levels and relative prosperity and these conditions enable the country to place a high priority on developing and implementing innovative mental health interventions for victims of violence and disaster. In this volume, Nathaniel Laor, MD, PhD, and his colleagues describe the Tel Aviv Model, a sophisticated systemic approach that gives the responsibility for integrating and operating all mental health services in a particular government-designated geographic region to the Mental Health Emergency Headquarters (MHEH). The MHEH oversees trauma training for mental health professionals and coordinates the mental health services of HMOs and municipal, national and army units in a single framework. To be effective, such a model must predate the emergency situation in which it will be used and must have well delineated responsibilities at each stage of an emergency, from the time of initial warning through the immediate aftermath of the event and the longer term monitoring and intervention. This approach is based on the premise, initially advanced by Pynoos, Goenjian and Steinberg,[15] that mental health professionals have the responsibility in times of disaster to facilitate the responses of the government, social service agency and healthcare institutions to the evolving needs of children and adults and to mediate the appropriate allocation of duties and resources.

The utility of a community wide systemic approach to prevent and reduce violence need not be limited to situations of chronic war or terrorism. Many communities in the United States have high levels of violence that co-occur with poverty and economic decline. There is generally a lag in time between violence and heightened trends of psychopathology among adults and the emergence of a similar co-occurrence of violence and psychopathology among children and adolescents. According to Pynoos and Steinberg, this intergenerational contagion can be predicted when there is no organized community or governmental response to outbreaks of violence by adults. Philip B. Uninsky, JD, provides positive evidence, however, that active and substantive interagency collaboration in implementing a continuum of empirically based programs with proven efficacy can measurably reduce juvenile violence and children's exposure to violence, and alleviate academic failure and underachievement. The Partnership for Results, a not-for-profit agency that administers a Safe Schools/Healthy Students federal grant to Cayuga County, New York, has achieved these results by developing a multi-system service planning and delivery framework that brings together educational, human services and law enforcement agencies through the flexible allocation of funding and a system for sharing client information across relevant agencies while protecting privacy. However, improvements in the functioning of children as the result of community-wide interventions are not always predictable. Greg J. Duncan, PhD, and his coauthors describe a residential mobility program that relocated families with young children to safer neighborhoods. Mental health improvements in this program were observed for girls but not for boys.

A community's ability to implement programs with empirically demonstrated efficacy to alleviate the problems associated with children's exposure to violence raises the question of how to develop those programs in the first place. While in the United States it is often taken as axiomatic that empirically based programs automatically ensure clinical success in the community, this view is not shared universally.[16] It is important not to overstate the contributions that rigorous laboratory-based research can make to the well-being of children traumatized by violence. While randomized controlled trials are undoubtedly the "gold standard" in proving a causal relationship between treatment and outcome, because they eliminate selection bias by neutralizing the influence of extraneous factors, their potential liabilities are seldom elucidated. These liabilities include the following:

- strategies become common knowledge and influence "treatment as usual" in uncontrolled ways, possibly diluting or eliminating effect size by affecting the counterfactual (ie, what clients would be receiving if they were not in the treatment group)
- the related problems of standardizing what happens within the control group because participants are free to engage in a variety of treatments that may include similar components to those being tested in the treatment group
- difficulty securing client adherence
- flawed research designs that may lead to mistaken conclusions about treatment efficacy, including inappropriate generalization of the findings

An additional conundrum is that methodologically sound randomized controlled studies of the efficacy of treatment programs for traumatized children tend to have small sample sizes, clients with relatively homogeneous characteristics (because they are carefully selected for exposure to specific traumatic stressors), and a research design that minimizes attrition rates and places treatment in the hands of a small number of highly trained and motivated professional staff, who use standardized manuals and who are closely monitored for adherence to the treatment protocol. In contrast, the large and complex systems where community-based treatment is implemented usually serve heterogeneous populations of clients who have been exposed to a range of different traumas. In addition, treatment is generally delivered in this setting by a large number of providers (often a mixture of professional and lay practitioners) who may or may not be motivated to apply a new treatment. Conducting randomized controlled trials under these community-based conditions presents daunting problems of treatment standardization, adherence and attrition control, as well as major challenges to efforts to document treatment effectiveness. The cultural diversity of client populations in community-based treatment programs is another obstacle to translating the findings from one community to another, because the treatment approaches must be adapted to the specific values, customs, beliefs, practices and languages of the ethnic and racial groups in those communities.

Given these circumstances, searching for a unified message that integrates clinical and research considerations leads to the next question: Do randomized controlled trials demand methodological conditions that even the *best* large-scale, community-based studies cannot meet? There was general agreement among the Round Table participants that randomized controlled trials should be restricted to the evaluation of well established treatment approaches, because only such mature interventions can meet the essential condition of having treatment providers who are highly trained, experienced and motivated so that adherence to the intervention protocol is sufficiently high and attrition rate is reasonably low. Insisting that only the most rigorous research design can lead to usable knowledge may lead to the premature implementation of community-based clinical trials before these programmatic conditions have been met. The resulting failure to show treatment effects because of training and implementation problems may, in turn, lead to the erroneous conclusion that a particular treatment is not effective rather than to an acknowledgment that it has not been implemented effectively.

Fear among clinicians and community leaders that programs supported by tax dollars may not be funded unless they show empirical evidence of success stifles a genuine spirit of enquiry. Rejection of randomization in community treatment settings, notably among ethnic and racial groups that have been victimized historically, should be acknowledged and addressed as a legitimate response to the persistent mental health treatment gap for minorities and the poor.[17] In this climate, it is imperative to foster an atmosphere that greets all findings on treatment outcomes and program evaluations as worthwhile whenever they increase understanding, promote improvements in access to services, and enhance the standard of care — even if there is no clear-cut evidence of statistically significant treatment effectiveness or efficacy. Therefore, research on interventions and treatment outcomes should be conceptualized as cumulative long-term endeavors aimed at promoting best practice within the context of a strong and steady commitment to provide services and alleviate distress for traumatized children and their families.

Because of the enormous toll exacted by the pervasiveness of children's exposure to violence, the question of how best to mobilize trauma resources for children was a unifying priority for the Round Table participants. The strategies proposed by William W. Harris, PhD, and his colleagues that are described in this volume illustrate the generative value of solutions that transcend disciplinary boundaries and bring together clinical, research and public policy considerations. Public health screening is warranted for trauma-related symptoms in children who have been exposed to violence, because childhood traumatic stress meets all the following relevant screening criteria:

- it is serious
- early treatment makes a significant difference in outcomes
- it has a high prevalence
- the costs of the sequelae in terms of health problems, lost productivity, crime and other factors are high enough to offset the costs associated with screening, follow-up and treatment

Although much more research must be conducted and public health strategies must be developed before we can effectively and ethically screen children for trauma-related symptoms, screening measures are available and are being systematically evaluated. The problem of large numbers of unidentified and untreated children has serious implications for the children themselves, their families, and for society as a whole — and warrants taking systematic steps now to mobilize resources on their behalf. Some strategies proposed by Harris and his colleagues include the following:

- aggregate the various epidemiological studies to sort out the frequent overlap of children across different categories
- promote partnerships between trauma service providers and agencies
- reach out beyond the confines of trauma agencies and programs to find the children where they live and spend time, in settings such as childcare centers and schools, foster care homes, the juvenile justice system, domestic violence shelters and shelters for runaway youth
- develop and engage in continuous evaluation of best practice strategies
- explore the opportunities for and barriers to government support for these activities

Highlighting child trauma as a significant public health problem through an educational campaign targeted to the public at large, as well as elected officials and their staffs, is recommended as a key strategy. Such a campaign must emphasize the serious societal and personal consequences of failing to address the needs of traumatized children. Greater awareness in all sectors of society of the plight of traumatized children and the eventual fallout to society if these children are left untreated could lead to the long-awaited enactment by Congress of the Mental Health Parity law. This law would require enhanced access to services for children traumatized by violence and their families.

Within every sector of the population — regardless of age, ethnicity and socioeconomic status — there are children who have been exposed to violence. Undoubtedly, minorities and the poor are disproportionately affected and have the least access to services. There is an urgent need to increase the number of available treatment programs, enhance the quality of care and train professionals and paraprofessionals across service delivery systems to enable them to provide appropriate care and/or refer clients as needed to mental health programs and providers that specialize in trauma. Congress has recognized the importance of taking action by authorizing the creation of the National Child Traumatic Stress Network (NCTSN), sponsored by the Substance Abuse and Mental Health Services Administration (SAMHSA). The Network is comprised of more than 50 centers across the country, many of which are represented by the authors of the chapters in this book, that provide treatment and other services to traumatized children and their families and disseminate best practices to community agencies nationwide.

In summary, this Pediatric Round Table provided a valuable opportunity to bridge disciplinary boundaries and engage in a collective dialogue about strategies to address the problem of child exposure to violence from a variety of perspectives. Ultimately, it is our hope that practitioners from these diverse disciplines will consider the material presented in this publication as food for thought and action, and will speak with one strong voice and act collaboratively on behalf of traumatized children everywhere.

References

1. Rutter M. Resilience reconsidered: conceptual considerations, empirical findings, and policy implications. In: Shonkoff JP, Meisels SJ, eds. *Handbook of Early Childhood Intervention.* Cambridge England: Cambridge University Press; 2000:651-682.
2. Rutter M, Sroufe LA. Developmental psychopathology: concepts and challenges. *Development and Psychopathology.* 2000;12:265-296.
3. Sameroff AJ. Developmental systems and psychopathology. *Development and Psychopathology.* 2000;12:297-312.
4. Lynch M, Cicchetti D. An ecological-transactional analysis of children and contexts: the longitudinal interplay among child maltreatment, community violence, and children's symptomatology. *Development and Psychopathology.* 1998;10:235-257.
5. Hughes HM, Parkinson D, Vargo M. Witnessing spouse abuse and experiencing physical abuse: a "double whammy"? *Journal of Family Violence.* 1989;4:197-209.
6. Mayr E. The evolution of living systems. *Proceedings of the National Academy of Sciences.* 1964;51: 934-941.
7. Sroufe LA. Pathways to adaptation and maladaptation: psychopathology as developmental deviation. In: Cicchetti D, ed. *Rochester Symposium on Developmental Psychopathology.* Vol. I. The Emergence of a Discipline. Hillsdale, NJ: Erlbaum; 1989:13-40.
8. Cicchetti D, Sroufe LA. The past as prologue to the future: the times, they've been a-changin'. *Development and Psychopathology.* 2000;12:255-264.
9. van der Kolk BA, Pelcovitz D, Roth S, Mandel FS, McFarlane A, Herman JL. Dissociation, somatization, and affect dysregulation: the complexity of adaption to trauma. *American Journal of Psychiatry.* 1996;153:83-93.
10. Cohen and the Work Group on Quality Issues. Practice parameters for the assessment and treatment of children and adolescents with posttraumatic stress disorder. *Journal of the American Academy of Child and Adolescent Psychiatry.* 1998;37:4S-26S.
11. Groves BM. *Children Who See Too Much: Lessons From the Child Witness to Violence Project.* Boston, Mass: Beacon Press; 2002.
12. Lieberman AF, Van Horn P. Attachment, trauma, and domestic violence: implications for child custody. *Child and Adolescent Psychiatric Clinics of North America.* 1998;7:423-443.

13. Van Horn P, Hitchens. DJ Partnerships for young children in court: how judges shape collaborations serving traumatized children. In: Osofsky JD, ed. *Young Children and Trauma: Intervention and Treatment.* New York, NY: The Guilford Press; 2004:242-259.
14. Larrieu JA, Zeanah, CH. Treating parent-infant relationships in the context of maltreatment: an integrated systems approach. In: Sameroff AJ, Mc Donough SC, Rosenblum KL, eds. *Treating Parent-Infant Relationship Problems.* New York, NY: The Guilford Press; 2004:243-264.
15. Pynoos RS, Goenjian AK, Steinberg AM. A public mental health approach to the postdisaster treatment of children and adolescents. *Child and Adolescent Psychiatric Clinics of North America.* 1998; 7:195-210.
16. Roth A, Fonagy P. *What Works for Whom? A Critical Review of Psychotherapy Research.* New York, NY: The Guilford Press; 2005.
17. President's New Freedom Commission on Mental Health Final Report. *Achieving the Promise: Transforming Mental Health Care in America.* DHHS Pub. No. SMA-03-3832. Rockville, Md: Department of Health and Human Services; 2003.